FRENCH AND ITALIAN STOICISMS

Also Available from Bloomsbury

German Stoicisms: From Hegel to Sloterdijk, ed. Kurt Lampe
and Andrew Benjamin (forthcoming)
The Art of Living Well, Paul van Tongeren, trans. by Thomas Heij
The Selected Writings of Pierre Hadot, trans. by Matthew Sharpe and Federico Testa

FRENCH AND ITALIAN STOICISMS

From Sartre to Agamben

Edited by
Kurt Lampe and Janae Sholtz

BLOOMSBURY ACADEMIC
LONDON • NEW YORK • OXFORD • NEW DELHI • SYDNEY

BLOOMSBURY ACADEMIC
Bloomsbury Publishing Plc
50 Bedford Square, London, WC1B 3DP, UK
1385 Broadway, New York, NY 10018, USA
29 Earlsfort Terrace, Dublin 2, Ireland

BLOOMSBURY, BLOOMSBURY ACADEMIC and the Diana logo are trademarks
of Bloomsbury Publishing Plc

First published in Great Britain 2021
This paperback edition published in 2022

Copyright © Kurt Lampe and Janae Sholtz, 2021

Kurt Lampe and Janae Sholtz have asserted their rights under the Copyright,
Designs and Patents Act, 1988, to be identified as Editors of this work.

"Galien : la réduction à l'homonymie par l'écriture" from *L'Effet sophistique*
by Barbara Cassin © Editions Gallimard, Paris, 1995.

Chapter 10 © Editions Gallimard, Paris, 1995: "Galien: la réduction à l'homonymie par l'écriture"
from *L'Effet sophistique* by Barbara Cassin

For legal purposes the Acknowledgments on p. ix constitute an extension
of this copyright page.

Cover design by Charlotte Daniels
Cover images: Jean Paul Sartre © Granger Historical Picture Archive / Alamy. Julia Kristeva © Patrick
BOX / Gamma-Rapho / Getty Images. Bust of Zeno © Jeanette Dietl / Shutterstock. Column illustration
© iStock. Column ruins by All Bong on Unsplash. Background by Mockaroon on Unsplash.

All rights reserved. No part of this publication may be reproduced or transmitted in any form
or by any means, electronic or mechanical, including photocopying, recording, or any information
storage or retrieval system, without prior permission in writing from the publishers.

Bloomsbury Publishing Plc does not have any control over, or responsibility for, any third-party websites
referred to or in this book. All internet addresses given in this book were correct at the time of
going to press. The author and publisher regret any inconvenience caused if addresses have changed
or sites have ceased to exist, but can accept no responsibility for any such changes.

A catalogue record for this book is available from the British Library.

Library of Congress Cataloging-in-Publication Data

Names: Lampe, Kurt, 1977-editor. | Sholtz, Janae, editor.
Title: French and Italian Stoicisms: from Sartre to Agamben / edited by Kurt Lampe and Janae Sholtz.
Description: London; New York: Bloomsbury Academic, 2020. |
Includes bibliographical references and index. | Summary: "The importance of Stoicism for Gilles
Deleuze's Logic of Sense and Michel Foucault's Hermeneutics of the Subject and The Care of the
Self is well known. However, few students of either classics or philosophy are aware of the
breadth of French and Italian receptions of Stoicism. This book firstly presents this broad
field to readers, and secondly advances it by renewing dialogues with ancient Stoic texts.
The authors in this volume, who combine expertise in continental and Hellenistic philosophy,
challenge our understanding of both modern and ancient concepts, arguments, exercises,
and therapies. It conceives of Stoicism as a vital strand of philosophy which contributes to the
life of contemporary thought. Flowing through the sustained, varied engagement with Stoicism
by continental thinkers, this volume covers Jean-Paul Sartre, Gilles Deleuze, Michel Foucault,
Julia Kristeva, Alain Badiou, Émile Bréhier, Barbara Cassin, Giorgio Agamben, and Pierre Hadot.
Stoic sources addressed range from doxography and well-known authors like Epictetus
and Seneca to more obscure authorites like Musonius Rufus and Cornutus"– Provided by publisher.
Identifiers: LCCN 2020019578 (print) | LCCN 2020019579 (ebook) |
ISBN 9781350082038 (hardback) | ISBN 9781350082045 (ebook) | ISBN 9781350082045 (epub)
Subjects: LCSH: Stoics. | Philosophy, French–20th century. | Philosophy, Italian–20th century.
Classification: LCC B528.F74 2020 (print) | LCC B528 (ebook) | DDC 194–dc23
LC record available at https://lccn.loc.gov/2020019578
LC ebook record available at https://lccn.loc.gov/2020019579

ISBN: HB: 978-1-3500-8203-8
PB: 978-1-3502-0401-0
ePDF: 978-1-3500-8204-5
eBook: 978-1-3500-8205-2

Typeset by Deanta Publishing Services, Chennai, India

To find out more about our authors and books visit www.bloomsbury.com
and sign up for our newsletters.

CONTENTS

List of Figures	vii
A Note on Translation	viii
Acknowledgment	ix
Abbreviations	x

Chapter 1
INTRODUCTION: STOICISM, LANGUAGE, AND FREEDOM 1
Kurt Lampe

Chapter 2
SARTRE, STOICISM, AND THE PROBLEM OF MORAL RESPONSIBILITY
(FROM 1939 TO 1948) 15
Olivier D'Jeranian, trans. by O. D'Jeranian and Kurt Lampe

Chapter 3
SARTREAN ONTOLOGY AND THE STOIC THEORY OF INCORPOREALS 35
Laurent Husson and Suzanne Husson, trans. by Kurt Lampe

Chapter 4
DELEUZIAN EXERCISES AND THE INVERSION OF STOICISM 53
Janae Sholtz

Chapter 5
HOW AND WHY DID BADIOU BEAT DELEUZE WITH A STOIC STICK 75
Thomas Bénatouïl

Chapter 6
JULIA KRISTEVA, STOICISM, AND THE "TRUE LIFE OF INTERPRETATIONS" 93
Kurt Lampe

Chapter 7
INDIFFERENCE *VERSUS* AFFIRMATION: MICHEL FOUCAULT ON THE
STOIC IDEA OF LIFE AS A TEST 113
John Sellars

Chapter 8
VERIDICTION AND *PARRHESIA*: THE COMPLEX CASE OF STOICISM
    AND ITS READING BY M. FOUCAULT   127
Valéry Laurand

Chapter 9
STOICISM: POLITICAL RESISTANCE OR RETREAT?
    FOUCAULT AND ARENDT   143
Michael Ure

Chapter 10
STOICISM, AMBIGUITY, AND THE DECISION OF SENSE   161
    Barbara Cassin, trans. by Steven Corcoran and Kurt Lampe,
    with an Introduction by Kurt Lampe

Chapter 11
ONTOLOGY AND LANGUAGE, BETWEEN CHRYSIPPUS AND AGAMBEN   177
    Nicoletta di Vita, trans. by Kurt Lampe

Chapter 12
MAKING USE OF AGAMBEN'S "STOIC PROVIDENCE-FATE
    APPARATUS": A READING OF SENECA'S *CONSOLATION TO POLYBIUS*   195
    Clifford A. Robinson

Chapter 13
PIERRE HADOT: STOICISM AS A WAY OF LIFE   215
    Matthew Sharpe

Contributors   235
Index   237

FIGURE

10.1 Phōnē, Lexis, *and* Logos　　　　　　　　　　　　　　　167

TABLE

13.1 Hadot's Epictetan "key" to (later Roman) Stoicism as a way of life　　　222

A Note on Translation

Chapters 2, 3, 10, and 11 were originally written in French. Their authors are discussing primary sources written not only in French and English but also in ancient Greek, Latin, Italian, and German. Because translation is already a matter of interpretation, I considered it unwise to adopt published English translations of the sources they are quoting (where they exist). My translation is therefore based on four principles: first, I have consulted the sources quoted in the original language; second, I have compared this with the way the authors have rendered these sources into French; third, I have borne in mind existing anglophone conventions around technical terms. For instance, with respect to ancient Greek and Roman Stoic sources, in almost all cases I have followed the conventions established by Anthony Long and David Sedley's seminal sourcebook and commentary, *The Hellenistic Philosophers* (1986). The fourth step was of course to ask the authors themselves to critique and verify my translations.

The only generalization worth mentioning is that I have attempted to disambiguate French *signification* and *sens* throughout, since the distinction is sometimes philosophically significant. I have accordingly translated *signification* as "meaning" wherever appropriate; in some contexts, I have instead used "signification." I have translated *sens* as "sense" rather than "meaning."

Kurt Lampe

ACKNOWLEDGMENT

This volume began life as one half of a networking project funded by the Arts and Humanities Research Council of the United Kingdom in 2016 under the title "Continental Stoicisms: Beyond Reason and Wellbeing." We are grateful for their support.

ABBREVIATIONS

Cic.	Cicero
Fat.	*De Fato* (*On Fate*)
Fin.	*De Finibus* (*On Ends*)
ND	*De Natura Deorum* (*On the Nature of the Gods*)
Off.	*De Officiis* (*On Obligations*)
Tusc.	*Tusculanae Disputationes* (*Tusculan Disputations*)
DL	Diogenes Laertius, *Lives of the Illustrious Philosophers*
Epict.	Epictetus
Ench.	*Enchiridon* (i.e., *Manual*)
Diss.	*Dissertationes* (i.e., *Discourses*)
LS	A. A. Long and D. N. Sedley (1986), *The Hellenistic Philosophers*, 2 vols., Cambridge: Cambridge University Press.
MA	Marcus Aurelius
SE *M.*	Sextus Empiricus, *Adversus Mathematicos* (*Against the Professors*)
Sen.	Seneca
Ben.	*De Beneficiis* (*On Benefits*)
Ep. Mor.	*Epistulae Morales* (*Moral Letters*)
Prov.	*De Providentia* (*On Providence*)
Tranq.	*De Tranquillitate* (*On Tranquillity*)
SVF	Hans von Arnim (1903–5), *Stoicorum Veterum Fragmenta*, 4 vols., Leipzig: Teubner.

Chapter 1

INTRODUCTION

STOICISM, LANGUAGE, AND FREEDOM

Kurt Lampe

1 The Meaning(s) of the Stoic Tradition

What is the significance of the Stoic tradition? That, of course, is an unwieldy question: the concepts, arguments, doctrines, mental and practical techniques, and everything else that travels under the label "Stoicism" have meant different things to different people. Today we have an increasingly detailed understanding of the aspects of ancient Stoic theory preserved by surviving ancient Greek and Roman sources. The academic study of this evidence, which until the 1980s was concentrated in German and French scholarship, is now flourishing in anglophone universities as well. There is also a growing body of research about the reception of Stoicism from antiquity until today (e.g., Spanneut 1973; Colish 1990; Neymeyr, Schmidt, and Zimmerman 2008; Sellars 2016). Perhaps more surprisingly, in the last decade "modern Stoicism" has become a powerful international movement, bringing together scholars of antiquity, psychotherapists (especially from cognitive-behavioral backgrounds), and a broad public interested in living philosophically.[1]

Dwelling briefly on this movement will shed some light on how the reception of Stoicism in "continental (European) philosophy" enriches its significance. While it is hazardous to generalize, the following quotation from the front cover of Donald Robertson's excellent *Stoicism and the Art of Happiness* is both concise and representative: "What is Stoicism? Practical wisdom and resilience building techniques. Take control—understand what you can and can't change" (2013). Let me expand this a bit. The modern Stoic is enjoined to become mindful of the contents of her consciousness (e.g., words, images, sensory and bodily feelings, emotions, and impulses), to articulate these in propositional form, to weigh these propositions against a series of guidelines (e.g., that we must focus on what we can control, namely our thoughts, and that behaving virtuously is more satisfying and valuable than wealth, status, or any other goals external to our behavior), to harmonize and systematize them, and in this way to view herself as someone progressing toward greater happiness, goodness, and concord with other people and the world (cf. Robertson 2013: 10). There is no doubt that this approach is well grounded in the ancient texts and accurately captures core intentions of many ancient practitioners. However, we should also remark that modern Stoics emphasize some aspects of the ancient evidence and downplay or repudiate others—avowedly and deliberately so, in fact (Vernon and LeBon 2014; Chakrapani 2018). For this chapter's purposes, it suffices to mention two of these partialities. The first is that, in proclaiming humankind's "natural rationality," they set aside the myriad epistemological, psychological, sociopolitical, and metaphysical questions raised by the endeavor to express truthfully in language the content of thought and the structure of reality.[2] The second is that, in declaring that our thoughts are "under our control," they beg questions about both external and internal determinism and freedom.[3]

Now contrast the following passage from a section called "In the Garden of Epictetus" in *The Education of the Stoic* by the Portuguese author Fernando Pessoa (1888–1935):

> "The pleasant sight of these fruits and the coolness given off by these leafy trees are yet other solicitations of nature," said the Master, "encouraging us to abandon ourselves to the higher delights of a serene mind.... Sit still with me, and meditate on how useless effort us, how alien the will, and on how our very meditation is no more useful than effort, and no more our own than the will."
> (Pessoa 2005: 51)

Since Pessoa (or rather his heteronym, the Baron of Teive) puts these words into Epictetus's mouth, he implicitly questions to what extent anything is "under our control," including our thoughts: "Our very meditation," he muses, "is ... no more our own than the will." We could relate this to the ancient Stoics' own attempts, given their commitment to universal causal determinism, to explain in what sense our decisions belong to us (LS 55, 62; cf. Bobzien 1998: 234–411). Pessoa's Epictetus also doubts whether we can know or express any truths, which is one reason he considers the very meditation he performs "useless." Later he explains that we can neither know nature, despite its tantalizing "solicitations," nor express what we think (2005: 52). Once again, this can be related to ancient Stoic doctrines: their standards of knowledge and correct reasoning are so lofty they have to defend the possibility of their attainment (as we can now read in what may be Chrysippus's own words [Alessandrelli and Ranocchia 2017]).[4] So the Baudelairean attitude of Pessoa's Epictetus, though antithetical to that of the ancient Stoics, can nevertheless be read as an intelligible reaction to their teachings, albeit one colored by personal idiosyncrasies and a specific moment in literary history.[5]

Pessoa was a younger contemporary of Jean-Paul Sartre, the earliest modern philosopher addressed in the present volume, and features prominently in *Handbook of Inaesthetics* by Alain Badiou, at the opposite chronological end of our coverage. The two broad themes I have just identified in the quotation from his work, which I shall encapsulate under the headings "language" and "freedom," recur frequently in French and Italian reception of Stoicism. This reception tradition, it should be emphasized, is a complement rather than a competitor to modern Stoicism. One of the French authors concerned, Pierre Hadot, is frequently cited in modern Stoic literature. As Matthew Sharpe elucidates, Hadot's readings incorporate both prior German and French scholarship and a range of philosophical influences (Sharpe, Ch. 13). Nevertheless, it remains true that continental philosophers tend to develop the meaning of the ancient evidence with greater creative latitude than modern Stoics. On the one hand, they explain aspects of Stoic practice differently than the practitioners themselves, and in this respect expand our understanding of the Stoic life. On the other, they discover significance in theorems that the original theorists would probably disavow, and in that respect envisage ways of living "Stoicism" quite different from those practiced in the ancient world or the mainstream of the modern Stoic movement.

I will not attempt to survey the chapters to come in the remainder of this introduction. Instead, I will selectively use and supplement their research and arguments in order to comment briefly on how modern French and Italian philosophers' engagement with Stoicism allows them to raise subtle and important questions about language and freedom.

2 Language

The foundational figure for continental responses to Stoic philosophy of language is Émile Bréhier (1876–1952), chair of the History of Ancient and Modern Philosophy at the Sorbonne and successor to Henri Bergson at the Académie des sciences morales et politiques. Bréhier's research interests were extremely far ranging, but Stoicism particularly fascinated him both intellectually and practically, as Henri-Charles Puech eulogized:

> This intransigent rationality, which was nevertheless life-affirming and profoundly human, this austere discipline of self-mastery, this ideal of wisdom founded on the accord of philosophical autonomy with the rhythm of the universe, inspired in him both sympathy and admiration. (1952: xxvi)[6]

Bréhier's doctoral *thèse complementaire*, the first edition of which reached publication in 1907 (third edition 1962), was on *La théorie des incorporels dans l'ancien stoïcisme* ("The Theory of Incorporeals in Ancient Stoicism")—a topic which had begun attracting attention in the 1880s, and which von Arnim's collection of fragments in 1903–5 made substantially more accessible.[7] The metaphysics of "sayables" (*lekta*) feature prominently here, as indeed in Wolfhart Totschnig's recent defence of Bréhier's core position (Totschnig 2013). But Bréhier's formulations have generated echoes far beyond specialist scholarship. Consider the terminology he uses to highlight the Stoic distinction between bodies, which are beings and have causal power, and the effects of bodies, which are nonbeing, incorporeal sayables:

> These results of the action of beings, which the Stoics were perhaps the first to perceive in this form, are what we today would call "facts" or "events" (*des faits*

ou des événements): a bastard concept that is neither that of a being nor of one of its properties, but what is said and asserted about being. (1962: 13)

Note two aspects of Bréhier's interpretation of Stoic sayables. First, he problematizes their relationship with the bodies that cause them (when they are conceived as effects, LS 55A-D) or to which they refer (when they are conceived as the content of thoughts, LS 33). We will see below that this problem expands to encompass their relation to the signifiers that express them, the speech acts that enunciate them, and the speakers who think and say them. Second, he elevates this problem to the status of a metaphysical principle. It is in this connection that he speaks of "'facts' or 'events,'" which are caused by beings, yet whose connection to those beings is unstable: they "play" on the "surface" of being (1962: 12–13, 60–3). This way of presenting the Stoic theory of sayables has ethical and political consequences, as the evental metaphysics of Deleuze, Badiou, and other contemporary continental philosophers demonstrates. Although these aspects are tightly intertwined, for the sake of exposition I will present them separately.

Let me begin with language and the event. It is well known that Gilles Deleuze took inspiration from Bréhier's interpretation of the Stoic theory of sayables when elaborating his metaphysics of the chaosmic Event in *The Logic of Sense*, which coordinates ideal significations, bodily intensities, and enunciative attitudes.[8] (Deleuze was also influenced by Bréhier's successor, Victor Goldschmidt, on whom see further below.) It has not been recognized until now that Sartre had preceded Deleuze in this respect, as Laurent and Suzanne Husson demonstrate in this volume. Sartre enthusiastically followed Bréhier's lectures at the Sorbonne, and his loan record at the École Normale Supérieure from 1926 to 1928 includes both ancient Stoic texts and French and German scholarship on the school. While it cannot be argued that Stoicism plays a major role in *Being and Nothingness*, it is noteworthy that Sartre alludes to Stoic doctrine precisely when, in the "metaphysical outlooks" of that book's conclusion, he postulates a type of being that would unify the for-itself and the in-itself. Such a being, the Hussons argue, would be analogous to the Stoic category of "somethings" (LS 27A-D), and its foundation in the absolute in-itself's "ontological act" would correspond to the thinking of Stoic God (L. and S. Husson, Ch. 3). At the opposite end of the century, Thomas Bénatouïl shows how part of Alain Badiou's polemic in *Deleuze: The Clamor of Being* revolves around a closely related issue. Badiou's strategy is to tendentiously pigeonhole Deleuze as a Stoic. Among Badiou's moves is to claim that the ostensibly Stoic theory of evental sense (i.e., the sayable) makes it impossible to defend the univocity of being, which is supposed to underpin Deleuze's radical ethics and politics. A true radical, Badiou argues, must return to Plato (Bénatouïl, Ch. 5).

Now let us consider how the Stoic sayable has been appropriated for theorizing the relations among bodies, signifiers, thought, and speech. Of course, Deleuze's *Logic of Sense* is once again central to this story. But he is far from the only continental thinker involved. For example, the psychoanalyst Jacques Lacan, whose theories are an important point of reference for *The Logic of Sense*, appears in turn to take inspiration from it. In the wake of the publication of *Logic of Sense* in 1968, Lacan experiments with connecting the Stoic *lekton* to his own ideas about the signifier, *objet a*, *lalangue* [*sic*], and the transference (Lacan 1970a: 9–11, b: 19; c: 55–6, 61, 68, 1985 [delivered 1975]: 11–12, cf. 2007 [delivered January 21, 1970]: 60–1).[9] It may not be coincidental that the classicist and philosopher Barbara Cassin has also been deeply influenced by Lacan. In her discussion of the Stoics' analysis of ambiguity, she argues that their distinction between the dynamics of vocal sound (which is bodily) and the dynamics of significations (which are incorporeal) blocks the demand that speakers aim to signify one and the same thing, for themselves and others, with univocal correspondence to material referents. Since this demand implies a regulatory norm, blocking it creates an opportunity—whether or not most Stoic practitioners take advantage of it—for ethical and political reorientation (Cassin, Ch. 10).

Julia Kristeva approaches Stoic philosophy of language from a similar theoretical orientation, but arrives at less sympathetic conclusions. This is in large measure because her numerous remarks on Stoicism, while indebted to Bréhier, are more influenced by Goldschmidt. In his magisterial *Le système stoïcien et l'idée de temps* (The stoic system and the idea of time 1953), Goldschmit develops a vision of the Stoic aspiration to incorporate divine totality and eternity in the "events" of human thought, volition, and action. This leads Kristeva to infer that Stoicism freezes the relations among signifier, signified, and referent, and then again between antecedent and consequent propositions. This has the effect of repressing what she calls the "semiotic" and "imaginary" dimensions of language, which strangles creativity and singularity. In my chapter I return to lesser-known ancient Stoic texts in order to evaluate Kristeva's claims. While she illuminates one temptation for Stoics, I argue that imaginary and semiotic creativity play a larger role in ancient Stoic thinking than she acknowledges—and that this deserves further consideration in modern Stoicism (Lampe, Ch. 6).

If the interpretations of the sayable by Deleuze, Lacan, Cassin, and Kristeva overlap in many particulars, Giorgio Agamben's reception—though undertaken in full knowledge of the work of Bréhier, Goldschmidt, and Deleuze—marks a substantially new departure. Nicoletta di Vita explores in her chapter how Agamben's scattered discussions culminate in the long chapter "On the Sayable and the Idea" in *Che cos'è la filosofia?* (*What Is Philosophy* 2016: 57–122), where he argues that the sayable just is "the fact of language" (di Vita, Ch. 11)—in other words, speech as a potentiality that human beings must actualize, withdraw from, or be deprived of in various ways. Agamben incorporates a philologically detailed meditation on Stoic and Platonic texts into his ongoing investigation of what is presupposed and singularized by every act of speaking.

3 Freedom

The theme of freedom is connected to those of language and knowledge. In the 1920s and 1930s "Alain" (Émile Chartier, 1868–1951) popularized an association between Stoicism and his own ideas about the will, truth, and responsibility, which go back to his own and Victor Brochard's scholarship on Stoic epistemology in the 1880s and 1890s (Bénatouïl 2017: 361–2). Alain's "Stoic attitude" exerted considerable influence over Jean-Paul Sartre, as Olivier D'Jeranian shows. More specifically, D'Jeranian traces how Sartre comes to terms with the Epictetan dyad of "what is up to us" and "what is not up to us" during the 1940s. In a nutshell, Sartre eventually incorporates "what is not up to us" in his own philosophy as "the situation," which is factitious rather than natural, fated, or providential. He then transforms "what is up to us" so that it no longer connotes our capacity to affirm a situation as an opportunity for behaving virtuously, but rather our ability to "assume" and "surpass" that situation toward a "free project," rather than affirming that situation as an opportunity for behaving virtuously (D'Jeranian, Ch. 2).

Sartre's ethics also bear a surprising resemblance to Goldschmidt's influential vision of Stoicism. Consider Goldschmidt's description of the relation between Stoic wisdom and the singular acts through which it is expressed:

> However, if he receives the theme for his action from external circumstances, the sage by no means depends on them. . . . Which amounts to saying . . . that potentiality is higher than actuality, because it is an infinite potentiality for all possible acts. . . . The singular act reveals the entirety of a potentiality that infinitely surpasses it. (1953: 152–3)

For Goldschmidt, "surpassing" the present toward eternity and totality, which involves a kind of "freedom," is central to Stoic practice. He explicitly compares this with Sartrean ethics: "One could compare the 'spontaneity' of the 'for-itself' in Sartre to the [Stoic] present of freedom, where ethical initiative (*hormē* . . .), which ceaselessly renews itself, is located" (1953: 191 n.2; cf. 124 n. 3, 213 n. 5). Of course, it remains the case that this free "surpassing . . . of all concrete determinations" (1953: 191 n.2; cf. 124 n. 3, 213 n. 5) is nevertheless governed by cosmic law, which prescribes every event in the universe (1953: 89, 156). However, responding elsewhere to Heidegger, Goldschmidt asserts "there would be some naivety . . . and plenty of imperialism" in asserting, from the supposedly universal vantage point of existential phenomenology, that the Stoic way of relating to nature and god is "inauthentic" (1953: 54). Later he goes so far as to suggest that we can view Epictetus's reconciliation of "care" (*epimeleia*) with "steadiness" (*eustatheia*) as a way of unifying what Heidegger calls "the double sense of care" (1953: 177–8, citing Ep. *Diss.* 2.5.9 and Heidegger 1962: §42 H199). In other words, by combining free responsibility for finite events with appropriation of an infinite divine law, Stoicism configures in its own way the same issues as the two Heideggerian faces of care, namely "thrownness" and "projection." One might even argue, developing statements by Deleuze and Paul Veyne (Deleuze 2004: 148–9; Veyne 2003: 181 n. 80), that Senecan tragedy dramatizes the tension this creates (cf. Lampe 2018).

Deleuze scarcely mentions "freedom" in his reading of Stoicism, but what he does say is very indebted to Goldschmidt. Goldschmidt writes the following in his discussion of "the use of impressions":

Since we cannot, like god, go from intention to act in the same instant, since the act [i.e., the event] is given to us first, it will suffice in this same instant to follow the inverse pathway and make the act (what does not depend on us) coincide with the intention (which depends on us fully). We must "accept" the event and want it. (Goldschmidt 1953: 100)

For Deleuze, the Stoic sage aims to articulate and assent to "cataleptic impressions"[10] that "envelope" the differential sense of an event (2004: 163–7). This is what Deleuze calls "counter-actualization." For a Stoic it is the sense of divine thought that must be counteractualized. Deleuze instead relates counteractualization to the psychoanalytic "phantasm." This is where he speaks of freedom: "It is here that our greatest freedom lies—the freedom by which we develop and lead the event to its completion and transmutation, and finally become masters of actualizations and causes" (2004: 243). In good Stoic fashion, he construes "freedom" in what we can loosely call a "psychological" sense; in other words, he makes it primarily a matter of the agent's relation to her own passions and actions (Bobzien 1998: 338–45). That said, it must be added that Deleuze envisages a very different way of relating to passions and actions than the ancient Stoics did. As Janae Sholtz shows, a Deleuzean neo-Stoicism (especially if it were nourished by Deleuze's later collaborations with Félix Guattari) would continue to revolve around techniques of self-cultivation, which we could call the pursuit of freedom; but "habituation" would be replaced with "experimentation," and the moderation of emotions (impassivity and eupathy) with their "intensification" and "amplification." Underlying these changes is the shift from an implicit theory of self as an "inner citadel" to Deleuze's valorization of "nomadic subjectivity" and the impersonal (Sholtz, Ch. 4).

Perhaps the most sustained discussion of freedom in the continental reception of Stoicism is that by Michel Foucault (esp. 1990, 2005). This bears emphasizing, since anglophone classicists and historians of ancient philosophy often overlook Foucault's philosophical agenda, which tends to disappear behind his philological and historical commentary (cf. Ure, Ch. 9). In the final years of his life, Foucault had come to see the continuity of his oeuvre in investigating how, given that "governmentality" (the operations of power) pervades "subjectivation" (the formation of subjectivity) and "veridiction" (the constitution of truths), we can nevertheless resist domination and incapacitation (Foucault 1990: 3–7, 1996: esp. 432–49, 2010: 2–6, 2011: 8–9, 65–8). If he emphasizes the priority of self-care over knowing and governing oneself and others in Stoicism (esp. 2005: 250–69, 455–62), it is not primarily in order to make claims about the conceptualization of "the self,"[11] but rather because he suspects this model of subjectivation can facilitate a kind of freedom *under the circumstances in which he is living*. Thus, his hyperbolic assertion that "there is no first or final point of resistance to political power other than the relationship one has to oneself" (which he softens in a subsequent interview) must be taken with its immediate prequel: "I think we may have to suspect that we find it impossible today to constitute an ethic of the self, even though it may be an urgent, fundamental, and politically indispensable task" (2005: 252, cf. 1996: 448).

Several chapters in this volume explore Foucault's search for freedom in Stoic practices. Michael Ure confronts Foucault's praise of Stoicism with Hannah Arendt's critique. Arendt and Foucault loosely agree about the harmful effects of managerial governmentality in modern liberal states. But Arendt, drawing on a Hegelian tradition to which Sartre was also heir, argues that Stoicism positively saps resistance to political domination. Foucault rightly objects that Stoics by no means encourage withdrawal from political activity, contrary to Arendt's assertions. But Ure finds little evidence that ancient Stoicism equipped its practitioners to resist political domination (Ure, Ch. 9).

By way of confirmation, one might adduce David Sedley's reconstruction of how philosophical commitments influenced the plot against the "tyranny" of Julius Caesar in 44 BCE. Contrary to the impression given by Shakespeare, Brutus was motivated by Antiochean rather than Stoic principles. A fascinating report in Plutarch's *Life of Brutus* (12.3-4) underpins Sedley's contention that "it is far from being the case that Brutus was even a Stoic-sympathizer. . . . It will turn out to be no accident at all that the conspirators did not even include any known Stoics" (1997: 44). "For a Stoic," Sedley explains, "freedom is first and foremost a personal matter, exclusive to the wise, who can count on preserving it under any political conditions" (50). Whether for this or other reasons, the ancient Stoic political imagination was often dull and sometimes downright establishmentarian (cf. Lampe, Ch. 6).

On the other hand, the activity of Roman Stoics, like Thrasea Paetus, Musonius Rufus, and Helvidius Priscus, arguably amounts to political resistance in a sense both Foucault and Arendt would recognize, even though it eschews violent regime change. Consider the following dialogue between Helvidius Priscus and the emperor Vespasian imagined by Epictetus:

> When Vespasian sent to him and forbade him from entering the Senate, he answered, "It's in your power not to allow me to be a Senator. But as long as I am, I must go in." "Fine, then go in, but stay silent." "Don't call upon me, and I'll stay silent." "But I have to call upon you." "And I have to say what seems right." "But if you say it, I'll kill you." "So when did I tell you I was immortal? You'll do your part, and I'll do mine. Your part is to kill, mine to die without trembling; yours to exile, mine to depart without distress." So what good did Priscus do, being just one person? Well, what good does the purple do to the garment? What else than stand out as purple and display itself as a fine model for other people? (*Diss.* 1.2.19-22)

In his chapter, John Sellars confirms Foucault's assertion that Roman Stoics often view life as a heroic "test" (Sellars, Ch. 7). If Priscus was enacting such a test with Vespasian, one could argue that it was futile: he was in fact killed by the emperor, whose behavior remained unchanged. We could even follow Lacan's claims about Stoic "masochism," and suggest that Priscus's unconscious goal was to *encourage* Vespasian to "lay down the law" (Lampe 2013: 192–7). But it is worth considering more carefully Epictetus's claim that Priscus's solitary resistance nevertheless "did good" (ὠφέλησε) and "was displayed as a fine model for other people" (τοῖς ἄλλοις δὲ καλὸν παράδειγμα ἔκκειται).

Let me briefly sketch a reading of how Priscus exercises a kind of freedom. For a Foucauldian, the principal question is not how Priscus responds to the emperor's explicit commands, but rather how he relates to the considerations that implicitly give those commands meaning and force. In this instance, those considerations include the value of execution, exile, fear, and distress, and the privileges and obligations of an emperor, senator, or citizen. If we bear in mind the historical contexts, we will appreciate that these are subtler than they might appear to most modern readers. At this time the Roman Empire was once again recovering from several years of civil war and the swift, violent deaths of four emperors (ca. 67–69 CE). As it had under Augustus, this recovery involved an array of practical and symbolic measures. In both respects Helvidius Priscus, as both senator and praetor, clashed with the new emperor. For example, he argued that it was the senate, not the emperor, which should control the treasury and address the deficit created by the wars, and he both initiated and performed the most conspicuous ceremonial role in the postwar restoration of the central shrine of the Roman state, namely the temple of Jupiter, Juno, and Minerva on the Capitoline hill (Tac. *Hist.* 4.5-9, 4.53; Malitz 1985; Wardle 1996). It would thus be entirely incorrect to claim that Helvidius only concerned himself with "inner freedom," and did nothing to oppose the actual and external operations of imperial power. What a Foucauldian reading adds here is the suggestion that it is by caring for himself, constantly trying to discern how to be a more virtuous senator, praetor, and human being under complex and demanding political circumstances, that Priscus finds the leverage to reconfigure governmentality's "mobile field of force relations" (Foucault 1998: 95–6). This concern allows him to disregard the considerations that Vespasian hopes will govern his decisions, such as that death is bad and opposing the emperor is pointless. For Priscus, the question is instead whether a certain attitude toward execution or the emperor allows him to perfect "the person he is" (Frede 2007). By focusing on this question, Priscus not only deflects Vespasian's attempt at control but also exerts influence over others—as attested not only by Epictetus's commemoration but also by the lost biography of Herennius Senecio (another Stoic, himself executed by Domitian; on the "Stoic resistance," see Syme 1991).

Perhaps it is therefore best to maintain a middle position: Arendt is right that Stoicism *sometimes* motivates aquiescence and complicity, but Foucault is also right that prioritizing the self's relation to itself *sometimes* nourishes political resistance. In fact, I suggest that recognizing this ambivalent potential in Stoic politics is very important for modern practitioners, since it can help them avoid pitfalls and cultivate the tradition's best potentials.

The example of Priscus raises another issue for Stoicism and freedom. If he evades imperial influence by prioritizing the effort to become a more just and courageous version of himself, does he not thereby risk "subjection" to precisely those normalizing ideals of "justice" and "courage?" To put it another way, cannot the pressure to "be brave" and "pursue justice," both as internalized ideals and as exhortations from like-minded friends, in itself become controlling and oppressive? One way to approach this problem is via Foucault's final seminar on *parrhēsia* (2011), which may be translated "saying everything" or "free speech." While some commentators have been apologetic about this seminar, which Foucault completed while dying of AIDS, Valéry Laurand finds it surprisingly useful for interpreting *parrhēsia* in the works of Seneca, Musonius Rufus, and Marcus Aurelius. *Parrhēsia* is both a mechanism of self-care and a testament to a certain mode of relating to oneself and others. It is this "testimonial" dimension which leads Foucault to view it as a kind of "truth-telling." This truth-telling is not a matter of embodying preexistent "true" propositions; it aims to "be truthful" without being grounded in certain knowledge. For this reason, at least in part, it avoids subjecting its speaker to the kind of norms that would constrain her freedom. In fact, Laurand argues that Stoic *parrhēsia*, because it takes careful account of circumstances and addressees, is a better candidate for "the reality of philosophy" than the Cynicism championed by Foucault. In other words, Laurand speculates that Stoicism could offer a model of philosophical "free speech" as "truth-telling" that constitutes political action (Laurand, Ch. 8).

A great deal could be said about freedom and Stoicism following Foucault, but I shall restrict myself to two brief notes. The first concerns Bernard Stiegler, a philosopher best known for his work on "technics": in other words, the acquisition and practice of skills (or "techniques"), their material and digital supports ("technology"), and their psychical, social, and institutional frameworks. Terms borrowed from Senecan Stoicism feature prominently in Stiegler's transformation of Foucault's "care of the self" into "therapeutics" of the capacity to "take care" (see especially Stiegler 2010).[12] Second, Clifford Robinson explores Agamben's remarks about a Stoic "providence-fate apparatus" in *The Kingdom and the Glory* (Agamben 2011). Agamben's concept of an "apparatus" emerges from his critical reading of Foucault (Agamben 2009). Responding critically to Agamben, Robinson argues that "zones of indifference" in Stoic cosmology permit Seneca to elude (at least in part) the incapacitating effects of the emperor Claudius's sovereign power (Robinson, Ch. 12).

4 Conclusion

In this short introduction, I have attempted just one way of synthesizing the meanings of French and Italian reception of Stoicism over the last century. I have chosen it because it creates the possibility of dialogue about big ideas between continental philosophy and not only modern Stoicism but also mainstream anglophone scholarship. The question of how these readings challenge and enrich interpretations of both ancient Stoic and modern continental philosophies is addressed by the contributors to this volume in a variety of provocative and creative ways. Their array of backgrounds and breadth of expertise enable them to illuminate a wide array of interchanges with Stoicism (see also the companion volume in this series, *German Stoicisms: from Nietzsche to Sloterdijk* [Lampe and Benjamin]). Still, much remains to be explored, and our hope is that this volume stands as a launch point for these future inquiries.

Notes

1. The digital epicenter of this movement is the Modern Stoicism website (https://modernstoicism.com) and the associated Facebook open group, which as of July 18, 2019, had 50,616 members.
2. As Janae Sholtz rightly suggests to me, this also disregards the complexity and diversity of human "nature."
3. Robertson addresses this briefly (2013: 82–4); Long proposes modern Stoicism should creatively embrace ancient physics as "cosmic connectedness" (2018).
4. Alessandrelli and Ranocchia, in their edition, commentary, and Italian translation of columns 104–10 of Papyrus Herculanensis 1020, argue that Chrysippus is its most likely author (2017: 8–10).
5. Note that I am not claiming Pessoa knew Stoic theory in any detail. The reading I sketch here is deliberately charitable.
6. All translations in this chapter from French, Latin, and ancient Greek texts are my own, unless a published translation is cited.
7. Bréhier acknowledges several predecessors (1962: 2 n.3); cf. Bénatouïl (2017: 364).
8. See the scholarship cited by Bénatouïl and Sholtz in this volume. In an as-yet unpublished paper, which he informs me is destined to become the introduction to a new edition of Bréhier, Jean-Baptiste Gourinat critiques Bréhier's influence on Deleuze's understanding of Stoicism (2016).
9. To the best of my knowledge, no one has yet explored whether Lacan's shifting claims about Stoic philosophy of language are philosophically interesting or can be related convincingly to the evidence.
10. Deleuze calls them "comprehensive representations," which is simply a matter of translation conventions. What anglophone scholars typically call an "impression," French scholars usually call a *représentation* (Greek *phantasia*); and while anglophone scholars often transliterate ancient Greek *katalēptikē*, French scholars translate it *compréhensive*.
11. Even Inwood 2005: 322–52, despite his subtle attention to controversies in Foucauldian interpretation (esp. 329–32), focuses on claims that are tangential to Foucault's real concerns.
12. I am preparing a publication on Stiegler, Foucault, and Seneca.

Bibliography

Agamben, G. (2009), *What Is an Apparatus? and Other Essays*, trans. D. Kishik and S. Pedatella, Stanford: Stanford University Press.

Agamben, G. (2011), *The Kingdom and the Glory: For a Theological Genealogy of Economy and Government*, trans. Lorenzo Chiesa with Matteo Mandari, Stanford: Stanford University Press.

Agamben, G. (2016), *Che cos'è la filosofia?* Macerata: Quodlibet.

Alessandrelli, M. and G. Ranocchia, eds. (2017), *Scrittore Stoico Anonimo, Opera Incerta (PHerc. 1020), Coll. 104-112*, Rome: ILIESI digitale. Accessed at http://www.pherc.eu/publications.html.

Badiou, A. (2000), *Deleuze: The Clamor of Being*, trans. L. Burchill, Minneapolis: University of Minnesota.

Badiou, A. (2005), *Handbook of Inaesthetics*, trans. A. Toscano, Stanford: Stanford University Press.
Bénatouïl, T. (2017), "Stoicism and Twentieth-Century French Philosophy," in J. Sellars (ed.), *The Routledge Handbook of the Stoic Tradition*, 360–73, London: Routledge.
Bobzien, S. (1998), *Determinism and Freedom in Stoic Philosophy*, Oxford: Oxford University Press.
Bréhier, É. (1962), *La théorie des incorporels dans l'ancien stoïcisme*, 3rd ed., Paris: Librairie philosophique J. Vrin.
Chakrapani, C. (2018), "Stripping the Dead Bark off of Orthodox Stoicism," *Modern Stoicism*, October 17. https://modernstoicism.com/stoic-minimalism-stripping-the-dead-bark-off-orthodox-stoicism-by-chuck-chakrapani/ (accessed February 12, 2019).
Colish, M. (1990), *The Stoic Tradition from Antiquity to the Middle Ages*, 2 vols, Leiden: Brill.
Deleuze, G. (2004), *The Logic of Sense*, trans. M. Lester with C. Stivale, ed. C. V. Boundas, London: Bloomsbury.
Foucault, M. (1990), *The History of Sexuality Volume Three: The Care of the Self*, trans. R. Hurley, London: Penguin.
Foucault, M. (1996), *Foucault Live: Collected Interviews, 1961-1984*, ed. Sylvère Lotringer, trans. Lysa Hochroth and John Johnston, New York: Semiotext(e).
Foucault, M. (1998), *The History of Sexuality Volume One: The Will to Knowledge*, trans. R. Hurley, London: Penguin.
Foucault, M. (2005), *The Hermeneutics of the Subject. Lectures at the Collège de France 1981-1982*, ed. F. Gros, trans. G. Burchell, New York: Picador.
Foucault, M. (2010), *The Government of Self and Others: Lectures at the Collège de France 1982-1983*, ed. Frédéric Gros, trans. Graham Burchell, Basingstoke: Palgrave Macmillan.
Foucault, M. (2011), *The Courage of Truth. The Government of Self and Others II: Lectures at the Collège de France 1983-1984*, ed. Frédéric Gros, trans. Graham Burchell, Basingstoke: Palgrave Macmillan.
Frede, M. (2007), "A Notion of a Person in Epictetus," in T. Scaltsas and A. Mason (eds.), *The Philosophy of Epictetus*, 153–68, Oxford: Oxford University Press.
Goldschmidt, V. (1953), *Le système stoïcien et l'idée de temps*, Paris: Vrin.
Gourinat, J.-B. (2016), "*L'arbre verdoie*: The Influence of Bréhier's *Théorie des incorporels* on Deleuze," *Stoicism and French Philosophy: From Sartre to Badiou*, Bristol (United Kingdom), January 4.
Heidegger, M. (1962), *Being and Time*, trans. J. Macquarrie and E. Robinson, London: Harper Perennial.
Inwood, B. (2005), *Reading Seneca: Stoic Philosophy at Rome*, Oxford: Oxford University Press.
Lacan, J. (1970a), *Écrits*, Collection Points, Paris: Éditions du Seuil.
Lacan, J. (1970b), "Préface," in Anike Rifflet-Lemaire, *Jacques Lacan*, 9–20, Brussels: Charles Dessart.
Lacan, J. (1970c), "Radiophonie," *Scilicet* 2 (3): 55–90.
Lacan, J. (1985), "Le *symptôme*," *Le Bloc-notes de la psychanalyse* 5: 5–23.
Lacan, J. (2007), *The Other Side of Psychoanalysis: The Seminar of Jacques Lacan, Book XVII*, trans. Russell Grigg, New York: Norton.
Lampe, K. (2013), "Obeying Your Father: Stoic Mythology between Myth and Masochism," in V. Zajko and E. O'Gorman (eds.), *Classical Myth and Psychoanalysis: Ancient and Modern Stories of the Self*, 183–98, Oxford: Oxford University Press.

Lampe, K. (2018), "Philosophy, Psychology, and the Gods in Seneca's *Hercules Furens*," *Philosophia: Yearbook of the Research Center for Greek Philosophy at the University of Athens* 48: 233–52.

Lampe, K. and A. Benjamin (forthcoming), *German Stoicisms: from Nietzsche to Sloterdijk*, London: Bloomsbury.

Long, A. A. (2018), "Stoicisms Ancient and Modern," *Modern Stoicism*, October 6. https://modernstoicism.com/stoicisms-ancient-and-modern-by-tony-a-a-long/ (accessed July 18, 2019).

Malitz, J. (1985), "Helvidius Priscus und Vespasian. Zur Geschichte der 'stoischen' Senatsopposition," *Hermes* 113 (2): 231–46.

Neymeyr, B., J. Schmidt, and B. Zimmerman, eds. (2008), *Stoizismus in der europäischen Philosophie, Literatur, Kunst, und Politik*, 2 vols, Berlin: De Gruyter.

Pessoa, F. (2005), *The Education of the Stoic: The Only Manuscript of the Baron of Teive*, trans. R. Zenith, Cambridge, MA: Exact Change.

Puech, H.-C. (1952), "Allocution de M. Henri-Charles Puech, Président de l'Association," *Revue des Études Grecques* 65 (306–8): 20–33.

Robertson, D. (2013), *Stoicism and the Art of Happiness*, London: Hodder & Stoughton.

Sellars, J. (2016), *The Routledge Handbook of the Stoic Tradition*, London: Routledge.

Sedley, David (1997), "The Ethics of Brutus and Cassius," *The Journal of Roman Studies* 87: 41–53.

Spanneut, M. (1973), *Permanence du stoïcisme: de Zénon à Malraux*, Gembloux: Éditions J. Duculot.

Stiegler, B. (2010), *Taking Care of Youth and the Generations*, trans. S. Barker, Stanford: Stanford University Press.

Syme, R. (1991), "A Political Group," in A. R. Birley (ed.), *Roman Papers: VII*, 568–87, Oxford: Oxford University Press.

Totschnig, W. (2013), "Bodies and Their Effects: The Stoics on Causation and Incorporeals," *Archiv für Geschichte der Philosophie* 95 (2): 119–47.

Vernon, T. and M. LeBon (2014), "Do You Need God to Be a Stoic?" *Modern Stoicism*, November 26. https://modernstoicism.com/the-debate-do-you-need-god-to-be-a-stoic/ (accessed February 12, 2019).

Veyne, P. (2003), *Seneca: The Life of a Stoic*, New York: Routledge.

Wardle, D. (1996), "Helvidius Priscus and the Restoration of the Capitol," *Historia: Zeitschrift für Alte Geschichte* 45 (2): 208–22.

Chapter 2

SARTRE, STOICISM, AND THE PROBLEM OF MORAL RESPONSIBILITY (FROM 1939 TO 1948)

By Olivier D'Jeranian, trans. by O. D'Jeranian and Kurt Lampe[1]

1 Sartre's Complex Relationship with Stoicism

In this chapter I will try to reveal some signs of a secret use of Stoicism by Jean-Paul Sartre in his writings from the 1940s involving one of his most important philosophical preoccupations, ethical responsibility. I shall mostly concern myself with *L'Être et le néant* (*Being and Nothingness*, published in 1943)[2] and two unfinished works, which were not published during his lifetime: *Carnets de la drôle de Guerre* (*Diaries from a Phoney War*, written in 1939–40 [Sartre 1995a]) and *Cahiers pour une morale* (*Notebooks for an Ethics*, written in 1947–8 [Sartre 1983a]).

Many elements would seem to reveal a conflict between Sartre's existentialist philosophy and Stoicism. However, Sartre's frequent references to the Stoics, and the "stoic" attitude he says he adopted, attest to a real influence in regards to his ethical philosophy. The two unfinished writings framing *Being and Nothingness* contain important clues about two different types of connections with Stoicism with regard to the philosophical problem of ethical responsibility, which Sartre connects with the problem of "commitment" (*engagement*). In the *Diaries*, the philosopher's optimistic attitude had given way to a critique of Stoicism unmasked as a "psychological trick" fundamentally opposed to "authenticity" (1995a: 19–20), an ethical concept used by Sartre until 1948. In the *Notebooks*, Stoicism will, however, be criticized more directly because it maintained a form of complicity with the established order in the name of an "abstract freedom."

These texts show that before and after *Being and Nothingness*, Sartre wrestles with Stoicism in order to build an ethical philosophy in accordance with his onto-phenomenology. And we know that at the end of this book, the French philosopher concludes that no ethics could be derived from the analysis he has developed over more than seven hundred pages. If this final section is itself very problematic, this statement represents a positive failure, which recalls the dilemma he had to manage with the Stoics. On the one hand, Sartre seems entirely to endorse Stoic ethical doctrine (or rather the Stoic "attitude") and begins to call it "authenticity." On the other hand, assuming that "human reality" (i.e., "the for-itself") is, by definition, opposed to "being" (i.e., "the in-itself"), the simple fact that one wants "to be authentic" is an inauthentic position (a "bad faith," as he called it later). This is because "the for-itself" is a "nothing" and never could be a "being." The "bad faith" appears when someone tells himself that he is determined as the "beings" are determined. So, it is a way consciousness uses to hide its real nature from itself and to avoid the anguish of the burden of freedom and the maximum responsibilities implied by choices which must be made.

At this point, it seems that there is a real conflict between ethical and onto-phenomenological analysis in Sartre's philosophy. But that does not mean that he had to choose between two philosophical matters or preoccupations, and surely not that he rejected Stoicism entirely. In fact, the Sartrean definition of freedom, which he used from 1939 and again in *Being and Nothingness*, is fundamentally linked to the definition of "human reality." And this ontological analysis of freedom betrays his deep affinity for Stoicism, because freedom is for him negatively linked to a situation to which we are called, or rather "summoned," in order to commit ourselves by making choices and assuming our duties in action, but without any transcendent values to guide ourselves.

For ten years, Jean-Paul Sartre built his ethical and ontological philosophy by means of a very critical, personal, and secret debate with Stoicism, and the real importance it developed in his philosophy of commitment and responsibility shows in return that Stoicism is not—as we are used to thinking and as Sartre was also obviously used to thinking at the beginning of his enquiry—a philosophy of retreat and disengagement. Although sometimes denounced by Sartre as an "ethics of convenience" (1983b: 458), as a mere "psychological machination" (1995a: 29–30), or, in a more political aspect influenced by Hegelian dialectic, as a blind servility and a complicity with the master (1983a: 402), Stoicism seems at first to have been considered by the philosopher as an interior disposition, essentially psychological, which can and must be associated with authenticity (1995a: 68–9). But, on October 13, 1939, the necessary connection between Stoicism and authenticity is broken:

> No doubt curious consequence of this Stoicism, of which I do not know any more today if I approve it or if I want to get rid of it for the sake of authenticity. (1995a: 124)

But it was only on November 27 that Sartre struck the fatal blow:

> In any case, the Stoic is a pragmatist who uses violence and self-deception to achieve his goal. What to do then? Well, we must rather suffer and whine and cry but never veil the value of things. Authenticity requires us to cry a little. Authenticity is true fidelity to oneself. (1995a: 241)

A few years later, the *Notebooks* will contrast Stoicism and authenticity more directly. But does this mean that Sartre's hesitation between an ethics of authenticity and an ethics of responsibility is at the root of his complex relationship with Stoicism?

I hope here to shed light on the critical evolution of Sartre's relationship to Stoicism from the *Diaries* to the *Notebooks*, showing how this doctrine fuels and structures the moral problem.³ I will show that Stoic ethical categories—and especially the ethical dualism of Epictetus: of that which does and does not depend on us—were able to serve as theoretical bases for Sartre's thoughts about responsibility and commitment, albeit bases from which Sartre distinguished his own positions by negation. Thus the appropriation of Stoicism by the French philosopher will have been accomplished in several stages, starting with the *Diaries* and continuing through the *Notebooks*.⁴ Writing the *Diaries* permitted Sartre to elaborate a conception of responsibility understood as a response to a situation that calls a person to choose, that is to say to engage himself authentically by "assuming," "shouldering," or "taking on" (*assumer*) what does not depend on him. But it is precisely at this point that Sartre's dialogue with Stoicism makes sense and brings into play the relationship between what depends on us, that is "our choice" or "original project," and what does not depend on us, that is the "situation." The Stoic position, which first appears in the *Notebooks* as a psychological posture, analogous to emotion, gradually reveals itself as an ontological position whose ethical stakes overlap with Sartre's preoccupations. His criticism becomes an essential component of the "true ethics" (an "ethics of absolute human responsibility" [Scanzio 2000: 57]) discovered during the writing of the *Diaries*⁵ by the elimination of ethics of convenience, such as Stoicism, as evidenced by the conclusion of *The Age of Reason*:

> Already the time-tested ethics discreetly offered their services: there was disillusioned epicureanism, smiling indulgence, resignation, the spirit of seriousness, Stoicism, everything that allows one to enjoy, minute by minute, as a connoisseur, a failed life. (1981: 729)

Sartre blames the Stoics for having established a relationship of mutual exclusion between what depends on us and what does not depend on us, producing at the same time a philosophy of passive acceptance, helpless, optimistic and joyous resignation, irresponsibility, collaboration with the established order and, finally, disengagement in inauthenticity. But if the onto-phenomenological analyses made by Sartre in *Being and Nothingness* are unable to produce an ethics (see the Conclusion, 2011: 673–4)—even if they constantly insist on the ethical requirement linked to the ontological status of human responsibility—they nevertheless realize the synthesis of Stoic dualism by developing a concept of fundamentally alienated freedom. In other words, what depends on us, that is freedom, would have for its opposite, as literal negative, that which does not depend on us, that is our situation, our birth, our past, our surroundings, and so on. As Juliette Simont has pointed out,⁶ Sartre's criticism targets the problem of "assumption." If Sartre, who perceives Stoicism as inherently inauthentic, does not reject it entirely, it remains to know what he is able to preserve. I will hypothesize here that the problematic presence of Stoicism in the unpublished writings of the 1940s testifies to a new use of this ancient system of thought, summoned to answer Sartre's preoccupations of that time, and to Stoicism's decisive influence in Sartre's constitution of the ethical and existentialist problem.

2 Acceptance and Realization in War Diaries: Notebooks from a Phoney War

The very first pages of the *Diaries* show a gradual abandonment of Sartre's "Stoic optimism" during the war. Over the course of three months, his positive association of Stoicism with authenticity gave way to condemnation. Sartre's attack on the Stoic attitude contains two complementary sides. The first one is psychological: Stoicism is a "conspiracy" (a machination), a "trick" which finally betrays an inauthentic position; the structure of this critique prefigures Sartre's later theorization of bad faith. The second is "existential": the Stoic is accused of denying his being in a situation when he determines the situation as external to him (when he places it in the field of οὐκ ἐφ'ἡμῖν: what is not up to us). The complementarity of these two sides is revealed by Sartre when he defines his own attitude at the time of military mobilization—showing that the philosophical problem is, above all, a very personal matter for Sartre. His "stoic optimism" is a pure and simple denial of the fundamental aspect of human reality that makes of it a "committed facticity." For a human being to accept or reject war is ultimately to refrain from living his being-in-the-world, since the war is, as Sartre says, "a way of existing for the world and for me, who am in the world" (1995a: 59). This abstraction from the world, in a pure freedom, would indeed mean changing oneself rather than the world (as Descartes said), in a general refusal to act upon it.

The link between Stoicism and emotion is quite obvious at first sight. Emotion, as Sartre conceives it, is "a certain manner of apprehending the world" (1995b: 71), but also "a transformation of the world" when the latter appears "so urgent and so difficult" (1995b: 79). In emotion, consciousness "transforms itself in order to transform the object" (1995b: 79), because it is unable to seize the object that is creating an intolerable tension. As Sartre puts it,

> In emotion, it's the body that, directed by consciousness, changes its relations to the world, in order that the world change its qualities. If emotion is a game, it's a game in which we believe. (1995b: 82)

In emotion, consciousness denies an object in the exterior world, going "as far as to annihilate itself in order to annihilate the object along with itself" (1995b: 85). This is why "the emotional crisis," Sartre writes, is "abandonment of responsibility, magical exaggeration of the world's difficulties" (1995b: 86–7). By representing to himself the object in the world, initially perceived as terrifying, *as* an indifferent, and by manipulating his impressions so that they become "tolerable," does not the Stoic attempt to transform the world through a passive transformation of his own consciousness? Does he not flee from his responsibilities, faced with a world that he continues to perceive, *in reality*, as "too difficult?"[7]

But this is not the angle of attack chosen by Sartre. Far from merely referring to a Stoic emotional "attitude," he highlights its ontological significance. As Juliette Simont shows, for Sartre both Stoicism and emotion imply a "rupture of the synthetic and conflictual relation with being" (Simont 1998: 80). In his *Sketch for a Theory of the Emotions*, Sartre had already indicated that emotion, because it is an *attitude*, a *posture*, implies an apprehension of the world in the mode of "magic" (Sartre 1995b: 82-3), and should not be understood as an accident of consciousness, but rather as a "mode of existence of consciousness, one of the ways in which it is understood . . . its being-in-the-world" (Sartre 1995b: 116). But what makes the Stoic attitude a posture more than an emotion according to the *Sketch* is that it quickly falls from itself—hence the ironic title of "Tribulations of a Stoic" (1995a: 20, 98)—first when Sartre is faced with the pure gratuitousness of mobilization and then through his gradual understanding of the "world of the war." The phrase "phoney war" reveals the Stoic Sartre's inability to overcome the gratuitousness of mobilization and the mediocrity of the current situation:

> Always the tribulations of a Stoic. When I left the Beaver [i.e. Simone de Beauvoir], on September 2nd, I left for harder and better than this tranquil mediocrity. Now I am contaminated, rotten. (note of September 18, 1939, 1995a: 36)

This "ghost war"[8] prevents the Stoic Sartre from believing in his own images and gradually creates in him the feeling of freedom in his anxiety when faced with *nothing*. Stoicism is actually unable to produce the "magic" of emotion, and stands revealed as an inauthentic position, precisely because the phoney war thwarts the kind of optimism that has meaning only when a situation is considered as a test, an obstacle by which a person must bring himself to realization. In other words, when Sartre was faced with war as daily boredom, avoiding the "objective situation" no longer made sense and accepting the war as a disaster, as inhuman, as a "war-cholera" finally gave way to understanding "being in the world":

> The war, which I first knew as the mythical reign of the conservative virtues, then, during my readings, as an inhuman and terrorized tremor of the bowels, as something too hard for man, which consequently diminished him, became, on the contrary, a very profitable anguish, by whose favor one could better understand his being in the world. . . . It was suddenly revealed to be a modality of being-in-the-world, perhaps the most propitious for feeling and understanding this being-in-the-world. (1995a: 89).

To accept the inhuman situation as material to be used in the exhibition of virtue, as the Stoics do, is to refuse to see in it a first "commitment," which would disqualify in advance any acceptance as well as any refusal. Sartre also denounces what he calls the "Stoic refusal" of the French philosopher "Alain" (Émile-August Chartier) during the First World War, because it prevents Alain from "living and understanding war as authenticity" (1995a: 90). In others words, actively refusing the war in which a person is in any event "invested" appears as denying responsibility, taking an inauthentic position toward a war that is structurally inseparable from the human reality which is "abandoned" in it. This is why Alain's posture paradoxically coincides with that of the Stoic, who, although his attitude may appear contrary to active refusal, also assumes that war is an evil foreign to humankind and, consequently, that one does not have to commit oneself to it. Just as the Stoic optimist (Sartre) does not make a commitment in the war but leaves the matter to the military authorities as to his doctors, the Stoic objector (Alain) refuses any military commitment in the name of human dignity. But if Alain, in Sartre's opinion, refuses not so much the war as the "military system," and if the war is not the cataclysmic and terrifying ordeal that would have proved the Stoic grandeur of Sartre's soul, it becomes necessary to "understand the situation" in order to live it fully (1995a: 90–1; cf. Alain 1995 [orig. 1921]: 60).

Now, what phenomenological descriptions of "the world of war" reveal is the deep change in the destination of the original meaning of objects: those which served to protect life now serve to destroy it, in their "secret and sinister meaning" (1995a: 22–3). War is therefore both dehumanizing and structurally essential to "committed human reality" and that's why any Stoic behavior, any optimistic attitude or rejection of the war, falls into abstract freedom—and then human dignity is destined for failure. War can no longer be this test, this adventure "coming to complete my destiny," and this "source of experience" for a person (1995a: 25–6).

The question that arises concerns the Stoic acceptance of this situation as an opportunity for him to "realize" in order to achieve and complete human dignity (or rather his "virtue"). However, it appears that ethical commitment, in order to be authentic, has to be connected to a good understanding of ontological commitment. To "accept the war" is above all to believe that we can take advantage of it as part of any situation. To "refuse it" is to believe we can save human dignity with pacifism. But, in both cases, it is clear that the posture involved is an optimistic illusion, since it rests on the premise that we could preserve and passively realize the human dignity that any object of war is specifically intended to destroy.

To explain this, Sartre uses a quote from Brice Parain: "If you make war, you accept it, so you are an accomplice" (1995a: 58). In other words, since to accept is to be an accomplice and to go to war is to accept it, to go to war is to be an accomplice. But this is, for Sartre, a fallacy: whoever refuses the war (e.g., the deserter) makes it just as much as the one who accepts it, and he is also an accomplice, although he follows different paths. He makes war in the mode of desertion, and he "plays his part in it."

Where the Stoics argued that it is not up to us to choose the role, but only to play it well,[9] Sartre shows that the role is rather the result of a choice made about a fated situation. Parrain's error of reasoning is that it is vain to accept or refuse being-in-the-world, as if it could depend on us. Complicity is a condition of being human since, whatever happens, a person "collaborates" with events. It is not an *effect* of being it but its proper *fact*: it is out of our reach. As Sartre points out, the idea of enduring war as a microbial disease is absurd, since war happens by men and to men, it is human reality. It is nothing that descends from outside on men, like an inane storm, but an organized and intimate change in their being, one of the possible beings of human reality. It should neither be endured as a microbial evil that torments me without my being complicit, nor condemned as the consequence of the bad will of a few. It must be seen not as an evil done to me, but as an evil *which I am*. The war is me. This is my being-in-the-world, the world-to-me. (1995a: 101)

At this stage, Sartre actually gets very close to Marcus Aurelius's position, for instance at *Meditations* 8.46:

Nothing can happen to anyone which is not a human accident; nor to a cow, which is not a bovine accident; nor to a vine, which is not an accident of the vine; nor to a stone, which is not proper to a stone. If then what happens to each thing is both normal and natural, why should you complain? For the common nature brings nothing to you which isn't endurable.

Likewise, Sartre shows that nothing that does not depend on us can be considered as an accident:

Moreover everything which happens to me is *mine*. By this we must understand first of all that I am always equal to what happens to me as a man, for what happens to a man through other men and through himself can only be human. . . . Thus there are no accidents in life; a community's event which suddenly bursts forth and involves me in it does not come from the outside. If I am mobilized in a war, this war is my war; it is in my image and I deserve it. I deserve it first because I could always get out of it by suicide or by desertion; these ultimate possibilities are those which must always be present for us when there is a question of envisaging a situation. (2011: 598–9)

Here Sartre shows that there is no event which is not commensurate with humanity. But, where Marcus Aurelius insists that any event that happens to a person is "human" by virtue of universal nature, which makes us bear nothing unbearable, Sartre believes instead that events which are structurally "inhuman" (such as war or a disease) become "human" in that they engage our responsibility when they "come to us." It is again by Marcus Aurelius (6.42) that he seems to be inspired when he says that complicity is a condition of humankind since, whatever happens, we "collaborate" with events.

We understand that for Sartre, human responsibility is affiliated with the burden of freedom, the anxiety of having to maintain the values that would not exist without our concrete commitment in the world. For Marcus Aurelius, it is obviously different: responsibility is devoid of anxiety, because it is established on a universal, providential, and rational nature that insures people the opportunity to achieve virtue. The Stoic does not carry the "weight of the world on his shoulders," as Sartre says in *Being and Nothingness* (2011: 598–600), so it is unclear what the assumption of responsibilities can mean for him. For the Stoics, what does not depend on us (e.g., war) is the object or, better, the "material" of what depends on us, that is "the use of impressions" (Epictetus, *passim*). Ultimately, the field of the οὐκ ἐφ'ἡμῖν (not in our power) is grounded in the field of the ἐφ'ἡμῖν (in our power) by the free use of impressions—the "faculty of choosing" or *prohairesis* (as Epictetus defines it)—which has the immediate effect of isolating the freedom of fate by making it our means of achieving virtue or, in other words, of achieving voluntary accordance with nature.

If the Stoics assume, with a certain optimism, this natural collaboration with events, we can suppose that they do it at the price of an ethical dualism that Sartre interprets liberally (1) as an ontological dualism—the separation between what depends on us and what does not depend on us—and (2) as an assertion that the world is providentially and thus rationally organized and animated by a divine will. Sartre obviously rejected the latter hypothesis, but it is not clear that he did the same for the former. I would suggest rather that it is a different orientation of the οὐκ ἐφ'ἡμῖν (that which does not depend on us) that Sartre has fully integrated with the human reality as its own "condition," whereas the Stoics distinguished it as an "opportunity." In other words, if the Stoics consider war as another opportunity to activate or "realize" a person's humanity by voluntary accordance with nature, Sartre sees a more fundamental and ontological commitment through which decisions and the actions may make sense. The criticism of Stoicism is made at two levels that must not be confused. On the one hand, the point is to show the absurdity of an active rejection of war. Psychologically, the Stoic's "defensive" optimism is even more dubious in that it seems to protect Sartre from the anguish of freedom, whose existential underside is the comprehension of the factitious but necessary "investment" of human reality. This analysis leads Sartre, in a long note of October 3, 1939 (1995a: 90–1), to return to his dilemma:

> I found myself at a crossroads between the Stoic refusal that all my ethical notions taught me to want and authenticity—and I tried to get rid of one in favor of another. I think I begin to understand now: the nature of the war is to be hateful and men that trigger it are criminals. Moreover, it is a historical accident, an always avoidable contingency. But once this contingency *arrives*, it becomes a vantage point that man realizes and understands through his being-in-the-world (because this being-in-the-world is *in danger*). Better yet, it is the being-in-the-world of man that is human reality itself from the perspective of fragility, of the absurd and of despair, but thereby set in relief. We must therefore live war without denial, which does not mean we do not hate it, because its nature is to be hated. It must be lived in the hateful and authenticity. In short, the change in my views is the following: I took war for an inhuman disorder that fell on man, I see now that it is a hateful but orderly and human situation, it is one of the modes of being-in-the-world of man.

This passage continues the discussion of a specific form of Stoicism that Sartre attributes to Alain. The "Stoic refusal à la Chartier" refuses itself in war by refusing war as an inhuman situation. Ultimately, Sartre reproaches Alain for not living the war, not realizing it, and keeping his "eyes closed" (1995a: 90). When writing the first book of the *Diaries*, Sartre clarifies his thoughts on the attitude to be adopted toward war. Stoic avoidance (by acceptance or refusal) and "realization" of the existential (authenticity) can only be opposed by reference to the situation. As Sartre points out, Alain's "Stoicism is imported from peace to war"; it "would rather be an ethics of peace, inapplicable in war." This refusal is "Stoic" since it builds itself on three complementary and equally false ideas: (1) war is a bad thing when it involves violence toward others, an external evil which does not depend on us; (2) war is inhuman; and (3) it is possible to save human dignity in spite of it. Most probably seduced by this idea, Sartre gets rid of it gradually by considering that the "sinister and secret meaning" (1995a: 22–3) of the world of war is the destruction of objects and therefore dehumanization, but that war does not come from the outside as an inhuman evil which would be necessary to endure (in Stoic acceptance) or to eliminate or desert (in Stoic refusal); war is human reality, and it is a fate necessary to assume as its own condition. By saying "I am the war," however, Sartre seems to introduce what does not depend on us at the heart of human reality, understanding what depends on us as an act of assuming this very fate. The thing stamped "not in our power" is not so much the "material" of the thing stamped "in our power" as the density of its own being, so to speak; it is not so much an opportunity for achievement as the condition of achievement's meaningfulness. Thus it is no longer a question of accepting or refusing it, but rather of assuming it (1995a: 177).

As pointed out by Juliette Simont (1995), whereas Stoicism is "dualizing" posture, authenticity is a "totalizing," and considers human reality as being-in-the-world or in *situation*, that is in its fundamental duplicity: necessarily both gratuitous and free. In other words, the authentic posture sees the possibilities of human reality as being, in this specific case, *of* war, through what Sartre calls "pre-ontological understanding" (1995a: 60). But human reality's complete understanding of itself, in the mode of non-complicit reflection, implies apprehending the interrelations of the ἐφ'ἡμῖν and the οὐκ ἐφ'ἡμῖν.

One could say against Sartre that Epictetus also "totalizes," since "external materials" merely refer us to a free use of impressions by our faculty of choosing. Therefore the thing stamped οὐκ ἐφ'ἡμῖν is dependent on the thing stamped ἐφ'ἡμῖν, from which it receives its negative determination. The Stoic sage paradoxically reaffirms his freedom in the agreement of his will with that of god. The Stoic posture "totalizes" freedom by conceiving every event, every thing and every representation, as material for free use. The world becomes for humans the place of appearance and exercise of our own free usage. By contrast, the Sartrean idea of "assumption" implies a totalization in the sense of alienation, since the aim is to understand that any attitude necessarily indexes itself to an unchosen situation, which structures free choice ontologically. In other words, where the Stoics make our fundamental freedom prior to our servility, Sartre makes our fundamental estrangement prior to our freedom, reversing at the same time the sense of responsibility. Being responsible no longer means responding freely by making good use of what does not depend on us; rather, it means freely embracing what does not depend on us as the essential condition of our freedom.

To the Stoic idea that any "circumstance" (περίστασις),[10] which provides unavoidable "materials" and "themes" to the people in it, is an appropriate and undifferentiated ground for the deployment of virtue,[11] Sartre opposes the idea of *situation* as alienating. As I have shown, for Sartre, the point is not so much to separate the field of what depends on us from what does not depend on us, but rather to index the former to the latter. The "situation" is therefore essential for achieving freedom for both Sartre and the Stoics, but apparently in opposite fashions. For a Stoic like Epictetus, each circumstance is an indifferent opportunity for free use, a call from Zeus for a human answer. This call is relayed by the rational structure of the cosmos, which allows us to realize virtue, the *telos*, or the "end" of Stoic ethics (DL 7.67-9). The condition of possibility for the use of indifferents is the rational structure of the world, which passes through each event as an expression of divine will. Each circumstance is conducive to the proper use of reason by virtue of the "kinship" of reason (συγγένεια) that humans have with the cosmos or Zeus.[12] The world is a playground for the sage, and war, for example, becomes an adventure in which he "realizes" his own humanity. This may be the point where Sartre's critique of Stoicism in the *Diaries* is most evident, since *realization* can only be brought about by taking into account the total duplicity of human reality, and not in a detachment whose sole aim would be to neutralize its original investment by so many "jesuitical [i.e. quibbling, dissembling] strategies."[13] Therefore, it cannot be a question of *realizing yourself* through the occasion of war (Stoicism), but rather of "making yourself at war" by making war (1995a: 125).

As a result, Epictetus's ethical dualism leads to the erasure of the specificity of the situation of war by keeping us away from our various "roles." It is indeed forgetting the existential—and thus essential—break produced by the change in the situation (the transition from civilian life to military life through mobilization).[14] Stoics believed they could maintain human dignity *in all circumstances*, because *calamitas occasio virtutis est* (misfortune is virtue's opportunity).[15] They conceptualize human realization *through* the indifferent situation and not *in* it, in a use of the situation that tends toward passive acceptance. This conception is based on the idea that every event is the rational and providential manifestation of divine will. But, as Sartre shows, war dehumanizes, and it is impossible to assert any dignity there, because it is "abjection of man, liberation of transcendental consciousness, breaking with 'life,' the presence of death, anonymity of individual and place" (1995a: 125).

This "great irrational" of war (1995a: 136) recalls notions of absurdity and contingency, but Sartre stipulates that war is not a fatality that is blind and foreign to human volition. Moreover, he considers that it was the actions of people in peacetime that caused the war, because "war is an ignominy and an absurdity that can only happen through people's laziness and cowardice" (1995a: 244). If war is not a foreign fatality but belongs to the order of these "great irrationals," it is because war was "possible" during the years of peace and Sartre did nothing to avoid it. At this point in his analysis, "being-in-war depends on what was 'being-for'" war, that is the situation of peace, and people were-for-war ever since they were born: "Every moment of my life," Sartre confesses, "even in peace, was a being-for-war eluded, covered, deferred, but a being-for-war anyway" (1995a: 137). Here, Sartre's thought seems to be in dialogue with Stoic fatalism. It is remarkable that by making war a "great irrational" at no time did the analyses of the *Diaries* consider changing the structure of what is not up to us (i.e., the war). Interestingly, Sartrean "assumption" is defined by reference to Stoic "acceptance" and appears to be the only possible outcome of being-in-war as an "authentic" realization of its condition:

> Not *to accept* what happens to you. That's too much and not enough. To *assume* it (when you've understood that nothing can happen to you except by your own hand), in others words to adopt it as one's own, exactly *as if* one had given it oneself by decree, and, accepting that responsibility, to make it an opportunity for new advances, *as if* that were why one had given it to oneself. This "as if" is not a lie, but derives from the intolerable human condition, at once its own cause and without foundation, so that it's no judge of what happens to it but all that does happen to it can do so only by its own hand and within its responsibility. (1995a: 296)

That "nothing can happen to you except by your own hand" means here that what does not depend on us, which the Stoics had made the occasion for virtue and the object of acceptance, is actually the very condition of human reality itself. The ontological field of responsibility that Sartre seems to describe here becomes the very object of acceptance. To put it in the vocabulary of *Being and Nothingness* (Section IV.1.III), responsibility, or "consciousness (of) being the incontestable author of an event or object," (1) is overwhelming precisely because human reality "carries the world on his shoulders," because it is through it that there is a world, and (2) is not acceptance but the "logical embrace of the consequences of our freedom." The assumption of the "commitment that I am" implies knowing myself as the author of what happens to me and knowing myself as "primitive absurd fact":

> Thus completely free, indistinguishable from the period of which I chose to be the meaning, as profoundly responsible for the war as if I had declared it myself, unable to live without integrating it into my situation, commit myself entirely and mark it with my seal, I must be without remorse or regrets as I am without excuse, because, from the moment of my emergence into being, I carry the weight of the world by myself alone without anything or any person being able to lighten it. (2011: 600)

3 Being and Nothingness *and the Stoic Conception of Freedom*

These discrete traces of a critique of Stoicism in *Being and Nothingness* tell us that, far from abandoning it at the time of *Diaries*, Sartre gave it a prominent place in the elaboration of an ontology of freedom. We know that Sartre inherited from

Émile Bréhier analysis of the Stoic concepts of "sayable" (λεκτὸν) and incorporeal, which he linked in the *Diaries* (February 1940, 1995a: 395–9) to the question of the origin of nothingness. Thus, the first evocation of Stoicism in *Being and Nothingness* continues the developments of *Notebook* XI (February 1940):

> Is negation, as the structure of the judicative proposition, at the origin of nothingness? Or, on the contrary, is it nothingness, as the structure of the real, which is the origin and foundation of negation? (2011: 41)

If nothingness were to come from a negation, and therefore from a judgment attributable to us (2011: 40), its reality would be nothing. Nothingness would then be equivalent to nothing, as the fact that "paper is not porous" is nothing in the sense that this negation is to be put "in the account of my mind" (1995a: 395). According to Sartre, this position corresponds to the Stoic concept of the λεκτὸν, or "sayable," and it is against this position that he develops the thesis according to which nothingness is a structure of reality and even the foundation of negation.[16]

Let us recall that the sayable is one of four species the Stoics call "incorporeals." The incorporeal is a nonbeing, or rather a without-body (ἀσώματον), since Stoics maintain that only bodies are beings. Whatever exists can produce and undergo effects; now, only bodies have this power; therefore, there are only bodies (σώματα). Bodies are "beings" (ὄντα), because they are causes, while their effects are incorporeals. Although they belong to the category "something" (τί), the effects of these bodily causes are non-existents (μὴ ὄντα). Thus bodies are always causes to other bodies of an incorporeal effect, as the knife is the cause to the apple of an incorporeal event, "being cut." This event-effect is an incomplete sayable when it is in the form of a "predicate" (κατηγόρημα), such as "cut," but complete when in the form of a proposition (ἀξίωμα), such as "the apple is cut." Inasmuch as it is incorporeal, the sayable does not possess the same ontological solidity as its cause, which *is* because it is bodily.[17]

Because the incorporeal sayable affects neither the body that causes it nor the body that undergoes it, it is an "unreal" modification of bodies, like the fact that the apple "is cut" does not affect the apple *in its being* (because "be cut" is an incorporeal predicate). But the fact that the predicate "be cut" is a *nothing* (a nonbeing) does not imply for the Stoics that it is unreal in the sense of "not somethings" (οὔτινα). For the Stoics, the incorporeal predicate is nothing in the sense of "not beings" (μὴ ὄντα). Sartre's reading tends to *de-realize* the Stoic sayable, a path that Deleuze would follow after him.[18] By viewing the sayable as something unreal, and the negation it implies as a nothing, Sartre forgets the fine metaphysical distinction the Stoics draw between the "existence" of bodies and the "subsistence" of incorporeals. Be that as it may, Sartre's interpretation, although it is inaccurate, is significant for Sartre's existentialist philosophy and in particular for his conception of freedom.

Nothingness must be "given to the heart of being" because it cannot be conceived either outside being or inside being; its origin can only be that of a being by which nothing comes to things, a being that nihilates the in-itself. In *Notebook*

XI, it was consciousness; in *Being and Nothingness*, it will be human reality, or freedom, because only this being has the possibility "to be nihilated." It alone in "its own nothingness" (2011: 57) can "secrete a nothingness which isolates it" (2011: 59) from its relation with being (the for-itself). Sartre rejects here the Stoic position on the grounds that the negation proper to the sayable implies a simple external determination, a psychic event that maintains a synthetic unity with the denied in an unreal mode. When he seeks to define freedom, Sartre contrasts the negation proper to human reality with the intangible production of the effect in the Stoic conception of causation, which he conceives as "unreal": "the being by which nothingness comes to the world cannot produce nothingness by remaining indifferent to this production, like the Stoic cause which produces its effect without being altered" (2011: 57).

In other words, the Stoics would have understood that a human being has the faculty of producing, as a cause, a "nothingness which isolates her" from being, that is, an incorporeal (an unreal). But they would have made a mistake in hypostasizing freedom by giving it the solidity of an in-itself, that is a body. Stoic materialism, which clearly distinguishes the body and the incorporeal with regard to being and nonbeing, does not allow us to think the synthetic unity of these two terms, invest human reality, or derive that reality from the void that it is and that it secretes. It is for this reason that Stoicism cannot be a Sartrean existentialism, because it makes nothingness a *nil* (a verbal and superfluous negation) and not an "ontological characteristic" of the being it requires.

If "all negation supposes a certain mode of synthetic unity of the realities that it denies" (1995a: 397), as Sartre says, then it is in the unity of what Epictetus would have wrongly separated that the problem of freedom is solvable. The Stoic essentialization of freedom and the conception of negation as a mere *sayable*, conceived as an undifferentiated relationship between the denier and the denied, would then have direct ethical consequences.

Indeed, if the duality between what depends on us and what does not depend on us is strictly ethical, it is remarkable that the "problem of freedom" (2011: 59) involves these ethical categories as ontological structures. By distorting the Stoics's ethical dualism, by making the οὐκ ἐφ'ἡμῖν the ontological support of the ἐφ'ἡμῖν, Sartre seems to make the condemnation of human reality to facticity an ontological ethical responsibility to assume, but without providing any transcendent value to guide us. This assumption reveals the *situation* in the choice it makes of it.[19] The synthesis of what depends on us and what does not depend on us is more presumed than explained in the *Diaries*, but it is now quite clear why imaginary abstraction of the world amounts to changing yourself rather than the world, in a general refusal to act upon it. But in considering the burden of responsibility as what "remains" to be assumed, does not Sartre come back to the Stoic attitude that only aimed to accept what happens to us as not dependent on us? On the other hand, assuming that human dignity cannot be maintained in wartime, how can we reconcile the need to be authentic in war, to make oneself while making it, while the deep, secret, sinister sense of war is precisely that of destruction and dehumanization? It is these questions that the *Notebooks* try to answer.

4 The Final Critique of Stoicism in the Notebooks for an Ethics

In the *Notebooks*, "assumption" is understood above all in terms of "surpassing" (*dépassement*). It is a question of maintaining what happens to me, of preserving it for free change, and of "surpassing" it. Sartre therefore breaks more radically with Stoicism, viewing it as an attempt to take refuge in ideal and mystified freedom. But this criticism paradoxically will assume a more direct use of Stoic ethical categories (directly quoted in Greek in the text).[20] In the *Notebooks*, Stoicism appears as an escape from the situation and a "pure negativity," an escape into abstract freedom. This links Sartre's analysis to Hegelian conclusions about Stoicism as a form of "freedom of self-consciousness," a "conscious manifestation in the history of the Spirit" (Hegel 1977: §199–202), an "internal refusal" in the form of "objective obedience" (Sartre 1983a: 274), since the Stoic

> accepts in order to be able to refuse. He wants what he does not want in order to be able not to want what he wants. In deflecting responsibility onto the other, he helps recognize the freedom of the other as unconditioned and maintaining in him an ineffective refusal, he limits his personal freedom to an abstract position taking. (Sartre 1983a: 275)

By proclaiming an ethics of passivity and withdrawal—a negative attitude toward the real—the Stoic is dangerous in that he is an accomplice of the established order that he tends to maintain:

> The flight from the historical and the concrete into the universal and the eternal is a category of escape that we constantly find. It's still a complicity with the Master and that's why other slaves will refuse Stoicism in the name of their concrete humanity as slaves. Nevertheless, Stoicism can only refuse in the name of revolt, and if the slave refuses Stoicism without revolting, it is to fall into the other type of complicity, one where he lets himself drown in the world established by the Master. (Sartre 1983a: 402)

The psychological and onto-phenomenological analyses of *Diaries* and *Being and Nothingness* led Sartre to consider Stoicism as an ethics of passivity and withdrawal, a negative attitude toward the real, in that the slave is reinforced in its character as a passive concrete object left in the hands of the Master, while "the universe of the master is not touched" (Sartre 1983a: 402). This criticism also announces the general position of the commentators of Stoicism during the postwar years. For Sartre, it is Epictetus tortured by his master who demands a human dignity, a "right," a recognition on the part of the master, and this affirmation, inasmuch as it is a "pure abstract possibility" and not a decision of new values in the world in taking action, is finally "concrete adherence to the order established by the Master" (Sartre 1983a: 402).

This is the reason why Sartre endeavors to subtly distinguish Stoic *refusal* (*refus*) from Stoic *resignation* (*résignation*). The latter is the "installation in me of the freedom of the Other," while Stoic refusal is "purely symbolic" and a measure of my helplessness (Sartre 1983a: 344). We find here, transposed to the Hegelian theme of recognition in the dialectic of the master and the slave, the criticism formulated in the *Diaries* with respect to the Stoic who believes in maintaining and realizing humanity (with virtue and wisdom) through a hateful and dehumanizing situation such as war. But, in the *Notebooks*, Stoicism is dangerous in that it is an accomplice of the established order which it tends to maintain. Stoicism is thus seen by Sartre, in the *Notebooks*, as an "instrument" of the slave's "complicit acceptance" of his "inessentiality" (Sartre 1983a: 405–6).

This does not mean that Sartre has returned to Brice Parain's syllogism: making war entails being its accomplice. As we have shown, the criticism in the *Diaries* was that making war depends on the being of war and that all making or doing is a stance bringing about a fundamental and structural complicity of human reality with the situation it invests. However, the Stoic does not concretely accept his situation as oppressed or as a soldier (he accomplishes his task with zeal). Only if he understands that he refuses it in the abstract does he stand at attention to release the negativity of his "pure consciousness," to no longer "be this tense object" at attention, but to remain a man despite the insults and blows of his superior (Sartre 1983a: 402). Moreover, these blows and insults are, for him, the opportunity to realize his freedom in the abstract (and not in the concrete, in action). On the other hand, his complicity with the oppressor, or the dehumanizing enterprise of man, does not depend on doing (a servile task or act of war, for example), but on attempts that are "inner and idealistic."

If Stoicism is characterized as an "escape into the abstract," the "assumption" proposed by Sartre must aim at a change of situation. In the *Diaries*, we noted that the ἐφ'ἡμῖν was posterior to the οὐκ ἐφ'ἡμῖν as the two sides of the same human reality, which raised the problem of a demand for ontological responsibility toward a dehumanizing situation. But, in the *Notebooks*, it is no longer a question of "existential living" for realizing yourself in the situation, of being authentic, of making yourself in making the situation, but of changing it. In other words, Sartre no longer makes the situation an opportunity for realization, as he did when agreeing with Stoicism, but an opportunity for change:

> So there is truth in an ethics [i.e. Stoicism] that puts human greatness in accepting the inevitable and destiny. But it is incomplete because we must assume it only to change it. Not adopt the disease, not settle in it, but live it in accordance with the standards for remaining human. (Sartre 1983a: 448)

The example of disease shows well enough Sartre's change from the *Diaries*: the dehumanizing "great irrational" must be adopted to be changed, in order to live in a concrete, nonabstract humanity. But it supposes that the situation can contain within itself the possibility of emancipation, and therefore, a "human" life. This supposes, on the part of the "diseased" person (or the slave, the soldier), a refusal of the Stoic attitude in the name of the "concrete" humanity of human reality. What must be assumed is not the possibility of disappearing from the former situation (e.g., of ill health). The violence of the disease can indeed violently crush the sick man who, if he refuses it in the name of some human dignity lost with his former state, will only try to endure it by diligently carrying out his "role of sick person." It is hard not to see the real point of Stoicism here. But, as Sartre underlines, the former possibilities are not removed but replaced by new ones which should be assumed:

> Possibilities with regard to my disease (being a good or a bad patient), possibilities relative to my condition (still earning a living, etc.), a sick man has neither more nor less possibilities than one of good health; he has his range of possibles like the other, and he has to decide based on his situation, that is to say, to assume his sick condition in order to surpass it (towards recovery or towards a sick human life with new horizons). In other words, the disease is a condition in which man is free and without excuses again. He has to take responsibility for his illness. His illness is an excuse for not achieving his non-sick possibilities, but it is not an excuse for not achieving his possibilities of being an ill man, which are as numerous. Still, he did not want his disease and must now want it. [. . .] What is not up to him (οὐκ ἐφ'ὑμῖν) is the sudden removal of possibilities. What is up to him (ἐφ'ὑμῖν) is the immediate invention of a new project *across* the sudden removal. And as we must necessarily assume something in order to change it, the romantic rejection of the disease by the sick is totally ineffective. (1983a: 448)

The dependence of the "immediate invention of a new project" on the disease as a "sudden removal of possibilities" is the same as that outlined in the *Diaries*. But now it is a question of changing the structure of what is not up to us in order to restore a human meaning in "an additional commitment" (1983a: 449). Knowing that disease or war, for example, can only effectively dehumanize man, "assumption" means (1) acceptance of the suppression [οὐκ ἐφ'ἡμῖν] of a possible which has elapsed and (2) invention, within the οὐκ ἐφ'ἡμῖν "accepted," of new possibilities. In other words, it is a matter of the responsibility of man to reinvent his humanity within a determining and dehumanizing situation, which means surpassing the οὐκ ἐφ'ἡμῖν toward humanity or assigning "beyond" this assumed fatality a "project" toward freedom.

This move of resumption and surpassing of the situation can now appear to us as a reform of ancient Stoicism, for which every situation is an opportunity for the realization of humanity and for surpassing in virtue through an ethical commitment. Note that, in Stoicism, this would probably have been envisaged already by Marcus Aurelius, who seems to bring to completion the doctrine of "reservation" (ὑπεξαίρεσις or *exceptio*)[21] with the notion of the "reversal" of the obstacle (περιτροπή) (MA V.20, 8.35; see Brunschwig 2005). This means that, for Marcus Aurelius, human perfection always accomplishes itself through a technical and an intelligent use of circumstances, and, more generally, of all foreign "materials," transforming the obstacle into an auxiliary.

The remaining difference between Sartre and the Stoics rests upon the ontological presuppositions allowing this commitment in the world and with others, which seems to constitute in both cases the maximum responsibility. So, whereas Stoicism's aim was above all to "live in accordance [with nature],"[22] that is to say with Epictetus, to accord ἐφ'ἡμῖν with οὐκ ἐφ'ἡμῖν in order to achieve the humanity of man, Sartre's version of Stoicism in the *Notebooks* is to invent a project through the situation, in order to achieve "an additional commitment" of human reality (1983a: 449). This means that every circumstance contains the possibility of its own emancipation, for Sartre as for the Stoics, because it is entirely penetrated by the freedom of man who has the possibility, and then the duty, to realize his humanity through it. But if, for the Stoics, that possibility was relayed by the providential and rational structure of the cosmos as a possibility of the world, for Sartre it would be fully guaranteed by the transcendence of human reality (the for-itself) which maintains its values out of nothing, because, for Sartre, a human being is nothing other than this possibility "by which nothingness comes into the world" (2011: 59).

Notes

1 A previous version of some of this material appeared as D'Jeranian 2016. The author would like to thank Charles Arden for his proofreading and his invaluable help.
2 In which Sartre discusses the Stoics's conception of freedom. On this point, see D'Jeranian 2017.
3 On the constitution and incompleteness of Sartre's ethics, I refer to Jeanson 1965 (orig.1947), and Scanzio 2000.
4 This appropriation would cover the period from 1939 to 1948, hence Sartre's confession to Michel Contat, in *Situations* X: "I've always had sympathy for the Stoics" (1976: 135).
5 On the state of the moral question in Sartre at the time of writing the *Diaries*, see Scanzio 2000: chap. II.
6 See Simont 1995: 175–93, 1998: 80–1.
7 One thinks particularly of Marcus Aurelius, who codified these techniques of the use of impressions imagined by Epictetus. Faced with a compelling and distressing impression (e.g., Epict. *Ench.* 1.5), these psychological techniques aim to give shape to the real, to change our perspective (MA 6.13; also 4.50, 6.24, 7.19, 7.48, 8.25, 37; 9.30, 12.27), to strip the impression bare (3.11, 6.3, 8.21, 22, 24, 12.8), or to devalue it (10.18, 10.19).
8 See the note of September 18, 1939: "The ghost war. A war in the style of Kafka. I cannot feel it, it's running away. The press releases do not mention our losses. I did not see any wounded" (1995a: 35).
9 Compare Epict. *Diss.* 2.5.13-14; 4.2; *Ench.* 17; MA 10.8; Cicero, *Off.* 1.107.
10 Because Zeus supplied us with the equipment to face them (Epict., *Diss.* 1.6.37, 2.1. 28; see the comparison with the athlete, 1.18.21. 1.24.2, 29, 34-36), the difficult circumstances, which sadden us generally (*Diss.* 2.16.16-17), exercise and train us, as it was the case for Heracles (*Diss.* 1.6.31, 1.24.1). For Marcus Aurelius the difficulties are in me and not outside (see 9.13), which is why "one mustn't abandon philosophy, no matter what the circumstances" (9.41).
11 See Seneca *Tranq.* 13.

12 See Epictetus *Diss.* 1.6.10, 1.10.10, 3.5.10, 3.13.7, 4.1.100 et 103; 4.7.6.
13 See his note of November 27, 1939, 1995a: 240–1. We find such techniques implemented by Marcus Aurelius, as detailed above (n. 7).
14 "In short, from my point of view, being-in-war would be a second life that would be given to me in another world and that I would have to live completely without relation to my other life (my principal life)" (1995a: 125).
15 Sen. *Prov.* 4.6. See too *Tranq.* 10.4. Cf. Epictetus, *Diss.* 3.20.9-12; fr. 21; and MA 6.50.
16 Sartre's relationship with Bréhier and engagement with the theory of sayables is discussed further by L. and S. Husson in this volume.
17 See LS 27, 33, 55A-G; SVF I.89, 146; SVF II.194, 196, 319, 329, 331, 341, 344, 347, 387, 525. On sayables, see Bréhier 1962 (esp. 62, where he reduces all incorporeals to the sayable), Long 1971, Frede 1994, Brunschwig 1995.
18 See Sholtz and Bénatouïl in this volume.
19 Cf. 2011: 599: "So if I preferred war to death or dishonor, everything happens as if I bore full responsibility for this war."
20 Sartre quotes Greek technical terms from Stoicism twenty-one times.
21 Cf. Epict. *Ench.* 2.2; fr. 27 (= MA 11.37); Seneca, *Ben.* 4.34, 4.39; *Tranq.* 13. 2-3; MA 4.1, V.20, 6.50; SVF III.564.
22 See for example Cic. *Fin.* 3.60-61.

Bibliography

Alain (1995 [1921]), *Mars ou la guerre jugée*, Paris: Folio.
Bréhier, É. (1962), *La théorie des incorporels dans l'ancien stoïcisme*, 3rd ed., Paris: Librairie philosophique J. Vrin.
Brunschwig, J. (1995), "Sur une façon stoïcienne de ne pas être," in *Études sur les philosophies hellénistiques: Épicurisme, stoïcisme, scepticisme*, 251–68, Paris: Presses Universitaires de France.
Brunschwig, J. (2005), "Sur deux notions de l'éthique stoïcienne. De la 'réserve' au 'renversement'," in J.-B. Gourinat (ed.) and G. Romeyer Dherbey (dir.), *Les Stoïciens*, 357–80, Paris, Vrin.
D'Jeranian, O. (2016), "L'usage sartrien du stoïcisme, dans les *Diaries de la drôle de guerre* et les *Notebooks pour une morale*," *Dialogue, Canadian Philosophical Review* 55 (2): 287–311.
D'Jeranian, O. (2017), "Le stoïcisme caché de *Being and Nothingness*," in Aminian Tabrizi (ed.), *Etudes sartriennes (n°21), Penser avec Sartre aujourd'hui*, 149–76, Paris: Classiques Garnier.
Frede, M. (1994), "The Stoic Notion of a lekton," in Stephen Everson (ed.), *Companions to Ancient Thought 3: Language*, 109–28, Cambridge: Cambridge University Press.
Hegel, G. W. F. (1977), *Phenomenology of Spirit*, trans. A. V. Miller, Oxford: Oxford University Press.
Jeanson, F. (1965 [1947]), *Le problème moral et la pensée de Sartre*, Paris: Seuil.
Long, A. A. (1971), "Language and Thought in Stoicism," in *Problems in Stoicism*, 75–113, London, The Athlone Press.
Sartre, J.-P. (1976), *Situations* X, Paris: Gallimard.
Sartre, J.-P. (1981), *Oeuvres romanesques*, ed. Michel Contat and Michel Rybalka, Paris: Gallimard.

Sartre, J.-P. (1983a), *Cahiers pour une morale*, Paris: Gallimard.
Sartre, J.-P. (1983b), *Lettres au Castor et aux quelques autres, Tome 2*, ed. Simone de Beauvoir, Paris: Gallimard.
Sartre, J.-P. (1995a), *Carnets de la drôle de guerre septembre 1939 – mars 1940*, ed. Arlette Elkaïm Sartre, Paris: Gallimard.
Sartre, J.-P. (1995b [1938]), *Esquisse d'une théorie des émotions*, Paris: Hermann.
Sartre, J. P. (2011), *L'être et le néant*, Paris: Gallimard.
Scanzio, F. (2000), *Sartre et la morale. La réflexion sartrienne sur la morale de 1932 à 1952*, Naples: Vivarium.
Simont, J. (1995), "'Se vaincre soi-même plutôt que la fortune.' Le stoïcisme chez Sartre et Deleuze," *Études sartriennes*, no. 6: 175–93.
Simont, J. (1998), *Jean-Paul Sartre. Un demi-siècle de liberté*, Bruxelles/Paris: De Boeck.

Chapter 3

SARTREAN ONTOLOGY AND THE STOIC THEORY OF INCORPOREALS

by Laurent Husson and Suzanne Husson, trans. by Kurt Lampe

1 Sartre's Ontological Project and Stoic Ontology[1]

1.1 Sartre's Ontological Project and Classical Ontology

Although he reshaped it considerably, especially under Heidegger's influence and in line with his own philosophical convictions, Sartre inherited from Heidegger the idea that ontology is one of the elements of philosophy and indeed its foundation. This idea goes back to Aristotle, who distinguishes, at the heart of the theoretical sciences, between "first philosophy" (the study of separate and unchanging beings, also called "theology") and "second philosophy" (the study of substances in motion, also called "physics") (*Met.* E.1 1026a10-32). As we know, the status of this first science in Aristotle is very problematic: it is sometimes presented as the science of first causes, or of being *qua* being, or finally of unchanging and therefore divine substances.[2] However, this tension regarding definition did not become clear in France until 1962, thanks to the work of Pierre Aubenque. The young Sartre therefore inherited a traditional reading of Aristotle, which sees in the latter's metaphysics a unified study of "being *qua* being" and of first causes—something which Heidegger, well after *Being and Time*, had encapsulated and critiqued under the name of "onto-theology." It would even be possible to discover there the traditional questions about the soul, the world, and god belonging to *metaphysica specialis*.

Thus, in its subtitle *An Essay on Phenomenological Ontology*, *Being and Nothingness* represents—from the point of view of the classical dualism between being and phenomenon—an oxymoron. However, from the phenomenological point of view, it revisits Heidegger's project in *Being and Time*, which is indissociable from a "destruction of ontology." Clearly the issue here is the sense of being, such that at the end of *Being and Nothingness*, the project of a metaphysics or more precisely of a *metaphysica generalis* (in the classical sense of the term[3]) is revisited. Moreover, the study of the two modalities of being (in-itself and for-itself) leads to a subject proper to *metaphysica specialis*, namely the determination of the *ens causa sui* as the failed foundation of the in-itself by itself and as the ideal of being at which the for-itself aims in its own foundational project. In this way, it is revealed that the study of being (its scission into two modalities and their articulation) concerns being as a totality and that this total being first appears in the ideal of the being which is its own cause. It is therefore this total being's pretentions to reality that are studied in the conclusion to *Being and Nothingness*. This is not merely a conceptual study, as the question had been posed at the end of the Introduction, but an ontological one (2011: 668–9)—and in this respect, as we shall see, it joins the Stoic perspective.

1.2 Stoic Materialist Ontology and Its Break with the Platonic-Aristotelian Tradition

The Stoics, for their part, took a position at odds with that of Aristotle. Because they identified being with corporeality, they automatically denied the distinction between first and second philosophy. If we can only ascribe being to bodies, because they alone act and receive action,[4] then the conception of purely changeless reality is an illusion. Thus, if we frame the question in Aristotelian terms, it is physics that is first philosophy, since for the Stagirite "if there is no other substance beside those constituted by nature, physics would be first science."[5]

Physics will be the study, not of being conceived in a general manner ("*qua* being"), but "of the *kosmos* and what is found in it" (Aet. I Preface 2 = LS 26A): in other words, bodily beings, their internal constitution (substance and qualities), and their reciprocal and cyclical transformations. At the same time, this physics will be a theology.[6] In this way, even if commentators permit themselves recourse to the expressions "Stoic ontology" or even "Stoic metaphysics," in fact Stoic thinking about being explodes the categories that would constitute ontology or metaphysics. Nevertheless, even if Stoicism denies a beyond to physics, it cannot avoid having to think about something that falls outside of it.

According to a well-known doctrine, the Stoics distinguished the category of "being" from that of "subsistence" (διαιροῦνται κατὰ γένη τό τε ὂν καὶ τὸ ὑφεστός, LS 27F = SVF II.322). The category of τὸ ὑφεστός (what subsists), by contrast with τό ὄν (what is), takes its name from the verb ὑφίστημι. It consists of incorporeals, of which the Stoics distinguish four species: time, sayable (*lekton*), void, and place (LS 27D). Corporeals (beings) and incorporeals (subsistents) are ultimately ranged under a supreme category, "something" (τὸ τί, SVF II.329-334, LS 27A-D), which therefore subsumes being and nonbeing, since incorporeals "are not" (SVF II.335).

1.3 The Place of Incorporeals in Stoic Ontology

Where do the Stoics study incorporeals, that is, nonbeings? First, the privileged locus is obviously dialectic, with the study of *lekta*, of signifieds. As Plutarch notes, although (Stoic) philosophers frequently make predicates and conditional and conjunctive propositions their objects of study, and assign them to the logical part of philosophy, they nevertheless declare them nonbeings.[7] At first glance, we might think that this is neither surprising nor worrying for the Stoic edifice: among the "theoretical" disciplines, physics studies beings, and, alongside it, dialectic concerns itself with what we say and think about being. Insofar as these signifieds do not fall within being, dialectic concerns itself with what is not, but which is all the same a "something" that refers to being.

However, the other three incorporeals (time, place, and void) are "naturally"— we might say—addressed by physics, since all three of them are connected to bodies or to the movements of bodies. Place is "what is completely occupied by a being, or what can be occupied by a being and is entirely occupied by one or by several" (SVF II.503 = LS 49A), while void is "what is capable of being occupied by a being but isn't occupied" (SVF II.505 = LS 49B).[8] Movement "is a change in place, either in whole or in part" (SVF II 492; cf. SVF III, Apol. Sel. 7), and time is an interval of movement (κινήσεως διάστημα, SVF I.93, II.509 = LS 51A). In this way, and certainly against their inclination, the Stoics found themselves unable to conceive of what for them is a full and continuous being without referring to forms of nonbeing. Nor does it suffice to expel the void outside of the established *kosmos*: nonbeing endures as time and as place, without which it is impossible to think about movement. In this way human reasoning is unable to think about being without referring to nonbeing.

Is this penumbra of nonbeing that necessarily accompanies the thought of being merely human,[9] or must it also be attributed to divine thought? If the active cause is both a body immanent in all the parts of the universe and rational and providential, it must be able to think the events it causes, which are themselves sayables and not beings (LS 55A-E). Thus it cannot cause them without thinking them for itself, without which no *logos* would be possible. If we posited a hiatus between human and divine rationality, such that the former could not dispense with nonbeing, while the latter, while remaining a final rational order, would unfold without thinking its own movements, like Aristotle's final cause among beings devoid of sensation (*Met.* 12.7), then we would lose what rightly differentiates Aristotelian and Stoic teleologies, namely the existence of an ethical community shared by humans and gods, and, in particular, by the god who encompasses and governs the rest, the "designing fire," present as "breath" (*pneuma*) in the established cosmos: Zeus (LS 46). Suppose that we did not share with the gods, and therefore with the cosmic god, the same self-aware rationality, articulating judgments in accordance with sayables, and thinking the incorporeals connected to movement. It would then be difficult to believe that the gods were our co-citizens in the cosmic city and that we could, for example, assent to their volition, since, without judgment on their part, there could be no question for them of assent or volition, except perhaps in a metaphorical sense. Thus the Stoic universe, in its various phases, is supposed to be a plenum of being, which satisfies the Parmenidean requirement of the continuity of being—it is not more here than there or less here than there (Parm. fragm. 8, 22-5). It is nevertheless conscious and conscious of itself as a totality; otherwise it could not exercise Providence. But this cannot happen without an intervention of nonbeing, without recourse to incorporeals.

We might say, from a Sartrean point of view, that Stoicism is not only one example among others of the misguided effort to think an in-itself-for-itself as totality but also—by means of the place it accords to nonbeing—a sign of what ontology needs in order to break free from this effort.

This appears to be the principal reason why the convergence of the Stoic theory of incorporeals with Sartre's ontology of negation particularly merits investigation, and why Stoic incorporeals were destined, so to speak, to attract Sartre's attention. However, this "destiny" was also the result of contingent encounters.

2 Sartre's Readings of Stoicism before Being and Nothingness

Sartre's loan record at the library of the École Nationale Supérieure on the rue d'Ulm from November 1924 to June 1928 displays a solid education in classical philosophy (Plato and Aristotle) starting already in 1924–5, independent of his preparation for the *agrégation* in 1927–8, when Plato was on the program.[10] From his first year at the ENS we note loans not only of canonical works but also of the canonical commentaries of the period (Léon Robin [1923] for Plato and Octave Hamelin [1920] for Aristotle). He also directed his reading toward Hellenistic philosophy with Lucretius and Guyau's *La Morale d'Epicure* (1878) at the end of this first year. The Stoics appear later, in April 1926, when Marcus Aurelius and Epictetus are taken out, and the Sceptics make their entry in May 1927, when there are loans of Brochard's book (1887) and Cicero's *Academica* in the original Latin.

We also know that during his schooling at the ENS, Sartre very rarely visited the Sorbonne except in order to attend Émile Bréhier's courses on the Stoics, which particularly interested him (Sartre 1981: xliii). As far as his loan records go, this influence only appears in April 1928, at which time he appears to have relaxed his rigorous study of Plato in order to briefly take out Bréhier's *Chrysippe* (1910), von Arnim's SVF (1903–24), and Cicero's *De Natura Deorum*. More surprisingly, he also took out Karl Reinhardt's *Poseidonios* (1921, in German) and Brochard's *Études de Philosophie Ancienne et Moderne*, in which two articles are consecrated to Stoic logic (Brochard 1912: 221–51). Admittedly, we have not found any sign that Sartre took out Bréhier's book on incorporeals (which first appeared in 1908), but our reading of Sartre's text will show that Bréhier's analyses undoubtedly guided Sartre's understanding of this aspect of Stoic thought, first and foremost in his approach to the Stoic *lekton*.

3 Stoic Incorporeals in Being and Nothingness

3.1 An Explicit Incorporeal: The Lekton

The Stoics distinguished the signified (σημαινόμενον) from the signifier (σημαῖνον) and from "what happens to be there" (τυγχάνον, LS 33B = SVF II.166). The signifier is a body (a mass of air structured by a certain tension, which permits articulation); "what happens to be there," namely the referent, is another body; and, finally, the signified, in other words the *lekton*, is incorporeal. For example, the hand, whatever its arrangement, is a body, but the content of the proposition "the hand is cut off" is an incorporeal. As an incorporeal, it is of course a nonbeing situated between two existent bodies, namely the sonorous sign and the reality to which the signified refers. In his discussion, Bréhier places particular emphasis on this innovative and paradoxical aspect of Stoic logic, though perhaps he exaggerates this feature with formulations whose spirit we rediscover in Sartre. Thus, in his second chapter, which is devoted to the theory of "sayables," he makes the following comment:

> Judgment alone is true, in effect. Now, judgment is a sayable, and the sayable is an incorporeal. So right from the start, we find ourselves in non-being. True things, and by obvious analogy false things, namely simple or complex judgments, "are not anything." (Bréhier 1962: 20–1)

In his footnote, Bréhier refers to the text by Plutarch that we have already cited (n.7), but he forces the translation: the Stoics do not say that judgments "are not anything," but that they are not beings (*êtres*) or existents (*étants*) (ὄντα δ' οὐ λέγουσιν εἶναι). They are "somethings"; they belong to this supreme category of "something" that subsumes beings and incorporeals. In his desire to acknowledge the originality of Stoicism, Bréhier appears to push Stoic nonbeings toward a nothingness that would almost correspond to "not something." How then does Sartre use the *lekton*?

In Sartre, this notion appears explicitly at the beginning of the first part of *Being and Nothingness*, precisely in the context of an interrogation of the problem of nothingness.[11] The end of the Introduction identifies the ontological implications of modern thought's tendency to reduce the dualism of being and phenomenon. For this it focuses on the most advanced form of this reduction, namely phenomenology. Now, for Sartre, at the end of the Introduction, this reduction leads to another dualism, that of the being-in-itself as the being of phenomena and the being-for-itself as the being of consciousness. The being of consciousness can be discerned in its specificity in the structure of intentionality and what Sartre calls the "pre-reflective cogito." It is then defined as transparency to itself, "absolute of existence," "pure appearance," and "having nothing substantial" (Sartre 2011: 23). However, this first type of being is not sufficient and cannot account for the reality "of a concrete and full presence which is not that of consciousness" (Sartre 2011: 27). In order to account for this, it is necessary to identify another type of being, whose characteristics can be discerned in the very heart of the experience of this presence. This being is defined by Sartre as "being-in-itself," and its primary characteristics are given as follows: "Being is. Being is in itself. Being is what it is" (2011: 33). The first point refers us to the fact that being is not derived from the possible or the necessary and that it is therefore contingent in a particular sense. The second refers us to being's internal structure, an immanence that comes before all determination and all affirmation, for which reason it is impossible to apply a system of categories to being. The third refers us to its co-determination with that which is not it. Being-in-itself possesses an absolute solidity: it is "full positivity," which means that it knows no alterity and "never posits itself as *other* than an other being; it cannot support any relation with the other" (Sartre 2011: 33). This third trait refers us to being's indifference to determination, and particularly to external determination, a dimension which will be very important for the theory of nonbeing and its relation to the Stoic theory of incorporeals.

This ontological dualism between two types of being, namely the in-itself and the for-itself, poses the double problem of their connection and their unity. However, consideration of the in-itself does not open any pathways forward and that of the for-itself is too little developed in the Introduction to furnish any. It is only in Part I that a pathway appears, that of the presence of nonbeing in the heart of the de facto unity of being (such as it manifests in the structure of being-in-the-world). Nonbeing appears as a specific dimension, whose status and origin require investigation. The first approach shows that every dimension of nonbeing is inscribed in the human relationship to being and the essentially interrogative character of this relationship: it presupposes the possibility of a "no" (Sartre 2011: 39). The exteriority of this "no" with regard to the previously established ontological determinations leads Sartre to question whether the *lekton* is a "type of existence" (Sartre 2011: 41) adequate for characterizing the negative dimension, capable of appearing as a correlate of every interrogation, inasmuch as this correlate presents itself in the form of a judgment:

> Negation would simply be a quality of judgment and the expectation of the questioner would be an expectation of a judgment-response. As for nothingness, its origin would be in negative judgments, it would be a concept establishing the transcendent unity of all these judgments, a propositional function of the type: "X is not."
>
> Thus negation would be "at the end" of the judicative act without being, for all that, "in being." It is like an unreal inserted between two full realities, neither of which claims it: when being-in-itself is asked about negation, it refers to judgment, since it is only what it is—and judgment, a psychic positivity in its entirety, refers to being, since judgment articulates a negation concerning being, which is therefore transcendent. Negation, the result of concrete psychical operations, sustained in its existence by these very operations, unable to exist by itself, has the existence of a noematic correlate: its *esse* resides wholly in its *percipi*. And nothingness, the conceptual unity of negative judgments, could not have the least reality, unless it were that the Stoics confer on their "lecton [*sic*]." Can we accept this conclusion? (Sartre 2011: 40–1)

The *lekton* which, for the Stoics, is a nonbeing correlate of every judgment (*axiōma*), regardless of whether it is affirmative or negative, is mobilized by Sartre to think the status of nothingness as the correlate of negation. Sartre's reasoning is as follows: nothingness cannot supervene on being merely as the correlate of a negative judgment, since otherwise it would have the same status as a Stoic *lekton*.

Sartre refuses such a reduction to the dimension of subjectivity (the *lekton* being assimilated, in this perspective, to Husserl's noema in its unreal character). On the one hand, judgment is merely one form derived from a more fundamental "pre-judicative" attitude (Sartre 2011: 41); while on the other, as a psychical phenomenon, it cannot explain the upsurge of nonbeing, since, taken on its own, it partakes of being as "a concrete psychical event" (Sartre 2011: 45). This latter point resembles the manner in which, for the Stoics, the act of judging is an internal movement of the soul, which is a body, and therefore a being. The question of the origin of nothingness therefore remains untouched. Yet this does not stop Stoicism from being a meaningful point of reference, as further convergences with other types of incorporeals will show. The incorporeals' dimension of nonbeing, borrowed as much from Bréhier as from the Stoics, is radicalized, rendered more problematic, but not evacuated as meaningless.

3.2 Some "Implicit" Incorporeals: Space and Time

Beyond his explicit reference to the *lekton* and with the exception of incidental references to *sunkhusis*[12] (Sartre 2011: 202) and *pneuma* (Sartre 2011: 532), Sartre's direct references to the Stoics always return to existential and ethical problems. However, nonbeing is central to Sartre's thought, and *Being and Time* as a whole deploys an entire system of figures for nothingness.

One thinks in particular of "nihilation" as the inner structure of consciousness (Sartre 2011: 116), of so-called internal negation (Sartre 2011: 311) as an original relation of consciousness to being and as foundation for the asymmetrical unity of the in-itself and the for-itself. However, it is in the form of "external negation"—which leaves "untouched" the beings to whose determination it contributes (Sartre 2011: 122, 219)—that we encounter space and time. These are not the subject of a single continuous discussion, but rather of one differentiated according to various levels of analysis.[13]

Although space is a determination and framework of spatial determinations for each *this*, it is merely a nonbeing: not a way of differentiating being, but, on the contrary, of manifesting its indifference (Sartre 2011: 220-1). Just as, for the Stoics, bodies are not affected in their internal dynamism by incorporeals, Sartre's being-in-itself, because of its "solidity," is indifferent to all which is not it. For this reason, every being that exists in the manner of the in-itself is itself indifferent to that which is not it in its very being.[14] In this way space is simply the manner in which, at the heart of the world, concrete in-itselfs are indifferent to what is not them, in accordance with their type of being. Neither the in-itself nor the for-itself are space, which, as geometric space, is merely "pure nothingness" that leaves being-in-itself untouched and realizes the indifference of being (Sartre 2011: 536).

For their part, the Stoics distinguished void from place and space. The void is "what is capable of being occupied by a being but isn't occupied, or an interval (διάστημα) empty of body, or an interval that isn't occupied by a body"; place is "what is occupied by a being and coextensive with what occupies it"; and as for space, it is "an interval that is in part occupied by a body, in part unoccupied," or else "the place of the largest body" (SVF II.505 = LS 49B). We find an echo of these definitions when Sartre, following Heidegger, discusses distance as a so-called *négatité*: a structure of nonbeing that is constitutive of the concrete real (Sartre 2011: 58). Moreover, it would probably be possible to extend this comparison to other Stoic definitions.

But as Bréhier emphasizes, Stoic space, whether it be empty (void) or full (place), is distinct from Aristotelian space in that it does not in itself possess any determinations, such as up or down (Bréhier 1962: 46–7). With regard to "inactive and impassive" void, Bréhier explains: "It is without action on the bodies that are in it, and attracts them neither one way nor the other; the position of bodies is thus determined not by some properties of the void in which they find themselves, but by their own nature" (1962: 47). Consequently place does not define the movement of the first elements of bodies, as in Aristotle, but "the place of body is the result of this internal activity. This attribute is determined by the very nature of body and not by its position relative to another" (Bréhier 1962: 41). Place remains a nonbeing, a mere object of thought that "here plays a role analogous to the ideality of space in Kant's thought. Nor does place affect the nature of beings; it acts so little upon nature that for Kant it does not affect the thing in itself" (1962: 44). For Sartre,

> human reality is that through which something like a place comes to things. . . . Geometrical space, in other words the pure reciprocity of spatial relations, is a pure nothingness. . . . The only concrete positioning that can reveal itself to me is absolute extension, that is to say precisely that which is defined by my own place as the center from which distances are reckoned absolutely from the object to myself, without reciprocity. (Sartre 2011: 536)[15]

With regard to time, we can enumerate at least five figures in Sartre,[16] only some of which (the time of the world and its objectification) can be connected to the Stoics's physical temporality. Time was defined by Zeno as "the interval of all movement," while for Chrysippus it is "the interval of the movement of the world" (SVF II.510 = LS 51A). It nevertheless remains an incorporeal, so that, as Bréhier reminds us, the Stoics "deprived time of any real existence, and as a result, of any action upon beings" (1962: 59).

For Sartre, the time of the world or "universal time," which reveals itself immediately as "objective temporality" (2011: 240), is the reflection onto being of the original temporality of the for-itself. Moreover, it represents the atemporality of being-in-itself. Time is therefore apprehended "*on* being, like a pure reflection that plays on the surface of being without the possibility of modifying it" (2011: 242). In so doing it "appears like the shimmer of nothingness on the surface of a strictly atemporal being" (2011: 253). There is thus an "absolute, ghostly kind of nothingness [*néantité*] in time" (2011: 242).

Thus for Sartre, as for Stoicism, time and space are nonbeings—with reference to being-in-itself for Sartre and to being as body for the Stoics.[17] Yet the case of void is more problematic.

3.3 Void: A Special Case?

Void cannot in its own right be an object of study for Sartre, since the concept had been appropriated by scientific physics, and Sartre's concepts are pre-physical. In fact, correct understanding of the problem of void entails distinguishing two levels: the anthropological and the cosmological, or—to put it another way—the intramundane level and that of the totality of being. We could say that the void, when taken as a singular instance, is also a kind of negation. It is connected to questioning as a permanent possibility of nothingness (that there is nothing here), inasmuch as we can grasp it as a particular form of absence,[18] the analysis of which occupies the first part of *Being and Time*. This intramundane void would be that of the vase in which there is nothing, the place where what you are looking for does not appear, and so on. For Sartre, this intramundane dimension is essential,[19] and distinct from the extramundane, the void as an infinite milieu. But in order to address this second dimension, first we must elaborate some metaphysical perspectives.

4 From Nihilation to Totality: Toward the Question of the pan *and the* holon

4.1 Nihilation

In fact all the comparisons we have just made depend on an essential point, which we have set aside until now. It is a matter of relating an ontological interpretation to a strictly modern transcendental problem (and method), even if Sartre's relation to this problem is consistently polemical. Thus the structures of space, temporality, and the system of secondary intramundane structures—like void, distance, and absence—are *ultimately* analyzed from a genetic perspective, as having their origin in the for-itself, since the latter is, in its immanent structure, nihilation, and as a fundamental relation to being, internal negation. The secondary structures depend upon being-in-the-world as a synthetic structure of human existence. Now, human existence has another relation to spatiality and temporality: there is a spatialization of the for-itself because, by its existence, it gives itself its own situation and constitutes the meaning of that situation, while the temporalization of the for-itself is its most intimate structure. However, this peculiarity makes this spatiality and temporality neither merely subjective categories nor beings. It is always a matter of nonbeing, but a nonbeing that is to itself its own nothingness and that gives sense and reference to the negations of the world.

Nevertheless, this departure from ancient philosophical frameworks does not invalidate our preceding reflections. Indeed, it is with regard to the upsurge of the for-itself that Sartre hazards some propositions he calls "metaphysical," which shift his perspective: the for-itself would be the result of the in-itself's effort to found itself, which would lead us to a "radical reversal of idealism" (Sartre 2011: 253)—even if this reversal continues to be marked by a fundamental ambiguity—and to an ontology of singularity and the event, which is not unrelated to what has been ascribed to the Stoics. Although Sartre's critiques in *Being and Nothingness* are generally directed at modern philosophy, once it becomes a matter of surpassing the structures of the for-itself, implicit and explicit allusions to ancient philosophy return forcefully in his metaphysical outlooks. For example, Sartre uses the Platonic category of the "other," citing the *Sophist*, in order to express the status and the logic of nothingness in relation to being: "There is no being for consciousness outside of precisely this obligation, to be an intuition that reveals something. What does this mean, if not that consciousness is the Platonic *Other*?" (2011: 261). If we now try to envision the total unity of being—which includes the in-itself, the for-itself as nothingness, and the combination of what comes to being through the for-itself and what has the status of external negation (the determinations of what is)—we will find ourselves facing a problem like that introduced into Stoic cosmology by the theory of incorporeals: in other words, the problem of the *pan* and the *holon*.

4.2 The pan *and the* holon

We know that the Stoics distinguished "the whole" (ὅλον), which is identical with the world as it is constituted, from "the all" (πᾶν), which is the sum of the cosmos and the void (SVF II.522-24; LS 44A). Plutarch shows himself to be particularly sensitive to the difficulties introduced by the concept of "the all" (*On Common Conceptions* 1073d = SVF II.525). Since it is made up of both a body and an incorporeal, its status is problematic for the Stoics: it is neither a body nor an incorporeal. Plutarch objects that it follows "that the all (πᾶν) is a non-being," since the Stoics only give the name "being" to bodies. Moreover, whereas bodies act and receive action, the *pan* neither acts nor receives action. To these considerations can be added yet more paradoxes, which the Stoics embraced, such as that the *pan* is neither at rest nor in motion, neither animate nor inanimate. The all is certainly "something," since it is an object of thought for the physicist, but it outstrips the two fundamental classes of bodies and incorporeals, beings and nonbeings.

With regard to Sartre, two issues should be addressed here. The first is the constitution of a void beyond or outside the world, and the second is that of the totality. The problem of extramundane void is taken up at several places (Sartre 2011: 51-3, 217-18, 670): first in a polemical manner, then in a genetic manner, before being interrogated from the point of view of the totality.

The polemical aspect is connected to Sartre's interpretation of Heidegger's "What Is Metaphysics?" in classic cosmological terms. Heideggerian nothingness is then viewed as a complement to being, an "infinite milieu where being would be in suspense" (Sartre 2011: 56), which approaches the Stoic conception. Sartre must show that this dimension is not pertinent to the upsurge from nonbeing; yet at the same time, it represents a real phenomenon that must be accounted for, once we have explained the origin of nothingness as decompression of being surging up at the origin of being.

3. Sartrean Ontology and the Stoic Theory of Incorporeals

The second discussion of the extramundane void accomplishes precisely this genetic explanation, when Sartre explains how nonbeing appears "alongside the world":

> In this way knowledge is *the world*. To speak like Heidegger, the world and outside of it, *nothing* [*rien*]. Except this "nothing" is not originally that in which human reality emerges. This *nothing* is human reality itself. . . . Indeed, apprehending the world already makes appear *alongside the world* a nothingness that supports and frames this totality . . . but this nothingness *is* nothing [*n'est* rien] other than human reality apprehending itself as excluded from being. (Sartre 2011: 217–18)

This enables Sartre to rephrase the formulae made famous by Heidegger in "What Is Metaphysics?," namely "and nothing besides"; "and nothing further"; "and beyond that, nothing" (Heidegger 1993: 47). These formulae issue from the classic question, "How does it come about that there is something rather than nothing?" (cited by Sartre 2011: 52). This modality of appearance of nonbeing "alongside the world" is subsequently revisited in the light of various analytical registers. For each categorization that might challenge the realist position Sartre wants to establish, the counterargument is the same: it is a matter of showing that with regard to the senses, to instrumentality, and to meaning, nothing—on the strictly ontological plane—intervenes between being and consciousness, unless it be a nonbeing that neither adds nor removes anything from being.

Finally, the third discussion figures in the metaphysical outlooks of *Being and Nothingness* and tackles the problem explicitly in the course of answering one of the questions posed in the Introduction: "For what reason do [these two types of being] both belong to *being* in general?" (Sartre 2011: 32):

> The for-itself is without doubt nihilation, but as nihilation, it is; it is in *a priori* unity with the in-itself. Thus the Greeks regularly distinguished the cosmic reality they named τὸ πᾶν from the totality made up of this reality and the infinite void that surrounds it—a totality that they named τὸ ὅλον. Of course, we have been able to call the for-itself a nothing and declare that there is nothing "outside" of the in-itself, unless it were a reflection of this nothing that is itself polarized and defined by the in-itself inasmuch as it is precisely the nothingness of this in-itself. But here as in Greek philosophy, a question must be posed: what should we call "real?" To what should we attribute "being?" To the cosmos, or to what we were just calling τὸ ὅλον? To the pure in-itself, or to the in-itself surrounded by this sheath of nothingness that we have designated as the for-itself? (2011: 670)

What is immediately striking is Sartre's inversion of the sense of *pan* and *holon* in Stoicism,[20] since the task of conceptualizing the totality formed by the being and its "sheath of nothingness" is assigned to the *holon*. We will not explore the reasons that led Sartre to grasp the "real" as *holon* and to establish on this basis the possibility of thinking about a third type of being,[21] which he calls the *phenomenon*, the only phenomenon being "the world," simultaneously in-itself and for-itself without being the in-itself-for-itself (2011: 672–3). Instead, we will simply note several elements that can be compared with Stoic cosmology. First, as we have just seen, by affirming the unicity of the "phenomenon" Sartre elaborates a cosmology of singularity, just as Stoic cosmology understands the universe as a single body. This dimension of singularity is one of the fundamental issues in the philosophy of Sartre. However, it has generally been viewed from the perspective of human existence. Here Sartre is close to a project announced in a letter to Simone de Beauvoir. In this letter, he envisages the project of an "ontics" (*une ontique*), which would lead to an "absolute neo-realism" (Sartre 1983: 51–6).

5 Being and Nothingness *between God and the World: Perspectives and Convergences*

That last idea leads us to question the relationship between the two ontologies more globally, inasmuch as both are ontologies of the individual and for this reason encounter the same problems. It is by considering one of these problems, that of the unity of being and the void (or of non-being), that we would like to finish.

5.1 On the Unity of Being and Nothingness

It seems that Sartre responds in a way to the contradictions that the Stoics, according to Bréhier (1962: 49–50), had encountered in the impossibility of thinking the unity of cosmos and void. To this end, he still affirms the internal univocal connection, on the side of the for-itself, between being and nothingness *qua* for-itself. Nothingness, which cannot unfold in all its forms except on the basis of an original nihilation of being, is therefore connected internally to it, not given to it as an addition. In effect,

> In the case of internal negation for-itself-in-itself [the for-itself *knows* being in *not making itself be* being], the relationship is not reciprocal, and I am simultaneously one of the terms of the relationship and the relationship itself. I apprehend being, I *am* apprehension of being, I am *only* apprehension of being. And the being that I apprehend is not posited *against* me so as to apprehend me in turn. (Sartre 2011: 672)

If we follow Sartre's line of thought, we will conclude that the Stoics missed the particularity of internal negation because they did not begin with the in-itself as the original determination, but rather with bodies. There cannot be body except starting from the configuration of being-in-the-world, following the original nihilation of the in-itself that the existence of consciousness forces us to postulate. Bodies are posterior to nihilation, and it is not possible to conceive of nihilation by starting from bodies without committing a *hysteron proteron*. One must choose: either you start from bodies in their contexture as in-itself, and then you cannot extract the nonbeing that, in a certain manner, does not come from bodies and is prior to them; or else you want to think nonbeing, but then you must start from the primary ontological form, namely the in-itself, and from its failed moment of self-foundation—what Sartre calls the "ontological act" (2011: 115), which constitutes being as "individual adventure" (2011: 669). Thus it is only by going back to the in-itself as such that we can think its internal unity with nonbeing, by starting from the metaphysical hypothesis of the upsurge of consciousness as nihilation, as the result of being's effort to found itself and the appearance of nothingness in the world (2011: 114–15).[22] Nevertheless, is there not, in the very heart of Stoicism, a direct answer to the question of the origin of negation?

5.2 The Stoic God, Possible Source of Negation

We can in fact ask the Stoics the question Sartre posed at the beginning of *Being in Time*: "Is negation as structure of the judicative proposition at the origin of nothingness, or is it rather nothingness, as structure of the real, which is the origin and the foundation of negation?" (2011: 41)

Contrary to what happens in Sartre, for the Stoics negation is inseparable from its place in logic, namely the negative proposition. This itself belongs to dialectic. Indeed, when it comes to defining simple propositions, Diogenes Laertius's presentation begins with negative propositions:

> Among simply propositions, the negative is that which consists of a negation and a proposition, e.g. "Not: it is day." One species of this is the double negative. This is the negative of a negative, e.g. "Not: it is not day." It posits "It is day."[23]

Thus it is not only the case that negation is connected to the proposition but also that we cannot study the proposition without negation. In effect, negation commands the proposition as a whole and is placed before it (οὐχὶ ἡμέρα ἐστίν, "Not: it is day"); when the negative particle is inserted into the proposition, such as between the noun and the verb, we are no longer dealing with a negative proposition, but rather with an affirmation.[24] Moreover, the negative particle on its own is merely a part of discourse. Therefore, it cannot be a complete sayable (in other words, a proposition), and it is not even clear that it is a *lekton* at all, since the canonical examples of incomplete sayables all consist of attributes.[25] In fact, it is difficult even to know where to locate the negative particle among the five parts of *logos* identified by Chrysippus and Diogenes of Babylon (noun, appellative, verb, conjunction, and article: DL 7.57-8 = SVF II.147 and III Diog. 22). The element that cannot be conjugated or declined is the conjunction, which is defined as "a case-less part of language, which conjoins the parts of language" (DL 7.58). However, it is difficult to include the negative particle in this class, since it does not precisely join parts of a *logos*, but rather commands that *logos* as a whole (Cavini 1985: 49). Nevertheless, given that, unlike Aristotle, the Stoics assert that particles signify independently of the proposition to which they belong (Gourinat 2000: 154–5), it is plausible to think the same holds for negation, whether or not it is a conjunction. What could be its signification? The origin of negation is the act of a rational soul that denies: "The proposition takes its name from the fact that it is proposed or rejected, since he who says 'It is day' appears to propose that it is day" (DL 7.65 = SVF II.193).[26] The origin of negation is indeed the soul's act of rejection of a state of affairs, an act which, inasmuch as it is a change in the internal tension of a body, is simultaneously a something and a being. And what the negation signifies is that toward which the rejection points, namely the truth of the contradictory of the denied proposition (Cavini 1985: 50).

Therefore we must return to the act by which the soul is able to articulate negative propositions, and it is by this act that negations (in the sense of negative propositions) become something. But does this mean that if humankind did not exist, negative *lekta* not only would be nonbeings but would be nothing—in other words, would not even be somethings? Such an alternative would be true only if the human soul were the only to deny. We might suspect that this is indeed the case, since the place of negation is dialectic. Since the goal of dialectic is the avoid errors, what use could it be to a god?[27] Just as god is a continuous reality, could he not govern the world by proceeding from affirmation to affirmation? In fact, he cannot: even without dialectic, it remains true that divine reason needs to deny things. Divine providence—and this is this is an essential argument for theodicy—is such that good things cannot exist without bad things that are contrary to them: the two must necessarily coexist.[28] Now, unless we assert that divinity intends and wants the good without ever contemplating the bad as such, and therefore is ignorant of it, it is reasonable to impute to god thought of what is bad. Once divine thought contemplates what is bad, it must refuse it, and this act of refusal entails denying that it is good. Divine rationality cannot administer the cosmos without denying, without positing for itself (via an internal *logos*) negative *lekta*. Not only does god need *lekta*, and so nonbeings, in order to think, but he cannot think without denying. Nothing therefore prevents him from thinking nonbeing as such, that is the incorporeal as nonbeing opposed to being, or from being the agency through which the incorporeal as such becomes something. In any case, nonbeing is not to be situated outside of god, but in his very activity.

5.3 Of God, of the World, and of Being: Final Convergences

The central question of god and the world thus appears at both the beginning and the end of these two ontologies. It is at the beginning inasmuch as we could ultimately bring together the Stoic God, who is identical to being and the origin of nonbeing, with Sartre's concrete being-in-itself, taken at the moment of the absolute event of its foundation. Suppose that we set aside Stoic bodily determination and its interpretation, in accordance with the difference in Sartre between being and nothingness, between the absolute in-itself and intramundane in-itselfs. Suppose also that we set aside Sartre's Cartesian conception of God, and return to the Stoic idea of a cause indifferent to its effect.[29] Do we not then find an analogous movement in both philosophies, a production of nothingness by being (whether this nothingness be called "incorporeal" or "consciousness"), where this production is itself invested by being, nothingness is derived from being, and incorporeals have no sense except in relation to bodies?

If we now approach this issue from the other side, that of the world, the shared anti-essentialism of these two ontologies of the individual, namely Sartre's first ontology and Stoic corporealism, leads to a conception of being that is both general and singular. In this way Sartre's third ontological category, the "phenomenon … provided with two dimensions of being, the dimension in-itself and the dimension for-itself" (Sartre 2011: 673), could resonate with the Stoic category of "something."

However, this parallel between Sartre and Stoicism involves an element that perhaps marks its limits, that is, the affirmation of the nonexistence of god, who has no place in Sartre's cosmology. Furthermore, what Sartre calls the *holon* (whole)—like what the Stoics call the *pan* (all)—is not a unity, but the mark of the impossibility of any complete unity or integration. The totality is permanently "in a state of disintegration in relation to an ideal synthesis" (Sartre 2011: 671). This ideal synthesis is none other than the *ens causa sui*, which from an anthropological perspective we would call God.

6 Conclusion: Ontology and Ethics

Thus we can see that the debate between Sartre and the Stoics involves not only ethics but also ontology. These two can be brought together, as we will suggest by way of conclusion. On the one hand, we have an ontology that sets out from god as body in order to achieve an ethics of freedom as self-mastery, in connection with a cosmology of the whole and universal harmony. On the other hand, a decapitated ontology where freedom as nonbeing becomes not someone who joins the order of destiny but someone who faces it as a situation that must be embraced and a sense that must be determined in and by committed action.

Notes

1. We would like to thank all the participants of the workshop on Stoicism and French Philosophy for their stimulating interventions and especially Kurt Lampe for the considerable effort he has devoted to translation.
2. *Met.* 1.1-2, 4.1, 6.1 (it equally appears as the science of substance and its causes in 4.2 and the science of axioms in 6.3).
3. And not in the sense that Sartre gives this term in the conclusion of *Being and Nothingness* (2011: 667–9).
4. "For they only call bodies beings, since doing and undergoing belong to what is" (ὄντα γὰρ μόνα τὰ σώματα καλοῦσιν, ἐπειδὴ ὄντος τὸ ποιεῖν τι καὶ πάσχειν, Plut. *Comm. not.* 1073d = SVF II.525). Here the Stoics take over the Platonic "definition" of being from the *Sophist* (247e).

5 εἰ μὲν οὖν μὴ ἔστι τις ἑτέρα οὐσία παρὰ τὰς φύσει συνεστηκυίας, ἡ φυσικὴ ἂν εἴη πρώτη ἐπιστήμη, Arist. *Met.* E.1 1026a27-29. This obviously does not mean that physics was conceived by the Stoics as the first part of philosophy: their biological metaphors for the three parts of philosophy (dialectic, ethics, and physics) suggest an interdependence but not always a hierarchy (SVF II.35-39). Moreover, the debate regarding their pedagogical sequencing (SVF II.39-44) should not be entirely conflated with this question about their hierarchy.

6 If wisdom is the science of divine and human things (SVF II.35-36), physics is the part of philosophy that corresponds to the science of divine things (SVF II.42 = LS 26C, SVF II.44).

7 Plut. *Not. comm.* 1074d = SVF II 335: οὐδὲν οὖν ἔτι δεῖ λέγειν τὸν χρόνον, τὸ κατηγόρημα, τὸ ἀξίωμα, τὸ συνημμένον, τὸ συμπεπλεγμένον· οἷς χρῶνται μὲν μάλιστα τῶν φιλοσόφων, ὄντα δ' οὐ λέγουσιν εἶναι.

8 Regarding place and void, see further below.

9 Recall that spoken discourse is nothing more than translation into sound of internal discourse (SVF II.135).

10 Our warmest gratitude to Stéphane Toulouse et Sandrine Iraci for their help in consulting the borrowing archives of the ENS.

11 The term appears twice in *Being and Nothingness* (2011: 41), with the spelling "lecton." This passage was first elaborated in *Carnets de la drôle de guerre* (*War Diaries: Notebooks from a Phoney War*, 1995: 395-6). The connection there between the *lekton* and the original nihilation of being is clearer (three explicit citations) than in *Being and Nothingness*. The *lekton* is used there to summarize the classic philosophical position regarding negation.

12 This term is used to describe the soul's mode of being, which is characterized by an interpenetration of parts (LS 48C).

13 See especially Sartre 2011: 220-1, 293-4, 305-6, 346-7, 535-41.

14 There are particular figures: "abolitions," "apparitions," and movement. However, these figures are comprehended at first as internal determinations of the in-itself (Sartre 2011: 243-4, 248-50).

15 Here we are in a specific analytical register, namely that of the human meaning of things for freedom and the manner in which such a meaning affects being-in-itself or, to borrow Sartre's terminology, the "brute existent." Now, what human freedom adds to being is "a meaning" given by the end pursued. Now, this meaning is the fruit of freedom, in other words of a certain nihilation, a dissociation from the chain of causes and motives, which introduces a "nihilating coloration of the given" (Sartre 2011: 523).

16 There is original temporality (Sartre 2011: 142-85), the historicity of temporality as it reveals itself to reflection (2011: 193), psychic temporality (2011: 193-5), the time of the world (2011: 240-52), simultaneity and physical time (2011: 306). A final figure is that of the time of freedom, with a reworking of historicity and recuperation of the figure of the instant (2011: 510-12).

17 However, Sartre's in-itself must not be carelessly assimilated to Stoic body. The Sartrean body is an intramundane determination that concerns existence, not being. Some corporeal attributes, including the internal dynamism of bodies and cosmos, cannot be ascribed to being-in-itself, whose character of being in-itself prevents any affirmation about itself except the for-itself's decompression of being.

18 The difference between void and absence is related to the manner in which, for Sartre, absence is always human (Sartre 2011: 43-5, 317-20, 382).

19 This is the basis of his polemical argument against Heidegger.
20 At least in Bréhier's interpretation and analysis of this topic (1962: 49–51).
21 Sartre's inversion is perhaps related to his awareness of the connection constituting the Whole. In Plato, whom Sartre had read intensively, the term *holon* designates the totality, which is constituted by an internal connection (this is the term used in *Parmenides* and *Sophist* in particular), which Plato opposes to *to pan* as the simple sum of parts. Likewise, in *Theaetetus* 204a-205a, it is this distinction between the sum (*to pan*) and the whole (*to holon*) that serves as the point of departure for a discussion of the problem of their identity in terms of quantity.
22 The distinction between ontology and metaphysics is one of the essential aspects of the "metaphysical outlooks" in the conclusion of *Being and Nothingness* (Sartre 2011: 669).
23 DL 7.69. See the discussion by Gourinat 2000: 211 n.2, whose reconstruction of the text we follow: <καὶ τῶν μὲν ἁπλῶν ἀξιωμάτων, ἀποφατικὸν μὲν ἐστιν τὸ συνεστὸς ἐξ ἀποφάσεως> καὶ ἀποφατικὸν μὲν οἷον "οὐχὶ ἡμέρα ἐστίν." εἶδος δὲ τούτου τὸ ὑπεραποφατικόν. ὑπεραποφατικὸν δ' ἐστὶν ἀποφατικοῦ ἀποφατικόν, οἷον "οὐχὶ ἡμέρα <οὐκ> ἔστι"· τίθησι δὲ τὸ "ἡμέρα ἐστίν." Compare the text at SVF II.204, LS 34K.
24 When I say "It is not day," I am affirming the truth of this proposition, but when I say, "Not: it is day," I am denying the truth of the proposition that follows. See Gourinat 2000: 211–13, Cavini 1985: 49–50.
25 A complete sayable must be grammatically finished (cf. Alessandrelli 2013: 119–20), which clearly could not be the case with the negative particle, whose incompleteness is obvious. Furthermore, the list of incomplete sayables includes "predicates, accidents, and whatever is obtained by their division" (Philo of Alex. *De Agricultura* 139 = SVF II.182). Thus negation, which is neither a predicate nor an accidental attribute, is not found here.
26 ὠνόμασται δὲ τὸ ἀξίωμα ἀπὸ τοῦ ἀξιοῦσθαι ἢ ἀθετεῖσθαι· ὁ γὰρ λέγων Ἡμέρα ἐστίν, ἀξιοῦν δοκεῖ τὸ ἡμέραν εἶναι. Compare the translation of Gourinat 2000: 195.
27 When it was said, "If there were dialectic among the gods, it would be no other than that of Chrysippus" (DL 7.180), the implication was that the gods have no need of dialectic.
28 As Chrysippus elaborated in his treaty *On Providence* (Aulus Gellius 7.1 = SVF II.1169 = LS 54Q).
29 Sartre alludes to this doctrine, although in a different context (2011: 427).

Bibliography

Alessandrelli, M. (2013), *Il problema del lekton nello stoicismo antico. Origine e statuto di una nozione controversa*, Florence: Olschki.
Aubenque, P. (1962), *Le problème de l'être chez Aristote*, Paris: PUF.
Bréhier, E. (1910), *Chrysippe*, Paris: Librairie Félix Alcan.
Bréhier, E. (1962), *La théorie des incorporels dans l'ancien stoïcisme*, 3rd ed., Paris: Librairie philosophique J. Vrin.
Brochard, V. (1887), *Les Sceptiques grecs*, Paris: Impr. nationale.
Brochard, V. (1912), *Études de philosophie ancienne et de philosophie moderne*, Paris: Librairie Félix Alcan.
Cavini, W. (1985), "La negazione di frase nelle logica greca," in W. Cavini, M. C. Donnini Macciò, M. S. Funghi, and D. Manetti (eds.), *Studi su papiri greci di logica e medicina*, 7–126, Florence: Olschki.

Gourinat, J.-B. (2000), *La dialectique des stoïciens*, Paris: Vrin.
Guyau, J. M. (1878), *La Morale d'Épicure et ses rapports avec les doctrines contemporaines*, Paris: Éd. Germer Baillière.
Hamelin, O. (1920), *Le système d'Aristote*, Paris: Librairie Félix Alcan.
Heidegger, M. (1993), "What Is Metaphysics?," trans. D. F. Krell, in D. F. Krell (ed.), *Basic Writings*, 45–57, London: Routledge.
Reinhardt, K. (1921), *Poseidonios*, Munich: G. H. Beck'sche Verlagsbuchhandlung.
Robin, L. (1923), *La Pensée grecque et les origines de l'esprit scientifique*, Paris: La Renaissance du Livre.
Sartre, J. P. (1981), *Œuvres romanesques*, Paris: Gallimard.
Sartre, J. P. (1983), *Lettres au Castor et à quelques autres*, tome 2, Paris: Gallimard.
Sartre, J. P. (1995), *Carnets de la drôle de guerre*, 2nd rev. ed., Paris: Gallimard.
Sartre, J. P. (2011), *L'être et le néant*, Paris: Gallimard.
Von Arnim, J. (1903–1924), *Stoicorum Veterum Fragmenta*, Leipzig: Teubner.

Chapter 4

DELEUZIAN EXERCISES AND THE INVERSION OF STOICISM

Janae Sholtz

In *Logic of Sense* Deleuze explicitly aligns his thinking on sense and event with the Stoics, elaborating upon the Stoic distinction between causal bodies and incorporeal effects to accommodate his ontology of the virtual and the actual, praising the Stoics as the only ethical position worth pursuing. Commentary on the Deleuze/Stoic connection generally centers around passages concerning the significance of Stoic incorporeals, as they relate to what Deleuze calls the metaphysics of surfaces as an explanation of sense-making.[1] Less has been written about Deleuze's claim concerning Stoic ethics,[2] linked as it is to the characterization of ethics as "becoming worthy of the event"(1990: 149). Thus, it is worth pursuing the question of just how much of Stoic ethics, generally considered an ethics of perfection of rational disposition, obtains in Deleuze's appropriation. Deleuze finds a counterpart in the Stoics to his desire to liberate ethics from views of morality based on transcendent truths and universal principles,[3] preferring rather an ethological/ontological view of ethics—ethics as a practice of living in conformity with life, immanence, or cosmic order.[4] Yet, I argue that Deleuze's ethics offers a transformed understanding of Stoic *oikeiōsis*[5] and necessitates a re-formulation of spiritual exercises and practices proper to ethics.

Of course, there is some question as to whether Deleuze actually incorporates a faithful or classical interpretation of the Stoics.[6] Deleuze explicitly understands Stoicism as providing a logic of surfaces and an ethics of the event (Deleuze 1990: 5–6, 143)—yet no similar language of surfaces appears in Stoic thought, and the notion of event plays a much smaller role.[7] Likewise, in his discussion of incorporeal effects, Deleuze emphasizes *lekta* at the expense of other incorporeals (void, place, time), perhaps, as Sellars has criticized, extrapolating features of some incorporeals to *lekta* in a way that might suit his purpose but does not necessarily follow from the texts.[8] One of the main impediments, to my mind, in fitting Stoic ethics to a Deleuzian framework is the seeming incompatibility between visions of the subject and its relation to the cosmos, particularly in relation to the idea of a rationally ordered cosmos and the goal of the perfection of reason as the *telos* of ethics. As such, a further goal of this chapter is to reconcile aspects of Deleuze's philosophy that seem in tension with, or divergent from, certain Stoic principles, and by doing so, contemplate the way that Deleuze's philosophy, while intimately bound to Stoicism, reflects its inversion in relation to the passions (amplification and intensification) and spiritual exercises (experimentation).

As highlighted, Deleuze claims that the only true ethics is the ethics of the event, which he understands as *becoming worthy of what happens to us*. This ethical prerogative bears resemblance to a fundamental Stoic mantra: don't seek to have events happen as you wish but wish them to happen as they do happen. Of course, this mantra is intimately tied to the Stoic sense of fate[9] that events are the effects of a network of necessarily connected causes. Thus, our human prerogative should be to make peace, so to speak, with the causal order and, moreover, try to understand and become aware of our place in it. In *What Is Philosophy*, Deleuze invokes the concept of fate: "There is no other ethic than the *amor fati* of philosophy" (1994: 159), and he repeats the famous formula of *Logic of Sense*: "to become worthy of the event" (1994: 160).[10] The questions that arise from these statements are: How do we *become worthy* of what happens? What do we *mean* by "what happens to us?" and what is the sense of *willing* involved here?

In Stoicism, this principle (to will events as they happen) is derived from Zeno's fundamental ethical insight and moral end—to live in agreement with Nature. Combined with Stoic physics, this leads to a very specific understanding of how to live. The Stoics held the view that the cosmos is fully material, causally determined, and rationally (divinely) ordered. Cosmologically, the Stoics believed that the universe is a unified, finite whole composed of two principles, one active (reason/God) and one passive (matter), both of which are corporeal. The active principle is "life-giving, rational, creative, and directive" (Inwood 2003: 129) and causes all the attributes of bodies: their qualifications, dispositions, and relative dispositions. The Stoic argument for thoroughgoing materialism extends from Zeno, who posited that in order for something to exist, it must be part of causal relations, and, as Zeno says, "it was quite impossible for anything to be acted on by something entirely without body" (LS 45A). This conjunction of rational principle and materiality is the basis for not only Stoic determinism but also their insistence on the rational order of the universe, which, moreover, guarantees that fate itself is providential (the ultimate cause is God). In other words, given that the laws of nature are synonymous with the cosmic reason of God, the goodness (and purposefulness) of the universe is guaranteed. Living in agreement with nature means that we cultivate our rational natures to be in line with this rational order as much as possible. This is possible because of what the Stoics refer to as *oikeiōsis*, which indicates a process of appropriation, whereby Nature appropriates the organism to its telos, and the organism, as part of nature, self-appropriates itself to its telos. Acting rationally is to do those things that accord with one's nature and facilitate the health of the organism, and, as we shall see, explicitly means a movement beyond both passions and affectations, a life internally regulated as closely as possible to the rational nature of the universe.

Thus, to become *worthy* of what happens to us, from a Stoic standpoint, is bound up with ascending to the most rational part of our natures and accepting/ understanding the dictates of fate. The Stoics derive multiple guiding principles from this and recommend a series of practical and spiritual activities, several of which involve proper objects and direction of desire—namely to will only that which is within our power.

Willing is understood as rational impulse, the result of assenting through careful application of judgment and reason to impressions. As Marcus Aurelius writes, "The rational nature goes well when it assents to nothing false or unclear among its impressions . . . when it generates desires and inclinations for only those things that are in our power, and when it welcomes everything apportioned to it by common nature" (MA 8.7). The things that are in our control are essentially our mental states, our opinions, desires, aversions, and emotions, while the things not in our control are essentially those things external to us, which are subject to the immutable laws of nature. Assent should be given only to those impressions that are *kataleptic* (clear and distinct and in conformity with the natural order of causes); this forms the basis of an ethical practice.

Generally, it is agreed that this emphasis on assent comprises the realm of freedom in Stoic ethics. Thus, what is *within our power* is the very fact of assent and control over our reactions and inner dispositions. Since one must modulate beliefs about the good and bad that inform one's impulses and actions to accord with Nature, and the only things that can be considered good or bad are moral virtues or excellences of character, which correspond to the virtuous expression of a rational nature in line with the divinely ordered cosmos, anything that disrupts the inner tranquillity brought about by our resonance with the greater rational whole should be discarded or controlled. This is why the Stoics view *pathē* (passions) negatively, as misjudgments about things that we should consider with indifference. For instance, the expression of anger toward someone who has lied to us or stolen something is an improper reaction to these states of affairs, as these things are out of our control. These are bad judgments and therefore unnecessary passions.[11] Moreover, regulating our desires and controlling our emotions is a kind of freedom, in that it makes us more capable to appreciate the whole and not be carried away from the truth by false impulses.

This practice requires a kind of mental, or spiritual, discipline—as Hadot says, "to apply the rules of discernment to inner representations . . . so that nothing that is not objective may infiltrate" (Hadot 1998: 35–6), and the Stoics develop spiritual exercises in order to do just this. These spiritual exercises consist of reflecting or meditating on one's daily experiences—to identify falsely imposed value judgments—keeping in mind fundamental principles through daily repetition and imaginatively invoking a view of the cosmos and relation to it that extends beyond our everyday, self-interested, and banal experience (31). Deleuze's constant reflection on philosophy's illusions, value judgments, and his creative repetition of images and concepts to evoke the plane of immanence are counterparts, writ large, to these spiritual exercises, and his constant vigilance and examination of the foundations for our concepts and thought reveals a deep affinity with the Stoics's style and practice of philosophy. As with the Stoics, these exercises are aimed not merely at the theoretical but toward realizing a transformation of one's vision of the world, which is meant to be lived and practised (21). The twist, as we shall see, is that what Deleuze understands as impediments are, inversely, the very constructs upon which the Stoics rely.

For Deleuze, spiritual exercises would also be linked to experimentation, which must be devised to intensify experience rather than be met with indifference. His spiritual exercises are meant to bring us into contact with a cosmos of immanent forces and intensities:

> Precisely because the plane of immanence is prephilosophical . . . it implies a sort of groping experimentation and its layout resorts to measures that are not very respectable, rational, or reasonable. These orders belong to the order of dreams, of pathological processes, esoteric experiences, drunkenness, and excess. (Deleuze and Guattari 1994: 41)

Because of his immanent metaphysics, these will be techniques of disorientation, discontinuity, displacement, and disruption, not as conduits to revelation of a spiritual realm but as revelation of immanent cosmic force.[12]

As the second emphasis in Stoic ethics, "willing only that which is within one's power" also suggests that we must carefully assess and understand the causal chain of events, recognizing that events occurring in relation to external bodies are not up to us but, in order to make good judgments, understanding as much of the causal network as possible. The Stoics held that the perfect sage would have a grasp of the ordering principles of nature and how everything connects together, thus making her beliefs firm and unshakeable in their accordance with nature.

> The content of this knowledge . . . is the awareness of the rationality, teleology, and providentiality of cosmic divine rationality as it manifests itself in the constitution and functioning of terrestrial living beings, and, further, the understanding of how human rational action can be in accordance with, mirror, and promote this cosmic rationality. (Betegh 2003: 299)

In this sense, emphasizing what is or is not up to us is a way of conforming one's life to the natural, material order; the sage must devote herself to greater understanding of the cosmos as a whole, relinquishing a view concentrated on one's small sphere of personal interest. It is this imperative that leads Epictetus and Aurelius, for instance, to posit the need to develop what Sellars has called a cosmic perspective.

The impasse is that human judgment is normally based on a necessarily limited perspective, whereas the aim of a cosmic perspective requires moving beyond the sphere of self—to "observe the cosmos free from such human judgments" (Sellars 1999: 18). Even more importantly, this clarity seems essential to actually being able to live in agreement with Nature, moving beyond individual concerns toward a geo-historical perspective in which we see ourselves as part of the totality, subject to all of the processes of Nature (Sellars 2006: 164). Sellars's position is that the Stoics were aware of this impasse and devised certain Stoic exercises, such as meditating on the impermanence of all things (1999: 12), in order to facilitate this dissolution of the boundary between Self and Nature and that this is an essential element of Stoic ethics existing in tandem with the logical concerns for right reason and judgment.

Deleuze endorses a similar division between judgments/sense (logic) and attention to the cosmic perspective (physics), and Sellars even designates *Logic of Sense* as related to the first pole and *A Thousand Plateaus* as concerned with the second, making the case for a holistic approach to his ethics. My contention is that these poles, though derived from Stoicism, are also the place of Deleuze's inversion of Stoicism. In order to fully appreciate how, we must extend Sellars claim of the need to look at Deleuze's corpus as a whole, including not only these two references but other elements of Deleuze's own writings and also by engaging the significance of other figures within Deleuze's alternative lineage of immanent ontology. I will begin by parsing through several points of dislocation between Deleuze and the Stoics's ethical accounts, specifically when understood in relation to the processes of actualization and counteractualization originating from his earlier work.

1 Actualization, Counteractualization, and the Intensive Field

Though willing the event has often been associated with the purely logical or virtual (metaphysical surface),[13] I am interested in examining the event from Deleuze's stance toward its bodily incorporation, as integral to the ethics of being worthy of the event. Deleuze says that the Stoic sage is one who "understands the pure event ... [and] also wills the embodiment and the actualization of the pure incorporeal event in a state of affairs and in his or her own body and flesh" (Deleuze 1990: 146), raising the question of whether (and how) willing the event concerns both the logical and the physical pole of the Stoic division.

Deleuze paraphrases Émile Bréhier's *La théorie des incorporels dans l'ancien stoïcisme* (1962: 13), in saying that the Stoics were the first to "radically distinguish" two planes of being (1990: 5): bodies and states of affairs (which exist) and incorporeals (which subsist), and it is true that *Logic of Sense* is primarily focused on explicating the sense of the logical pole of this division. The incorporeals that Deleuze focuses upon are *lekta*, as logical or dialectical attributes. He describes these as subsisting or inhering in states of affairs that result from bodies, expressed as verbs, and existing at the limit or surface of being. They designate a way of being and are intimately connected to bodies—growing, becoming smaller, being cut. For Deleuze, this Stoic distribution implies "an entirely new cleavage of the causal relation" (1990: 6). On the plane of being/bodies, they refer causes to causes, while at the surface, bodies are the causes of incorporeal surface effects, which, again following Bréhier, can be multiplied infinitely: "a multiplicity of incorporeal beings without connection or end" (Bréhier 1962: 13). Effects can be referred to effects, and proliferate, as it were, at the "surface of being" (Bréhier 1962: 13). This new distribution upheaves philosophical categorization and reverses Platonic metaphysics that privileges the reality of the Idea. For the Stoics, states of affairs, quantities, and qualities are beings (bodies) and are contrasted to the extra-being of sense, which, as incorporeal, is a nonexisting entity—and which Deleuze links to the virtual. Thus, we are set to understand the event topologically as an infinite series of effects, frolicking at the surface of being, always referring back to a material foundation, though as non-resembling expressions (proliferations) of it.

Deleuze also attributes the relationship between the two levels to the Stoics: "Stoics' strength lay in making a line of separation pass—no longer between the sensible and the intelligible, or between the soul and the body, but where no one had seen it before—between physical depth and metaphysical surface" (Deleuze and Parnet 2002: 63), which begs the question of what kind of relationality this is. There are two interpretations of Deleuze's position here: (1) that order of causation is unidirectional, from material causes to effects and (2) that this *passage between* goes beyond a one-way cause/effect relationship. This debate hinges upon the elusive power of what Deleuze calls the quasi-cause, which he attributes to incorporeal effects, as an alternative type of causality that is somehow outside of the system of actual (physical) causal relations. The latter view, which will be mine, suggests Deleuze's emphasis on quasi-causality as an important factor in the differences between Stoicism and Deleuze.

Deleuze gets the notion of quasi-causality from Bréhier's reading of Stoic logic, wherein Bréhier distinguishes "real" corporeal being from "the plane of facts" at the surface of being (1962: 13). In relation to this surface, Bréhier refers to reason's "spontaneity" as an "active cause" (16) which constructs significations,[14] and, though this is most certainly the impetus for Deleuze's notion of the "quasi-cause," I believe it also marks a divergence, in that Deleuze attributes this "spontaneity" to a more primary disparity, the heterogeneity between series, which affects reason rather than extending from it—in essence, a nonsense within sense. It is this disparity that explains the proliferation of "a multiplicity of incorporeal beings without connection or end" (1962: 13) and which Deleuze links to the idea of the quasi-cause.

Deleuze describes the quasi-cause as a mark of difference between heterogeneous series, the unequal and/or the aleatory, and, though there are a few commentators who agree that Deleuze's interpretation of quasi-cause is compatible with the Stoics, many have suggested that his utilization of this term is idiosyncratic[15] and that he attributes more power to this feature than most Stoic scholars are willing to concede. While it is generally agreed that the quasi-cause indicates some kind of causal relationship that involves the virtual (sense or event) and the actual, intensive plenum (the realm of bodies),[16] there is much debate over whether Deleuze's interpretation accurately portrays incorporeals as having a "kind of autonomy with respect to Stoic bodies/beings" (Bennett 2015b: 3) (i.e., can they generate other effects), and, further, whether effects, as quasi-causes, affect how we interact with the world. As Bennett explains, the mainstream interpretation of incorporeals is that they have a subordinate relation to bodies, an asymmetrical dependence (2015b: 4), yet he goes on to argue that some commentators read this relationship as reciprocal (see Boeri 2001; Bobzien 1998). Deleuze's formulation of quasi-causality operates similarly to suggest that incorporeals are not merely "sterile byproducts of causal relations" but, instead, exercise their own power (Bennett

2015b: 5). Bennett associates this power with the logic of events, maintaining that at the level of the event (still incorporeal), there is a proliferative capability that goes beyond or happens irrespective of corporeal bodies "among event-effects themselves" (2015b: 7). Roffe reiterates this reading, endorsing Bennett's view that quasi-causality pertains only to the level of virtual events: "Events belong together, each making sense of each other, providing a point of view from which the other is able to be expressed" (2017: 284). This new causality resituates other events (285) but has nothing to do with the dynamic interactions of the Actual. I believe we should push this notion of the passage between physical depth and metaphysical surface farther.

To some extent, Roffe provides the connective tissue between my reading and Bennett's.[17] He reads the quasi-causal developmentally, claiming that, while in *Logic of Sense*, under the influence of the Stoics, Deleuze introduces the quasi-cause to make sense of the nature of compatibility and incompatibility between events—a strictly horizontal account of interactions between metaphysical surface events. In *Anti-Oedipus* the quasi-cause becomes vertical, expressing modality according to which intensive social inscriptions come to bear on social processes of connection. In other words, the quasi-cause is a problem in being rather than effect (Roffe 2017: 289), that is not merely residing within the incorporeal. Roffe also wants to push the limitations placed on quasi-causality; he just locates this later in Deleuze's thinking with Guattari in *Anti-Oedipus*, where he claims the quasi-cause is related to a kind of vertical causality which operates between the intensive plenum and the metaphysical surface. What Roffe locates in *Anti-Oedipus*, I want to insist, is already there in *Logic of Sense*, partly because I read the process of dramatization, developed in *Difference and Repetition*, as re-emerging in the discussion of counteractualization in *Logic of Sense*, rather than returning via *Anti-Oedipus* (see Sholtz 2016).

In the following passage Deleuze utilizes the theory of the event to propose another affinity with Stoic philosophy—that of fate. Yet, it is here that one may begin to see the possible impact of a reformulated emphasis on quasi-causality:

> The event is not what occurs (an accident), it is inside what occurs, the purely expressed. It signals and awaits us . . . to become worthy of what happens to us, and thus to will and *release* the event, to become the offspring of one's own events, and thereby to be reborn, to have one more birth. (1990: 149–50, my emphasis)

Though the language seems related to an idea of fate and acceptance in a Stoic manner, it is also within this passage that we can also see Deleuze diverging from Stoicism. We can easily assimilate the willing of (or even assenting to) the event to Stoic ethics, but what does it mean to release the event? Here is where I believe the full impact of the quasi-causality of effects comes back into play. One thing often lost in treatments of Deleuze's event is the ineluctable double-sidedness that the surface implies: "A doubling which . . . permits sense, at the surface, to be distributed to both sides" (1990: 125).

Deleuze reintroduces the question of bodies and passions in light of Stoic physics as an ethics of bodies, acknowledging that the event cannot be grasped or willed without it being referred to the corporeal cause from which it results, as well as the unity of causes (1990: 124). He calls this divination a tracing of lines and points that appear on surfaces (143). Effects act as signs of relations, forces, and intensities occurring between and within bodies. Deleuze says that it is by following the border that one passes from bodies to the incorporeal, releasing the incorporeal double and multiplying the method of expression. In *A Thousand Plateaus*, this process of tracing takes an even more materialist bent and becomes associated with the cosmic artisan, as one who is sensitive to cosmic flows and intensities (Deleuze and Guattari 1987: 223–9, 345). Dramatization is this act of retracing or miming of the event, and it follows that this method not only wills the event as it is but allows for more of its release.[18] Thus, the activity, though tracing the incorporeal sign, is a matter of opening up more potentialities for bodily encounters to be actualized.

This could be interpreted as purely metaphysical activity: "to extract sense and create identifiable states" (Lundy 2012: 45), yet Deleuze also writes that the more that events traverse the entire, depthless extension, the more they affect bodies which they cut and bruise (1990: 10), implying not only that "they provide the infinitive sense or organizational structure by which individuation occurs" (Lundy 2012: 45), but that they have some role in the actualization of bodies. In other words, incorporeal events do play a role in the selection involved in actualization of particular bodies out of the dynamic processes of the intensive plenum (in terms of which of these will be expressed): "As long as the surface holds, not only will sense be unfolded, but it will also partake of the quasi-cause attached to it. It, in turn, brings about individuation and all that ensues in a process of determination of bodies" (1990: 126). The depth has the power to organize surfaces, but Deleuze insists that it is the surface—the locus of the quasi-cause—which is like a theater for the reshuffling of singularities, condensations, and fusions (1990: 125). "The event re-patterns a system" (Protevi 2006) in much the same way that abstract machines operate in the framing of assemblages and relations later in *A Thousand Plateaus*.

The idea of quasi-cause is idiosyncratic to Deleuze in that it requires an appeal to these processes of actualization and counteractualization. Incorporeal surface effects are quasi-causes in the sense that through their proliferation, combination, or relations, they bring more unactualized potentialities, understood as the intensities and forces, to the surface. Thus, they do not actually cause in the Stoic sense, but they do quasi-cause the emergence or expression of that which already exists in an intensive state—as individuations and determinations—only now as re-patterned actualizations.

What I am suggesting is that, aside from the logical compatibility of effects/events which assures "the full autonomy of the effect" (1990: 95), in order to fully understand this elusive "power" of quasi-causality, one has to take into consideration the factors of actualization and counteractualization connected as they are to the logic of the individuation (generation of bodies out of the dynamic processes of the intensive plenum); and, in terms of "becoming worthy of the event," it is counteractualization that really holds crucial import. In fact, Boundas goes as far as saying "it is this process that reveals the true meaning of 'becoming worthy of the event'—the spinal cord of Deleuze's ethics" (2006: 17). The fact is that the event is always virtual *and* involved in processes of actualization and counteractualization. As Boundas remarks, "Deleuze situates freedom in the space of contradiction between the sterility and impassiveness of the virtual event and the event's resourcefulness in engendering actual states of affairs (Deleuze 1990: 4–11)" (2009: 223). It allows us to recognize the infinite play that is possible at the surface and between the surface and the depth. Becoming worthy of what happens to us is to exceed that which has been actualized, idea or state of affair, in order to recognize that what happens to us is a constant interplay with the virtual reservoir, that which is excessive to the event in any instant—a constant demand not to hypostasize existence.

Thus, excess is a central feature of the event—an excess that is only contingently actualized and which opens up a realm of chance and indeterminacy not present in Stoic ontology.[19] The event is a "paradoxical element, intervening as nonsense or as an aleatory point, and operating as a quasi-cause" (1990: 95). Yes, it is the case that this event is incorporeal, but it also intervenes on the intensive plenum of pre-individuated forces which form the immanent field out of which bodies arise. More will be said about how this field differs from the materialist, cosmological picture of the Stoics in the next section, but for now, we can relate this to the difference between being and becoming—bodies do not preexist their relations, and bodies do not exhaust the excessivity of immanence, thus there is a connection back to effects wherein they provide illumination of different potential relations and a framework for making those connections.

Willing the event is willing the release of more of the event; this is what is at stake in so many of Deleuze's invocations to make oneself a bodywithoutorgans (BwO), to dismantle the Self,[20] and to become worthy of the Event. Deleuze has said that we need more resistance to the present—let us interpret that in light of what we have just said to mean that resistance to the present means resisting interpreting the real only in terms of the actualized. Then we have a new way of conceiving what it means to be worthy of what happens to us, or as Colebrook says, "The true sense of freedom (is) an embrace of the virtual that is not limited to the possibilities that are contained within our present point of view" (2002: 171). Willing is a kind of *prosochē*, a "continuous vigilance and presence of mind" (Hadot 1995: 84) but one directed toward the infinite excessiveness of the event—to extract (counteractualize) more and more of the event in order that it may be incorporated into states of affairs.

Summarily, what is at stake in our guiding is the following: (1) to become worthy of the event equals traversing the event; (2) willing implies a kind of selection, not just assent; the actor/sage occupies the instant, represents and comprehends this instant, and in so doing selects (limits) the event in such a way that makes the instant all the more intense (147); (3) releasing the event means accessing more of the virtual event. What remains is to explore the final element of the quote:

(4) to become the offspring of one's own events, to be reborn. This is related to the Deleuzian imperative to overcoming the transcendental illusion of the Self, indicating a process of dismantling the boundaries of the Self, and is the (inverted) conceptual counterpart to the Stoic goal of eliminating the boundaries between the self and the cosmos. Before attending to this final element of becoming worthy of the event, it is important to have a sense of how the Stoics and Deleuze conceive both the human and what is beyond the human—their accounts of the cosmos. Looking more closely at the ways self and cosmos are differentially conceived gives us a clearer path toward a Deleuzian ethics.

2 Stoic and Deleuzian Conceptions of Self—Inverting Oikeiōsis

In order to further examine the inversion between Stoicism and Deleuze, we must look more closely at their different conceptions of the self. Though it is rather uncontroversial to claim that the Stoics identify reason as the key characteristic of the human soul (LS 63D), let's look at the consideration of the Stoic self which is provided by Hadot in *The Inner Citadel* and the relation of the higher self to a cosmic perspective therein. The self becomes aware of itself as an island of freedom in the midst of a great sea of necessity when the phenomena of nature are stripped of all adjectives so that it appears in its nudity and savage beauty, which would be the perspective of universal Nature and the flow of eternal metamorphoses (1998: 112).

Accomplishing this cosmic perspective requires a delimitation of the self, or rather the elimination of certain nonessential elements of the higher self. Hadot calls this delimitation of the Self the fundamental activity of Stoicism (1998: 120); it reflects a complete transformation of self-consciousness. The guiding principle is that anything that is subject to external causality must be delimited. Then there are circles of exteriority which must not enter into consideration of the true self and its realm of freedom, each of which corresponds to Stoic doctrine concerning those which should be considered as indifferents, including the body as subject to physical laws and the domain of involuntary emotions, which arise from the body and are conceived as a first shock to the soul that cannot be avoided with the help of reason (117). By delimiting the self from these, the self becomes aware that it stands outside of this flux but, in so doing, now wants and acts only according to reason, purifying the higher self that is aligned to the Rational world soul (LS: 396). The higher self is purified of pathos, aligned with reason, and revels in the intellect—its *good sense*.

As we have seen, the Stoic view of *oikeiōsis* assumes the good nature of thought in terms of its *a priori* nature as well as its *telos*—its natural orientation toward truth and reason. Deleuze, on the other hand, understands the rational, self-contained self to be a transcendental illusion, and the image of thought that it relies upon as in need of critique. According to him, good sense indicates a particular distribution of faculties that relies on assumptions of unification, identification, and recognition. Deleuze views the assumption of good sense as pragmatic, rather than expressing a metaphysical reality. Good will and good sense merely overlay the human desire for stability and order onto reality. When good sense sees

4. Deleuzian Exercises and the Inversion of Stoicism 63

differences, it wills that the differences eventually equalize or annul themselves (see Lawlor 2012: 106–12). Good sense thus "affirms that in all things there is a determinable sense or direction" (Deleuze 1990: 1). It *wills* the taming of our interaction with radical differences and the becoming/s of immanent existence. To truly be worthy of the event, rather than willing the erasure of differences, willing the event would perhaps multiply them, affirming the irreducible heterogeneity of what Deleuze calls "paradoxical agency" (Deleuze 1990: 40: see Lawlor 2012: 111).

Deleuze's image of thought is not one of harmonious agreement between faculties but of each faculty being taken to its limit, by and through external provocation. The judgments that must be overcome are the very endorsement of this good and common sense of a rational, higher self, as these "crush thought under an image which is that of the Same and the Similar in representation, but profoundly betrays what it means to think" (Deleuze 1994: 167)—an image which obscures the true nature of thought as an encounter with difference rather than of representation. Therefore, dismantling the self is not just a matter of moving beyond our personal perspective, interests, or desires to recognize our place in a larger whole, but a matter of overcoming a certain image of thought that assumes common sense and the good nature of sense (desire for truth): "There would seem to be an absolute incompatibility between a notion of making the self an inner citadel . . . and dismantling the self" (Skrebowski 2005: 11). The former subscribes to a natural resemblance between the Self and Nature, while the latter unlinks thought from the bonds of a transcendent principle and allows thought to think its own genetic conditions out of an impersonal and inhuman transcendental field.

Yet I want to claim that Deleuze actually takes the Stoic imperative to become one with, or correspond to, the cosmic to its ultimate, logical conclusion. Rather than accepting the Stoic vision of a rational organizing principle in the cosmos, Deleuze proffers a view of nature as self-differing, generative, and indeterminate.[21] Understood through this lens, the seeming incompatibility between Deleuze's dismantling of the self and the edict to live according to nature resolves itself, as thought must think its self-differing genesis and renewal as aligned with this wholly impersonal, nonrational, and indeterminate cosmic flux rather than stand outside of it—an inversion of Stoicism, but a form of *oikeiōsis* nonetheless.

The inversion reflected in Deleuze's dismantling of the Self requires the reversal of the Stoic priority of self-control and the concomitant disciplining of the passions or desire—supporting Deleuze's accentuation of the practices of experimentation and the proliferating of desires/(active) passions: "Do not count upon thought to ensure the relative necessity of what it thinks. Rather, count upon the contingency of the encounter with that which forces thought to raise up the absolute necessity of an act or thought or passion to think" (Deleuze 1994: 176). What this implies is that, rather than the delimitation described by Hadot, dismantling the Self is a method of exploring *and surpassing* limits of our being, which would be inherently externally oriented and which operates through exposure rather than closure.

> Acquiring knowledge of the powers of the body in order to discover in a parallel fashion, powers of the mind that escape consciousness . . . to discover more in

the body than we know and hence more in the mind than we are conscious of. (Deleuze 1988: 90)

Deleuze presents this becoming, and thus dissolution, of the Self as a matter of passages and fluctuations of intensity, which is to say, an affective engagement with the world. Obviously, this is always a processual and partial dismantling—Deleuze and Guattari caution of moving too fast and of various kinds of radical or full eviscerations (like alcoholism or suicide) which would be counter to life itself. The goal would be allowing these fluctuations and disturbances to flow over and through us, effectively *letting them in*, in order to transform and thus incessantly dismantle hypostasized formations and identities we tend to associate with of ourselves. Remembering Deleuze's imperative to release the event, affect is the enacting of a cut or tear in the surface, an encounter that forcefully re-opens the pulsating, primary order from whence sense and surface arises. Deleuzian spiritual exercises would involve the consideration of affect and desire as virtues rather than things to be avoided or delayed. Understanding or becoming sensitive to affective engagements, rather than attempting to limit or eradicate them, is important for improving or enhancing our knowledge of the world and our place in it. On this issue, Deleuze is more in line with Nietzsche than the Stoics, as Nietzsche understood that it was by participating in the superabundance of life, intensifying our vulnerability to chance and risk, that we grow and learn (the Great Health). As Ure explains, one of Nietzsche's main critiques of Stoicism is that their insistence on indifference especially in relation to our passions "cuts us off from the learning process that the passions facilitate" (2016: 298).

Spinoza, who Deleuze identifies as his predecessor, also reserves a more positive role for the passions and body and has a similar view of the edifying potential of encounters, which is explained in terms of the increase or decrease in one's power to act and think (to affect and be affected). And this is a crucial difference: the emphasis placed on affect and the attunement to the body, rather than indifference toward it, which indicates the relation between an affecting body and an affected body, and, by extrapolation, centers upon the importance rather than indifference toward the body as both the site of passage of intensity and the locus of these transformations. Rather than ethics being characterized by a movement beyond passions and affectations, it "is a movement oriented by encounters ... not based on autonomy and self-containment, the quelling of external impingements, but through engagements that enhance or deplete one's powers of bodies and thought to act and be acted upon" (Grosz 2017: 56). Positively, this means that affections and passions are utilized, rather than eschewed, as part of a practical ethology whose goal is to "denounce all that separates us from life" (Deleuze 1988: 26), that is separates us from our power (*conatus*).

Now, in what seems to be a correlate to Stoicism, Spinoza delineates actions, as a power of acting (originating from the individual), from passions, as a power of being acted upon (originating from an external source). For Spinoza, passive passions are those linked to inadequate ideas (separation from real causes), while active or joyful passions (those in which external bodies are in agreement with mine) are those corresponding to adequate ideas, which, very similarly to the Stoics, means that there is a clear understanding of real causes, which, in turn, leads to the increase of our capacity to act, active joy. Thus, their acquisition entails bringing the passions in line with a rational order. While passions, in general, separate us from our power of acting, they can also increase our power to be affected (Deleuze 1988: 27), and, when we have encounters which enter into agreement with our own body, they produce joyful passions that lead us "to the point of transmutation . . . that will make us worthy of action, of active joys" (28) which pertain to rational acquisition or more perfect understanding. In other words, a prima facie reading of Spinoza would suggest that passions are a necessary and an ineliminable part of what "makes us worthy" of action and life *but* are to be surpassed in view of a more rational acquisition of the concept. Deleuze's uptake of Spinoza (see 1988) actually complexifies this particular understanding of the role of affect.

On the prior view, increase of power and the corresponding active joy pertain to moving beyond sad passions (and some might say even joyful passions), which differs from Deleuze's appropriation on several counts. First, although Deleuze advocates the promotion of joyful passions and, ultimately, active joy, as Ruddick points out and I agree, Deleuze extends Spinoza's argument for exploring the passions to *all* affects. Thus Deleuze is not merely focused on the move from passive to active (or the discovery of common notions that this implies), but instead "more complex determinations of a range of emotional [and affective] registers" (Ruddick 2010: 35) and their creative potential.[22] In other words, there is a shift in viewing affect as edifying our thought to actually creating new modes of thought and as exploration of the immanence of affective life as such. Though perhaps less apparent when reading Deleuze solely on Spinoza, this becomes clear when combined with his insistence on the creative potential of aesthetic encounters, whose power lies in their ability to disrupt and confound us. Relatedly, Deleuze would not be satisfied by an account of *eupatheiai* (good passions), as related to Stoic virtue or Spinozist correlation to adequate ideas, that merely associates them with becoming more rationally ordered or conceptually clear: "The aim is not to make something known to us but to understand our power of knowing" (Deleuze 1988: 83). At several points in his discussion of Spinoza, Deleuze points to a kind of knowledge beyond Reason (intuitive intellect) (58) or toward a mode of thinking beyond the Idea (that of conatus and affect) (59). "Kinds of knowledge are modes of existence, because knowing embraces the types of consciousness and the types of affects that correspond to it" (82). Second, this interpretation also neglects the pervasive way that Deleuze advocates affirmation of the encounters as a provocation in and of itself (as a power of shame to catapult us beyond ourselves/ our I and what we "think" we know/are, that is, our stupidity[23]).

Rather than [solely] a *telos* toward rational, adequate ideas—what Ruddick insinuates is the recuperation of a "Stoic moment in Spinoza's passions" (2010: 36)—the Deleuzian *ethos* is guided by the desire to increase affective capacities and create new capacities. It is *thanks to* these passions that we move to more understanding and knowledge, but Deleuze is quick to point out that this knowledge is in service of *life*, of understanding our singular existence as an ongoing and infinite process (being worthy of the event as it is infinite and never ending).

In this respect, Deleuze takes the more Nietzschean view that passions and affects should be cultivated in order to learn more about the unknown—essentially embracing risk and contingency in the acknowledgment that our purview should be to explore more of what we can become, to discover and create, rather than assume a coherence between an already known rational nature and ourselves: "The genesis of thought is not a model of the same, but a co-creation of something unforeseen" (Ruddick 2010: 36). There is value in every encounter in that they force us to think beyond recognition, ungrounding thought. Deleuze recognizes the importance of passive affects and bodily encounters in moving us beyond ourselves: "It is a matter of acquiring knowledge of the body in order to discover in parallel fashion, powers of the mind that escape consciousness" (Deleuze 1988: 90). The immediate visceral experience of an encounter (passive affect) actually creates changes on and through bodies, potentially engendering different perceptual fields and modes of thought. Encountering new affects, shocking affects, spurs thought to create new concepts, and thus to introduce new ways of being into the social sphere. Moreover, the rise and fall, these fluctuations, of affect are the very process by which the individual becomes worthy of the event or immanently related to the cosmos. This process of exploration is a counteractualization which leads to greater understanding of the cosmic and greater empowerment of ourselves. This represents a further reorientation of the Spinozist ethos toward Deleuze's full throttle embrace of experimentation.

Deleuze's emphasis on affections, desires, and passions also constitutes a reorientation of living in agreement, a new *oikeiōsis*. As I have mentioned, the Stoics associated *oikeiōsis* with self-preservation and perfection of the normative self, deriving the notion from observing how organisms are fitted to their environment, and linking this to humanity's greatest capacity—to reason. For Deleuze, preservation is rather expressed as increase in the capacity to be affected and to affect: "Each tries equally to preserve himself, and has as much right as he has power, given the affections that actually exercise his capacity to be affected" (Deleuze 1990: 258). Here, Deleuze is endorsing the basic premise of living in agreement, but this phrase has now become compatible with what Deleuze thinks should guide us: affects which both enhance the power (potential) of the body and lead us to know what these potentials are, spurring us to new thoughts and new bodily configurations. What differentiates the wise from the foolish is the type of affectations of which they are capable.

3 From Spiritual Exercises to Experimentation

In order to experience the Event, Deleuze advocates the dismantling of the Self—a dismantling which differs dramatically from the dissolving of boundaries between Self and Nature implied by the Stoics. Counteractualizing or releasing the event, if it is to be an engagement with the virtuality of the Idea/Event, needs the dissolution of the subject—*the I must counteractualize itself*. In other words, the dismantling of the self has to precede the dissolution of boundary between Self and the cosmos, which Deleuze might say still remains in the realm of the actual. This is an idiosyncratic idea of rebirth that it is predicated on a kind of death, the perpetual and incessant experience of the dissolution of subjectivity into the event. This is position that we find both in *Difference and Repetition* and *Logic of Sense*, where Deleuze calls for the dissolution of self as a kind of performance which would allow the individual to re-engage the intensive plenum. Working through or contemplating the double-ness of death, as an incongruent interface between the empirical event and transcendental instance, is a kind of Deleuzian spiritual exercise, which initiates what he calls a "radical reversal . . . [that] loosens my hold upon myself by casting me out of my power" (Deleuze 1994: 148). It is the very practice of contemplating the incommensurability of the two faces of death that constitutes a method of cracking the self, wherein the illusory boundaries of the Self's identity and resemblance fall away in light of the affirmation of the intensive plenum and pure connectivity. Hence death is affirmed as generative becoming beyond the Self. This is another instance of the importance of what Spinoza might call the confusion of the passive—these affections that have not been fully incorporated into the active and thus confound our sense of assurance. It is also an instance where Deleuze most clearly moves beyond the sole ethical aim of increasing power, in service of what seems to be the higher order of becoming worthy of the event itself. Submitting ourselves to the crack is a necessary component because living in agreement is placing oneself into the flow of the cosmic, not obtaining a final resting place—for thought or for ourselves.

This is a spiritual exercise, the outcome of which is to transform the individual perspective into a perspective of the absolutely and infinitely singular, not the universal. As well, this is merely a step necessary to engage in a more "appropriate" relation with immanence. The dismantling of the subject loosens the psychic boundaries in order that one begin the work of making oneself a bodywithoutorgans by engaging more acutely with the fluctuations of intensity of the plane of immanence. Willing that one *become* an event is thus the deeper sense of becoming worthy of the event, which brings us to the issue of experimentation.

Willing the event is to engage in a way of life directed by the intent to take the event to its limit, to always experience more of the event. But if the event is infinite, the limit would be limitless. Deleuze wants us "to explore all distances" (Deleuze 1990: 210), transforming ourselves through the process, rather than succumb to any particular actualization of the event and resign ourselves to our "fate" in a limited fashion. As Bowden says, given the ongoing nature of the sense-event, Deleuze translates the Stoic desire to live according to nature to mean living in accordance with the event, which never finishes coming about (Bowden 2011: 45). This is a process of affirming as much of the event as we can stand to experience and perpetual transgression as *the* way of life—the Nietzschean element of affirmation melds with Stoic acceptance of fate.

Deleuze's emphasis on experimentation (spiritual *and* bodily) is integral to his ontology of the event:

> The sage waits for the event, understands the pure event in its eternal truth, independently of its spatio-temporal actualizations, as something eternally yet-to-come and always already passed. But, at the same time, the sage also wills the embodiment and the actualization of the pure incorporeal event in states of affairs and in his or her own body and flesh. (Deleuze 1990: 146).

This quote suggests that, for Deleuze, experimentation is a matter of imbricating ourselves in immanence (material existence). This correlates to Deleuze's penchant for Spinoza's claim that no one has yet determined what the body can do. As we have seen, we primarily come to know the body indirectly, through being affected. Moreover, passive (external) affectations are what allow us to go beyond what we already "know."

Attempts to capture the flows of desire and infinite powers of the event can be disastrous: Artaud's madness or Fitzgerald's alcoholism. This prompts Deleuze to question whether we should limit ourselves to the counteractualization of an event that would not include actual physical destruction:

> To will the event, how could we not also will its full actualization in a corporeal mixture . . .? If the order of the surface is itself cracked, how could it not itself break up, how is it to be prevented from precipitating destruction . . . how can we prevent deep life from becoming a demolition job? (Deleuze 1990: 183)

But then Deleuze flips the question: Are we merely to speak of these risks taken to the body and to the extremities of psychic awareness while remaining on the shore? These individuals who succeeded in communicating something of the event only did so through great risk and bodily vulnerability. Remaining at the shore, as a spectator, is not an option. The fine line between tracing the incorporeal crack at the surface and letting this crack deepen exists in tandem with the inscription on bodies: "The eternal truth of the event is grasped only if the event is also inscribed in the flesh" (Deleuze 1990: 188). The metaphor of the crack is illustrative in that it invokes the metaphysical surface of thought and instructs us to move beyond this purely ideational plane. Thought must be quickened through the return of exteriority and the depth of the body. The crack, by which we can understand the dismantling of the Self, makes possible the release of the underlying forces and affects that compose the depth (body and materiality) from which the surface is generated. Deleuze likens the greatest health to an open wound—living on the surface of a sheer exposure to the outside and suffering the intensification of this moment.

The construction of the bodywithoutorgans corresponds to this open wound—letting chaos in to remake our bodies and our thoughts. Making a BwO is described as a process of freeing of intensities, which is initiated through the fracture of self and reason (Deleuze and Guattari 1987: 158). One can see how Deleuze's revision of the image of thought as a genetic provocation of the faculties inverts the priority of rational judgment by positing a more fundamental level of experience that must be accounted for (i.e., affect), issuing in his imperative to think that

4. Deleuzian Exercises and the Inversion of Stoicism 69

which is unthought. It is the level of affect, which is found in those intensities that pass between bodies and the variations and resonances between them. But Deleuze is clear; making a BwO is "not a notion or a concept but a practice, a set of practices" (Deleuze and Guattari 1987: 149–50), sustained through pursuit of intense embodied experiences. In this way, affect is synonymous with the force of encounter, and experimentations calibrate our awareness to movements of becoming.

Deleuze's is a method of repetition and imagination that disciplines us against certain transcendental illusions. It is a method of miming that reminds us of the externality of thought. It is a method informed by the nature of the event, which allows us to place ourselves within its ebbs and flows in order that we become worthy of that event. It is a method of counteractualization, which releases the event. Finally, it is a method of experimentation, which places our bodies at risk in order to experience and transgress the apparent limits thereof.

For the Stoics, all beings participate in rational being, while for Deleuze, all beings are part of the immanent field of forces and intensity. Whereas Stoic immanence is governed by rational order, Deleuzian immanence is characterized by contingent becoming. What is appropriate is that there is nothing proper—immanence is living a singular life, attentive to the particularity of the assemblage of forces that one finds oneself in at any particular moment. We are most appropriate when we are swept into the immanent flow of life. Eradication of the fiction of the subject/self—to become impersonal—is to be more in line with the fluidity of immanence. Living in accordance would be to live in a constant state of intensification, experimentation, and becoming.

Notes

1 Williams (2008) elucidates the relation between the language and the event, philosophy as event, and how the metaphysics of the surface relates to the Deleuzian impersonal transcendental field, singularities, and genesis; Widder (2011) focuses on the importance of incorporeals; Bowden (2011) emphasizes the influence of the Stoics distinction between incorporeal meaning/effects and corporeal bodies in Deleuze's characterization of sense as the "fourth dimension" of language, as well as devoting attention to the importance of Stoic ethics; Johnson (2017) provides an excellent account of the significance of incorporeals for Deleuze's account of sense.
2 Notable exceptions: Sellars (2006) says that by examining his *oeuvre* as a whole one can discern a deeper affinity with Stoicism. Reynolds (2007) approaches Deleuze's ethics of the event as a matter of recognizing the irreconcilable rupture between the transcendental and the empirical that reflects the heterogeneity between certain aspects of time (147–8); Lawlor (2012) writes about the significance of being worthy of the event. Bennet (2015a, b) writes on the significance Stoic Fate and quasi-causality for Deleuzian ethics.
3 The priority of immanence over transcendence is a fundamental feature of Deleuze's thought, as seen in his 1966 article "*Renverser le platonisme*," in his insistence on the plane of immanence in *A Thousand Plateaus* (1987), and in his last book, *Immanence:*

A Life. Many commentators have linked this priority to his ethics. See, for instance, Lorraine (2011) and Smith (2007).
4 As Johnson notes, Deleuze finds preferable figures whose philosophies evince an entailment of ethics from ontology (2017: 285, ft. 21). Ansell-Pearson describes Deleuze as committed to affirmative naturalism, linking "together physics and ethics as a way of providing an emancipatory and affirmative philosophy of life" (2014: 121).
5 The Stoics appeal to *oikeiōsis* (DL 7.85-6; Seneca Letters 121.6-15), postulating the naturalness of certain capacities and the recognition of what belongs to oneself. Klein explains that the Stoic *oikeiōsis*, as an original impulse to that which is appropriate the entity, is often explained in terms of self-preservative instincts of animals, but that since human beings' particular natural capacity is to reason, what is appropriate to us is to seek beyond mere instinct toward *understanding* the cosmos (2016: 148).
6 Deleuze's interpretation relies heavily on Bréhier 1962 [orig. 1908] and Goldschmidt 1953 (Widder 2011: 103).
7 The Stoics do speak of "events" (*gignomena*) as incorporeals (Alexander of Aphrodisias, *Fat*. 181.13-182.20), but do not make them central features of their philosophy.
8 See Sellars (2006); Long and Sedley also separate *lekta* from other incorporeals (LS 51H).
9 In *De Fato*, Cicero identifies fate with antecedent causes: no motion is without a cause, all happens by preceding causes, everything happens by fate (20–21). Further, Alexander of Aphrodisias argues for the necessary connectedness of all causes, otherwise "the universe would be torn apart" (*Fat*. 192).
10 Deleuze is partial to Nietzsche's conception of *amor fati*, which is to say the affirmation of the aleatory encounter rather than mere acceptance.
11 Sedley (2003) identifies Chrysippus's use of moral failings and passions as synonymous (21). Gill (2003) attributes to Seneca the view that emotions need to be extirpated not just moderated (49).
12 For more on Deleuze's experimentation and spiritual exercises, see my article, "Bataille and Deleuze's Peculiar *Askesis*: Techniques of Transgression, Meditation, and Dramatisation" (Sholtz 2020).
13 For commentators who associate the event with the virtual *tout court*, willing the event must be related solely to thought. See Sellars 2006: 160; also Bennett 2015b).
14 Kurt Lampe remarks on this thoroughly in Chapter 6 of this volume, seeing it as an essential opening for Kristeva's reading of the Stoics.
15 Massumi (1992) calls it a neologism; Angelova (2006) calls it a "strange term of Deleuze's own coinage" (121); James (2008) dubs it "one of the rare heavy and clumsy concepts in Deleuze's work" (130).
16 The relation of the intensive with bodies may seem strange as the philosophic tradition associates material substance with extension, but in *Difference and Repetition* Deleuze uses the intensive when referring to bare materiality "while spatio-temporal dynamisms suggest a materialist 'plane of immanence,' a pre-individual continuum of matter—energy flows, these remain undifferentiated until incarnating a particular set of differential relations as the solution to a particular problematic Idea" (Sholtz 2016: 53). Part of this comes from the problem of mapping these terms across texts (as the Virtual is related to the pre-individuated/pre-actualized in *Difference and Repetition*, yet aligned with the metaphysical surface in *Logic of Sense*), but I want to maintain the idea of the intensive plenum, as the plane of immanence, out of which bodies become fully actualized. In *Difference and Repetition*, where Deleuze is interested specifically in

the process of formation (different/ciation), everything that is undetermined would be associated with virtuality, whereas he seems to split the Actual and Virtual in *Logic of Sense* more clearly between corporeal (physical plane) and incorporeal (metaphysical plane). I would advocate that this proves rather than confounds my point, as the plane of immanence suggests that the inseparability of the actual and virtual, corporeal and incorporeal—they must be thought as ineluctably intertwined and in relation.

17 Even Bennett suggests that "incorporeal transformations shift what things in the world the proposition supposedly refers" (2015b: 16), which, in turn, would shift concrete social contexts.

18 In *Difference and Repetition*, dramatization is part of an ontological process of different/ciation, where spatiotemporal dynamisms are dramatized (actualized); in *Logic of Sense*, dramatization is linked to counteractualization, reflecting a doubling of dramatization; making the event one's own has to do with ideal selections (tracings) from the event. See Sholtz 2016.

19 There may be ways that even this might be reconciled with Stoicism. Chrysippus's discussion of hidden causes could account for those things which are unexplainable via directly observable causal chains (see Galen, *De placitis* 348, 16–8). Alexander of Aphrodisias's reference to "swarm of causes" (*smênos aitiôn*) (*Fat.* 192,18) has also been invoked to counter simplistic notions of linear causality in Stoic determinism (see Meyer 2009: 73).

20 The dismantling of the Self is not total annihilation of the individual, but indicates that there are preconceptions about the self-contained, metaphysically defined Self (*the self as transcendental illusion*) that limit our ability to make new connections and relations or understand the constant interplay between ourselves and the world. I have reserved capitalization of Self for this sense (with respect to Deleuze).

21 The difference between Stoic and Deleuzian ontology represents another instance of inversion, one which, unfortunately, cannot be adequately developed within the scope of this chapter. Summarily, Deleuze would reject a cosmos governed by divine order, opting rather for an impersonal plane of forces and intensities which includes chaos, chance, and disorder (Deleuze and Guattari 1983: 140). My sense is that this divergence has to be explained in terms of advances in physics itself—a project that I am currently undertaking within an interdisciplinary research group (*supported by the SSHRC*) on Deleuze and cosmology, consisting of philosophers, Alain Beaulieu and myself, and physicists, Gennady Chitov and Ubi Wichoski (see https://www3.laurent ian.ca/deleuzecosmo/).

22 This becomes more apparent in Deleuze's later essay on Spinoza (1997), where he attributes, even to Spinoza, a more complex relation to affect and passions—one that exceeds the goal of developing common notions and revels in the expression, struggles, and liberations of affective life itself (146).

23 Deleuze characterizes stupidity as the unrealized assumption of a transcendental ground, especially in terms of the ego (1994: 152).

Bibliography

Angelova, E. (2006), "Quasi-Causality in Deleuze," *Symposium* 10 (1): 117–33.

Ansell-Pearson, K. (2014), "Affirmative Naturalism: Deleuze and Epicureanism," *Cosmos and History: The Journal of Natural and Social Philosophy* 10 (2): 121–37.

Aurelius, M. (1997), *Meditations*, trans. George Long, Mineaola: Dover Publications.
Bennett, M. J. (2015a), "Cicero's *De Fato* in Deleuze's *Logic of Sense*," *Deleuze Studies* 9 (1): 25–58.
Bennett, M. J. (2015b), "Deleuze's Concept of 'Quasi-Causality' and Its Greek Sources," unpublished paper. Available at https://www.academia.edu/ 9062058/Deleuzes_Concept_of_Quasi-Causality_and_its_Greek_Sources (accessed May 29, 2018).
Betegh, G. (2003), "Cosmological Ethics in the Timaeus and Early Stoicism," *Studies in Ancient Philosophy* 26: 273–302.
Bobzien, S. (1998), *Determinism and Freedom in Stoic Philosophy*, Oxford: Clarendon.
Boeri, M. D. (2001), "The Stoics on Bodies and Incorporeals," *The Review of Metaphysics* 54 (4): 723–52.
Boundas, C. V., ed. (2006), *Deleuze and Philosophy*, Edinburgh: Edinburgh University Press.
Boundas, C. V. (2009), "Gilles Deleuze and the Problem of Freedom," in E. W. Holland, D. W. Smith, and C. J. Stivale (eds.), *Gilles Deleuze: Image and Text*, Great Britain: Continuum International.
Bowden, S. (2011), *The Priority of Events: Deleuze's Logic of Sense*, Edinburgh: Edinburgh University Press.
Bréhier, É. (1962), *La théorie des incorporels dans l'ancien stoïcisme*, 3rd ed., Paris: Vrin.
Colebrook, C. (2002), *Understanding Deleuze*, Australia: Allen & Unwin.
Deleuze, G. (1966), "Renverser le platonisme," *Revue de Métaphysique et de Morale* 71: 436–438, republished in Deleuze (1969).
Deleuze, G. (1983), *Nietzsche and Philosophy*, trans. H. Tomlinson, New York: Columbia University Press.
Deleuze, G. (1988), *Spinoza: Practical Philosophy*, trans. R. Hurley, San Francisco: City Lights Publishers.
Deleuze, G. (1990), *Logic of Sense*, trans. M. Lester, New York: Columbia University Press.
Deleuze, G. (1994), *Difference and Repetition*, trans. P. Patton, New York: Columbia University Press.
Deleuze, G. (1997), *Essays Critical and Clinical*, trans. D. Smith and M. Greco, Minneapolis: University of Minneapolis Press.
Deleuze, G. and F. Guattari (1983 [1972]), *Anti-Oedipus: Capitalism and Schizophrenia*, trans. R. Hurley, M. Seem, and H. R. Lane, Minneapolis: University of Minnesota Press.
Deleuze, G. and F. Guattari (1987), *A Thousand Plateaus: Capitalism and Schizophrenia*, trans. B. Massumi, Minneapolis: University of Minnesota Press.
Deleuze, G. and F. Guattari (1994), *What Is Philosophy?*, New York: Columbia University Press.
Deleuze, G. and C. Parnet (2002), *Dialogues II*, trans. B. Habberjam, E. R. Albert, and H. Tomlinson, New York: Columbia University Press.
Epictetus (2004), *Enchiridion*, Mineola: Dover Publications.
Gill, C. (2003), "The School in the Roman Imperial Period," in B. Inwood (ed.), *The Cambridge Companion to the Stoics*, 33–58, Cambridge: Cambridge University Press.
Goldschmidt, V. (1953), *Le système stoïcien et l'idée de temps*, Paris: Vrin.
Grosz, E. (2017), *The Incorporeal: Ontology, Ethics, and the Limits of Materialism*, New York: Columbia University Press.
Hadot, P. (1995), *Philosophy as a Way of Life*, Oxford: Blackwell Publishing.

Hadot, P. (1998), *The Inner Citadel: The Meditations of Marcus Aurelius*, trans. Michael Chase, Cambridge, MA: Harvard University Press.
Inwood, B., ed. (2003), *The Cambridge Companion to the Stoics*, Cambridge: Cambridge University Press.
Johnson, B. E. (2014), *The Role Ethics of Epictetus: Stoicism in Ordinary Life*, Minneapolis: Lexington Books.
Johnson, R. (2017), "On the Surface: The Deleuze-Stoicism Encounter," in Abraham Jacob Greenstine and Ryan J. Johnson (eds.), *Contemporary Encounters with Ancient Metaphysics*, 270–88, Edinburgh: Edinburgh University Press.
Klein, J. (2016), "The Stoic Argument from *oikeiōsis*," *Oxford Studies in Ancient Philosophy* 50: 143–200.
Lawlor, L. (2012), "Phenomenology and Metaphysics, and Chaos: On the Fragility of the Event in Deleuze," in D. Smith and H. Somers-Hall (eds.), *Cambridge Companion to Deleuze*, 103–25, Cambridge: Cambridge University Press.
Long, A. A. and D. N. Sedley (1987), *The Hellenistic Philosophers*, 2 vols., Cambridge: Cambridge University Press.
Lorraine, T. (2011), *Deleuze and Guattari's Immanent Ethics: Theory, Subjectivity, and Duration*, New York: State University of New York Press.
Lundy, C. (2012), *History and Becoming: Deleuze's Philosophy of Creativity*, Edinburgh: Edinburgh University Press.
Massumi, B. (1992), *A User's Guide to Capitalism and Schizophrenia: Deviations from Deleuze and Guattari*. Cambridge, MA: MIT Press.
Meyer, S. (2009), "Chain of Causes: What Is Stoic Fate?" in R. Salles (ed.), *God and Cosmos in Stoicism*, 71–90, Oxford: Oxford University Press.
Protevi, J. (2006), "Deleuze, Guattari, and Emergence," *Paragraph: A Journal of Modern Critical Theory* 29 (2): 19–39.
Reynolds, J. (2007), "Wounds and Scars: *Deleuze* on the Time and Ethics of the Event," *Deleuze Studies* 1 (2): 144–66.
Roffe, J. (April 2017), "Deleuze's Concept of Quasi-Cause," *Deleuze Studies* 11 (2): 278–94.
Ruddick, S. (2010), "The Politics of Affect: Spinoza in the Work of Deleuze and Negri," *Theory, Culture & Society* 27 (4): 21–45.
Sedley, D. (2003), "The School from Zeno to Arius Didymus," in B. Inwood (ed.), *The Cambridge Companion to the Stoics*, 7–32, Cambridge: Cambridge University Press.
Sellars, J. (1999), "The Point of View of the Cosmos: Deleuze, Romanticism, Stoicism," *Pli* 8: 1–24.
Sellars, J. (2006), "An Ethics of the Event: Deleuze's Stoicism," *Angelaki* 3 (2): 157–71.
Sholtz, J. (2016), "Dramatisation as a Life Practice," *Deleuze Studies* 10 (1): 50–69.
Sholtz, J. (2020), "Bataille and Deleuze's Peculiar *Askesis*: Techniques of Transgression, Meditation, and Dramatisation," *Deleuze and Guattari Studies* 14 (2): 199–228.
Skrebowski, L. (2005), "Dismantling the Self: Deleuze, Stoicism and Spiritual Exercises." Available at https://www.scribd.com/document/37883973/skrebowskistoicsessay (accessed June 2018).
Smith, D. (2007), "Deleuze and the Question of Desire: Toward an Immanent Theory of Ethics," *Parrhesia* 2: 66–78.
Ure, M. (2016), "Stoicism in Nineteenth-Century German Philosophy," in John Sellars (ed.), *The Routledge Handbook of the Stoic Tradition*, 287–303, New York: Routledge Taylor & Francis Group.

Widder, N. (2011), "Matter as Simulacrum; Thought as Phantasm; Body as Event," in Joe Hughes and Lauren Guillaume (eds.), *Deleuze and the Body*, 96–116, Edinburgh: Edinburgh Press.

Williams, J. (2008), *Gilles Deleuze's Logic of Sense: A Critical Guide and Introduction*, Edinburgh: Edinburgh Press.

Chapter 5

HOW AND WHY DID BADIOU BEAT DELEUZE WITH A STOIC STICK?[1]

Thomas Bénatouïl

Two years after Gilles Deleuze's death in 1995, Alain Badiou published a small book *Deleuze: la clameur de l'être* (*The Clamor of Being*). Although it looked like an introduction to Deleuze's thought, the book was meant as a substitute for the *disputatio* book that Badiou wanted to write with Deleuze following a correspondence they had, which Deleuze ended. It seems fair to say that the book caused an uproar among French Deleuzians,[2] and rightly so, since they were an explicit target of Badiou, who immediately criticizes a common "image of Deleuze" (1997: 17–18) or the "*doxa*" which developed around his works (30). Badiou claims that, contrary to this "image" or "doxa," Deleuze was in fact a classical metaphysician, whose thought is characterized by three positions or orientations, which I will call Badiou's three ascriptions since they have been much disputed:

1. Deleuze's philosophy is organized around a metaphysics of the One.
2. It proposes an ethics of thought that requires dispossession and asceticism.
3. It is systematic and abstract. (2000a: 17)

While it is very difficult to resist assessing and criticizing this portrayal of Deleuze, I doubt this is the most interesting approach, not only because it has already been tried by many authors[3] but also because it is very clear that Badiou is himself engaging in a debate with Deleuze, an assessment of his system and of its inspirations from the point of view of his own doctrine: he is no historian of philosophy, even in this little book entirely devoted to Deleuze. There are, in fact, several other texts by Badiou about Deleuze, a few older and most of them more recent,[4] in which he is usually much more critical. In this paper, I will refer only to *The Clamor of Being* and to Badiou's *Logiques des mondes* (*Logics of Worlds*, 2006a) and focus on the role played by Stoicism in Badiou's critical view of Deleuze.

While Stoicism is a major reference in *Logique du sens* (Deleuze 1969), it is scarcely present in later works, where one can find only brief allusions to aspects of Stoicism already analyzed in *The Logic of Sense*.[5] By contrast, Stoicism is often mentioned in *The Clamor of Being*. In the first chapter, Stoicism is put forward when he introduces the second ascription, asceticism:

> However paradoxical the attribute may seem, applied to someone who claims to draw his inspiration above all from Nietzsche . . . it is necessary to uphold that the condition of thought, for Deleuze, is ascetic. This is what radically explains the kinship of Deleuze and the Stoics, other than the fact that they also thought of Being directly as totality. (Badiou 2000a: 13)

Badiou clearly casts Deleuze as a neo-Stoic. The first two ascriptions (listed on the previous page) also hold for Stoicism, and this explains Deleuze's attraction to Stoicism. My claim is that this "explanation" works equally well and perhaps even better the other way around: these analogies between Deleuze and the Stoics throw significant light on Badiou's views about Deleuze (and his own kinship with Plato). Hence, I will first highlight how Stoicism is crucial to Badiou's portrayal of Deleuze. I will then try to show how Badiou uses Stoicism to turn Deleuze against himself, as if Deleuze had betrayed his original philosophical inspiration. This will finally lead me to suggest that Badiou's argument with Deleuze is strictly analogous to the refutation of Stoicism devised by ancient Platonism.

1 The One-All and the Stoic Sticker

Badiou claims to derive his view of Deleuze's philosophy as a metaphysics of the One from Deleuze's advocacy of the "univocity of being." From the fact that Deleuze says that Being is said of all beings with one and the same sense, Badiou concludes that, for Deleuze, beings are only expressive modalities of the One:[6] "The multiple acceptations of being must be understood as a multiple that is formal, while the One alone is real" (2000a: 25). As for the Stoic dimension of this metaphysics of the One, it stems from its roots:

> The thesis of the univocity of Being guides Deleuze's entire relation to the history of philosophy. His companions, his references, his preferred cases-of-thought are indeed found in those who have explicitly maintained that being has "a single voice": Duns Scotus, who is perhaps the most radical . . . the Stoics, who referred their doctrine of the proposition to the contingent coherence of the One-All; Spinoza, obviously . . . Nietzsche . . . Bergson. It is hence possible to "read" historically the thesis of univocity, and this is indeed why Deleuze became the (apparent) historian of certain philosophers: they were cases of the univocity of Being. (2000a: 24)

Yet, there is an odd one out to be spotted in this historical picture: Deleuze never refers to the Stoics as proponents of the univocity of being. He would not have been mistaken if he did, since they claim that all beings are bodies and that incorporeals are not beings, but the Stoics are not mentioned on a par with Duns Scotus, Spinoza, and Nietzsche by Deleuze (1968: 58–60). Badiou's justification of his mention of the Stoics's connection with univocity of being is itself puzzling: how is the Stoic logic of propositions related to the coherence of the One-All? Badiou perhaps refers to the fact that, in *Difference and Repetition* (1968: 58–9), Deleuze uses an analysis of the ontological proposition which is similar to his Stoic analysis of propositions in *The Logic of Sense* (1990a: 12–22). But the two accounts are quite different: the latter is general and more complex, while the former is focused on the "ontological proposition" and applied to univocity of being as common to many authors. And there is no connection made (by Deleuze) between the ontological proposition or univocity of being and the Stoic cosmos.

Still, univocity of being is indeed advocated in *The Logic of Sense*, specifically in the twenty-fifth series: "Of Univocity" (1990a: 177–80), and this is probably why Badiou includes Stoicism in his historical list. It is indeed from the same series that Badiou draws also his main evidence about Deleuze's metaphysics of the One, focusing on a passage he quotes several times (2000a: 11, 20, 24–5, 119–20). However, in this text (1969: 210–1, translated in 1990a: 179–80), Deleuze does not refer to a totality of beings, or to the Stoic *cosmos* as a coherent entity, but to the unification of all events into one event. This is worth explaining in some detail.

Taken out of context and from a strictly Stoic point of view, Deleuze's definition of Being as "the unique event in which all events communicate" (1990a: 180) is puzzling, because it seems to conflate what exists or beings (bodies) and what subsists (incorporeal events) (1990a: 5). But this conflation is explicitly avoided by Deleuze: "It would be a mistake to confuse the univocity of Being to the extent that it is said with the pseudo-univocity of everything about which it is said" (1990a: 180). Deleuze insists that univocity is not the identity or unity of beings, but a feature of sense, which is what happens to and what is said of these things.[7] Univocity translates into oneness or uniqueness only at the level of sense, that is at the "surface" of (corporeal) beings: "a single instance for all that exists" (1990a: 211).[8] Moreover, even at this level, Deleuze's references to "one single Event for all events" (1990a: 180) do not mean that there is one total Event in which the others dissolve themselves, converge, or even cohere. Deleuze explicitly disagrees with the Stoics (and Leibniz) about the "communication" between all events and conceives of them (after Nietzsche) as entering into *diverging* series forming "a 'chaosmos' and no longer a world" (1990a: 176), thus undercutting the Stoic notions of fate as the universal and unifying reason according to which all events happen.[9]

Badiou nevertheless sees Deleuze as "uphold[ing], in the manner of the Stoics, the virtual Totality or what Deleuze named a 'chaosmos'" (2000a: 4). Badiou might have a point that, however distinct from a convergence it might be, a communication between all events is a communion of sort and requires the One as an implicit principle,[10] but he conflates this One and the All into "the One-All" (2000a: 11).[11] Badiou consequently posits a unifying principle at both levels of Deleuze's ontology, and especially at the level of existing things, under the guise of the infinite power of Life, which expresses itself in every multiplicity. This is certainly the case for the Stoics, who hold the world, which includes all bodies, to be unified by Reason or God, which is the active (corporeal) principle sustaining all and every particular thing in existence and guaranteeing that, at the level of incorporeal sayables, all true propositions are consistent with each other. Hence, in the first quotation made above, Badiou is right to say that the Stoics "conceived of Being directly as a totality." But this is problematic as far as Deleuze is concerned, not only because, as we have just explained, Being is for Deleuze an incorporeal event in which all events communicate without converging but also, as shown by Villani (1998) or Roffe (2012: 7–10), because Deleuze refuses to see multiplicities as superficial expressions of a unique principle: his notion of multiplicity is directed against the couple one/multiple.[12]

Badiou's reading is restated and made more explicit in the section "The Event according to Deleuze" of *Logics of Worlds* (2009: 381–7), where Deleuze's concept of event in *The Logic of Sense* is analyzed into four axioms,[13] which are then reversed to define Badiou's conception of event. The first holds that the event expresses or reveals "the One amid the concatenation of multiplicities," or that it is "the concentration of the continuity of life, its intensification" (2009: 382). This accounts for the conflation between Being as event and beings (here named multiplicities or becomings) highlighted above. The second states that the event is never present, does not divide time, but is always what just happened or will happen. While the third axiom clearly acknowledges the two levels of Deleuze's Stoic ontology ("The nature of the event is other than that of the actions and passions of the body"), Badiou restates in his explanation that the event "intensifies" or "affects bodies" and thus disregards the very separation between events and bodies, effects and causes he claims to explain, since he sees events as acting upon bodies. The fourth axiom states that "a life is composed of the same single Event, despite all the variety that happens to it" (2009: 383). Badiou notes that the problem here is not the uniqueness of this event, because it has already been established by the previous axioms. Hence, the unity of all events in one is just the replication of the unification of Life or Becoming by itself, just as the consistency of all true complete (incorporeal) sayables is the expression of the unity of the (corporeal) world through divine reason in Stoicism.

Before listing these four axioms, Badiou notes that Deleuze explained his concept of event in *The Logic of Sense* "in the company of the Stoics. This sets the tone: the 'event' must comply with the inflexible discipline of the All, from which Stoicism takes its bearings. Between 'event' and 'fate' there must be a subjective reciprocation of sorts" (2009: 282).

This quote perfectly spells out how the reference to Stoicism operates in Badiou's interpretation of Deleuze: by contamination. Stoicism is used to make seemingly un- or anti-Deleuzian readings of Deleuze *stick*. If Deleuze was inspired by some doctrines of the Stoics, then he must have tacitly agreed with other aspects of their doctrine.[14] Deleuze's alleged kinship with the Stoics is used by Badiou to pin some of their positions on Deleuze, as Badiou's second ascription should make clear.

2 More Stoicism: Asceticism and Monotony

There is at least a whole chapter of *The Logic of Sense* about Stoic ethics, but Badiou does not mention it when he casts Deleuze as an "ascetic thinker."[15] Still, the reference to Stoicism is essential to this description, as seen in our first quotation.

What does Badiou mean by "asceticism"? Mainly it requires going beyond one's individuality: "Thinking is not the spontaneous effusion of a personal capacity. It is the power, won only with the greatest difficulty, *against* oneself, of being constrained to the world's play" (2000a: 12, after quoting Deleuze 1990a: 73).

This has two consequences according to Badiou. First, that "Deleuze's conception of thought is profoundly aristocratic. Thought only exists in hierarchized space" (2000a: 12), because it is a process accessed only by a few "ascetic" persons. This is an attack on the image of Deleuze as a nomadic or anarchist thinker (2000a: 13 and 69-70, see also 2009: 387). Second and much more paradoxical, Deleuze turns out to be a philosopher of death, because death is the paradigm of all events as dissolution of my identity in the impersonal flow of Life. In *Logics of Worlds*, Badiou says that death is common to phenomenology and vitalism (he mentions Bergson and Deleuze) as "the attestation of finite existence, which is simply a modality of an infinite over-existence, or of a power of the One which we only experience through its reverse" (2009: 268). Badiou's second ascription turns out to be dependent upon the first.

While it is true that Deleuze advocates the dismantling of the subject by impersonal vital processes, he never connects death with finite existence: death is not a sign of my being part of something bigger than myself, but a sign of my being composed of impersonal or pre-individual singularities or events. ("It dies like it rains.") Badiou has a point about death as the Deleuzian paradigm of the contrast between singularity and personal identity (or subjectivity), but Deleuze warned, at least in later texts, about misinterpreting this connection: "But a life should not have to be enclosed in the simple moment when individual life confronts universal death. *A life* is everywhere, in every moment which a living subject traverses and which is measured by the objects that have been experienced, an immanent life carrying along the events or singularities that are merely actualized in subjects and objects" (2006: 387).[16]

As textual evidence of his second ascription, Badiou quotes a passage of *The Logic of Sense* (1990a: 153), which he terms "a veritable hymn to Death [...] slipping effortlessly in the footsteps of Blanchot" (Badiou 2000a: 14).[17] But he also makes the ascription stick by referring it again to Stoicism: "The result is that this philosophy of life is essentially, just like Stoicism (but not at all like Spinozism, despite the reverence in which Deleuze holds Spinoza) a philosophy of death" (2000a: 13).[18]

As for the third ascription (systematicity), it drew fewer objections than the previous two from Deleuze's followers, probably because Deleuze himself claimed to agree with such a classical definition of philosophy.[19] Badiou does not mention Stoicism to support this ascription, perhaps because he does not realize that Stoicism was the first philosophy to claim to be a "system."[20] Deleuze approvingly emphasizes the tight connection between Stoic ethics, logic, and physics (highlighted in Goldschmidt 1953), but it does not mean that he shares this structural conception of a system:

> I believe in philosophy as a system. The notion of system which I find unpleasant is one whose coordinates are the Identical, the Similar, and the Analogous. Leibniz was the first, I think, to identify system and philosophy. In the sense he

gives the term, I am all in favor of it. Thus, questions that address "the death of philosophy" or "going beyond philosophy" have never inspired me. I consider myself a classic philosopher. For me, the system must not only be in perpetual heterogeneity, it must also be *heterogenesis*, which as far as I can tell, has never been tried. (Deleuze 2006: 361)

Badiou's third ascription goes, in turn, beyond systematicity in a structural sense but also against Deleuze's notion of a system of heterogeneity. Badiou holds the often-celebrated thematic diversity of Deleuze's books to be superficial. While Deleuze always starts with concrete "cases" (as Badiou terms them), such as the works of a philosopher, a painter, a writer, or movie-directors, they are not objects of thought to Deleuze, and he does not analyze them for their own sake (according to Badiou): they are occasions to constrain thought into thinking, ascetic exercises, so to speak. Badiou sees proof of that in the "monotony" of Deleuze's *œuvre*: all his books are supposed to operate with a very limited stock of concepts repeating themselves under various names. Accordingly, there is only one system re-engendering itself in all of Deleuze's works. This allows Badiou to use Deleuze's two volumes about cinema and his books about Leibniz and Foucault on a par with *The Logic of Sense* or *Difference and Repetition* in order to reconstruct Deleuze's ontology. It is as if Badiou took Deleuze's approach to other thinkers or artists to be similar to Stoic allegory, which was mocked by its adversaries as a method allowing the Stoics to rediscover their own physics in Hesiod, Homer and all the various myths.[21]

I will not discuss this approach to Deleuze's method and philosophy, but note only that in *The Clamor of Being* and later texts, Badiou consciously ignores the works written with Félix Guattari (2000b: 210), as if Deleuze's thought had not evolved after *The Logic of Sense* through this collaboration.[22] *Anti-Oedipus* and *A Thousand Plateaus* develop theories which are surely different from the structuralist approach offered in *The Logic of Sense*, especially concerning the signifier[23] and psychoanalysis, and this had consequences as far as ontology is concerned, as Deleuze himself acknowledged (Deleuze and Parnet 1987: 16–18, Deleuze 2006: 65–6)—calling *A Thousand Plateaus* "the book dedicated to multiplicities in themselves" (2006: 362). Even if one conceded to Badiou that Deleuze started as a neo-Stoic, one would still need to prove that he remained one. The repeated reference to Stoicism in Badiou's interpretation is also a way of turning *The Logic of Sense* into a canonic presentation of Deleuze's metaphysics. It is in this book that Badiou finds his main evidence in favor of his first two ascriptions.[24] While many important doctrines of Deleuze, like the overturning of Platonism, univocity of being, eternal recurrence or the notions of singularity and problem, are already present in *The Logic of Sense*, others are not. As for the references used in *The Logic of Sense*, many are not, so to speak, canonical from the point of view of Deleuze's history of philosophy: Kant, Spinoza, and Bergson are absent and, instead, we have the Stoics, Husserl, or Sartre.[25]

In *Dialogues*, when Deleuze explains how he started doing the history of philosophy by focusing on authors he liked for their marginal status, he lists Lucretius, Spinoza, Hume, Nietzsche, and Bergson (Deleuze and Parnet 1987: 15). The Stoics are not named, although they are later discussed, after Hume and

Spinoza, in the same book (Deleuze and Parnet 1987: 62–6). For Deleuze, the Stoics are probably like Leibniz: they had wonderful concepts, they are fascinating antiplatonists, hence they are not enemies, like Plato, Descartes, or Hegel, but they clearly do not belong to the group of Deleuze's philosophical heroes. From its introduction (2000a: 4 quoted above) to the last pages of his short book, Badiou nevertheless keeps making Deleuze the heir of as many Stoic legacies as possible: "The Stoics, Spinoza, Nietzsche, Bergson, as well as Deleuze himself will construct the fold of the unfolding, will refold, will virtualize" (2000a: 101).

3 Spinoza as the Foot-in-the-Monist-Door

One might however object that Badiou could have made many of his ascriptions stick by using Deleuze's official pantheon. In fact, he does just that in his book; Spinoza, Bergson, and Nietzsche are mentioned at least as often as the Stoics by Badiou. For example, it is not difficult to make a case that an admirer of Spinoza such as Deleuze cannot be a pure advocate of multiplicity or singularity, since Spinoza's philosophy posits one single Substance.[26] And the same could be said for asceticism, which, as far as Badiou's understanding of this notion is concerned, could easily be connected to the third type of knowledge in Spinoza. Badiou does indeed sometimes uses Spinoza in this way, for example in *Logics of Worlds*:

> Deleuze's idea of the event [as having an "eternal truth"] should have persuaded him to follow Spinoza—who he elects as the "Christ of philosophy"—right to the end, and to name the unique Event in which becomings are diffracted as "God." God the sole Event where all becomings diffract themselves. (2009: 386).

The reference to Spinoza helps to pin a religious attitude on Deleuze, but note that this is done explicitly ("Deleuze should have. . .") and that this chapter opens with an analogous use of Stoicism, which was quoted and analyzed above. One could find other similar remarks in *The Clamor of Being*, for example when Bergson and the God of Spinoza (Nature) are mentioned to introduce Bernanos's phrase "All is grace," which is supposed to summarize Deleuze's attitude about reality: "For what is, is nothing other than the grace of the All" (2000a: 97).[27] But, here again, Stoicism is not far off, since Badiou continues like this:

> This wager governed Deleuze's creative Stoicism throughout the inhuman experience of the loss of breath [an allusion to Deleuze's illness], of immobilized life ("all is grace," even to die). But it was already apparent in his oblique, although concentrated, way of participating in institutional or collective peripeteias with what I would like to call an indifferent cheerfulness ("What does it matter?"). This shows the power of Deleuze's philosophical choice. (200aa: 97)

While Spinoza and Stoicism are often referred to by Badiou to support the same aspects of his interpretation of Deleuze, they are not always aligned. Stoicism is sometimes used by Badiou to contrast Deleuze with Spinoza in *The Clamor of Being*. This is explicit in the ascription of a philosophy of death to Deleuze previously quoted. Badiou opposes this purportedly Stoic inspiration to Spinoza's famous and probably anti-Senecan claim that "a free man thinks of death least of all things, and his wisdom is a meditation not of death but of life" (*Ethics* 4, prop. 67).

I would like to suggest that this contrast is operating implicitly in other ascriptions by Badiou. The best example is the conclusion of his close analysis of Deleuze's distinction between the virtual and the actual. According to Badiou, Deleuze's claim that the virtual is real is inspired by Bergson but leads to a problem because Deleuze wants to maintain the univocity of being. He must consequently hold that the virtual and the actual are distinct but impossible to distinguish: the reality of the virtual, according to Badiou, leads to the unreality of the actual, which is another way of saying that only the One is real.[28] Badiou comments:

> The more Deleuze attempts to wrest the virtual from irreality, indetermination, and nonobjectivity, the more irreal, undetermined, and finally nonobjective the actual (or beings) becomes, because it is the Two and not the One that is instated. And when the only way of saving—despite everything—the One, is by the reconciling and obscure metaphor of the "mutual image," one says to oneself that, most decidedly, the virtual is no better than the finality of which it is the inversion (it determines the destiny of everything, instead of being that to which everything is destined). Let us be particularly harsh and invoke Spinoza against his major, and indeed sole, truly modern disciple: just like finality, the virtual is *ignorantiae asylum* [the refuge of ignorance]. (2000a: 53)

The description of virtuality as what "determines the destiny of everything" (*il destine tout*) is a transparent allusion to fate (*le destin*), which is well captured by the English translation. The Stoics were one of the main philosophical targets of Spinoza's famous refutation of theological finalism in the Appendix of the first part of his *Ethics*. These two elements suggest that Badiou is here implicitly blaming Deleuze for following the Stoics rather than Spinoza, as he did explicitly with regard to the status of death.[29]

The same strategy might also be implicit in Badiou's description of Deleuze's method as resisting the temptation to turn the distinction between activity and passivity (which is central to Spinoza, as emphasized by Deleuze himself) into a categorical dualism:

> One must never distribute or divide Being according to these two paths [activity and passivity]. One must never lose sight of the fact that, if, as we have shown, two names are always necessary to do univocity justice, these two names never operate any ontological division. (2000a: 34)

On some readings, Stoicism is based precisely on such a dualism, since it posits two independent principles for what exists, one active and one passive, matter and reason;[30] whereas Spinoza has only one Substance and uses activity and passivity as an immanent opposition.

Badiou seems therefore to picture Deleuze as oscillating between two versions of the univocity of being or monism, Stoicism and Spinozism, failing to achieve a non-dualistic version of this position and falling on the Stoic vitalist side. The use of this strategy can be confirmed and explained by the fact that Spinoza is acknowledged by Badiou in the first page of his book as the only philosophical reference he shares with Deleuze: "His canonical references (the Stoics, Hume, Nietzsche, Bergson . . .) were the opposite of my own (Plato, Hegel, Husserl) [. . .]. Spinoza was a point of intersection but 'his' Spinoza was (and still is) for me an un recognizable creature" (2000a: 1). As shown by Laerke (1999: 90–1), Badiou's approval of Spinoza is very different from Deleuze's and is based on the *more geometrico* exposition, and, one should add, the claim that "we feel and know by experience that we are eternal" (*Ethics* 5, prop. 23, scol., quoted in the conclusion of *Logics of Worlds*, 2009: 510). It is, so to speak, a Platonist Spinoza, who takes mathematics as the guide to ontology[31] and who claims to show how we can live as immortal beings.

4 Deleuze as a Platonist malgré lui

This Platonic inspiration, pervasive in Badiou's *oeuvre*, turns out to be crucial to understanding Badiou's use of Stoicism. His attempts to oppose Deleuze's Stoic perspective to his Spinozist inspiration is only part of a more general and more explicit argument to the effect that Deleuze did not succeed in "overturning Platonism," as he claimed (Deleuze, 1966),[32] and should have taken leave of Modernity's anti-Platonism. Badiou argues that Deleuze ends up accepting Plato's principles while claiming to overturn Platonism. Explaining this line of argument in Badiou's thought would require another paper, but one good instance of it can be highlighted here, since it concerns a topic already mentioned above: the relationship of multiple beings to the One.[33]

After showing that, for Deleuze, "the world of beings is the theater of the *simulacra* of being," Badiou notes:

> Strangely, this consequence has a Platonic, or even Neoplatonic, air to it. It is as though the paradoxical or supereminent One immanently engenders a procession of beings whose univocal sense it distributes, while they refer to its power and have only a semblance of being. But, in this case, what meaning is to be given to the Nietzchean program that Deleuze constantly validates: the overturning of Platonism? (2000a: 26)[34]

Then, after explaining Deleuze's understanding of Nietzsche's program, Badiou notes that Plato's view is actually not very far from Deleuze's view of sensible *simulacra* as not opposed to intelligible Ideas but differentiating them. He refers briefly to famous and problematic texts about the Good and the One in the *Republic* and the *Parmenides* and to his own ontological solution to these problems, which grants the One "a status of pure event." He then quotes *The Logic of Sense* about the free man capable of comprehending "every mortal event into one single Event" (1990a: 152) and comments: "One wonders whether this Event with a capital 'E' might not be Deleuze's Good. In light of the way it requires and founds the temperament of 'the free man,' this would seem probable" (2000a: 27). Thus, according to Badiou, Deleuze turns out to be a Platonist in spite of himself, subscribing not only to the status of the One as a principle but also unwittingly to the identity between the Good and the One.

I have explained above how Badiou reconstructs Deleuze's ontology by equating the All, Being, and the One (which belong to different levels according to the Stoics and to Deleuze). For someone familiar with ancient philosophy, this conflation is puzzling because ancient Platonists are adamant to distinguish the One from the All and even from Being. It is as if Badiou offered a pre-Platonic or Parmenidean notion of the One as the undifferentiated totality of Being. But, in fact, this is not *his* conception but the conception he ascribes to Deleuze and to Stoicism. It is, according to Badiou, the way in which they acknowledge that the One is required by any philosophical system, without being able to account consistently for it. As Badiou notes in the last page of his book, Deleuze was a pre-Socratic philosopher, a physicist, a "thinker of the All," and Plato "conducted a trial against philosophy construed as a Great Physics" (2000a: 102) by showing that only mathematics can lead us to a true conception of the One.

Accordingly, Badiou's own position, based on set-theory and Russell's paradox, is that there is no existing All but only multiplicities of multiplicities. As for the One, we have just seen that it is not part of being and cannot be identified with the All, which is an inconsistent notion. Badiou holds that all metaphysicians who do not subscribe to this Platonist view can neither posit the multiple nor the novelty of events in any serious sense. This is the ultimate reason why Badiou does not see any substantial difference between the Stoic coherent cosmos (governed by fate) and Deleuze's *chaosmos*: as long as there is a totality of being, the structure of this unity does not matter to him. To a Platonist, Lucretius's infinite universe (which is probably closer to Deleuze's than the Stoics's) is not that different from the Stoic unified world, since they are both corporeal throughout and lack any real unity (which can only be an incorporeal principle).

5 Overturning Stoicism as a Failed Platonism

At first sight, the use of Stoicism to make Badiou's three ascriptions stick and this platonization of Deleuze might seem wholly incompatible, but they in fact go hand in hand. As recent research on the ancient debate between Stoicism and imperial or late Platonists has shown, it is typical of Platonism to refute Stoicism by showing that it cannot succeed in grounding truth and science, justice and the good, or divine existence and providence (as it claims to do) on the basis of its materialist ontology, its empiricist epistemology, and its naturalistic ethics. From this perspective, Stoicism appears as an unstable or hypocritical, and ultimately impossible, compromise between incompatible positions. Consequently, it must renounce either its specific tenets (and choose the side of Platonism) or its philosophical aims (and choose the side of relativism).[35] This is why it can and must be characterized both as a naturalism (or vitalism, in Badiou's vocabulary), from the point of view of its basic tenets, and as a failed or awkward version of Platonism, from the point of view of the goals it claims to achieve. This whole argumentative strategy is hence based on at least two assumptions: (1) that Stoicism shares its fundamental philosophical orientations with Platonism (for instance, the distinction between opinion and knowledge, the identity between the good and the virtue, and the existence of a providential order of the world) and (2) that these orientations cannot be explained and defended without going beyond corporeal reality and the structure of language, that is to say, without positing eternal, intelligible entities.

Badiou describes the aim of philosophy in different terms, but his argument is entirely analogous. We have seen how he sometimes uses Spinoza to have Deleuze at least partly subscribe to these aims. Similarly, the ancient Platonists referred to Socrates, since he was a crucial authority for the Stoics as well, and could thus be used as a common ground to challenge the ability of Stoicism to satisfy Socratic philosophical standards. This is also why Badiou must base his ascriptions on notions which he shares with Deleuze, such as the One, asceticism, and the notion of system.[36] Moreover, Badiou stresses how Deleuze and he shared similar adversaries, both from a philosophical and a political point of view. While he briefly said that he and Deleuze belonged to different factions of the Left during *Mai 68* and that he wrote very polemical pieces about Deleuze and Guattari during these years (2000a: 2–3), Badiou nevertheless considers Deleuze to be more or less on the same side as himself, namely against phenomenology, analytic philosophy, and "the parliamentary moral doctrine of rights" (2000a: 98).[37]

Badiou's Platonism is based on a specific concept of events (and the One) as breaking from continuous becoming (and multiplicities, equated with beings) and as eternal truths, and he claims that Deleuze's Stoic notions of the One as the Virtual All and of events as superficial singularities cannot ground his Spinozist drive toward eternity or his political orientations. This is the meaning of Badiou's ambivalent praise of Deleuze's "unwavering love of the world" and refusal to judge it (2000a: 44). It is admirable, but it also prevents Deleuze from accounting for events (as absolute creations defining new and eternal truths) and for subjects (defined by Badiou through their faithfulness to these created truths). As a consequence, Deleuze's staunch resistance to "what threatens us" (according to Badiou), namely ordinary language, logic, and democratic ethics, turns out to be a weak resistance,[38] which cannot defend the eternal truths of events against the reign of capitalism and democratic opinion. The only true resistance is the one based on logic and mathematics and, hence, must "have recourse to the other tradition that ... goes back, not to Nietzsche and the Stoics, but to Descartes and Plato" (2000a: 99). To a Platonist, a coherent Stoic either turns into a sophist or defects.

6 Conclusion

If my account of Badiou's interpretation of Deleuze and its underlying strategy is correct, three types of objection can be (and have indeed been) leveled against Badiou on this score. First, one can challenge the characterization of Deleuze as a neo-Stoic on the grounds that Badiou overlooks the fact that Deleuze distances himself from Stoicism in various ways (explicitly or implicitly, in the works where he draws on Stoicism or in other later works where he changed his positions). Still, it will always remain an open question whether Deleuze can ultimately be considered to be Stoic, as Badiou and others think, or not. But, even conceding the portrait of Deleuze as a Stoic, one can also try and refute Badiou's claims that Deleuze did not succeed in elaborating (on his Stoic principles) as consistent and radical a democratic materialism as he (and Badiou alike) claimed to offer. Such a counterattack would be similar to the arguments offered by some ancient Stoics to the effect that Zeno's doctrine is a far more consistent and efficient defense of Socrates's central positions about virtue, dialectic or gods and the world than Plato's doctrine. Finally, one could challenge this common ground itself and deny that Deleuze shares crucial philosophical goals and concepts with Badiou. One would thus argue that their "images of thought," to borrow an important Deleuzian notion, are hardly similar. Just as, according to Deleuze, the Megarics, the Cynics, and the Stoics offered "a reorientation of all thought and what it means to think" directed against Plato's notion of philosophy as a conversion to a higher sphere of reality (Deleuze 1990a: 148–51), Deleuze is hardly interested in fidelity to truths or in political revolutions, and sketches with Guattari a politics centered on flight, minority, and resistance.

Notes

1. I thank Kurt Lampe, Clifford Robinson, and Janae Sholtz for their comments on this paper and bibliographical suggestions during the Bristol Conference and afterward.
2. See Alliez (1998), Gil (1998), and Villani (1998) which were all published in the same issue of *Futur antérieur*.
3. See previous note and Laerke (1999), Toscano (2000) which is a review of Badiou (2000a), Smith (2003: 431–8), Crockett (2013: 11–26) and Roffe (2012).
4. See Roffe (2012: 1–6) for a brief study of all these texts, which rightly emphasizes the differences between them, and Laerke (1999) about the chapter in *Court traité d'ontologie transitoire* (Badiou 2006b: 63–72).
5. References to Stoicism can be found in Deleuze (1968: 106), (1977: 77–81), and (1988: 71–2), Deleuze and Guattari (1980: 199) and (1992: 120). On Stoicism in Deleuze, see Bénatouïl (2003), Beaulieu (2005), Sellars (2006), Bowden (2005), and (2011: 15–5), Bénatouïl (2015) and several chapters in this volume.
6. This inference is quite problematic, as explained by Brassier (2000: 201), Smith (2003: 431–2), Roffe (2012: 6–23), and Laerke, who notes that "univocity means unity, but not oneness, because univocity is not a numerical determination" (2005: 13, n. 53). See also Laerke (1999).

7   "Being is Voice that is said [. . .] It occurs, therefore, as a unique event for everything that happens to the most diverse things" (1990a: 179). "Univocity raises and extracts Being, in order to distinguish it better from that in which it occurs and from that of which it is said. It wrests Being from beings [. . .] Univocal Being inheres in language and happens to things [. . .] Neither active, nor passive, univocal Being is neutral. It is *extra-Being*, that is, the minimum of Being common to the real, the possible, and the impossible" (1990a: 180).
8   Here the English translation does not capture the connection with Stoic ontology: Deleuze writes "*une seule insistance pour tout ce qui existe*" (1969: 211), where *insistance* refers back implicitly to the verb *insister*, which is one possible translation (with *subsister*) of *huphisthanai*, the verb Stoics used about incorporeals and distinguished from *huparchein*, which is usually translated by *exister*, a distinction which Deleuze mentions when he introduces events in *The Logic of Sense*: "On ne peut pas dire qu'ils existent, mais plutôt qu'ils subsistent ou insistent, ayant ce minimum d'être qui convient à ce qui n'est pas une chose, entité non existante" (1969: 13). This sentence might be taken to suggest that, for the Stoics, being is the genus of which existing things and subsisting entities are species or perhaps degrees/levels. This is not the case (and Deleuze refers more often and more adequately to incorporeals as *extra-beings*). The criteria of being, for the Stoics, are acting and being acted upon, hence only bodies (i.e., existing things) are beings. This point is crucial in the debate between Plato and the Stoics, as shown by Brunschwig (1988).
9   See Beaulieu (2005: 67–8), Sellars (2006: 167), and Roffe (2012: 114–19).
10 Brassier (2000: 202–3) offers an interesting account of why, from Badiou's perspective, "the Deleuzian invocation of pure Chance" amounts to affirming "the ineluctability of Fate" or, as Badiou writes in the context of a comparison between Deleuze and Heidegger, "Deleuze does not decipher any destiny, or, rather, for him destiny [*le destin*] is never anything other than the integral affirmation of chance" (2000a: 100).
11 See also Badiou (2000b: 198) about the many possible names of the One.
12 See Badiou (2000a: 10–11) and (2000b: 197–202), respectively, for an anticipation of and a detailed answer to this objection. Badiou criticizes in particular the opposition between multiplicities and sets, which Deleuze supposedly reduced to numerical multiplicities. For a criticism of Badiou's counter-objections and a thorough defense of Deleuze from the point of view of the history of mathematics, see Smith (2003).
13 On this analysis, see also Roffe (2012: 107–9).
14 I am not suggesting this principle is in itself wrong. When one conceives of philosophy as a system and when one recalls that the Stoics did, it is only natural to suspect that borrowing one tenet from Stoicism might not be possible without taking on board other Stoic tenets. Still, before ascribing these other unintended Stoic tenets to the borrower, it is necessary to assess the extent and method of the explicit borrowing and whether the borrower takes care of insulating it from other Stoic doctrines, as Deleuze does when he parts company with the Stoics in *The Logic of Sense* (1990a: 169–75).
15 Brassier (2000: 203), by contrast, notes correctly that Deleuze's reference to Stoic ethics and *amor fati* (1990a: 142–53) might be taken to support Badiou's reading of Deleuze's pure Chance as just another name for the necessity of Fate.
16 This text "Immanence: A Life" was published in September 1995 just before Deleuze's death. Some of its sentences can be read as answers to Badiou and one wonders whether they are echoes of Deleuze's correspondence with Badiou: see the last page

about the One and the last paragraph about the event of the wound in Joe Bousquet, which refers back to *Logique du sens*.

17 Badiou overlooks that Deleuze's phrasing emphasizes (much more than Blanchot's) how death can be turned against *itself*: see Villani (1998). Still, Deleuze writes in the previous page, commenting upon Blanchot: "It is in this way that death and its wound are not simply events among other events. Every event is like death, double and impersonal in its double" (1990a: 152). There is no doubt that death is a paradigm of sort for Deleuze here.

18 I come back below to this contrast drawn by Badiou between Deleuze and Stoicism on the one hand and Spinoza on the other.

19 See for instance Villani (1998).

20 Badiou (2015: 172) takes Aristotle to be the "inventor of the system" in the sense criticized by contemporary thought, and vitalism, from Nietzsche onward, to be one of the trends critical of this notion.

21 See for instance Cicero, *ND* 1.41.

22 This is a conscious move on the part of Badiou (2000b: 210). Note that the *Anti-Œdipus* was violently criticized by Badiou in his first texts about Deleuze, dating back to the 1960s and 1970s.

23 Sauvagnargues (2009: 188–94).

24 This is confirmed by *Logics of Worlds*: as noted above, Deleuze's philosophy is depicted as a metaphysics centered on the concept of event (2009: 382) and strictly opposed to Badiou's own ontology centered on the same concept. In fact, the concept of event is quite rare in Deleuze's later books, except in *The Fold: Leibniz and the Baroque* in which a short chapter is called "What is an event?" In Deleuze's middle works written with Guattari, the concept of *becoming* becomes much more important than the concept of event. See further Roffe (2012: 104–8) about "Deleuze's intermittent attention" to event, which contrasts with Badiou's focus on this concept in his own philosophy and in Deleuze's. For an introduction to Deleuze's philosophy from the point of view of the concept of event, see Zourabichvili (1994).

25 Hughes 2008 claims that Husserl's imprint on Deleuze extends way beyond *The Logic of Sense*. While I doubt this is the case, I am not suggesting that Husserl and other references central to *The Logic of Sense* become irrelevant in later works, just that they are not direct interlocutors anymore. For a thorough comparison between Sartre's, Deleuze's, and Husserl's approach to the Stoic notion of a sayable, see Majolino 2020.

26 See Badiou (2000b: 197–8), where he argues (against objections to his interpretation of Deleuze's doctrine as a metaphysics of the One) that, following Spinoza, *any* real philosophy approaches particular things *in order to* grasp Substance or the One and that Deleuze (like Stoicism, Spinoza, Bergson or Nietzsche) aims at a "new intuition of the power of the One."

27 Badiou also praises (somewhat ironically?) Deleuze for "an astonishing undertaking that consisted in integrally secularizing Bergsonism" (2000a: 99). For Badiou, Deleuze is ultimately a "religious" thinker (because of his equating truth with the One, of which we have no experience) and this is as always shown by his lineage: Stoicism, Spinoza, and Bergson.

28 About and against this analysis which takes the virtual as a founding or transcendental principle in Deleuze, see Laerke (1999: 87) and Laerke (2005: section 8).

29 In another chapter (2000a: 85), Badiou criticizes Deleuze's description of the All as "that which keeps [the set] open somewhere" or "which attaches it to the rest of the universe" as a "theoretical convenience" (*solution de facilité*), describes this attachment

as a "providential marking," and compares it to the doctrine of the two parts of the object, one virtual the other actual. Providence is again a typically Stoic position (especially in the context of a discussion of the ascetic way to the One justified by the nature of the All) which is criticized by Spinoza (in the same Appendix to *Ethics* I).

30 About dualism in stoicism, see Gourinat (2015).

31 See also this concluding remark in a later text on Deleuze: "The only thing we ask is how a player of thought, a thrower of dice like Deleuze, can so insistently claim filiation with Spinoza.... No doubt, like many interpreters, Deleuze neglects the function mathematics holds in Spinoza's ontology.... It is not an overstatement to say that for Spinoza mathematics only thinks Being, for mathematics alone consists completely of adequate ideas. This is what I sought to ascertain by placing Spinoza at a divide—yet another one—between Deleuze and myself" (Badiou 2006b: 71). For replies to this objection, see Laerke (1999) and Smith (2003, 435).

32 This paper was revised and republished in 1969 as an appendix in *Logique du sens*.

33 Another good example would be Badiou's argument over the status and nature of truth (2000a: 55–61), which proceeds exactly like his analysis of the One/beings distinction: Deleuze claims to overturn Platonism by criticizing truth, but what he opposes to truth is in fact similar to Plato's actual method (which is itself very different from Platonism), so much so that Deleuze turns out again to be "an involuntary Platonist" (2000a: 61).

34 See Ansel-Pearson (2002: 97–114) and Roffe (2012: 19–23) about Badiou's reading of Deleuze's ontology as platonist or emanative in this section of his book, which they aptly refute on the basis of Deleuze's critical analysis of Neoplatonist emanation (1990b: 178–85). Still, the metaphysics of the One Badiou ascribes to Deleuze seems to me to be quite different from neoplatonism, as shown by Badiou's privileged reference to Stoicism on this topic and by his insistence that Deleuze posits the One-All, which is very different from the Neoplatonist One. This is why I would not endorse Roffe's conclusion that Badiou "portrait[s] Deleuze as a neo-plotinian" (2012: 6), while agreeing with most other points made by Roffe. However, the fact that Badiou suggests several similarities between Deleuze and neoplatonism is indeed very significant, but it is in my view part of a larger strategy painting the neostoic Deleuze as incapable of constructing a coherent antiplatonist philosophical system, as I will argue in the last section of this chapter.

35 The best examples of this strategy in the field of ethics can be found in Cic. *Fin.* 4-5 and Plotinus *Enneads* 1.4. For epistemology, see the examples offered and analyzed in Bonazzi (2015). For cosmology and metaphysics, see Cic. *ND* 3 (inspired by Carneades's argument against Stoic theology), Plutarch, *The E at Delphi*, and Plotinus *Enneads* 2.4 and 3.1. These authors do not share the same platonist doctrines, but they can be shown to share an overall strategy against Stoicism and some philosophical orientations guiding this strategy.

36 Had Badiou ascribed to Deleuze "a philosophy of nature as a totality" and an "ethics based on *amor fati*," instead of "a metaphysics of the One," as "an ascetic ethics of thought," he could have pictured Deleuze as a neostoic just as easily. But it would have been much more difficult to show that Deleuze ultimately failed to reach his philosophical aims. Whereas describing him as using concepts and goals seemingly common to him and Badiou (and applicable to Stoicism and Platonism) and prepares the second step in which Deleuze is shown to offer only inconsistent or weak versions of them (see next paragraph).

37 In the preface to *Logics of Worlds*, Badiou describes Deleuze as having attempted to offer a path against "democratic materialism" (2009: 7), which is today's common sense and Badiou's ennemy (2009: 1–2). Badiou and Deleuze's philosophical orientations are supposed to be the same, while their paths may be "different and even perhaps opposed," but only one will turn out to be able to reach the intended destination (see next note). There is a similar allusion in the Badiou's last book, where Deleuze is said to have "come close to the dangers of a positivism of Life or of Totality [*positivisme vitaliste, ou de la Totalité*]," which is one of the dangers "facing philosophical progressivism" (2018: 35).
38 In other texts, Badiou is less generous and blames Deleuze for sharing various assumptions with phenomenology, linguistic philosophy, and democratic politics (2009: 268, 386). See Brassier (2000: 206–9) for an account of Badiou's doubts about the political implications of Deleuze's ontology.

Bibliography

Alliez, E. (1998), "Badiou/Deleuze," *Futur antérieur* 43, www.multitudes.net/Badiou-Deleuze/ (accessed January 2019).
Ansel-Pearson, K. (2002), *Philosophy and the Adventure of the Virtual*, London: Routledge.
Badiou, A. (1997), *Deleuze: La clameur de l'Etre*, Paris: Hachette.
Badiou, A. (2000a), *Deleuze: The Clamor of Being*, trans. L. Burchill, Minneapolis: University of Minnesota Press.
Badiou, A. (2000b), "Un, multiple, multiplicité(s)," *Multitudes* 1, www.multitudes.net/Un-multiple-multiplicite-s/ (accessed January 2019).
Badiou, A. (2006a), *Logiques des mondes. L'Être et l'événement, 2*, Paris: Seuil.
Badiou, A. (2006b), *Briefings on Existence: A Short Treatise on Transitory Ontology*, trans. N. Madarasz, Albany: State University of New York Press.
Badiou, A. (2009), *Logics of Worlds. Being and Event 2*, trans. A. Toscano, London: Continuum.
Badiou, A. (2015), "*Système du système*," *Les Temps Modernes* 682: 172–9.
Badiou, A. (2018), *L'immanence des vérités. L'être et l'événement 3*, Paris: Fayard.
Beaulieu, A. (2005), "Gilles Deleuze et les Stoïciens," in A. Beaulieu (ed.), *Gilles Deleuze, héritage philosophique*, 45–72, Paris: PUF.
Bénatouïl, T. (2003), "*Deleuze, Foucault: deux usages du stoïcisme*," in F. Gros and C. Lévy (eds.), *Foucault et la philosophie antique*, 17–49, Paris: Kimé.
Bénatouïl, T. (2015), "Stoicism and Twentieth Century French Philosophy," in J. Sellars (ed.), *Routledge Handbook of the Stoic Tradition*, 541–62, London: Routledge.
Bonazzi, M. (2015), *A la recherche des idées*, Paris: Vrin.
Bowden, S. (2005), "*Deleuze et les Stoïciens: une logique de l'événement*," *Bulletin de la Société Américaine de Philosophie de Langue Française* 15 (1): 72–97.
Bowden, S. (2011), *The Priority of Events: Deleuze's Logic of Sense*, Edinburgh: Edinburgh University Press.
Brassier, R. (2000), "Stellar Void or Cosmic Animal? Badiou and Deleuze on the Dice-Throw," *Pli* 10: 200–16.
Brunschwig, J. (1988), "La théorie stoïcienne du genre suprême," in J. Barnes and M. Mignucci (eds.), *Matter and Metaphysics*, Fourth Symposium Hellenisticum, 20–127, Napoli: Bibliopolis.

Crockett, C. (2013), *Deleuze beyond Badiou: Ontology, Multiplicity, and Event*, New York: Columbia University Press.
Deleuze, G. (1966), "Renverser le platonisme," *Revue de Métaphysique et de Morale* 71: 436–8, republished in Deleuze (1969).
Deleuze, G. (1968), *Différence et répétition*, Paris: Presses Universitaires de France.
Deleuze, G. (1969), *Logique du sens*, Paris: Minuit.
Deleuze, G. (1988), *Le Pli*, Paris: Minuit.
Deleuze, G. (1990a), *The Logic of Sense*, trans. M. Lester and C. Stivale, New York: Columbia University Press.
Deleuze, G. (1990b), *Expressionism in Philosophy*: Spinoza, trans. M. Joughin, New York: Zone Books.
Deleuze, G. (2006), *Two Regimes of Madness: Texts and 1975–1995*, ed. D. Lapoujade, trans. A. Hodges and M. Taormina, New York: Semiotext(e).
Deleuze, G. and C. Parnet (1977), 77–81.
Deleuze, G. and C. Parnet (1987), *Dialogues*, trans. H. Tomlinson and B. Habberjam, London: Athlone.
Deleuze, G. and F. Guattari (1980), *Mille Plateaux*, Paris: Minuit.
Deleuze, G. and F. Guattari (1992), *Qu'est-ce que la philosophie?*, Paris: Minuit.
Gil, José (1998), "Quatre méchantes notes sur un livre méchant," *Futur antérieur* 43, www.multitudes.net/Quatre-mechantes-notes-sur-un/ (accessed January 2019).
Goldschmidt, V. (1953), *Le Système stoïcien et l'idée de temps*, Paris: Vrin.
Gourinat, J.-B. (2015), "Les Stoïciens et le dualisme," *Chôra. Revue d'études anciennes et médiévales* 13: 165–84.
Hughes, J. (2008), *Deleuze and the Genesis of Representation*, London: Continuum.
Laerke, M. (1999), "The Voice and the Name: Spinoza in the Badiouian Critique of Deleuze," *Pli. The Warwick Journal of Philosophy* 8: 86–99.
Laerke, M. (2005), "Gilles Deleuze and the System of Nature and Philosophy," *Alegrar* 2, http://www.alegrar.com.br/02/mogensing.pdf (accessed December 2015).
Majolino C. (2020), "Back to the Meanings Themselves Husserl, Phenomenology and the Stoic Doctrine of the *Lekton*," in J. K. Larsen and P. R. Gilbert (eds.), *Phenomenological Interpretations of Ancient Philosophy*, Leiden: Brill.
Roffe, J. (2012), *Badiou's Deleuze*, Montreal and Kingston: McGill-Queen's University Press.
Sauvagnargues, A. (2009), *L'empirisme transcendantal*, Paris: Presses Universitaires de France.
Sellars, J. (2006), "An Ethics of the Event: Deleuze's Stoicism," *Angelaki: Journal of the Theoretical Humanities* 11: 157–71.
Smith, D. (2003), "Mathematics and the Theory of Multiplicities: Badiou and Deleuze Revisited," *The Southern Journal of Philosophy* 41: 411–49.
Toscano, A. (2000), "To Have Done with the End of Philosophy," *Pli* 9: 220–38.
Villani, A. (1998), "La Métaphysique de Deleuze," *Futur antérieur* 43, www.multitudes.net/La-metaphysique-de-Deleuze (accessed January 2019).
Zourabichvili, F. (1994), *La philosophie de l'événement*, Paris: Paris University Press

Chapter 6

JULIA KRISTEVA, STOICISM, AND THE
"TRUE LIFE OF INTERPRETATIONS"*

Kurt Lampe

Julia Kristeva (1941–) is a psychoanalyst, novelist, and cultural critic, whose work has exerted considerable influence over literary theory and feminist philosophy. Her engagement with Stoicism, unlike those of Gilles Deleuze and Michel Foucault, has hitherto gone completely unnoticed by classicists and historians of ancient philosophy. Yet she offers important criticisms of Stoic practical ethics, which she grounds in claims about Stoic philosophy of language and metaphysics. Precisely because she forces us to reflect on the depth psychology of Stoic reasoning, which Stoicism itself neglects, her provocations merit consideration by both scholars and modern Stoic practitioners.

My first objective in this chapter is to explain the scattered, elliptical, but insightful and coherent remarks about Stoicism Kristeva threads throughout her *oeuvre*.[1] These remarks are difficult to understand, both because they require familiarity with the audacious scholarship of Émile Bréhier and Victor Goldschmidt (the same scholars on whom Deleuze relies) and because Kristeva eschews dispassionate clarity in favor of affective involvement with the topics and situations on which she writes.[2] In other words, she *performs* her ethics of interpretation. "Interpretation," for Kristeva, designates an ethico-epistemic attitude, and the "true life of interpretations" designates a personally and politically healthy form of this attitude.

My second objective is to sketch a critical response to Kristeva's presentation. The point is certainly not to praise or condemn her accuracy, but rather to develop a new perspective on the "existential option" that the Stoic life has been or *could become* (Hadot 2002: 102, 114–15, 126–8).

1 Kristeva on the Stoic "Life of Interpretations"

In "Psychoanalysis and the Polis," Kristeva writes,

> I would say that interpretation as an epistemological and ethical attitude began with the Stoics. . . . Man, says Epictetus, is "born to contemplate God and his

---

* An earlier version of this chapter appeared.

works, and not only to contemplate them but also to interpret them. . . . 'To interpret'" in this context, and I think always, means "to make a connection." Thus the birth of interpretation is considered the birth of semiology, since the semiological sciences relate a sign (an event-sign) to a signified in order to act accordingly, consistently, consequently. (79)

This quotation makes clear the importance Kristeva attributes to Stoicism as the originary and preeminent example of a certain interpretive model. I will not address her assertion about the Stoics's chronological priority. What interests me is instead her claim that the Stoics's "epistemological and ethical attitude," which is revealed in their interpretive activity, can be encapsulated by the term "semiology," that is "making a connection" among three elements: an "event-sign," a "signified," and an action. What does that mean?

Before attempting to clarify this, it is best to complete the list of elements connected, according to Kristeva, in Stoic semiology. In "From One Identity to Another" she argues that "every language theory is predicated upon a conception of the subject that it explicitly posits, implies, or tries to deny" (1981a: 124). There she mentions Stoic language theory only in passing, saying that she will not "refer back to the stoic sage, who guaranteed both the sign's triad and the inductive conditional clause" (125). In this compressed reference, the phrase "inductive conditional clause" refers to the connections we have just seen among event-sign, signified, and action. We might think of this as the secondary level in Stoic semiology. I will explain it more thoroughly in a moment. But the term "sign's triad" introduces a prior semiotic level, which is internal to the event-sign: namely, the connections among a signifying phrase, a conceptual signification, and an external state of affairs. We might call this the primary level of Stoic semiology. Kristeva believes that Stoic semiology is an "epistemological and ethical attitude" of the accomplished philosopher who, as she says here, "guarantees" both the primary and the secondary levels of connectivity.

In order to understand this connectivity, we need to detour via Kristeva's beliefs about language.[3] For Kristeva, language ought to be the last in a series of mechanisms for mediating and managing the intensity of our needs, joys, and frustrations vis-à-vis other people. She expresses this by saying that the engine of language is "primal want" (1982a: 5, 35) or the archaic, sexual, maternal "Thing" (1989: 12-20, 1995: 62, 2009: 28).[4] To put it another way, the Thing represents our unnameable and overwhelming fascination, love, frustration, and hatred toward other people, which is fundamental to human experience. Our first, infantile way of relating to the Thing is via kinetic and sensorial rhythms and patterns, which Kristeva calls "the semiotic." These are experienced as an immediate relation to the maternal body as possessor of the Thing. But in the normative sequence of development, the child "abjects" this relation to the maternal body and invests its loves and hatreds in paternal signifiers instead—the "big Other" in place of the "(m)other." Kristeva calls this the "thetic break"; like Lacan, she designates the ensuing domain of signification "the symbolic." But Kristeva places greater emphasis than Lacan on the enduring importance of both semiotic patterns and "imaginary" polysemy within language, both of which she sees as supplements and potential rivals to signification as a means of negotiating our relation to the Thing.[5]

Let us look more closely at Kristeva's theory of thetic signification. Each thetic act not only connects a signifying phrase, a signification, and an external referent but also represents the "subject of enunciation" in her mediated interaction with the Thing.[6] For example, if I say "the Stoics are brilliant," on the one hand I am using a string of syllables, that is a signifying phrase, to express a symbolic signification. I am also connecting this symbolic signification with an external state of affairs, namely the actual being-brilliant of some group of philosophers. But on the other hand, I am positioning *myself*, the subject of enunciation, vis-à-vis the symbolic Other, of which my addressee is the present representative. I am struggling to say what I can never articulate, but which we might gloss as "you frustrate me," "I hate you," "I love you," "please satisfy me," and so on. To put it another way, beneath every illocutionary function, such as explaining, persuading, and so on, the foundational and unachievable illocutionary aim is to occupy a satisfying position vis-à-vis the Thing.

In fact, it is this illocutionary drive that brings together the three elements of the primary semiotic level in a complete utterance. In *Revolution in Poetic Language* Kristeva writes,

> There is no sign that is not thetic and every sign is already the germ of a "sentence" . . . . Stoic semiology, which was the first to formulate the matrix of the sign, had already established this complicity between sign and sentence, making them proofs of each other. (44)

Why does Kristeva say that "every sign is already the germ of a 'sentence?'" Because even if a child utters the proto-sign "woof-woof," she intends the sentence "*this is a woof-woof*"; it is in predication that the subject of enunciation appears. The child is enunciating this proposition *for* her caretaker in the hope of eliciting a response. "Yes," the father might say adoringly, "that *is* a woof-woof." Thus it is the "primal want" (for approval, for attention, for satisfaction) behind predicating enunciation that creates the "complicity between sign and sentence."

Next, we must explain why Kristeva claims that the Stoics themselves were "the first to formulate this matrix of the sign" and "had already established this complicity between sign and sentence." In order to reconstruct her sequence of thought, we must first recall that the Stoics anticipated the modern triad of sign, sense, and reference (Mates 1961: 19–26). For the Stoics written or spoken words do not designate bodies or bodily qualities.[7] Rather, a written or spoken "signifier" (≈ sign) designates an incorporeal "signified" (≈ sense), which expresses an impression made upon the speaker's soul by the bodily "bearer" (≈ referent) of this signified (LS 33B). The incorporeal signified may be thought of as an "event" or effect, which the speaker understands and asserts as a true or false "sayable" about the underlying bodily cause. Because they are incorporeal, these "sayable events" do not "exist"; they are not "beings." Rather, they are "somethings," which "subsist."[8] Thus the Stoics articulated something like what Kristeva calls "the sign's triad" or "the matrix of the sign."

Second, we must follow up Kristeva's vague reference to Émile Bréhier's pioneering study, *La théorie des incorporels dans l'ancien stoïcisme* (1962 [orig. 1908], cited by Kristeva 1984: 243 n. 49). According to Bréhier, Stoic metaphysics of language

> radically separates . . . two planes of being: on the one hand, deep and real being, force; on the other, the plane of facts, which play on the surface of being, and which constitute a multiplicity of incorporeal beings without connection or end (13).[9]

Later Bréhier speaks of reason's "spontaneity" as the "active cause" which "constructs" rational significations (1962: 16).[10] This is why Kristeva treats the Stoics as forerunners of her own psycholinguistics to the Stoics, as she reveals in saying they "had already established this complicity between sign and sentence." Because Bréhier says that facts "play on the surface of being," where reason operates "spontaneously," he opens a space between linguistic thought and the corporeal reality to which it refers. Into this gap Kristeva inserts the dynamism of the primal want, which closes it by conjoining signifying phrases, signified concepts, and bodily states of affairs in the process of enunciation.

We are now in a position to return to the secondary level of Stoic semiology and the Stoic sage's "guarantee" of the "inductive conditional clause," that is the connections among sign, signified, and action. Here we must begin by elucidating Kristeva's confusing terminology: at the secondary level, both "event-sign" and "signified" will refer to a primary triad, that is a signifying phrase, a conceptual signification, and an external state of affairs. In order to understand how, we must again follow up a vague citation in Kristeva's footnotes (1982b: 79 n. 1), this time to Victor Goldschmidt's *Le système stoïcien et l'idée de temps*. One of the key passages for Goldschmidt is section eight of Epictetus's *Enkhiridion*: "Don't search for events to happen as you want, but want events to happen as they do."[11] At the point where he introduces this quotation from the *Enkhiridion* (Goldschmidt 1953: 79), he also cites the same passage of Epictetus's *Discourses* as Kristeva. It is worth quoting Goldschmidt at some length, since his exact wording informs Kristeva's meaning.

> In order to "want events as they happen," we must know and understand them, we must *interpret* them. Man, says Epictetus, is born "to contemplate god and his works, and not only to contemplate them, but also to interpret them" [*Diss.* 1.6.19]. "Interpret" means make a connection. (1953: 79)

Recall now the quotation from Kristeva with which we began:

> Man, says Epictetus, is "born to contemplate God and his works, and not only to contemplate them but also to interpret them" [*Diss.* 1.6.19]. "To interpret" in this context, and I think always, means "to make a connection." (1982b: 79)

It is clear that Kristeva had Goldschmidt's book open to this page as she was writing. Understanding what Goldschmidt means by "making a connection," and what it has to do with "wanting events as they happen," will turn out to be essential for appreciating Kristeva's claims.

For Goldschmidt, the phrase "want what happens" encapsulates the fundamental aspiration of the Stoic life of interpretations, which is to align your volition with the reason of god, whose providential law is also the universal causal nexus of destiny. In other words, god's benevolent and rational plan determines absolutely every sayable event in the Stoic universe. Goldschmidt distinguishes two planes of interpretation in Stoic philosophy, which are two pathways toward cognitive and affective alignment with god. In the first pathway, "the two terms, when we're dealing with events, are separated in time: one, the event-sign, which we must 'interpret,' is given to us in the present" (79). Note here the term "event-sign," which Kristeva picks up: "The semiological sciences," she says, "relate a sign (an event-sign) to a signified in order to act accordingly." In this pathway the interpreter attempts to align her volition with god's by inferring, through her grasp of theology and physics, which future event will follow from the present event-sign. She then desires that divinely ordained future event.

But Goldschmidt believes that the emphasis in Stoicism falls instead on the second pathway. This is what Epictetus calls the "use of impressions," that is the cautious scrutiny of our thoughts about whatever is presently happening. In this pathway we do not connect a present event-sign to a future one, since this is often beyond our merely human capacity. Instead, acknowledging our cognitive limitations, we connect a present event-sign to an appropriate reaction on our part. As Goldschmidt says, "The use of impressions brings us already to action. Understanding an impression consists in knowing 'which virtue we should use in connection with the object that has produced it'" (1953: 123, quoting MA 3.2.3).

Let me illustrate this in terms of Stoic logic and moral psychology. As an example of an "event-sign," I will adapt a topic from the Roman Stoic Musonius Rufus (fr. XVIIIB): I am at dinner, and the host serves me bread and butter. Now, let us also imagine that I already have in my soul some Stoic beliefs, like that intemperate behavior is to be avoided. What, in this case, is the "inductive conditional clause" to which Kristeva refers, which connects an event-sign to a signified and consequently an action? It is something like this: "If I use too much butter, this is intemperate. If this is intemperate, it is to-be-avoided." Now, according to Stoic psychology, if I assent to the proposition "it is to be avoided," action follows immediately.[12] Thus in this example I have connected an event-sign, namely "I am eating bread and butter" to a complex signified, namely "using too much butter is to-be-avoided." Furthermore, I have connected this signified to an action: by assenting to its signification, I immediately choose not to use too much butter.

Now that we understand how Kristeva reads the Stoic model of interpretation, we are ready to appreciate her critical response. This comes across most clearly in a passage later in "Psychoanalysis and the Polis":

> The person through whom knowledge comes about is not mad, but (as the Stoics have indicated) he is (subject to) death. The time of accurate interpretation, that is, an interpretation in accordance with destiny (or the Other's Phallus), is a moment that includes and completes eternity; interpretation is consequently both happiness and death of time and of the subject: suicide. The transformation of sexual desire into the desire to know an object deprives the subject of this desire and abandons him or reveals him as subject to death. Interpretation, in its felicitous accuracy, expurgating passion and desire, reveals the interpreter as master of his will but at the same time as slave of death. Stoicism is . . . the last great pagan ideology, tributary of nature as mother, raised to the phallic rank of Destiny to be interpreted. (1982b: 83)

I will not attempt to address every facet of this dense, poetic passage. Rather, I will focus on three claims it advances about the Stoic model of interpretation. First, Stoic interpretation "includes and completes eternity." Second, it is a sort of "suicide" or death. These first two claims take their inspiration from Goldschmidt, but substantially transform the significance of his reading. Third, Stoic interpretation is an "ideology." This claim moves beyond the "epistemological and ethical attitude" of Stoicism in order to encompass its political implications.

It is best to deal with the first two claims together. The first, that Stoic interpretation "includes and completes eternity," rests on Goldschmidt's analysis of the interplay of the two pathways of Stoic interpretation. As we have just seen, for Goldschmidt it is because I know my limits that I do not attempt to understand the providential nexus of destiny, but rather focus on aligning my volition with god's within my immediate circumstances. Thus I put all my energy into buttering that bread as beautifully and virtuously as I can, for example.[13] Yet in "wanting what happens" in this limited way, I nevertheless integrate myself into the entire series of divinely willed events: the divine law that I obey in consuming dinner virtuously is the same law that governs nature (Goldschmidt 1953: 101, 156). In fact I am not other than god, for god pervades the entire universe as its active principle (LS 44B, 54A-B), and is particularly concentrated in rational souls (LS 47O.2). This is the key to understanding Stoic compatibilism: insofar as I manage to think and act in accord with nature, divinely determined events become my freely chosen actions. Thus, in a sense, the eternity of providence is telescoped into my action.

The second claim, that Stoic interpretation is somehow suicidal, emerges from the same trend in Goldschmidt's thinking. According to the Stoics, "Living in accordance with nature comes to be the end . . . engaging in no activity typically forbidden by the universal law, which is the right reason pervading everything and identical to Zeus, who is the director of the administration of existing things" (LS 63C, translation adapted). Furthermore, they insist that this end, which can also be called "happiness," can be completed in an instant (LS 63I, SVF 3.54). Goldschmidt explains that on the one hand, this is the instant in which the Stoic sage connects the event-sign with an action that is natural, reasonable, and in alignment with the "universal law" of Zeus. The concordance of sage and god in this instant is perfect; it cannot be improved by temporal extension. On the

6. Julia Kristeva, Stoicism, and the "True Life of Interpretations" 99

other hand, because the moral agent's initiative is integrated into god's enduring providence, this instant expands throughout time. Thus the moment of virtue satisfies our "desire for eternity" (1953: 205), and leaves nothing lacking from our happiness. As Goldschmidt perorates,

> The instant, as Marcus Aurelius had said, is able to contain and encompass the centuries of cosmic cycles. Thus the instant extends throughout the present of Zeus, like a drop of wine, according to Chrysippus, extends to the dimensions of the ocean and penetrates its entirety. (1953: 207; cf. 146–51, 198–207)

Goldschmidt's tone is rhapsodic, but Kristeva's appropriation of his reading transforms it into a pointed critique. For Kristeva, the eternity completed by the Stoic would be what she calls "time as project, teleology, linear and prospective unfolding; . . . time as history" (1981b: 17). The "teleological project" here is that of god, whose purpose has determined once and for all what is good and choice worthy. In effect, God's volition hypostasizes the symbolic values established for the speaking subject by the thetic break. In other words, divine law and reason are names given to the big Other of signifiers, in which the speaking subject has invested her drive energy at the moment of surrendering the narcissistic jouissance of the mother-child union. Kristeva believes this thetic break is experienced as a sacrifice or loss ("castration"), which reiterates and exacerbates the "primal want" underlying all interpersonal relations (2000: 76–85). When symbolic value is fixed once and for all, this loss becomes irremediable. This is why Kristeva calls the totalizing instant of Stoic interpretation a kind of suicide or death. "Time . . . in Western philosophy always refers to the time of *death*," she writes (2009: 44). The consequences for the subject of this totalization of value and time vary, but might include absence of affect, evacuation of meaning from the world, or compensatory, violent acting-out.[14]

The alternative for Kristeva is to avoid temporal finalization and evaluative totalization. She believes this is possible because, as I emphasized earlier, symbolic signification continues to be underpinned by semiotic articulation and imaginary polysemy, both of which go back to our non-linguistic relations to our primary caregivers. These a-signifying modes of relating, emoting, and enjoying combine with thetic signification in "vital" and "creative" speech, which Kristeva calls "significance" (*signifiance*). Examples in Kristeva's work include the speech of poets and literary authors in general, which she calls "a kind of second birth" (1984: 70); the discourse of literary appreciation, through which we participate in the "sharable singularity" of creative "genius" (2009: 29–41, 2000: 27–9); the speech of psychoanalysts, who avoid "playing dead and adopting a stoic apathy" (1995: 73) in order to make each analysis a "work of art" (1995: 34), combining thetic reason with counter-transferential jouissance (1995: 3–102, esp. 34–5, 1982b: 81, 83–4, 86–7, 2000: 62–4); the masochistic sublimation of Christian mystics (2009: 47–63); and—most controversially—the speech of maternal passion (2009: 42–7).[15] All of these modes of interpretation, of "making a connection," encourage the creativity and vitality supposedly choked off by Stoic totalization. In other words, they make it possible to initiate genuinely new beginnings, breaking the linear teleology of historical time; and they facilitate the sublimation of drive in language, imbuing language with affect and meaningfulness.

Kristeva's third claim is simply the politicized consequence of the first two, as is exemplified by her commentary on the *Republic* of the Stoic Zeno (1991: 57–63).[16] Given the totalization of symbolic value and exclusion of semiotic and imaginary interventions, Kristeva suggests that Stoic politics can only oscillate between two undesirable tendencies. On the one hand is the anomia of each individual's obedience to divine volition, which replaces positive law. This is how Kristeva interprets the testimony that Zeno permitted cannibalism and incest in his utopia.[17] On the other, institutionalizing values attributed to divine volition could lead to totalitarianism. To both of these Kristeva prefers a middle way, in which citizens preserve the creativity and vitality of desire and jouissance, which singularize them, but use their shared investment in symbolic signification to collaborate in constructing narratives and making decisions.[18] "The living political bond," she writes elsewhere, "understood and practiced as a sharing of creativity, calls upon the singularity of each person: Had 'one' forgotten this?" (2009: 13)

2 Response to Kristeva

I have now completed my clarification of Kristeva's reading of Stoicism and explanation of her critical response. In the remainder of this chapter I would like to offer some thoughts about the merits of Kristeva's criticism. In other words, I want to consider its importance for the growing number of people interested in Stoicism not only as an intriguing historical phenomenon, but as a source of guidance for pursuing well-being, resilience, or freedom.

I will first suggest that Kristeva's analysis sheds considerable light on *some* aspects of *some* Stoic texts. Let me begin with a general point of doctrine. One could plausibly argue that Stoic moral psychology revolves around a fundamental and nonrational drive, which is called *oikeiōsis*. No single word in English effectively translates of this word, though "appropriation" serves best. What it connotes is each organism's impulse to preserve and perfect its "constitution."[19] Seneca defines a constitution as "the hegemonic part of the soul disposed in a certain way toward the body" (*Ep. Mor.* 121.10).[20] The disposition of the hegemonic part of the soul toward the body is the sustaining principle of an animal's vital unity.[21] Every animal is "pleased with," "loves," "yearns for," and "thinks well" of this vital unity, which is the animal's self.[22] The character of this vital unity develops over time, so that a human infant, for example, appropriates a different constitution than she will as an adolescent, an adult, and so on (Sen., *Ep. Mor.* 121.14-18). Up to a certain stage this happens without cognitive mediation, just as other animals are supposedly impelled to preserve their own constitutions. But at a certain stage something changes in human beings. As Diogenes Laertius reports, "Since reason ... has been bestowed on rational beings, to live correctly in accordance with reason comes to be natural for them. For reason supervenes as the craftsman of impulse" (LS

57A). In other words, whereas animals are automatically impelled toward what will preserve their constitutions, in humans, reason should come to supervise impulses. Moreover, precisely this use of reason, since it is "natural" for mature human beings, becomes the central feature in their constitution and the primary object of appropriation (Sen. *Ep. Mor.* 121.14). The right and legitimate use of reason is to align our volition with that of Zeus, who, as we saw earlier, is identical with "right reason" (LS 63C). Thus, appropriation is designed to culminate in the resolve to perfect our reason, which means harmonizing it with divine Reason.

I would like to cautiously suggest a limited comparison between this developmental psychology and that of Kristeva. Granted, there is a striking difference between Kristeva's flexible thinking about the drives, which she sometimes expresses by referring to the "archaic Thing," and the Stoics's fundamental drive toward self-preservation and self-perfection. Nevertheless, there is a thought-provoking resemblance between key moments in the two developmental theories, namely the Stoic appropriation of reason and what Kristeva calls the thetic break. The thetic break marks the epochal shift of libidinal investment from parental bodies or associated sensations to symbolic signifiers. In a similar way, one could argue that in the Stoic account, appropriation of reason shifts the fundamental impetus from things to reasoning about things.

Let me explain. On the Stoic account, a child is immediately concerned with her own mental and bodily integrity, and even adults may be immediately concerned with the well-being of their children, friends, or spouses.[23] But in order for reason to fulfill its role as the "craftsman of impulse," we should not desire the well-being of our own bodies or those of our children, friends, or spouses for their own sakes. Rather, we should wish to act in conformity with universal law and right reason, and perceive that it is legitimate and reasonable (in most circumstances) to cherish our bodies, children, friends, and spouses. Thus reason would intervene as the primary object of appropriative feelings, in a sense estranging us from prior intimacies.

If there is anything to this reading, it could be taken to embed deep in Stoic theory some of the features criticized by Kristeva. Even if this comparison at the level of theory turns out to be indefensible, at the level of practice it is hard to deny that Stoics sometimes adopt the role of ideology police; according to Kristeva, "Wardens of repression and rationalizers of the social contract in its most solid substratum (discourse) . . . carry the Stoic tradition to its conclusion" (1981a: 24). There are innumerable examples of this, but for reasons of space I will provide just one.

The Stoic Hierocles writes that "we should guard the laws of our fatherland as if they were second gods of a kind, and live by their guidance" (70–3). In fact, "second gods" is a favorite simile for Hierocles, who also says we should treat our fatherland itself and our parents "like second gods" (68–9, 82–3). This is more than a simile, of course: it points toward divine law and reason as the preeminent elements in our own constitution. But for Kristeva, Stoic God is merely a hypostasis of repressive symbolic values. Thus it should come as no surprise when Hierocles writes,

> I for my part welcome Zaleucus, the [legendary] lawgiver of the Locrians, who made it law that anyone who proposed a new law should do it with a noose around his throat, so that he should be instantly strangled and die, unless he rearranged the original constitution of the state in a way that was most emphatically profitable to the community. (71)

And it is not only the laws that must be treated as second gods. Hierocles adds that "no less than the laws, customs must also be guarded, those that are truly ancestral. . . . Custom aims to be a kind of unwritten law, which has enrolled as its noble lawgiver the satisfaction of all those who make use of it" (17).

From a Kristevan perspective one might make two observations about these passages. First, Hierocles is indeed operating as a "warden of repression and rationalizer of the social contract": in effect, he makes the symbolic values enshrined in civic law and social custom unbreakable parameters for choice and action. Under the regime of Zaleucus, there is precious little room for creative renewal through a life-giving return to pre-rational jouissance and imagination. Who would risk democratic innovation, if the cost of any mistake were "that he should be instantly strangled and die?" Second, one might detect in this fantasy of violent reprisal, which is authorized by the legendary paternal lawgiver, the return of what has been repressed by Stoic rationalism. In other words, the energies excluded by the rigidification of symbolic value return as violent acting-out, even if only at the level of rhetoric.

These considerations lead me to suspect that Kristeva has identified a dangerous temptation within Stoicism, something excluded from the Greek and Roman Stoics's own self-understanding. However, in other ways I think that Kristeva's reading is very one-sided. These all come back to a fundamental error, namely her consistent reading of Stoic doctrines about virtue as straightforward descriptions of the lived experience of Stoicism. In fact, the ideal of virtue, which is embodied in the sage, operates rather as an organizing fantasy. Commentators in general pay too little attention to a fundamental contradiction within Stoicism: on the one hand, by explicit doctrine virtue can be achieved; on the other, by unbreakable convention no practitioner can claim that she has achieved virtue.[24] For this reason I think we should view Stoic virtue roughly as Jonathan Lear suggests we view Aristotelian contemplation. "Any form of life," Lear writes,

> will tend to generate a fantasy of what it is to get outside of that life. This is because life is experienced, consciously and unconsciously, as being lived under pressure—and it is correlative to that experience that there is a fantasy of release. (2000: 48–9)

Like Aristotle's fantasy of self-sufficient contemplation, the Stoic fantasy needs to be theoretically achievable in order to make life meaningful. In Kristeva's terms, this allows it to harness drive energy to symbolic significations. Yet it also needs to be practically unachievable, or else it would implode and give way to a new fantasy.

This insight has both general and specific consequences. The general consequence is that we should acknowledge how much creative improvisation is involved in the Stoic effort to live in harmony with divine volition. Although Stoics sometimes come across as vindictive agents of symbolic law, they also place a great deal of emphasis on circumstantial complexity. An infinite distance separates fidelity to general ethical guidelines from perception of the virtuous thing to do in any particular situation. This is why Stoics insist that all errors are equal (Arius Didymus 11o).[25] The sage must use her creative initiative in order to cross this chasm. Such creativity is emblematized by the unorthodox Stoic Aristo, who entirely rejects ethical guidelines, and focuses exclusively on the sage's "adventitous capacity" to respond to "opportunity" and "circumstance" (Boys-Stones 1996). But even within orthodox Stoicism, which aims to strike a balance between extemporaneity and principled foresight, the upshot is that *every* Stoic decision can in principle make room for creative interventions.

More specific consequences reveal themselves in those passages of Stoic texts in which the yearning to understand and imitate god becomes explicitly thematized. It is here more than anywhere that we might glimpse something like a relation to the archaic Thing, at the boundaries where a penumbra of drive energy suffuses thetic reasoning. I will offer just two examples.

The first comes from Musonius Rufus, who is perhaps the Stoic author most given to ideological policing. As I discuss elsewhere (forthcoming), his handling of sex, eating, and grooming is astoundingly sanctimonious. Yet events in Musonius's biography, such as his attempt to reason with Vitellius's troops during their march against Rome (nearly a fatal miscalculation: Tacitus, *Histories* 3.81), powerfully exemplify the demand for improvisation in the enactment of virtue. Moreover, his lectures are unusually rich in fantasies about divine volition, as I will exemplify with reference to *Concerning Nourishment*.[26]

In this discourse Musonius encourages his listeners to restrict their diet to uncooked vegetables and dairy products, but above all he exhorts them to avoid meat. "Nourishment from the plants of the earth," he claims, "is naturally suited to us . . . So is nourishment from animals that are not harmed, especially domestic animals . . . like ripe fruit, some vegetables, milk, cheese, and honeycombs" (XVIIIA 94.12-95.7). By contrast,

> He used to say that [nourishment by meat] was heavier and somehow impeded thought and cognition, because the rising vapors from it were muddier and darkened the soul. So people who eat a lot of meat appear to be slower of mind. (95.11-96.1)

Here we can see the beginnings of a rational justification for avoiding meat, which is grounded in physiology: when meat is digested, it produces "rising vapors" that impede cognition. From this perspective, Musonius is sketching an enthymeme grounded in symbolic values. This allows him to understand the world, and through that understanding to achieve satisfaction.[27] Yet we should also notice the prevalence of images of heaviness, slowness, muddiness, and darkness. This recalls the bodily depths which power abjection. Added to the reminiscences of ripe fruit, vegetables, milk, cheese, and honeycombs, it creates a rich sensual landscape. From this perspective, Musonius is discharging drive energy through a phantasmagoria of images that underpins or bypasses rational argumentation.

This interplay of reasoning and fantasy climaxes in an exhortation to imitate the celestial gods. "Since human beings are the most akin of earthly organisms to the gods," Musonius says,

> we should also be nourished in a manner most similar to them. Now, the exhalations of earth and water carried up to them are enough for the gods. So if we took the lightest and purest nourishment, he said, we would take the most similar nourishment to the gods. (96.1-6)

Let us pause and give this strangely literal comparison of human and divine nourishment due consideration. Like the preceding, it is structured by an enthymeme grounded in theoretical commitments. The Stoics certainly believe that humans are the earthly organisms most akin to the gods. Moreover, they believe that the foundation of this kinship is our shared rationality.[28] Even the physiology of our rational souls is similar: both are constituted by "breath," which is a compound of compacting moisture and expansive fire (LS 47G-H, J, O-Q). This helps to explain the role of "rising vapors" and "exhalations" in Musonius's comparison.[29] Within this breath the compacting moisture is responsible for inward tension, which stabilizes organic forms (LS I.288). The expansive fire is the intelligent, directive element; thus Zeno calls the sun a "fiery kindling from the vaporous rising of the sea" (SVF Zeno 121), and Zeus himself is defined as "intelligent, designing fire which methodically proceeds toward the creation of the world" (LS 46A.1). This helps to explain why Musonius counsels avoidance of "dark" and "heavy" meat. It is on the basis of these elemental homologies between human and celestial souls that Musonius infers we should prefer light, pure nourishment.

On the other hand, we should also acknowledge how semiotic investments may underpin this line of reasoning. In making vital heat and breath the signifiers of human kinship with the gods, Stoic theory already makes respiratory and circulatory rhythms a domain in which semiotic and symbolic investments can easily converge. In focusing particularly on nourishment, Musonius accentuates this convergence. Henceforth when I eat my rustic cheese and honey, I can think and feel that I am ingesting the rationality of the gods.[30] To put it in psychoanalytic terms, this is an example of oral introjection: beyond my rational alignment with god, I will be replaying a primal bodily relation to and identification with him. Perhaps some of the strangeness of Musonius's argument comes from the way in which this drive facilitation and imaginary fantasy combine with its implicit argumentative structure.[31]

I turn now to my final example, which comes from Cornutus's *Survey of Greek Theology*. This text belongs to a domain of Stoic literature that scholars have found enigmatic. Why, they wonder, are Stoics so interested in the myths, iconography, and even rituals of the Olympian pantheon, which their rational theology appears to render superfluous (Long 1992; Boys-Stones 2003: esp. 209–15; Algra 2009: 234–8; Lampe 2013)?

Kristeva's work points toward a new way of resolving this enigma. For Kristeva, allegory is a paradigmatic example of how "the imaginary" operates "like a tense link between Thing and Meaning, the unnameable and the proliferation of signs, the silent affect and the ideality that designates and goes beyond it" (1989: 100). In other words, imaginative constructions are halfway between symbolic signification and delirious proximity to the archaic Thing. The allegorical imagination both "disowns" the surface meaning, thus clinging to the archaic Thing, and makes associative leaps to symbolism via acoustic and visual images, thus generating new quasi-meanings—meanings in which we only halfway believe, but which we therefore enjoy more (or at least differently).[32]

Take Cornutus's discussion of the god Hermes. This discussion extends over six pages of the standard edition (20–6), encompassing etymology of his name and epithets, exegesis of his literary and statuary images, and observations about some aspects of his cult. What binds this discussion together is Cornutus's initial assertion that Hermes represents reason: "Hermes happens to be reason, which the gods sent to us from heaven, making humans alone of earthly animals rational, which is the best thing the gods themselves possess" (20.18-21).[33] This assertion is justified by the etymological derivation of the name *Hermēs* from the phrase *erein mēsasthai*, meaning "contrive to speak." This derivation grounds the entire fantasy that follows, which we might call an imaginary celebration of rationality.

I will pick out just three moments in this sublime fiction. The first is Cornutus's explanation of the epithet "Hermes of the golden rod." "Of the golden rod (*khrusorrhapis*)," Cornutus writes, "because a beating (*rhapismos*) from him is very precious, since timely admonitions and the attention of those who listen is worth a great deal" (21.15-8). In other words, verbal castigation is like being beaten with a golden rod! Hermes's rod (*rhabdos*) returns later in the discussion,

> "with which," as Homer writes, "he soothes the eyes of whomever he wishes," i.e. the eyes of the mind, "and arouses those who are dreaming" [Homer, *Iliad* 24.343-4]—for he's easily able both to encourage those who are slack and to sedate those who are excited. For the same reason people believed he sent dreams and was a prophet, turning impressions whichever way he wanted. (22.10-18)

In other words, Hermes's rod represents the power of words to magically stimulate, sedate, or generally lead listeners wherever the speaker wishes. If we permit ourselves to suspect this is slightly phallic, Cornutus will reward our audacity:

> The ancients made older, bearded statues of Hermes with erect genitals, but younger, smooth-cheeked statues with flaccid ones, letting it be surmised that in those of advanced age reason is generative and complete, but fruitless and incomplete in immature men. (23.16-22)

In other words, mature reason is like an *erect penis*; rational admonition is like a "very precious" beating with an erect golden penis; with this erect penis you can guide your listeners wherever you wish.

The foregoing allegory disowns the surface significations of these literary and visual representations of Hermes in order to think associatively about rationality instead. This thinking does not focus on the significations through which rationality is usually explained, such as "intellect," "language," "concepts," and "inferences." Rather, it approaches rationality via a series of images: the messenger of the gods, the golden rod, sending dreams, awakening from sleep, inspiring with foresight, delivering punishment, bearded statues with erect penises, and youthful statues with flaccid ones. Insofar as these images enchant, amuse, or unsettle the allegorist—effects enhanced by the cultural importance of Homer and religion—they modulate his relationship to the archaic Thing. This, in turn, will predispose him to bring together signifiers, significations, and referents in particular ways when he enunciates propositions about rationality. Thus Kristeva helps us to perceive that we should not set aside Stoic allegory as an embarrassing idiosyncrasy. Rather, we should recognize that this creative activity plays a dynamic part in the Stoic life of interpretation.

3 Conclusions

For Kristeva, as we saw in Section 1, the "true life of interpretations" is one in which each individual's rational conclusions are always amenable to revision from two directions: first, by engagement with the a-signifying internal forces of imaginary and semiotic jouissance; and second, by engagement with other people, including those people's imaginary and semiotic fantasies and compulsions. That is why Kristeva speaks of a "true life of interpretation*s* (in the plural)" (1982b: 37): she believes that healthy ethics and politics combine shared reason with a plurality of unreasonable and sometimes unshareable impulses.

From this perspective Kristeva criticizes the Stoic life as one that totalizes interpretation, thus impeding creative renewal, tolerance, and cooperation. In response, I have suggested in Section 2 that Kristeva is partly right: Stoics do sometimes display a proclivity toward ideological rigidity. But at the same time, parts of their "ideology" build in the sort of stimulus for creativity that Kristeva demands. Thus it should come as no surprise that fantastic confabulations appear in ancient Stoic literature, although these receive too little attention from historians of philosophy and modern Stoics.

If the preceding is sound, several consequences might follow for modern Stoicism:

(1) Alongside the emphasis on reforming beliefs in the cognitive-behavioral reception of Stoicism, we should give more explicit recognition to imaginative and semiotic elements. These are often present already. For

example, the *Stoic Week 2014 Handbook* introduces the exercise of "Morning Meditation" by saying,

> Marcus Aurelius talks about walking on your own to a quiet place at daybreak and meditating upon the stars and the rising Sun, preparing for the day ahead. You can also do this at home, sitting on the end of your bed, or standing in front of the mirror in your bathroom, *and still think of the sun rising against a backdrop of stars*. (Gill et al. 9; italics mine)

Compare Donald Robertson's re-description of the Stoic technique of "premeditation" as "imaginal exposure" (2014: 155–6). What merits greater reflection here is the sensory and imaginary dimension of cognitive exercises. In fact, one of the reasons that Stoicism is an important complement to cognitive-behavioral therapies is its imaginary richness.

(2) The emphasis on "technologies of the self" and "spiritual exercises" in the post-Foucauldian and post-Hadotian reception of Stoicism risks entanglement in the networks of power within which Foucault himself struggled to find a sort of immanent freedom. Stoic self-cultivation must not be reduced to any catalogue of exercises directed toward well-defined virtues. Rather, we should give more attention to collaborative improvisation.

(3) Rationalism today is often associated with secularism. By contrast, after Kristeva we can perceive in Stoicism the synergy between intense theoretical and practical reasoning and numinous aspirations. The same combination is apparent in Senecan tragedy (Lampe 2018) and in Stoic theorizing about divination, which have only recently received sustained and sympathetic attention (Struck 2017: 171–214). This makes Stoicism an interesting interlocutor for post-dogmatic anthropology and philosophy of religion (e.g., Magliocco 2007; Kearney 2011; Kripal 2017), particularly since it avoids the Abrahamic presuppositions that still dominate this field (Sikke 2017).

None of these suggestions will bring us to The Truth about either Kristeva or Stoicism. However, all of them could expand and enrich these spiritual, ethical, and political traditions of thought and action.

Notes

1 The following does not aspire to be an exhaustive index to Stoicism in Kristeva: 1981a: 24, 125, 1982b: 79–80, 83, 92, 1984: 40, 44, 1991: 56–63, 1995: 73, 82, 88, 2002: 74–5. I would also take Stoicism to be one inspiration for the "sad philosopher" of 2009: 41.
2 See the conclusion of "Psychoanalysis and the Polis": "I would like the above remarks to be taken both as a 'free association' and as the consequence of a certain position. I would want them to be considered not only an epistemological discussion but

3 My overview draws on all of Kristeva's works, but see especially 1984: 25–30, 43–56, 1989: 40–2, 2000: 32–90. I necessarily smooth over some variations in these accounts. Compare McAfee 2004: 13–27. Oliver 1993 remains an excellent introduction to Kristeva, but does not address language acquisition independently.
4 She puts this most carefully in *This Incredible Need to Believe*: "This *I* who speaks unveils himself to himself inasmuch as he is constructed in a vulnerable bond with a strange *object* or an ek-static *other*, an ab-ject: this is the *sexual thing* (others will say: the object of the sexual drive whose 'carrier wave' is the death drive)" (2009: 28).
5 Although Kristeva was profoundly influenced by Lacan, her training was not Lacanian (Kristeva 2011), and it is important not to conflate their ideas.
6 Kristeva of course borrows the distinction between "subject of enunciation" and "subject of the statement" from the linguist Émile Benveniste.
7 To be more precise, "complete sayables" (e.g., propositions) do not designate bodies. However, nouns and pronouns designate qualities, which are bodily (LS 33M).
8 For "event" (*pragma, sumbama, accidens*) see LS 33B.2-3, 33q (only in volume 2), Seneca *Ep. Mor.* 117.3. For effect, see LS 55A-D. For the basics of Stoic metaphysics, see LS 27.
9 All translations are my own. Goldschmidt expands on this line of interpretation when he compares a certain trend in the thought of Epictetus and Marcus Aurelius to Kantian critical idealism (1953: 119–21). Of course, this passage in Bréhier features prominently in Deleuze as well (2004: 8).
10 He is thinking in particular of concept formation and the testimony of DL 7.53. For recent discussions of the Stoic theory of concept formation, see Brittain (2005); Dyson (2009).
11 Goldschmidt relates this to Marcus Aurelius 7.23 ("Does something happen to me? I accept"), of which he says, "So we must 'accept' the event and want it" (100).
12 Strictly speaking the ensuing "impulse" will be directed at the *predicate* of the proposition "this is to-be-avoided." See SVF 3.91 = LS 33J; SVF 3.89; compare Arius Didymus *Ep.* 6c.
13 Goldschmidt aptly cites Epict. *Diss.* 1.7.32-33 (1953: 169 n. 1).
14 Note that, à propos of "the time of history," Kristeva adds, "A psychoanalyst would call this 'obsessional time,' recognizing in the mastery of time the true structure of the slave" (1981b: 17). In other words, she directly contradicts the Stoic claim that alignment with transcendent value equals freedom. Thus she also implies that Stoicism is basically an "obsessional" cultural structure. On the relation of obsessional neurosis to the symptoms I have just described, see especially 1995: 44–65.
15 The foregoing citations are merely illustrative: Kristeva revisits most of these themes many times across her works.
16 Zeno's *Republic* is lost, but various sources inform us about its contents. Here again it is worthwhile tracing a vague reference in one of Kristeva's footnotes (1991: 198 n. 31): her reading of Zeno's *Republic* and most (if not all) her exact citations of Greek and Roman texts turn out to derive from Voelke 1961: 114–31, 143–5, 152–62, 185–90.
17 For more recent scholarship on this topic, see Schofield (1999), Vogt (2008).
18 2009: 71–6. Kristeva makes a subtly different point in "Psychoanalysis and the Polis": there she emphasizes how effective political interpretation, like psychoanalytic

also a personal involvement (need I say one of desire?) in the dramas of thought, personality, and contemporary politics" (92).

19 The following summary presumes the continuity of what are sometimes distinguished as "self-appropriation" and "social appropriation." In this I agree with Brennan 2005: 154–68. Key testimonia regarding appropriation include DL 7.85-6 = LS 57A, Cic. *Fin.* 3.62-8 (excerpted by LS 57F), Seneca *Ep. Mor.* 121 (excerpted by LS 57B), Hierocles *Elements of Ethics* esp. VI-IX (excerpted by LS 57C, D, G), and Aulus Gellius 12.5.7 = SVF 3.181.

20 Ramelli helpfully connects this definition with Hierocles's explanation that the hegemonic part of every organism perceives all parts of both the organism's body and its soul (55, citing Hierocles *Elements of Ethics* IV.44-52 = p. 12-13). On this Stoic theory of "proprioception" see Long 1996.

21 "Relative disposition" is the fourth of the so-called Stoic ontological "categories" or "genera," on which see the testimony gathered at LS 29. Note also that virtue is defined as the soul in a certain disposition (Seneca *Ep. Mor.* 113.2). Compare Hierocles *El. Eth.* IV.27-53 = p. 12-13, which connects the "tensive movement" of the soul, which is a "sustaining power," with the organism's continuous and complete self-perception, which occurs by the oscillation of this tensive movement outward from the hegemonic part to the extremities and back again.

22 The Greek terms are *aresein* and *euarestein* (Hierocles *El .Eth.* VI.40-5 = p. 18-19), *sphodron himeron* (Hierocles *El .Eth.* VII.1-5 = p. 18-19), *philautias* (Hierocles *El .Eth.* VII.20-5 = p. 20-1), and *eunoētikōs* (Hierocles *El .Eth.* IX.5-9 = p. 24-5).

23 On bodily integrity, see LS 57A.1-3, Sen. *Ep. Mor.* 121.18-24, Hierocles *El. Eth.* VI.54-VII.50 = p. 18-21; on children, LS 57F.1; on friends, Hierocles *El. Eth.* 11.15-20 = p. 28-9; and on marriage, see Reydams-Schils 2005: 143–76.

24 This convention is never (to my knowledge) articulated, a silence that in itself deserves further analysis. The neo-Aristotelian Alexander of Aphrodisias attributes to the Stoics the claim that "there have been just one or two good men, as their fables maintain, like some absurd and unnatural creature rarer than the Ethiopian's phoenix" (LS 57N.2).

25 Similarly, an infinite distance separates vice from virtue: "Just as in the sea the man an arm's length from the surface is drowning no less than the one who has sunk five hundred fathoms, so even those who are getting close to virtue are no less in a state of vice than those who are far from it" (LS 61T).

26 See also my reading of Musonius's "masochistic" jubilation (2013: 192–7).

27 For Kristeva the object of "the need to believe" is "a truth that keeps me, makes me exist" (2009: 3); such a truth recalls the self-certainty of mother-child "oceanic feeling" or the loving support from the "imaginary father" (2009: 1–10).

28 A claim advanced in innumerable Stoic texts, for example, LS 57F.3, 63D-E, Epictetus *Diss.* 2.8.10-12.

29 Compare Seneca's paean to the nourishing "breaths" of the earth at *Natural Questions* 2.16.1-3.

30 In "A General Theory of Sacrifice," Vernant writes, "if one circumvents sacrifice . . . by consuming only undefiled food or by existing on odors only . . . it becomes possible to attain a state of total communion that can be taken just as easily as a return to the tender familiarity of all creatures of the Golden Age or as a descent into the chaos and confusion of savagery" (1991: 298).

31 "Uncanny strangeness" (*étrangeté inquiétante*, the French translation of Freud's *das Unheimliche*) is one of the many avatars of the archaic Thing (Kristeva 1991: 182–92; 214 n. 19).

32 "By shifting back and forth from the disowned meaning, still present just the same, of the remnants of antiquity for instance (thus, *Venus* or 'the royal crown') to the *literal* meaning that the Christian spiritualist context attributes to all things, allegory is a tenseness of meanings between their depression/depreciation and their signifying exaltation (*Venus* becomes the allegory of Christian love)" (1989: 101–2).

33 Reading *monon ton anthrōpon* where Lang prints *monon ton anthrōpōn*.

Bibliography

Algra, K. (2009), "Stoic Philosophical Theology and Graeco-Roman Religion," in R. Salles (ed.), *God and Cosmos in Stoicism*, 224–51, Oxford: Oxford University Press.

Arius Didymus (1999), *Epitome of Stoic Ethics*, ed. and trans. Arthur J. Pomeroy, Atlanta: Society for Biblical Literature.

Boys-Stones, G. (1996), "The ἐπελευστικὴ δύναμις in Aristo's Psychology of Action," *Phronesis* 41: 75–94.

Boys-Stones, G. (2003), "The Stoics' Two Types of Allegory," in G. Boys-Stones (ed.), *Metaphor, Allegory, and the Classical Tradition*, 189–216, Oxford: Oxford University Press.

Bréhier, É. (1962), *La théorie des incorporels dans l'ancien stoïcisme*, 3rd edn, Paris: Vrin.

Brennan, T. (2005), *The Stoic Life: Emotions, Duties, and Fate*, Oxford: Oxford University Press.

Brittain, C. (2005), "Common Sense: Concepts, Definitions and Meanings In and Out of the Stoa," in D. Frede and B. Inwood (eds.), *Language and Learning*, 164–209, Cambridge: Cambridge University Press.

Cornutus (1881), *Cornuti Theologiae Graecae Compendium*, ed. Carl Lang, Leipzig: Teubner.

Deleuze, G. (2004), *Logic of Sense*, trans. M. Lester with C. Stivale, ed. C.V. Boundas, London: Bloomsbury.

Dyson, H. (2009), *Prolepsis and Ennoia in the Early Stoa*, Berlin: De Gruyter.

Gill, C., P. Ussher, J. Sellars, T. Lebon, J. Evans, G. Garratt, and D. Robertson (2014), *Stoic Week 2014 Handbook: Live Like a Stoic for a Week*, http://modernstoicism.com/course/view.php?id=5&section=2 (accessed November 25, 2014).

Goldschmidt, V. (1953), *Le systeme stoïcien et l'idée de temps*, Paris: Vrin.

Hadot, P. (2002), *What Is Ancient Philosophy?* trans. M. Chase, Cambridge, MA: Belknap.

Hierocles (2009), *Hierocles the Stoic: Elements of Ethics, Fragments, and Excerpts*, ed. and comm. Ilaria Ramelli, trans. David Konstan, Atlanta: Society of Biblical Literature.

Kearney, R. (2011), *Anatheism: Return to God after God*, New York: Columbia.

Kripal, J. (2017), *The Secret Body: Erotic and Esoteric Currents in the History of Religions*, Chicago: University of Chicago Press.

Kristeva, J. (1981a), *Desire in Language: A Semiotic Approach to Literature and Art*, trans. L. S. Roudiez, Oxford: Blackwell.

Kristeva, J. (1981b), "Women's Time," trans. A. Jardine and H. Blake, *Signs* 7 (1): 13–35.

Kristeva, J. (1982a), *Powers of Horror: An Essay on Abjection*, trans. L. S. Roudiez, New York: Columbia University Press.

Kristeva, J. (1982b), "Psychoanalysis and the Polis," trans. M. Waller, *Critical Inquiry* 9 (1): 77–92.

Kristeva, J. (1984), *Revolution in Poetic Language*, trans. M. Waller, New York: Columbia University Press.

Kristeva, J. (1989), *Black Sun: Depression and Melancholia*, trans. L. S. Roudiez, New York: Columbia University Press.

Kristeva, J. (1991), *Strangers to Ourselves*, trans. L. S. Roudiez, New York: Harvester Wheatsheaf.

Kristeva, J. (1995), *New Maladies of the Soul*, trans. R. Guberman, New York: Columbia University Press.

Kristeva, J. (2000), *The Sense and Non-Sense of Revolt: The Powers and Limits of Psychoanalysis Volume 1*, trans. J. Herman, New York: Columbia University Press.

Kristeva, J. (2002), *Intimate Revolt: The Powers and Limits of Psychoanalysis Volume 2*, trans. J. Herman, New York: Columbia University Press.

Kristeva, J. (2009), *This Incredible Need to Believe*, trans. B. B. Brahic, New York: Columbia University Press.

Kristeva, J. (2011), "*Lacan ou la portée historique de la psychanalyse: Entretien avec Julia Kristeva*," http://www.kristeva.fr/lacan-le-point-septembre2011.html (accessed October 27, 2014).

Lampe, K. (2013), "Obeying Your Father: Stoic Theology between Myth and Masochism," in V. Zajko and E. O'Gorman (eds.), *Classical Myth and Psychoanalysis: Ancient and Modern Stories of the Self*, 183–98, Oxford: Oxford University Press.

Lampe, K. (2018), "Philosophy, Psychology, and the Gods in Seneca's *Hercules Furens*," *Philosophia: The Yearbook for the Research Centre for Greek Philosophy at Athens* 48: 233–52.

Lampe, K. (forthcoming), "Philosophy and Sex," in W. Shearin (ed.), *The Oxford Companion to Roman Philosophy*, New York: Oxford University Press.

Lear, J. (2000), *Happiness, Death, and the Remainder of Life*, Cambridge, MA: Harvard University Press.

Long, A. A. (1992), "Stoic Readings of Homer," in R. Lamberton and J. J. Keaney (eds.), *Homer's Ancient Readers*, 41–66, Princeton: Princeton University Press.

Long, A. A. (1996), "Hierocles on *oikeiōsis* and self-perception," in *Stoic Studies*, 250–63, Berkeley: University of California Press.

Magliocco, S. (2007), *Witching Culture: Folklore and Neo-Paganism in America*, Philadelphia: University of Pennsylvania.

Mates, B. (1961), *Stoic Logic*, Berkeley: University of California Press.

McAfee, N. (2004), *Julia Kristeva*, London: Routledge.

Musonius Rufus (1905), *Reliquiae*, ed. O. Hense, Leipzig: Teubner.

Oliver, K. (1993), *Reading Kristeva: Unraveling the Double-Bind*, Bloomington: Indiana University Press.

Reydams-Schils, G. (2005), *The Roman Stoics: Self, Responsibility, and Affection*, Chicago: University of Chicago.

Schofield, M. (1999), *The Stoic Idea of the City*, with a new forward by M. Nussbaum, Chicago: University of Chicago.

Sikke, S. (2017), "Rescuing Religion from Faith," in Paul Dreper and J. L. Schellenberg (eds.), *Renewing Philosophy of Religion: Exploratory Essay*, 15–32, Oxford: Oxford University Press.

Struck, P. (2017), *Divination and Human Nature: A Cognitive History of Intuition in Classical Antiquity*, Princeton: Princeton University Press.

Vernant, J. (1991), *Mortals and Immortals: Collected Essays*, ed. Froma I. Zeitlin, Princeton: Princeton University Press.
Voelke, A. (1961), *Les rapports avec autrui dans la philosophie grecque d'Aristote a Panétius*, Paris: Vrin.
Vogt, Katja M. (2008), *Law, Reason, and the Cosmic City: Political Philosophy in the Early Stoa*, Oxford: Oxford University Press.

Chapter 7

INDIFFERENCE *VERSUS* AFFIRMATION

MICHEL FOUCAULT ON THE STOIC IDEA OF LIFE AS A TEST

John Sellars

1 Indifference versus Affirmation

One popular image of the Stoic is of someone coldly indifferent to the world around them, dismissing everything that fate throws at them as irrelevant to their well-being.[1] External misfortunes are nothing to the Stoic, whose quality of life depends solely on their excellence of character (*SVF* 3.49). Virtue of character is the only thing that is genuinely good, while all external things and states of affairs are mere "indifferents" (*SVF* 3.117). Although some of these external things might be "preferred," they are ultimately of no concern because they do not add anything to the goodness of one's character. On this view, the Stoic adopts an attitude of indifference to all external events, whether beneficial or harmful, holding on to the central Stoic ethical claim that only virtue is truly good.

However, another image of the Stoic presents them as a naive optimist, claiming that all events that come to pass are the product of a divine providential force permeating Nature and identified with Reason (*SVF* 2.634). Everything that happens is part of this providential plan in the best of all possible worlds that is repeated again and again in an eternal recurrence of the same. Given this rational and providential ordering of events, the Stoic's fundamental attitude is one of affirmation, embracing everything that happens to them as part of the natural and divine order. Part of what it means to live in harmony with Nature is to welcome what Nature brings, no matter what that might be (*SVF* 3.4).

There is an apparent tension between these two Stoic attitudes, which we might call a Stoic attitude of indifference, on the one hand, and a Stoic attitude of affirmation, on the other. If the Stoic believes in blind fate, then they may well embrace indifference; if they believe in divine providence, then perhaps they ought to practice affirmation. The problem, of course, is that the Stoics identified fate with providence (*SVF* 2.933, 937), making that kind of distinction untenable within the context of their philosophical system. So how might we account for these two different attitudes so often associated with Stoicism? Is one simply a misrepresentation? If so, which one? Is it possible to reduce the distance between these two attitudes? Or do they reflect shifting attitudes within the Stoic tradition, held by different figures in different times? According to Michel Foucault, this apparent tension can be explained by positing a shift in attitude between the earlier Athenian Stoics and the later Roman Stoics.

2 Life as a Test

In his late works Foucault discussed a wide range of Stoic topics and texts within the context of a number of overlapping projects concerned with ancient practices of the self.[2] The most detailed discussions of Stoic material can be found in the lecture courses he delivered at the *Collège de France*, which were published after his death. Of these, his 1981–2 lecture course entitled *The Hermeneutics of the Subject* is especially rich in Stoic material.[3] It is here in the second hour of a lecture delivered on the March 17, 1982 (Foucault 2005: 437–52) that Foucault suggests that one of the defining characteristics of Stoicism in the Imperial period is the idea of approaching life as a test (*probatio*). For the Roman Stoics, unlike their Athenian predecessors, "life must be recognized, thought, lived, and practiced as a constant test" (2005: 437). Conceived in this way, external misfortunes ought not to be a matter of mere indifference, but rather welcomed as a contribution to ethical training.

This shift in attitude is, Foucault suggests, especially clear in the work of Seneca and Epictetus. For Seneca God the father loves like a father, with vigor, severity, and roughness (Foucault 2005: 438). This is indeed just how Seneca presents the Stoic God in his dialogue *On Providence*, a work that Foucault describes as "the basic text" for the idea of life as a test (Foucault 2005: 438). There, Seneca suggests that apparently adverse external events ought to be seen as opportunities to improve one's virtue. Someone who grasps the Stoic claim that Nature is providentially ordered will no longer see negative external events as misfortunes but will rather regard them as "training exercises" for virtue (*Prov.* 2.2). According to Seneca, the virtuous person will welcome whatever happens to them as an opportunity to train themselves, just as a wrestler will welcome opponents. In the case of the wrestler, it would be a bad thing only to face lesser opponents, for they would soon lose their skill. Only genuinely challenging opponents give the wrestler the opportunity to show their talents and improve their game. Seneca suggests that the same applies in the case of virtue. As Foucault comments, Seneca's God is a tough father who shows his love by testing and challenging his children. If someone accepts this idea, then their attitude toward misfortunes will be turned on its head. As Seneca puts it:

> I will show how things that seem bad are not. Now I say this: first, that those things that you call harsh, that you call adverse and detestable, are in the interest of the very men to whom they occur; next, that they occur in the interest of everyone, for whom the gods have greater concern than for individuals; and

after this, that the men to whom they occur are willing, and that if they are not willing, they are deserving of bad. (*Prov.* 3.1)

The person who cannot see that misfortunes are in fact good for them, Seneca says, will suffer something genuinely bad. This is not to claim that the external event will be itself bad; instead, by resisting the training that providential Nature brings, the person will fall out of harmony with Nature and suffer the sort of mental conflict that the Stoics hold is genuinely bad.

Seneca's wrestling analogy illustrates the idea that adverse events might be seen as a form of ethical training. To this he draws a further parallel with surgery, to highlight the way in which such events sometimes play the role of painful cures. These are however just two ways of thinking about the same events. The virtuous person and those making progress toward virtue will appreciate adverse events as forms of training—and so no longer see them as misfortunes—while non-virtuous people who fail to grasp the providential intent behind such events will still see them as misfortunes, and it is for these people that such events function as cures. Although it might not seem that way, Seneca suggests that ultimately the non-virtuous will benefit from their experiences of adversity.

It is at this point that Seneca introduces the idea of being put to the test by providence. He claims that people only find out their true character when tested by events. If people were never tested by adversity then they would never come to see how they would react in such situations. As he puts it, "No one will know what you were capable of—not even you yourself" (*Prov.* 4.3). It is only when being tested that a person finds out just how virtuous they really are. This is why anyone working toward virtue will welcome adversity. It reveals their state of progress and lets them see what they have learned. As Seneca sums it up, "Calamity is an opportunity for virtue" (*Prov.* 4.6). But even if the person making progress fails the test, they should still welcome it as further training for the next time. Seneca fleshes it out with some examples:

> How can I know how much spirit you have against poverty, if you are immersed in wealth? How can I know how much resilience you have against dishonor and infamy and being hated by the people, if you are living your old age amid applause, if you are followed by a popularity that cannot be assailed and someone turns minds favorably toward you? How do I know how calm your mind will be when you confront deprivation, if the children you have raised are there before your eyes? I have heard you when you were consoling others. I would have taken notice only if you had consoled yourself, if you had forbidden yourself to grieve. (*Prov.* 4.5)

No one can claim to possess virtue, Seneca insists, until they have demonstrated it during a test.

Having rehabilitated so-called misfortunes, Seneca goes on to question the value of things that people usually consider to be examples of good fortune. If misfortune is in fact a benefit, then "an excess of good fortune is exceedingly dangerous" (*Prov.* 4.10). In contrast to the benefits that misfortune brings, good fortune encourages complacency, weakness, and laziness. It makes people feel dependent on the external goods they enjoy, which will inevitably at some point get taken away.

It is worth stressing here that Seneca presupposes a specific conception of the self. The real self is someone's inner character; their body, by contrast, is less significant. Seneca seems to suggest that if providence damages someone's body via illness or hunger, then no real harm has happened, for the real self remains unaffected. However, if providence makes someone's life excessively comfortable, supplying all the needs of the body, that runs the risk of creating a genuine harm for their character, which will never be tested.

All this gives Seneca a ready response to the traditional problem of evil. In answer to the question of why good people suffer, Seneca can now say that it is right that the best people will be tested and trained the most. The better the person, the more adversity they should expect. At the same time he claims that it is important that apparent external goods—such as wealth and success—are distributed randomly among good and bad people, in order to make clear that these external things possess no inherent value:

> This is god's plan and the wise man's alike: to show that the things that the crowd desires and fears are neither good nor bad. But it will be clear that things he has allotted to no one but the good man are good, and that things he has imposed only on bad men are bad. [...] God has no better way of removing people's desire for things than by conferring them on the most disgraceful men and taking them away from the best men. (*Prov.* 5.1–2)

Here Seneca draws on the Stoic claim that all external things are neither good nor bad, and so deserve an attitude of indifference. But as we have seen, in *On Providence* as a whole Seneca proposes a far more positive attitude toward events. For the good person, seemingly bad events are in fact beneficial and so ought to be welcomed as such. For a bad person, those same events are also benefits, even if they do not comprehend this at the time. Thus, the correct attitude is one of affirmation, welcoming whatever happens. This attitude of affirmation is closely tied up with the idea of life as a test.

Seneca is not the only Stoic to develop this idea. Foucault also refers to Epictetus (2005: 440). In his *Discourses*, on the topic of how someone ought to contend with difficulties (*Diss.* 1.24), Epictetus suggests that one should think of God as a gymnasium trainer, matching people against tough opponents in order to help them to become Olympic champions. Difficulties are always opportunities and one ought to approach them just as a wrestler faces his next challenger. Echoing Seneca, Epictetus says that it is only when faced with difficulties that we find out what someone really amounts to (*Diss.* 1.24.1).

Commenting on these texts, Foucault suggests that there are two key ideas: first, that one is educated and tested throughout one's life—"life and training are co-extensive" (2005: 440)—and, second, that the test stands as a mark to distinguish the good from the wicked, for the good are tested and the wicked are not. He says:

> We should no longer consider these tests, these misfortunes, as evils. We are really forced to consider them as goods that we should benefit from and put to use in the individual's formation. We do not encounter a single difficulty that, precisely as difficulty, suffering, and misfortune, is not as such a good. (2005: 441)

Returning to Epictetus, we find in the *Discourses* the claim that it is possible to draw advantage from every external circumstance. The enemy who injures or insults someone is, once again, their wrestling partner who trains them in patience and in avoiding anger (*Diss*. 3.20.9). A wicked neighbor may be bad, but only for himself, not for anyone else, who can benefit from the moral training he unwittingly gives (*Diss*. 3.20.11). Similarly, whatever someone faces can be turned into a source of benefit and ultimately a source of happiness (*Diss*. 3.20.15), including poverty, illness, and even death. Perhaps with Socrates in mind, Epictetus describes death as potentially a moment of glory, an opportunity for someone to show by their deeds what sort of person it is who follows the will of Nature (*Diss*. 3.20.13).

3 *Athenian* versus *Roman Stoics*

Having presented this Roman Stoic theme of life as a continual test designed to benefit people, Foucault says that this is an important idea because it is very close to what he calls "a wholly traditional Stoic theme," but adds "and yet it is very different" (2005: 442). In what Foucault calls "classical Stoicism," by which he means the early Athenian Stoa, there is, he says, "a nullification of evil" grounded on the claim that all external events are indifferents (*adiaphora*). The key source that Foucault relies on here is Cicero's *Tusculan Disputations*. In a discussion about how best to comfort people in distress, Cicero reports the early Stoic claim that the best way to do this is "to teach the sufferer that what happened is not an evil at all" (*Tusc*. 3.76). Cicero attributes this view to Cleanthes (cf. *SVF* 1.576). He contrasts this Stoic view with other philosophical responses on offer, such as Peripatetic and Epicurean ones, but the differences between the various consolatory responses to the person in distress vary between teaching them that "what happened either is not a bad thing or is bad only in a very small degree" (*Tusc*. 3.77). In Cicero's summary of available philosophical opinions, no one proposes trying to show that what is bad is in fact beneficial to the sufferer. In general, Cicero seems doubtful about the Stoic position, both that it can remove distress from someone presently caught up in emotional turmoil and that all external events are neither good nor bad. If the early Stoics had argued that such adverse events were in fact beneficial, and so for all practical purposes good for us, it seems hard to imagine that Cicero would not have reported that view, if only to deride it as even more absurd. The early Stoic attitude of indifference is, for Cicero, noble but unrealistic; he may have been far less credulous about the Roman Stoic attitude of affirmation.

If we turn to his account of early Stoic ethics in *On Ends*, we see Cicero report the standard Stoic view that pain, illness, poverty, and the like are things for which the Stoic has good reasons to reject and to avoid so far as they can (*Fin*. 3.51). These are, of course, classified as things non-preferred (*apoproēgmenon*). Since, as Cicero puts it, "everyone by nature loves themselves," the appropriate action will be to pursue those things that accord with our nature, and reject those that do not (*Fin*. 3.59). Implicit in Cicero's account is a very naturalist understanding of what a human being is: illness and poverty harm people insofar as they are embodied, living beings. This is at one level perfectly consistent with what we know about Stoic physics and metaphysics: people are fundamentally bodies, because only bodies exist (*SVF* 1.90). By contrast, as we saw earlier with Seneca, the Roman Stoic view, with its focus on moral training, implicitly identifies the individual with their virtue or excellent character. This alone is the essential self, and what counts as beneficial or harmful is decided with reference to this moral character rather than to the person conceived as a physical, embodied organism.

We can see the way in which the early Stoic attitude of indifference derives from their value theory. Foucault also claims that for the Athenian Stoics the fact that events are part of a providential order of things is another reason not to count them as evil. However, for the Athenian Stoics, on Cicero's account that Foucault reports, even if I recognize an evil event as part of a divine providential plan, it still harms me (2005: 443). Illness, for instance, is a real harm to the individual *qua* biological, living being, even if not something bad in itself. That real harm is what makes it something non-preferred (*apoproēgmenon*). For the Roman Stoics, by contrast, such an event is transfigured into a good event "precisely inasmuch as it harms me" as Foucault puts it (2005: 443). He goes on to write:

> The transfiguration into good takes place at the very heart of the suffering caused, insofar as this suffering is actually recognized, lived, and practiced as such by the subject. [...] In the case of Epictetus [...] there is, if you like, another type of mutation due to the test attitude, which doubles and adds a value to every personal experience of suffering, pain, and misfortune, a value that is directly positive for us. This added value does not nullify the suffering; it attaches itself to it, rather, and makes use of it. It is insofar as it harms us that the evil is not an evil. (2005: 443)

In both cases the evil event is nullified. In early Athenian Stoicism it is nullified by reference to the whole through an intellectual process that leads to an attitude of indifference. In later, Roman Stoicism it is nullified by reference to oneself through a very personal process that leads to an attitude of affirmation. Consequently, Foucault suggests that this later, Roman Stoic attitude is "something quite fundamental and [he says], I think, very new with regard to what may be considered the general theoretical framework of Stoicism" (2005: 443). The tension that we opened with, between a Stoic attitude of indifference and one of affirmation, reflects a shift in attitude that took place at some point during the transmission of Stoicism from Athens to Rome; this is Foucault's important claim.

So, according to Foucault there is something strikingly new in Roman Stoicism. Foucault ends his discussion by making three general remarks on this new Stoic attitude (2005: 443–7). The first is that this Stoic testing by God is quite unlike the suffering inflicted by the Gods in Greek tragedy. Whereas that could be cruel and vindictive, the Stoic God of Seneca and Epictetus is benevolent and paternalistic. The second is that neither Seneca nor Epictetus tells us what this is a test for, if *all* of life is supposed to be a test. The third is that this Roman Stoic attitude was later taken up by Christianity. One can see in these remarks where perhaps Foucault's real interest lies: he is looking at Roman Stoicism as a stepping stone between pagan Greek culture and later Christian culture.[4] It is with the Roman Stoics, he suggests, that we find the seeds of themes that will later become prominent in Christianity.

We shall have to put that larger question about how the Roman Stoics fit into a story of developing attitudes toward the self, stretching from pagan Greece to early Christianity, to one side. It is certainly important for understanding Foucault's own project. In the present context, we shall remain focused on whether there was indeed a shift in attitude between the Athenian and the Roman Stoics.

4 Conceptions of the Self

At the beginning we saw that one way in which someone might try to account for a shift from an attitude of indifference to one of affirmation would be to suggest a change in emphasis from fate to providence: a Stoic who believes in blind fate may well adopt an attitude of indifference to the events that such fate brings, while a Stoic who believes in divine providence might be more likely to embrace an attitude of affirmation. However as we saw then, such a distinction is untenable given the Stoics's identification of fate with providence. That the Athenian Stoics— and in particular Cleanthes, who was their representative earlier—were committed to a belief in providence also seems to be beyond doubt (cf. *SVF* 1.527, 537). So, an appeal to a distinction between fate and providence will not help.

A more plausible explanation might be one that we touched on earlier, namely a shift in the conception of self. Implicit in Cicero's account of the early Stoic position was the claim that benefits and harms refer to the individual conceived as a living, embodied organism. Illness is a harm rather than a benefit because it undermines someone *qua* biological entity. This claim is built upon the Stoic theory of appropriation (*oikeiōsis*) with which Cicero opens his account of Stoic ethics in *On Ends*:

> Every animal, as soon as it is born [. . .], is concerned with itself, and takes care to preserve itself. It favours its constitution and whatever preserves its constitution, whereas it recoils from its destruction and whatever appears to promote its destruction. (*Fin.* 3.16)

For the early Stoa, then, people are first and foremost animals (*animal* in Cicero's Latin (*SVF* 3.182); *zōion* in the parallel account in DL 7.85, *SVF* 3.178). For the

Roman Stoics, by contrast, their notion of what benefits and what harms seems to be focused solely on the individual's virtue or character. On this account, the resilience and strength of character someone gains from battling a severe illness makes that illness a genuine benefit rather than a harm. This seems to imply a quite different conception of self.

Presented in these terms it does indeed look as if there might be a sharp division between the Athenian and the Roman Stoic attitudes, one that is grounded on different conceptions of the self. But we need to ask whether the division is so sharp. Did, for instance, the Roman Stoics disown or downplay the theory of *oikeiōsis* that presupposes a conception of the individual as an animal? Seneca certainly did not, as we can see in his *Letter* 121 (cf. *SVF* 3.184). There, he explicitly responds to the question we face here. In a discussion of animals' perception of their own constitution, in which he adopts what we might call a phenomenological account that prioritizes knowledge of being an embodied agent over theoretical understanding (*Ep.* 121.11), Seneca considers the following objection:

> You say that every animal from the outset is attached to its own constitution, but also that the human constitution is a rational one. Therefore the human being is attached to itself not as an animate creature but as a rational creature, for the human being is dear to itself by virtue of that part that makes it human. How, then, can a baby be attached to a rational constitution when it is not yet rational? (*Ep.* 121.14)

Seneca's response to this objection involves a lengthy account of human development (*Ep.* 121.15–24). Each stage of a human life has its own constitution, and these are different for babies, children, youths, and adults. The individual is attached to its present constitution, whatever that might at present be, and that will be an entirely natural and intuitive attitude (*Ep.* 121.15–16). Whatever the individual's present constitution might be, it is combined with "a natural instinct toward self-preservation" (*Ep.* 121.20). As Seneca puts it,

> Each animal is attached to its own preservation, it both seeks out what will be beneficial and avoids what will be harmful. Impulses toward useful things are natural, aversions to their opposites are also natural. (*Ep.* 121.21)

Frustratingly, Seneca does not address directly the first part of the imagined objection, namely the apparent tension between humans being attached to themselves as either an animate creature or a rational creature. Yet the response he gives does supply the building blocks for a more direct reply to that problem. First, it is clear that Seneca remains committed to Stoic naturalism and to the claim that humans are simply a type of animal. (At 121.3 he describes humans as produced by nature and superior to *other* animals (*animalibus ceteris*), acknowledging that human are themselves animals.) Second, it is also clear that an individual's sense of their own constitution will change over time as they develop and grow, and this change will not be the product of reflection, but rather something entirely intuitive. The rational adult will not reflect on the fact that now his rationality is an important part of his identity and must be preserved; rather, part of his being a rational adult will naturally and automatically include an instinct to preserve his rationality. Implicit, but only implicit, is the further claim that the rational adult will prioritize the preservation of their rationality over their survival as a living animal. (And perhaps as one gets older the desire to preserve the body that is by now naturally in a state of decline also declines.) As we have seen, that claim becomes all too explicit later in Epictetus, but it is already present in Cicero's account of early Stoic ethics when he describes the development of human concern from basic physical needs to a desire for consistency (*homologia*) and concordance (*Fin*. 3.21). Although this is a later development, Cicero says that "it is none the less the only thing to be sought in virtue of its own power and worth, whereas none of the primary objects of nature [i.e. food, shelter, etc] is to be sought on its own account" (*Fin*. 3.21).

All this suggests that trying to point to two quite distinct conceptions of the self in Athenian and Roman Stoicism in order to explain the shift in attitude from indifference to affirmation is unlikely to work. The difference, if there is one, is far more subtle and perhaps merely a matter of emphasis. The rational adult remains an embodied, biological organism with physical requirements, to which is added a sense of self as a rational being. On Seneca's account in *Letter* 121 these are not opposed but rather are parts of a single nature. While the rational adult will increasingly identify with their rational nature as their rationality develops, the extent to which this completely replaces (rather than augments) their existing sense of self as an embodied agent is harder to discern. It is of course worth remembering that all the training and testing that Seneca and Epictetus think adversity gives us is for the sake of improving our ability to act within the world and to enjoy our lives as embodied, living beings. As we have seen, both are fond of the analogy with wrestling when describing this sort of testing, emphasizing that the task at hand is about developing a set of skills for use in very physical situations. For both the Athenian and the Roman Stoics, then, humans are very much embodied beings in the world.

It looks, then, as if neither an appeal to a distinction between fate and providence nor an appeal to a distinction between different conceptions of the self will take us very far in understanding this shift in attitude from indifference to affirmation. Instead, perhaps we ought just to focus on this new Roman Stoic attitude of treating life as a test. This is what Foucault does in his discussion. Let us return to his account and add some comments.

5 *Life* as if *a Test*

In his account of the Roman Stoic attitude, Foucault says that it is important that misfortunes are experienced *as* misfortunes. As we saw earlier, Foucault claims that for Epictetus the test attitude does not nullify the suffering but adds a positive value to it (see 2005: 443, quoted above). This is an interesting claim by Foucault, but it needs to be qualified. The texts by both Seneca and Epictetus that Foucault discusses are addressed to philosophical novices who no doubt *would* have seen these events as misfortunes, but it is not clear that they *must* or even *ought* to be experienced as misfortunes. On the contrary, the thrust of the argument in both Seneca and Epictetus is that such events are precisely not misfortunes; they are benefits. Once someone sees this, they see that they *are* benefits unconditionally and ought to be experienced as such, with no hint of misfortune remaining. It is true that, for instance, illness may harm the body, but that harm is nothing compared to the benefit gained from the development or exercise of one's virtuous character. The benefit simply overwhelms the physical discomfort.

We might also ask how seriously we ought to take the language used by Seneca and Epictetus. When Seneca presents life's challenges as a test, is he seriously suggesting that they have been conceived as a test by a benevolent deity, or is he rather suggesting that we ought to approach those challenges *as if* sent as a test? The language that Seneca uses certainly makes this a possibility: when he says that the good person "thinks of adversities as training exercises" (*Prov.* 2.2), the key word is *putare*, which can mean "to think," "to suppose," "to regard," "to consider," "to imagine." At this point we might distinguish between three distinct beliefs that Foucault ascribes to Seneca:

i) a belief in divine providence;
ii) the belief that adverse situations train and test our character; and
iii) the belief that adverse situations are deliberately sent by a benevolent deity to train and test us.

Seneca may well be sincerely committed to a belief in providence, and he might also hold that adverse situations do benefit us, insofar as they do train and test our character, but neither of those beliefs necessarily commits him to the further claim that such adversities were conceived and sent as a test. Even so, it may be beneficial for us to think of them *as if* a test. It is important again to remember that in these texts both Seneca and Epictetus are addressing philosophical novices who are seeking guidance for how to cope with difficult situations; that is, they are offering practical advice rather than formally presenting their considered theological views. Indeed, in the opening paragraph of *On Providence* Seneca is explicit that he will not address theological questions about providence and God's interest in us (*Prov.* 1.1). The primary goal is to offer coping strategies, not to explain the intentions of Zeus. The image of God the benevolent father that we find in *On Providence* is, to quote one commentator, "hardly more than metaphor" (Setaioli 2014: 389). Seneca's God, according to the same commentator, "is not, and cannot be, a personal god" (Setaioli 2014: 389).

If we turn to Epictetus, we find something similar. In one especially relevant passage (*Diss.* 1.6.32), he writes, "what figure do you think Heracles would have made if there had not been a lion like the one they tell of, and a hydra, and a stag, and unjust and brutal men, whom he drove off and chased away?" Heracles could not have been Heracles without a continual stream of adversity,

Epictetus insists. Even if he could still have been Heracles, what benefit would that be without the appropriate trials in which to exercise his talents? Epictetus goes on to say that these trials "were of service to reveal Heracles' nature and exercise him" (*Diss.* 1.6.36). He then says that, having grasped this lesson, the philosophical novice ought to say "Bring on me now, O Zeus, whatever difficulty you will, for I have the means and resources granted to me by yourself to bring honour to myself through whatever may come to pass" (*Diss.* 1.6.37). In this discourse by Epictetus—which, like Seneca's essay, is entitled *On Providence*—the focus is likewise on extracting practical benefit from whatever happens, however apparently adverse. The invocation of Zeus may well be sincerely meant, but, as others have suggested in the case of Seneca, it may be little more than a metaphor, akin to present-day exclamations of "O God" every time something goes wrong.

In these contexts, then, it would perhaps be a mistake to place too much weight on references to divine actions. One could go further and for the sake of argument doubt the sincerity of Seneca's or Epictetus's belief in divine providence (although I leave that question open for the moment), without undermining the belief that adverse situations might benefit us. Indeed, later Friedrich Nietzsche held just that view, as he outlines in his *Assorted Opinions and Maxims* 343, which, it has been suggested, may be a gloss on a passage from one of Seneca's *Letters* (Ure 2016: 301, who compares it with Seneca, *Ep.* 9.18-19):

> If life has treated a man like a brigand, and has taken from him all it could in the way of honours, friends, adherents, health, possessions of all kinds, he may perhaps, after the first shock, discover that he is *richer* than before. For it is only now that he knows what is truly his, what no brigand is able to get his hands on; so that he perhaps emerges out of all this plundering and confusion wearing the noble aspect of a great landed proprietor. (Nietzsche 1986: 291)

Indeed, it is interesting to note that Nietzsche, one of Foucault's favorite authors, often takes up this Roman Stoic attitude of life as a test, while clearly having no philosophical commitment to any kind of belief in providence. In one of the "Maxims and Arrows" in *Twilight of the Idols*, he wrote, "*From the military school of life*—What does not kill me makes me stronger" (Nietzsche 1990: 33). It is difficult to know whether Nietzsche intended this positively or negatively, and it depends, of course, of whether he thought the military attitude was worthy of admiration. Even so, what this shows is that it is perfectly possible to hold this attitude of life as a test without being committed to a belief in divine providence. Foucault seems to take the two to be closely intertwined, perhaps as part of the narrative he wants to tell about the prehistory of certain Christian beliefs. In Seneca's *On Providence* they are presented as interrelated, but, as we have seen, there is no necessary connection, and Seneca's argument, at least in the opening sections, is more about how a good person relates to misfortunes rather than the source of those misfortunes (cf. *Prov.* 2.1). His argument is not that they were sent by providence, but rather that they are not misfortunes. Indeed, it has been commented that Seneca's essay is somewhat disappointing with regard to its response to the traditional problem of reconciling providence and misfortune (Setaioli 2014: 390). It is possible to approach every adverse situation as an opportunity to improve and test one's character without having to think that a benevolent deity conceived them for that purpose. One might, like Nietzsche (and, later, Deleuze), see them as the product of a blind fate to which one ought not to be unworthy, or one might, like Marcus Aurelius, reserve judgment on their cause—providence or atoms—and instead simply focus on how best to make use of what happens. In sum, this practical attitude of treating life as a test need not commit one to any specific claims about fate, providence, or the nature of the self.

6 Conclusions

Foucault's interest in the Roman Stoic idea of life as a test—an interest perhaps primed by his long-standing admiration of Nietzsche—sheds light on an important aspect of Roman Stoicism. His claim that this was something new, not prefigured by the Athenian Stoics, helps to bring into focus the ways in which the Roman Stoics made their own distinctive contribution to Stoic thought. His wider concerns in his late work with the historical development of conceptions of the self made him especially sensitive to these sorts of shift in attitude. However, as we have seen, it is difficult to give an adequate account of how or why this new attitude came about.

One final question worth asking is why Foucault thought this new attitude was so significant. His answer is that the rise of this idea of seeing the whole of life as a test highlights the Greco-Roman attitude of care of the self. Someone who thinks that they are continually being tested by every event that happens "must live one's life in such a way that one cares for the self at every moment" (2005: 448). This turns life into a perpetual concern for the self, focused on how one responds to events, rather than the events themselves. This is why, he suggests, the question of whether these really are tests sent by a benevolent deity falls into the background in Seneca and Epictetus:

> Between the rational God, who, in the order of the world, has set around me all the elements, the long chain of dangers and misfortunes, and myself, who will decipher these misfortunes as so many tests and exercises for me to perfect myself, between this God and myself, henceforth the issue is only myself. (2005: 448–9)

Foucault concludes by saying that "it seems to me that we have here a relatively important event in the history of Western subjectivity" (2005: 449). Foucault's Roman Stoics are not mere popular moralizers who fail to live up to the philosophical greatness of their Athenian predecessors; instead they stand as significant contributors to the development of the idea of the Subject.

Notes

1. For simplicity I cite early Stoic material from *SVF* (the standard abbreviation for von Arnim 1903–24), by volume and fragment number. For the later Stoics and other ancient authors, I cite using standard Latin abbreviations of titles of their works. For Seneca (*Prov.* and *Ep.*), I quote from the translations in Seneca 2014 and 2015. For Epictetus (*Diss.*), I quote from Epictetus 1995. For Cicero (*Tusc.* and *Fin.*), I quote from Cicero (2001 and 2002).
2. As Elden 2016 has shown, Foucault was engaged in three distinct projects in his final years, which were never fully disentangled from one another before the hasty publication of the second and third volumes of his *History of Sexuality*. These were (i) a history of sexuality, (ii) a genealogy of the modern subject, and (iii) an examination of ancient "technologies of the self." I have touched on this elsewhere in Sellars (2018) and Sellars (forthcoming).
3. This was first published in Foucault 2001 and is translated into English in Foucault 2005. For the sake of simplicity, I give references to the English translation only.
4. As I noted earlier, in Foucault's late work one of the central themes was a project to map a genealogy of the subject; see Foucault (2016: 22), with Sellars (2018: 15–16).

Bibliography

Arnim, H. von (1903–24), *Stoicorum Veterum Fragmenta*, 4 vols, Leipzig: Teubner.
Cicero, M. T. (2001), *On Moral Ends*, ed. J. Annas, trans. R. Woolf, Cambridge: Cambridge University Press.
Elden, S. (2016), *Foucault's Last Decade*, Cambridge: Polity.
Epictetus (1995), *The Discourses of Epictetus*, ed. C. Gill, trans. R. Hard, London: Dent.
Foucault, M. (2001), *L'herméneutique du sujet: Cours au Collège de France (1981–1982)*, Paris: Gallimard/Seuil.
Foucault, M. (2005), *The Hermeneutics of the Subject: Lectures at the Collège de France, 1981–82*, trans. G. Burchell, New York: Palgrave Macmillan.
Foucault, M. (2016), *About the Beginnings of The Hermeneutics of the Subject: Lectures at Dartmouth College, 1980*, trans. G. Burchell, Chicago: University of Chicago Press.
Nietzsche, F. (1986), *Human, All Too Human: A Book for Free Spirits*, trans. R. J. Hollingdale, Cambridge: Cambridge University Press.
Nietzsche, F. (1990), *Twilight of the Idols and The Anti-Christ*, trans. R. J. Hollingdale, Harmondsworth: Penguin.
Sellars, J. (2018), "Roman Stoic Mindfulness: An Ancient Technology of the Self," in M. Dennis and S. Werkhoven (eds.), *Ethics and Self-Cultivation: Historical and Contemporary Perspectives*, 15–29, New York: Routledge.
Sellars, J. (2020), "Self or Cosmos: Foucault *versus* Hadot," in M. Faustino and G. Ferraro (eds.), *The Late Foucault: Ethical and Political Questions*, London: Bloomsbury.
Seneca, L. A. (2014), *Hardship and Happiness*, trans. E. Fantham et al., Chicago: University of Chicago Press.
Seneca, L. A. (2015), *Letters on Ethics to Lucilius*, trans. M. Graver and A. A. Long, Chicago: University of Chicago Press.
Setaioli, A. (2014), "Physics III: Theology," in G. Damschen and A. Heil (eds.), *Brill's Companion to Seneca: Philosopher and Dramatist*, 379–401, Leiden: Brill.
Ure, M. (2016), "Stoicism in Nineteenth-Century German Philosophy," in J. Sellars (ed.), *The Routledge Handbook of the Stoic Tradition*, 287–302, Abingdon: Routledge.

Chapter 8

VERIDICTION AND *PARRHESIA*

THE COMPLEX CASE OF STOICISM AND
ITS READING BY M. FOUCAULT

Valéry Laurand

My chapter was born from a difficulty that I encountered in my study of Foucauldian *parrhēsia*—a difficulty I still experience today. I must confess that I am at a loss to understand the notion of "veridiction," especially in its relation to *parrhēsia*, which constitutes less a problem of truth, than truth-telling as a problem of shame, or concealment of thoughts. I fear that this obstacle in understanding is not ready to be overcome any time soon. Nevertheless, this chapter provides me with the opportunity to try and shed light on my problem, since I have rather intrepidly decided to undertake a reading of the extremely scarce occurrences of the word *parrhēsia* in Stoic writings in order to consider the Foucauldian notion of "veridiction." The challenge I have set myself requires that I follow the Foucauldian meaning of *parrhēsia*, in an attempt to find some residual echoes within Marcus Aurelius, Seneca and Musonius Rufus (there is just one occurrence of the word in Epictetus, which refers to the ideal Cynic, and my reading of Seneca will be based on the problem of the congruence between speech and acts).

I must admit something else: I have been surprised to see that these ancient Stoic texts were not altogether oblivious to a Foucauldian meaning of *parrhēsia*. Moreover, I believe that, more than a Platonic *parrhēsia*, or a Philodemian one, or a Plutarchian one, or even a Cynic one, Stoic *parrhēsia* fits rather well with Foucault's theory, and one might even argue that the echo-phenomenon could find its basis in a possible, however incomplete, legacy. I begin with a reading of Marcus Aurelius's uses of the notion of *parrhēsia* (I). Then, I try to apply the famous distinction between what is true and the truth to Foucauldian *parrhēsia* (II). This hypothesis leads me to an analysis of the meaning of the Foucauldian notion of the "Reality of Philosophy" (III).

I

Do not waste the balance of your life in impressions about other people, when you're not referring to some advantage of your fellows—for why do you rob yourself of something else which you might do? . . . I mean if you imagine what so and so is doing, and why; what he is saying or hiding in his heart or engineering, and every thought of the kind which leads you away from watching closely over your own hegemonic part? Rather you must, in the train of your thoughts, avoid what is merely casual and without purpose, and above all curiosity and malice; you must habituate yourself only to thoughts about which if someone were suddenly to ask: "What is in your mind now?" you would at once reply, quite frankly (*meta parrhēsias*), *this* or *that*; and so from the answer it would immediately be plain that all was simplicity and kindness, the thoughts of a social being, who disregards pleasurable, or to speak more generally luxurious imaginings or rivalry of any kind, or envy and suspicion or anything else about which you would blush to put into words that you had it in your head. A man so minded, putting off no longer to be one of the elect, is surely a priest and minister of gods, employing aright that which is seated within him.[1]

Μὴ κατατρίψῃς τὸ ὑπολειπόμενον τοῦ βίου μέρος ἐν ταῖς περὶ ἑτέρων φαντασίαις, ὁπόταν μὴ τὴν ἀναφορὰν ἐπί τι κοινωφελὲς ποιῇ· τί γὰρ ἄλλου ἔργου στέρῃ . . . τουτέστι φανταζόμενος τί ὁ δεῖνα πράσσει καὶ τίνος ἕνεκεν καὶ τί λέγει καὶ τί ἐνθυμεῖται καὶ τί τεχνάζεται καὶ ὅσα τοιαῦτα ποιεῖ ἀπορρέμβεσθαι τῆς τοῦ ἰδίου ἡγεμονικοῦ παρατηρήσεως. χρὴ μὲν οὖν καὶ τὸ εἰκῆ καὶ μάτην ἐν τῷ εἱρμῷ τῶν φαντασιῶν περιίστασθαι, πολὺ δὲ μάλιστα τὸ περίεργον καὶ κακόηθες, καὶ ἐθιστέον ἑαυτὸν μόνα φαντάζεσθαι, περὶ ὧν εἴ τις ἄφνω ἐπανέροιτο· τί νῦν διανοῇ; μετὰ παρρησίας παραχρῆμα ἂν ἀποκρίναιο ὅτι τὸ καὶ τό· ὡς ἐξ αὐτῶν εὐθὺς δῆλα εἶναι ὅτι πάντα ἁπλᾶ καὶ εὐμενῆ καὶ ζῴου κοινωνικοῦ καὶ ἀμελοῦντος ἡδονικῶν ἢ καθάπαξ ἀπολαυστικῶν φαντασμάτων ἢ φιλονεικίας τινὸς ἢ βασκανίας καὶ ὑποψίας ἢ ἄλλου τινός ἐφ' ᾧ ἂν ἐρυθριάσειας ἐξηγούμενος, ὅτι ἐν νῷ αὐτὸ εἶχες. ὁ γάρ τοι ἀνὴρ ὁ τοιοῦτος, οὐκ ἔτι ὑπερτιθέμενος τὸ ὡς ἐν ἀρίστοις ἤδη εἶναι, ἱερεύς τίς ἐστι καὶ ὑπουργὸς θεῶν, χρώμενος καὶ τῷ ἔνδον ἱδρυμένῳ αὐτοῦ. (MA 3.4.1-3)

In one of its rare occurrences in Marcus Aurelius's *Meditations* (there are only four), *parrhēsia* reveals itself more as a result than as a process. It stands as a testament to the purity of a mind that has freed itself from all vice, passions, and what one might call "bad thoughts." For one who is able to speak "with *parrhēsia*" (*meta parrhēsias*) has already achieved the moral goal (and such an end is achievable) of focusing not on others, but on oneself, on one's own governing faculty, and in so doing, having only simple and well-meaning or benevolent impressions.[2] Such a stance involves being able to prevent all other thoughts that would not refer to the simplicity of human nature (including, if need be, all considerations of general interest).

In a sense that is absolutely in keeping with the etymology of the term *parrhēsia* (that is to say: "to say everything"), to answer with frankness with what comes to mind signifies, in fact, to have nothing to hide, to be able to put forward everything you have in mind without blushing, to say everything one has in mind. (In the passage above, "to put into words," ἐξηγέομαι, means "to put forward," "to tell at length," "to expound in detail," here, the very bottom of one's thoughts, of one's heart; it also means, echoing the word ἡγεμονικόν or "hegemonic part," "to govern," to show that one can lead one's thoughts, one's impressions.) Someone who dares "to tell" is someone who is not ashamed. What remains striking is the fact that Marcus Aurelius's *parrhēsia* appears to be in contradiction with the Cynic Diogenes's (or for that matter with Callicles'), inasmuch as such *parrhēsia* would have nothing shocking or indecent to tell. Diogenes would certainly not blush at what he thinks or says, and he would allow himself to think or say things that Marcus Aurelius perhaps might not dare think. It is precisely because Diogenes can come out with the obscenest things without shame at the risk of shocking—a risk that he fully assumes—that his *parrhēsia* transforms the value of what is said: the obscene is no longer obscene as long as it is, precisely, said. Conversely, one might argue that, for Marcus Aurelius, some things might be thinkable and utterable (without shame), whereas others might not be so.

Such speech takes root in what might be called an achieved ideal (and, to a certain extent, easy to obtain, provided that one agrees to focus on oneself), whereby an individual is not only capable of withholding from spilling or transmitting onto others his own fears and thoughts (either by curiosity, or by imputing motives to others, etc.) but has also recovered within himself the basis on which he is seated and of which can make use (χρώμενος καὶ τῷ ἔνδον ἱδρυμένῳ αὐτοῦ).

Parrhesiastic speech comes from what each of us has to rediscover in his own self, which permits the "use of impressions," that is to say, the ability to lead a critical examination of an impression before giving to it one's assent, before including it in our train of thoughts (in this case, a favorable one). Such a use allows for the transformation of a "luxurious imagining" (an ἀπολαυστικὸν φάντασμα) into an "impression" (a φαντασία) which might be more disillusioned but which nonetheless endeavors to "refer to" (ἀναφορά) mere reality:[3]

> And, in matters of sexual intercourse, that it is attrition of an entrails and a convulsive expulsion of mere mucus. (MA 6.13)
>
> καὶ ἐπὶ τῶν κατὰ τὴν συνουσίαν ἐντερίου παράτριψις καὶ μετά τινος σπασμοῦ μυξαρίου ἔκκρισις.

It remains that this excerpt of a meditation testifies to Marcus Aurelius's global strategy, which is a question of remembering, of reminiscing, of repeating to oneself constantly the goal (I daren't say "ideal") one has to achieve. In this text, the expression "with *parrhēsia*" (μετὰ παρρησίας) attests to the achievement of the goal but does not constitute the goal itself (one could indeed think that someone educated could also speak with frankness, without having in mind the same things). This transpires in another use Marcus Aurelius makes of the word *parrhēsia*, on two occasions. In these instances, it is not a matter of using *parrhēsia*, but of tolerating it. From Diognetus, who was his professor, the emperor assures us that he has received τὸ ἀνέχεσθαι παρρησίας (MA 1.6.1.4), "the faculty to bear *parrhēsia*." In *Meditation* 6.30, the problem is to avoid being transformed into a Caesar (Ὅρα μὴ ἀποκαισαρωθῇς, 6.30.1), and Marcus gives the example of Antoninus, who "bore a frank opposition to his judgments and showed gratitude if better judgments were found" (καὶ τὸ ἀνέχεσθαι <τῶν> ἀντιβαινόντων παρρησιαστικῶς ταῖς γνώμαις αὐτοῦ καὶ χαίρειν εἴ τίς <τι> δεικνύοι κρεῖττον) (6.30.4). Both occurrences signify that one allows others to say everything they think (even if they have had no preliminary critical examination of their impressions), at the risk (that one has to assume patiently) of being put to the test of a criticism that might be opportune. Interestingly, as we note with the last occurrence of the word in the *Meditations*, such a *parrhēsia* might have pedagogical implications:

> After Tragedy Old Comedy was introduced, which through its instructive frankness and its reminder by actual plainness of language to avoid vanity was not without profit. (MA 11.6.2)
>
> μετὰ δὲ τὴν τραγῳδίαν ἡ ἀρχαία κωμῳδία παρήχθη, παιδαγωγικὴν παρρησίαν ἔχουσα καὶ τῆς ἀτυφίας οὐκ ἀχρήστως δι' αὐτῆς τῆς εὐθυρρημοσύνης ὑπομιμνήσκουσα.

The pair of words, παρρησία ("frankness") and εὐθυρρημοσύνη ("plainness of language"), undoubtedly refines our understanding of the former: *mutatis mutandis*, we encounter once again what is essential in the "use of impressions"— that is to say, getting the science of uncovering the nakedness (ἀπογυμνοῦν) of things, being capable of plainness of speech, in order to achieve the ability to say everything. Then, as Sophie Aubert-Baillot argues, "l'εὐθυρρημοσύνη is invested with a function that is simultaneously ethical and pedagogical, which relates it to παρρησία" (2015: 82–3).[4] *Parrhēsia* gains a psychagogic power, which leads it close to a master's *parrhēsia*, certainly similar to that which Marcus Aurelius was able to bear from Diognetus, a *parrhēsia* that reminds us (ὑπομιμνήσκω) of what matters most. Within that pair of words, we can understand *parrhēsia*, as Michel Foucault understood it in *The Hermeneutics of the Subject*, though his analysis bore on Epicurean *parrhēsia*, not only as frankness or freedom of speech (what here is implied, to a certain extent, in the word εὐθυρρημοσύνη) but also as a "a technical term—which allows the master to make a proper use, from the true things he knows, of that which is useful or effective for his disciple's work of transformation" (Foucault 2005: 242).[5]

The analysis of the occurrences of the word *parrhēsia* in Marcus Aurelius allows one to situate the concept as both a means of achieving a goal and as the witness of this achievement. As a means, it is someone else's speech, a master's, which one must learn to bear in order to progress. As an aim, it is the act of a subject who is able to express his thoughts. As I have already said, we must not be unaware of the status of the *Meditations*. They consist in both an exercise and a thought experiment. From this point of view, we could certainly recall what Foucault says about *l'Ecriture de soi* (Writing the Self), because *Meditations* appears to be an ethopoetic exercise. "The fashioning of accepted discourses, recognized as true, into rational principles of action," the writing of the *Meditations* consists in an "agent of the transformation of truth into *ethos* (*un opérateur de la transformation de la vérité en ethos*)" (Foucault 2001b: 1237). Marcus Aurelius speaks to himself as a master would speak to a disciple. What we have here is the progressor's continuing back and forth (which Seneca theorized in his *De Vita Beata*) between the sage's figure and what we could call the ethics of moral progression, where the problem is to find in oneself and use what constitutes the seat of self (*to hidrumenon*) and, in fact, also its basis. Marcus Aurelius's ethics of progression obviously matches the aim that Foucault designates as *hupomnēmata*:

> Withdrawing in to oneself, getting in touch with oneself, living with oneself, relying on oneself, benefitting from and enjoying oneself. Such is the aim of the *hupomnemata*: to make one's recollection of the fragmentary *logos*, transmitted through teaching, listening, or reading, a means of establishing a relationship of oneself with oneself, a relationship as adequate and accomplished as possible.
>
> *Se retirer en soi, s'atteindre soi-même, vivre avec soi-même, se suffire à soi-même, profiter et jouir de soi-même. Tel est bien l'objectif des* hupomnēmata : *faire de la recollection du logos fragmentaire et transmis par l'enseignement, l'écoute ou la lecture, un moyen pour l'établissement d'un rapport de soi à soi aussi adéquat et achevé que possible.* (Foucault 2001b: 1239)

We must, therefore, understand the nature of this *hidrumenon* (this "seat") that everybody can find in himself and make use of. I would hypothesize that *hidrumenon* is nothing but the hegemonic part, naturally established to judge and naturally able to criticize impressions. In our text, the problem arises from recovering the use of that hegemonic part, and I would add and adapt a Foucauldian judgment about the Stoic theory of "appropriation" (*oikeiōsis*):[6] if we have to "become again what we should have been but never were" (Foucault 2001a: 95), we have now to recover a faculty which has never been achieved and that we must elaborate via philosophical exercises.

Our question at present links with Foucault's: that is to say both the conditions of this elaboration and its goal. Obviously, the latter could be expressed in this way: Marcus Aurelius, in our first text, encourages himself (and his reader) to equip himself with the means for critical thinking (that is to say, the means for stringing together impressions—εἰρμός—impressions suitable to be strung together and that come from the thread—συγκλωθόμενα—of Fate). In short, *parrhēsia* proves a critical mind, which examines what it receives and what it elaborates from these impressions. Hence, if the goal consists in one becoming the minister of the gods, or in featuring already among the best, that goal is nothing but a correct elaboration of thought, achieved by focusing on the elaboration proper and on refocusing on the hegemonic part of the soul. The goal is involved within the progression and that progression does not involve anything new (This again echoes "Writing the Self": the matter does not consist in revealing hidden things, neither in finding any ideal, but in making one's own what has been already said or written by philosophers.) (Foucault 2001b: 1238; see also Luxon 2008: 381). Otherwise said, it is not a matter of achieving a transcendent ideal but of duly noting that this ideal is, in a way, already at hand, for it suffices, to achieve it, to simply look into oneself.

Such is *parrhēsia*: the witness of the relation between a person and his or herself, of an elaboration of the self when *parrhēsia* is addressed to others, and the agent of that elaboration when it is addressed by a master or by oneself as another to oneself. Obviously, that addressed *parrhēsia* poses a serious challenge (*parrhēsia* is mainly—historically in its political institutional functioning in Athenian democracy, as in its pedagogical functioning—a speech addressed to someone else), a challenge not entirely solved by the Stoic gap between sage's truth versus progressor's error, between two points of view. Marcus Aurelius addresses to himself, a progressor, thoughts of a sage who would have arrived safe and sound, who would know the truth, who would even be the truth, if we admit that a thought to which all impressions are linked has the firmness and assurance of a system—that is to say the truth, for a Stoic.

II

We must dwell upon this truth, both as something which has been achieved (since Marcus Aurelius's speech has, for him at least, a truth value, and since we can assume that he reminds himself of Stoic systematic truth) and as something yet to be achieved. Michel Foucault, it is well known, reads in *parrhēsia* a problem of truth-telling, "veridiction," and focuses his inquiry concerning *parrhēsia* on the notion of truth. He almost never speaks about sincerity (which could yet be a translation of the word *parrhēsia*, which would avoid—at least temporarily—the problem of truth), except when he says that sincerity is itself a criterion of truth (March 2, 1983, first hour),[7] or when he conflates, without any commentary, truth and sincerity in *Fearless Speech* (Foucault 2001c: 15). This truth, nevertheless, verges on a "being in truth" as regards oneself or others. Now, here is the main problem and the philosophical task: "being in truth" makes problematic the very notion of truth (and besides, Foucault, in *Fearless Speech*, opposes Cartesian evidence with parrhesiastic truth, an opposition that we can find also in the discussion that follows the course of February 3, 1982) (Foucault 2001a: 182–3). Such a simple Foucauldian expression as "the true life" in fact involves a redefinition of the very nature and structure of truth. In a nutshell, telling the truth and being in the truth are phrases that do not refer to the same model of truth. Foucault has not missed this point, but he leaves a sort of grey area in his discourse concerning *parrhēsia*. Thus, one can discern a notable change in the paradigm of truth (which Foucault talks of in his course of January 5, 1983, to be found at the beginning of *The Government of Self and Others*): broadly, from truth as a process of subjection (*assujetissement*), producing subjects of knowledge and normalizing conduct (the example here is madness as a matrix of knowledge, or norm of behavior, that builds a "normal" subject), to truth as "alethurgy": "the production of truth, the act by which truth is manifested" (Foucault 2011: 3, course of February 1, 1984), the act by which the subject, telling the truth, manifests himself; the act by which the subject is established by himself as himself and is recognized as telling the truth. However paradoxical in appearance, this act does not lead to normalization. To quote his cynic expression, it leads to the "scandal of the truth," which might appear to be a call for resistance against all norms because of the irreducible alterity it implies.

Hence, Michel Foucault goes from a thought of a subjected subject, a "subject effect," a passive subject, to a subject who forms his own relationship both with the truth and with himself—an ethical subject, a subject of ethics, an active subject of "the care of the self."[8] Beyond that change, when reading Foucault we are faced with a constant hesitation in the analysis of the problematics of alethurgy and in the definition of truth (whether it be in Foucault's readings of Plato, the Stoics, or the Cynics). He seems to hesitate between two models of truth (Terrel 2010: 179ff.). First, a truth that precedes the subject, who constitutes himself within the truth. One could find, *mutatis mutandis*, such a truth in the ethical, technical, and philosophical knowledge that Marcus Aurelius refers to when addressing himself (that is the case, for instance, concerning the parrhesiastic master who dares tell the truth or/and blame the others). Here, it is a matter of complying with a constituted knowledge that would underpin the practice of the truth and the way to model oneself on a true discourse. In short, to try to match words and actions, which is a *parrhēsia*'s criterion. This kind of truth gives rise to a balance between philosophical conduct and philosophy as a system of values approved by the experience and practice of a master. Second, this is a truth that would invent itself, and, by which, the subject could invent himself. This truth would neither consist in a balance between a system (of values, of knowledge, etc.) and a conduct (from a perspective where *parrhēsia* would be an adequacy between ideals and acts), nor would it be a mere expression of the rejection of norms (even an aestheticized one) used in a city (from the perspective where *parrhēsia* would be the expression of an "other life"—Foucault 2011: 184, 244-6). That would be the truth of oneself that is encouraged by Marcus Aurelius and that guides his interpretation of doctrines, or the truth that Seneca obtains when, in midstream, he assures his accusers in *De Vita Beata*:

> I am not a wise man, and I will not be one in order to feed your spite: so do not require me to be on a level with the best of men, but merely to be better than the worst: I am satisfied, if every day I take away something from my vices and correct my faults. I have not arrived at perfect soundness of mind, indeed, I never shall arrive at it: I compound palliatives rather than remedies for my gout, and am satisfied if it comes at rarer intervals—and does not shoot so painfully ... I speak of virtue, not of myself, and when I blame vices, I blame my own first of all: when I have the power, I shall live as I ought to do. (17.3-4; 18.1)[9]

> *Non sum sapiens et, ut malivolentiam tuam pascam, nec ero. Exige itaque a me, non ut optimis par sim, sed ut malis melior: hoc mihi satis est cotidie aliquid ex vitiis meis demere et errores meos obiurgare. Non perveni ad sanitatem, ne perveniam quidem; delenimenta magis quam remedia podagrae meae compono, contentus,*

> *si rarius accedit et si minus verminatur . . . De virtute, non de me loquor, et cum vitiis convicium facio, in primis meis facio: cum potuero, vivam, quomodo oportet.*

Where Marcus Aurelius situated himself within the realm of that which has been "already achieved," Seneca, and without doubt because of the different status of his speech, situates himself between two nonbeings: he is not sage and, clearly, he will not be such. So, why? Is it worth continuing to philosophize? Even if Seneca admits that he does not match an ideal, it remains that he can be delighted to move progressively toward himself. What precisely matters is the delight in the process and not the sorrow of a gap between oneself and an ideal which is just a fiction (even if it is possible to become a sage, it suffices, so to speak, to return to one's nature). To be among the best, as in Marcus Aurelius' meditation, is not what matters. Seneca chooses to make do with the comparative form: to be better than the worst suffices to find oneself on the road of progress. Is Seneca drawing here the picture of an eternal progressor, who, despite knowing the truth, will never be able to live up to it? Far from being an abstract principle of existence, which one should be in accordance with, in an external way, philosophy is a discourse which commits the whole being of his listener. All in all, the fact that Seneca intends to achieve philosophical aims using ideas which he endorses (hence the anaphoric repetition of "I will" at 20.3-5, as many philosophical decisions which commit the progressor) leads little by little to putting them into practice (and to understanding that he is actually worth more than he thinks he is). That manipulation of ideas has implications: the trainee-philosopher makes real attempts (20.2) to fit with his discourse. The very thing consists in assuming the principles in the first person and in being the embodiment of these principles. The progression is determined by this adherence—that Foucault calls the "circle of listening" (2008: 217).[10] It does not suffice to set a target; one must *want* to try to achieve it (20.5). That implies a crucial confidence, not first in oneself,[11] but in the experience of former philosophers who have gone down that road.

If the sage practices his virtue as a permanent state, the progressor tries it out as a precarious tendency that he has always to reinforce, hence the gap between a discourse which pedagogically provides a model of virtue and the actual state of the progressor, for whom virtue is an inchoate and feeble disposition. The gap between words and actions, while being plain, cannot procure a good measure for one's progress toward wisdom. The relevant measure, in order to appreciate the progress, consists in the awareness of the number of faults that have been avoided, thanks to philosophy. If the philosophical speech takes on the sage's point of view, according to which every insane person is wholly blameworthy (but still improvable), a judgment about the progression of such and such a progressor requires a change of perspective in such a way that a vicious act is compared not with its opposite, a virtuous act, but with another act of a similar, vicious nature. One must not evaluate a progressor according to his program (even if that program allows for an actual progression) but according to the effective path he in fact crosses.

I would like to propose a comparison, which may at first seem slightly artificial but which could possibly shed light upon the discourses, not only of

Seneca and Marcus Aurelius, but of Foucault as well. The comparison would be with a famous Stoic distinction between what *is true* and the truth. Clauses of philosophy can *be true*; it remains that the truth is nothing other than the absolutely stable state of a soul whose thoughts are firmly integrated in a systematic way. This comes close, I would argue, to the Marcus-Aurelian idea of a progressive integration of impressions in the train—εἱρμός—of thoughts. Additionally, such an integration will inevitably have an ethical effect in the shape of acts. Then, the formulated ideal of wisdom (as a transcendent ideal) could be equal to a set of true clauses (true, because validated by philosophy, as a system of dogmas), while the embodiment of these dogmas in a soul could be equal to the truth and differ in its ethopoetic effects. Then, the philosophical speech would not assume a legislative function, a body of doctrines that would provide a law to which one would conform. Instead, and this is not a play on words, philosophical speech would consist in a system of dogmas which could be judged and called "true," but the "truth" of which would consist in their effective integration, through an experience, in the individual conduct of a subject transformed by this experience. As Nancy Luxon remarks, "Parrhēsia's paideic techniques must not become an orthopaedy" (2008: 387).[12] This ideal sketched by the philosopher's words could be close to the "fictions" that Foucault refers to concerning the writing of his own books and the experience of self-reassessment they allow him to experience in his own life:

> So here is a book that functions as an experience, for its writer and for its reader, much more than as the demonstration of a historical truth. In order to have such an experience through this book, it is necessary that what it asserts is somehow "true," in terms of academic truth, historically verifiable. But what is essential is not found in the series of these true demonstrations or historically verifiable; it lies rather in the experience which the book permits us to have. And this experience is neither true nor false: it is always a fiction, something one constructs for oneself, which exists only after it has been made, not before; [it isn't something that is "true," but it has been a "reality".] That is the difficult relation with truth, entirely at stake in the way in which truth is found used inside an experience, not fastened to it, and which, within certain limits, destroys it. (Foucault 2001b: 864)[13]

What matters for Foucault, as a philosopher, an academic, and an author, is to write, not to fix knowledge, but to grasp what he calls in French *le processus du savoir* by opposition to *connaissance*. Foucault's clarification of his position on knowledge is important in this respect:

> When I use the word "knowledge" (*savoir*), I do so in order to distinguish it from *a* knowledge (*connaissance*). The former is the process through which the subject finds himself modified by what he knows, or rather by the labor performed in order to know. It is what permits the modification of the subject and the construction of the object.

> *Connaissance*, however, is the process which permits the multiplication of knowable objects, the development of their intelligibility, the understanding of their rationality, while the subject doing the investigation always remains the same. (Foucault 1991: 69–70)

Following the Stoic distinction that I referred to earlier, the Foucauldian *connaissances* could be equal to Stoic true clauses, while knowledge (*le savoir*) would aim at the truth, which could be analyzed as the Marc-Aurelian integration of critical ability. True clauses are not sufficient to modify a subject (Epictetus, for example, criticizes disciples who just "vomit" their knowledge without experiencing them and prefers those who have digested them[14]—digestion could be a way of *savoir*, an integration of clauses in the soul), while the truth of "true" clauses does not lie in them, but in the wise soul who incorporates them—and reduces them to their contingency (Long and Sedley 1987: 202). Thus from 1980, Foucault had established the basis of his future analysis of parrhēsia; this basis would receive the appellation of "veridiction."

III

Such a conception of truth as that which is split between a set of true statements, on the one hand, and a progressive embodiment of truth, on the other, in the shape of an exercise in critical examination of impressions, could prove fertile—first, because it makes me better understand the relationship between *parrhēsia* and truth, and second, because it provides elements that nourish a reflection concerning the nature of a philosophical thought experiment.

Foucault seems to deal with the significance of this experience in depth when, in the course of February 16, 1983, he speaks about "the reality of philosophy" (*le réel de la philosophie*). His notion enables us to proceed with distinctions concerning *parrhēsia*. If philosophy is "an act of veridiction which may perfectly well be mistaken and say the false moreover" (Foucault 2010: 228, 2008: 210), one must also retain that "the will to tell the truth is in its very reality," the "activity of telling the truth," and "this completely particular and singular act of veridiction" is philosophy proper (albeit within a formulation which could have been clearer, as it tries to bring the "will to tell the truth" closer to "truth-telling," while defining parrhēsia as an act, something Foucault explains, besides, in the beginning of *Fearless Speech*).[15] Parrhēsia consists in a "speech activity" which is not simply built on words (by which I mean, it is not a mere game inherent to language): it is, indeed, a *logos*, which produces an *ergon* ("work" or "task") within a political context:

> The reality, the test by which and through which philosophical veridiction will demonstrate its reality is the fact that it addresses itself, can address itself, and has the courage to address itself to whoever it is who exercises power. . . . It enters the political field in diverse ways, none of which is essential, but always

marking its specific difference in relation to other discourses. (Foucault 2011: 228–9, see Foucault 2009: 2010–11)

What makes the "truth" of that veridiction is determined threefold: first, the speaker's involvement in his own speech, second, the addressee of that speech, and third, its specificity. The first determining factor, the degree of the speaker's involvement, finds its measure in part within the ethopoetic function of discourse—this transforms the speaker's *ethos*, which is the *ergon* of the discourse, and in part within the risk that the speaker takes (a risk that depends both on his own discourse and on his interlocutor). It needs noting at this point that the preferred candidate for such an approach to *parrhēsia* (already in 1983, but it will become plain in 1984) is the Cynic's approach, rather than that of Socrates or Plato in the *Seventh Letter*. Symptomatically Foucault does not mention the noteworthy fact that *parrhēsia* becomes, for Philodemus, Musonius, Plutarch, and also for Philo, a way of handling that risk by minimizing it in order to maximize the impact of speech on the interlocutor: When Diogenes disregards the consequences of the violence of his words, the other philosophers try to find a way to preserve the bond with their interlocutor. So *parrhēsia* becomes a *technē stochastikē* (art of conjecture), for Philodemus, which allows truth-telling to others, but truth that others must precisely be able to hear (and understand). So, it is a truth that has been an object of reflection, not only about the circumstances of enunciation (the *kairos*), but also about the way of telling that truth. Here, we can question the effective conditions of the "reality of philosophy": Is the ethopoietic a speech which is unlikely to be heard? Does the "specifity" of *parrhēsia* consist in the Cynic's rashness in the name of "an other life," which risks jeopardizing the bond with the interlocutor and to become simply a "vomited true clause" without impact and finally void? (Here, the risk is assumed not only by the speaker but also by the truth, if truth cannot be understood as truth.)

I'll finish my chapter with an example of another view of the "reality of philosophy" from a Stoic philosopher, namely Musonius Rufus. After having quoted the famous Euripidean verses about *parrhēsia*, Musonius offers this analysis of a circumstantial *parrhēsia*:

> But I should say in rejoinder: "You are right, Euripides, when you say that it is the condition of a slave not to say what one thinks, at least when one ought to speak, for it is not always, nor everywhere, nor before everyone that we should say what we think. But that one point, it seems to me, is not well-taken, that exiles do not have freedom of speech, if to you freedom of speech means not suppressing whatever one chances to think. For it is not as exiles that men fear to say what they think, but as men afraid lest from speaking pain or death or punishment or some such other thing shall befall them. Fear is the cause of this, not exile. For to many people, nay to most, even though dwelling safely in their native city, fear of what seem to them dire consequences of free speech is present. However, the courageous man, in exile no less than at home, is dauntless in the face of all such fears; for that reason also he has the courage to say what he thinks equally at home or in exile." Such are the things one might reply to Euripides.

But tell me, my friend, when Diogenes was in exile at Athens, or when he was sold by pirates and came to Corinth, did anyone, Athenian or Corinthian, ever exhibit greater freedom of speech than he? And again, were any of his contemporaries freer than Diogenes? Why, even Xeniades, who bought him, he ruled as a master rules a slave. (Lutz 1949: 73–5)

ἐγὼ δὲ φαίην ἂν πρὸς τὸν Εὐριπίδην ὅτι, ὦ Εὐριπίδη, τοῦτο μὲν ὀρθῶς ὑπολαμβάνεις, ὡς δούλου ἐστίν, ἃ φρονεῖ μὴ λέγειν, ὅταν γε δέῃ λέγειν· οὐ γὰρ ἀεὶ καὶ πανταχοῦ καὶ πρὸς ὁντινοῦν λεκτέον ἃ φρονοῦμεν. ἐκεῖνο δὲ οὔ μοι δοκεῖς εὖ εἰρηκέναι, τὸ μὴ μετεῖναι τοῖς φεύγουσι παρρησίας, εἴπερ παρρησία σοι δοκεῖ τὸ μὴ σιγᾶν ἃ φρονῶν τυγχάνει τις. οὐ γὰρ οἱ φεύγοντες ὀκνοῦσι λέγειν ἃ φρονοῦσιν, ἀλλ' οἱ δεδιότες μὴ ἐκ τοῦ εἰπεῖν γένηται αὐτοῖς πόνος ἢ θάνατος ἢ ζημία ἤ τι τοιοῦτον ἕτερον. τοῦτο δὲ τὸ δέος μὰ Δία οὐχ ἡ φυγὴ ποιεῖ. πολλοῖς γὰρ ὑπάρχει καὶ τῶν ἐν τῇ πατρίδι ὄντων, μᾶλλον δὲ τοῖς πλείστοις, τὰ δοκοῦντα δεινὰ δεδιέναι. ὁ δὲ ἀνδρεῖος οὐδὲν ἧττον φυγὰς ὢν ἤπερ οἴκοι θαρρεῖ πρὸς ἅπαντα τὰ τοιαῦτα, διὸ καὶ λέγει ἃ φρονεῖ θαρρῶν οὐδὲν μᾶλλον ἢ ὅταν ᾖ μὴ φυγάς, ὅταν φεύγων τύχῃ. ταῦτα μὲν πρὸς Εὐριπίδην εἴποι τις ἄν· σὺ δ' εἰπέ μοι, ὦ ἑταῖρε, ὅτε Διογένης φεύγων ἦν Ἀθήνησιν, ἢ ὅτε πραθεὶς ὑπὸ τῶν λῃστῶν ἦλθεν εἰς Κόρινθον, ἆρα τότε πλείω παρρησίαν ἄλλος τις ἐπεδείξατο Διογένους ἢ Ἀθηναῖος ἢ Κορίνθιος; τί δ'; ἐλευθεριώτερος ἄλλος τις ἢ Διογένης τῶν τότε ἀνθρώπων ἦν; ὃς καὶ Ξενιάδου τοῦ πριαμένου αὐτὸν ὡς δεσπότης δούλου ἦρχεν. (Musonius 9.48.1-49.9)

τὸ μὴ σιγᾶν ἃ φρονῶν τυγχάνει τις: "not keeping quiet about things one chances to think." This negative definition allows a reevaluation of the problem of *parrhēsia*. Musonius's *parrhēsia* is no longer that which appears in Euripides's *Ion* (671-75), which was an attribute necessarily linked to the condition of citizen and opposed to the slave's servitude of speech. (Foucault discusses *parrhēsia* in *Ion* at length in *The Government of Self and Others*, 2010: 72–147.) In Musonius' view, *parrhēsia* is no longer conditioned by a political status. The opposition between a free citizen and a slave must be reevaluated (classically in Stoic thought). The wise man is the sole free man, while every insane person remains a slave, a slave to his own passions. If Musonius has shown that freedom requires a critical reevaluation of the objects of impulse and of the relationship between subject and objects and between individual and others, in this instance he puts forward that *parrhēsia* requires also a reinvestment of one's own discourse. One must pay attention to its circumstances: *parrhēsia* must not be used at all times, in all places, and before anyone. Musonius criticizes the Cynic *parrhēsia* (in a way that Plutarch investigates in greater depth in his *De Adulatore*). The critical evaluation of the conditions of use of *parrhēsia* is an integral part of *parrhēsia*. However, this necessary management of risk depends on circumstances external to the speech only at a secondary level. No political reasons (then alienating) should hinder *parrhēsia*, even if they necessarily affect the way in which it is used. Musonius distinguishes *parrhēsia* as an inalienable attribute from the conditions of its use. In other words, the choice of free speech depends only on the subject, who knows also how to speak according to the circumstances. Hence, no one could be deprived of *parrhēsia* in his own city. Yet, internal obstacles can destroy *parrhēsia*: shame, fear, anxiety, and so on.

I have tried to show, in the first part, that Marcus Aurelius's *parrhēsia* can be understood both as a critical process and as a result. As a result, it expresses a true speech and may be considered as a norm and standard of self-elaboration. According to Michel Foucault, *parrhēsia* can be also conceived as a critical process of self-elaboration and reflects that elaboration, which remains the key issue of what he calls "veridiction." The gap between what could appear as an ideal (the truth of *parrhēsia*) and the process by which a subject fulfills it still needs to be evaluated. That was the second part of my chapter. The reading of Seneca has led me to distinguish "true" from "truth." The former as clauses setting out an ideal, and the latter as progressive integration of this ideal in a subject (who becomes a subject through that integration): the truth of progress relies not so much on the enforcement of ideals but on the level of effort made to conform to them. That is, the philosophical experience trumps ideals, and it cannot be reduced to the mere application of ideals (as true as they are). Only the wise man, the truth embodied, knows how to use these ideals. Experience allows, according to Foucault, the digestion of true clauses thanks to the critical skills that they ensure. By experience, we move from "*a* knowledge" (*connaissance*) to the process of knowledge (*savoir*). Finally, the truth of a critical knowledge is expressed in the speech-acting of a philosopher facing the politician, what Foucault calls "the reality of philosophy."

If Foucauldian "veridiction" finally seems to me quite close to Stoic truth as embodiment of the system (such an integration entailing both a self-modification and the power to use dogmas according to the circumstances), it remains for me to evaluate, from the example of Musonius, the distance between a *parrhēsia* which expresses the "other life" of a Cynic forged through the experience of the violence of truth (the *parrhēsia* favored by Foucault) and a *parrhēsia* whose courage is always (by concern for efficiency of the speech) associated with the cautious consideration of circumstances of its use. It appears to me that Foucault, in this respect and compared to the Stoics, claims a radicalism which disrupts even more his conception of truth by making it absolute, while the Stoics maintain anchoring in, precisely, the reality of a life dealing with circumstances and norms of a given society. The question that arises is how far the truth should extend in the transgression of norms. In a Foucauldian view, *parrhēsia* is that experience of truth which should run the risk of destroying the true clauses by which it has been elaborated. Stoic philosophers did not make this radical step: for them, truth could be seen as Italian *sprezzatura*: it is not a question of inventing new norms, but a question of having incorporated norms to such an extent that the wise man can transcend them while complying with them.[16]

Notes

1 All English translations are adapted from Farquharson (1968).
2 Note that, in our text and entirely in accordance with Stoic theory, the word φαντασία ("impression," the way in which senses are impressed by things—impressors) is

contradictory to φάντασμα ("imagination," which is classically defined as "an empty attraction"—without impresser). See Long and Sedley (1987) 39B.

3   "οἷαι δὴ αὐταί εἰσιν αἱ φαντασίαι καθικνούμεναι αὐτῶν τῶν πραγμάτων καὶ διεξιοῦσαι δι' αὐτῶν—Surely these are excellent imaginations, going to the heart of actual facts and penetrating them so as to see the kind of thing they really are" (MA 6.13).

4   All translations from French are my own, unless otherwise noted.

5   From "cours du 10 février 1982" (Foucault 2001a: 232).

6   The Stoics maintained that all beings have an innate and natural drive to 'appropriate,' preserve, and nourish their own 'constitution,' that which makes them what they are. As human beings develop, this 'constitution' comes to encompass not only their bodies, but their reasoning capacity and social identity (Long and Sedley 1987: 346–54). Yet, all of them, mostly because of education, have broken early during childhood, with this natural drive.

7   Foucault 2010: 314. "Now we can obviously raise the following question. A speech without embellishment, a speech which employs the words, expressions, and phrases which come to mind, and a speech that the person who utters it believes to be true, would describe, for us at any rate, a sincere speech, but not necessarily a true speech, so how is it that, for Socrates or Plato, saying things without embellishment, as they come to mind, and while believing them to be true, is a criterion of truth?" (see Foucault 2008: 289).

8   Luxon says, "Rather than a 'knowing subjet,' produced in reference to a defined body of knowledge and some external order, the 'expressive subject' draws on the structural dynamics of parrhesiastic relationships to give ethopoetic content to her actions," and, in opposition to a Kantian way, she adds, "Rather than being urged 'dare to know,' individuals are encouraged to 'dare to act'" (2008: 379).

9   All translations from Seneca's *De Vita Beata* are from Stewart 1900.

10 *La philosophie ne peut s'adresser qu'à ceux qui veulent l'écouter* (Foucault 2010: 235): "Philosophy can only address itself to those who want to listen."

11 "Not to its own strength but to that of human nature" (*De vita beata* XX: 2).

12 "For parrhesia to provide a model of ethical self-governance, however, these practices must be able to form coherent subjects without these relationships being ones of discipline and constraint, and without objectifying the individual into a 'body of knowledge'" (Luxon 2008: 387).

13 English (partial) translation can be found in Foucault (1991: 36), which I have used to translate.

14 Epict., *Diss.* 3.21.1-6.

15 Foucault: "The specific 'speech activity' of the parrhesiastic enunciation thus takes the form: 'I am the one who thinks this and that.' I use the phrase 'speech activity' rather than John Searle's 'speech act' (or Austin's 'performative utterance') in order to distinguish the parrhesiastic utterance and its commitments from the usual sorts of commitment which obtain between someone and what he or she says. For, as we shall see, the commitment involved in *parrhesia* is linked to a certain social situation, to a difference of status between the speaker and his audience, to the fact that the *parrhesiastes* says something which is dangerous to himself and thus involves a risk, and so on" (2001c: 13).

16 I wish to thank warmly Prof. Catherine Lisak for her attentive and careful proofing and Janae Sholtz and Kurt Lampe for their helpful comments.

Bibliography

Aubert-Baillot, S. (2015), "*Un cas particulier de franc-parler (παρρησία): le parler droit (εὐθυρρημοσύνη) des Stoïciens,*" *Rhetorica* 31 (1): 71–96.

Farquharson, A. S. (1968), *The Meditations of the Emperor Marcus Antoninus*, Vol. 2, Oxford: Oxford Clarendon Press.

Foucault, M. (1991), *Remarks on Marx, Conversation with Duccio Trombadori*, New York: Semiotexts.

Foucault, M. (2001a), *L'Herméneutique du Sujet*, Paris: Gallimard.

Foucault, M. (2001b), *Dits et écrits II, 1976–1988*, Paris: Gallimard.

Foucault, M. (2001c), *Fearless Speech*, Los Angeles: Semiotext.

Foucault, M. (2005), *The Hermeneutics of the Subject*, New York: Palgrave Macmillan.

Foucault, M. (2008), *Le gouvernement de soi et des autres, Cours au collège de France, 1982–1983*, Paris: Seuil Gallimard.

Foucault, M. (2009), *Le courage de la vérité*, Paris: Gallimard.

Foucault, M. (2010), *The Government of Self and Others*, New York: Palgrave Macmillan.

Foucault, M. (2011), *The Courage of the Truth*, New York: Palgrave Macmillan.

Long, A. and D. Sedley (1987), *The Hellenistic Philosophers*, Cambridge: Cambridge University Press.

Lutz, C. (1949), "Musonius Rufus: The Roman Socrates," *Yale Classical Studies* 10: 3–147.

Luxon, N. (2008), "Ethics and Subjectivity - Practice of Self-Governance in the Late Lectures of Michel Foucault," *Political Theory* 36 (3): 377–402.

Seneca, L. A. (1912), *De Vita Beata*, trans. A. Stewart, London: Bell.

Terrel, J. (2010), *Politiques de Foucault*, Paris: PUF.

Chapter 9

STOICISM

POLITICAL RESISTANCE OR RETREAT? FOUCAULT AND ARENDT

Michael Ure

This chapter examines Michel Foucault and Hannah Arendt's reception of Roman Stoic ethics. Arendt and Foucault's analysis of Stoicism develops in the context of a remarkably similar analysis of modernity. Both argue that since the eighteenth century we have crossed the threshold of political modernity: governance, they claim, has become a matter of regulating life processes rather than protecting or facilitating freedom (see Agamben 1998; Dolan 2005; Blencowe 2010; Ucnik 2018). In the age of biopolitics, as Foucault calls it, "security" remains the decisive criterion of political legitimacy and the aim of governance. For Arendt, this is less the security of the juridical subject against violence than "the security which permits the undisturbed development of the life process of society as a whole" (Arendt 1968: 150). On their account, political modernity is not a domain of freedom, as Arendt imagined it was for the ancient Athenians, but is oriented toward the total administration of life processes for the sake of population security and health.[1]

Despite sharing what we might call this biopolitical account of modernity, Arendt and Foucault radically diverge in their analysis of how we might overcome the breach between freedom and politics. One of their key differences comes to light in their mutually incompatible reception of Roman Stoicism.[2] Drawing on Hellenistic philosophies, especially Roman Stoicism, Foucault argues that reconstituting their ethic of the self's relationship to itself "is an urgent, fundamental and politically indispensable task," if it is true that "there is no first or final point of resistance to political power other than in the relationship one has to oneself" (2005: 252).[3] Foucault claims that reconfiguring the ancient care of the self is somehow essential to contemporary political resistance. On the other hand, following Hegel, Arendt argues that, in response to the decline of political freedom in the late Roman Empire, the Roman Stoics invented the idea of absolute freedom within oneself and in doing so set the seal on what she sees as a strictly nonpolitical concept of freedom. Arendt therefore deplores Stoicism for legitimating the claim that freedom resides in the self's relationship to itself rather than in the political domain. If, as she maintains, Roman Stoics developed a "nonpolitical" concept of freedom, their philosophy is the very last place we should look to challenge biopolitics. On her analysis, this project requires restoring the political domain as a space of freedom, not fleeing inward to escape the total administration of life.

Yet, Foucault shows that ancient Stoic ethical practices did have recognizably political aims or effects: viz., the cultivation of civic virtue. As Diogenes Laertius puts it, "The Stoics say that the wise man will take part in politics, if nothing hinders him ... since ... he will restrain vice and promote virtue" (Laertius 1925: 7.121). We should not therefore consider its ethics of the care of the self as merely an anti-political flight from the world. At the same time, however, it remains the case that Foucault fails to demonstrate that these practices are among the indispensable means for motivating political resistance. Put simply, Stoic practices of the self exclusively aim at cultivating virtue (*aretē*), or rational self-sufficiency, not the desire to exercise political power.

I develop this argument first by examining Foucault's late "return" to the theme of self-cultivation and his attempt to differentiate the Hellenistic, and especially Stoic, ethics of the self from Platonic and Christian practices. In Section 2, I outline Arendt's Hegelian-inspired rejection of Stoicism as a flight from the political domain and Foucault's justifiable criticisms of this indictment of Stoic freedom as purely nonpolitical. In Section 3, I show how Foucault correctly challenges this Arendtian conception of Stoic ethics as a retreat from politics. In the final section, however, I suggest that while Foucault demonstrates that Stoic ethics is compatible with the cultivation of natural and civic virtues, he does not establish that it can facilitate political resistance, as he conceives it. Indeed, I argue in close that on closer examination the Stoic ideal of rational self-sufficiency is in fact antithetical to political resistance.

1. Foucault Return to the Subject

Let us first briefly consider Foucault's path toward his late interest in the ethics of the care of the self. In his 1971 essay, "Nietzsche, Genealogy and History," Foucault sketches the genealogical method he later applied in his ground-breaking and disconcerting critique of modern disciplinary power. Foucault explicitly acknowledges the Nietzschean aims and methods of his historical studies of modern institutions and practices:

> "If I wanted to be pretentious, I would use the term 'genealogy of morals' as the general title of what I am doing" (1980: 53). He also describes *Discipline and Punish* as a "genealogy of the 'modern soul' ... a soul born out of the methods of punishment, supervision and constraint." (1975: 29)

Many critics argue that Foucault's embrace of Nietzsche's genealogical method necessarily entailed an endorsement of one or another Nietzschean concept of liberation. Foucault founded his Nietzschean critique of modernity, so his critics assumed, on a Dionysian ideal of transgressive, excess expenditure (Bataille) or an elitist, experimentalist and socially indifferent aesthetic of self-fashioning (Baudelaire) (see Wolin 2006). Foucault's Nietzschean ethics, they argue, underpin his alleged rejection of the modern liberal state, liberal norms, and the modern disciplinary practices that he identifies as creating docile, self-disciplined, moralized subjects. Like Nietzsche, Foucault seems to object to modern power regimes because they create Nietzschean "last men" so thoroughly adapted to their environment that they are incapable of the untrammeled, excessive expenditure of force. While many of Foucault's critics shared his concern about the domination of instrumental rationality and its construction of a compulsive identity, they did not, as he seemed to, denounce subjectivity, the self's relation to itself, as a principle of domination. As Dews put it:

> There can be no doubt that the central intention of this form of genealogy, as it is developed in Foucault's work from *Madness and Civilization* to *History of Sexuality* is to dissolve the link—inherited by the Marxist tradition from German Idealism—between consciousness, self-reflection and freedom—and to deny that there is any progressive political potential in the ideal of the autonomous subject. (1987: 160)

It seemed clear to his critics that, as a Nietzschean genealogist, Foucault diagnosed the self-reflexive moral subject as a sick animal born of coercion and discipline, a symptom of nihilism and decadence.

Yet, of course, in his later works Foucault returns to the subject, reconsidering the self's relationship to itself in his work on the Greco-Roman philosophies and their arts of living. In his late works on ethics, Foucault recognizes that his earlier notion of the subject as a mere effect of power constituted one of the major deficiencies in his thinking, and it was precisely to the Hellenistic ethics of the self that he turned in thinking about an alternative to the juridical and disciplinary models of selfhood. Hellenistic ethics, he suggests, centers on the self's relationship to itself. Even if, as Veyne observes, Foucault thought it would be undesirable and impossible to resuscitate Greek ethics, he nonetheless

> considered one of its elements, namely the idea of a work of the self on the self, to be capable of reacquiring a contemporary meaning, in the manner of one of those pagan temple columns that are occasionally reutilized in more recent structures. We can guess at what might emerge from this diagnosis: the self, taking itself as a work to be accomplished, could sustain an ethics that is no longer supported by either tradition or reason; as an artist of itself, the self would enjoy that autonomy that modernity can no longer do without. (Veyne quoted in Davidson 2005: 128)

Foucault suggests that our skepticism about the Hellenistic ethical principles of "caring for oneself," "withdrawing into oneself," or "being in oneself as a fortress" derive from deeply entrenched contemporary prejudices. We refuse to give the Hellenistic ethics of the self-positive value, to make the injunctions to "exalt oneself," or "to devote oneself to oneself," the basis of a morality (2005: 13), he argues, partly because we assume that it necessarily constitutes a withdrawal of the individual from collective morality and worldly politics (2005: 13).

In the modern European philosophical tradition this prejudice stems from the eighteenth-century German philhellenic tradition, with its privileging of the Greek ideal over Latin Rome (Butler 1935 [2012]), which found its locus classicus in Hegel's characterization of Stoicism as a retreat inwards prompted by the alleged demise of the Greek *polis* (see Hegel 1977; Ure 2016). Foucault aims to free us from this prejudice and, in doing so, give positive value to the Hellenistic ethics of the care of the self. Against the entrenched view, Foucault aims to show that reconstituting the ethics of the care of the self is important to contemporary movements that seek to resist or reverse political power. Liberation movements, he suggests, suffer from the fact that they do not want to base themselves on religious beliefs, legal imperatives, or allegedly objective, scientific norms, yet they lack an alternative principle on which to base the elaboration of a new political ethics (Foucault 1984: 343). Foucault maintains that a reconstituted ethics of the care of the self might answer to this need.

His late lectures make it clear then that Foucault had too quickly been made the apologist of an aesthetics of existence or a morality that consisted in a call to systematic transgression. Indeed, his critics failed to heed Foucault's own explicit warnings against anachronistically treating the ancient care of the self as "a sort of moral dandyism," insisting that it was the basis for "extremely strict moralities" (Foucault 2005: 12–13; see also Hadot 1995: 206–13; Hadot 2011: 136; Agamben 2016; Gros 2005: 530; Sellars 2019).

In these late lectures, Foucault does not reject the principle of subjectivity or agency, but through a genealogy of ethics he seeks to identify alternatives to modern subjectivity. He came to see that, while Nietzsche's genealogy of morals and his own genealogy of the modern soul may have exposed the origins, limits and dangers of one particular model of the self's relationship to itself, it by no means exhausted our storehouse of ethical models of self-cultivation. In his late genealogy of ancient ethics Foucault discovers a whole range of alternative ethical relationships of self to self: "A treasury of devices, techniques, ideas and procedures, and so on, that cannot exactly be reactivated, but at least . . . constitute, a certain point of view, which can be a very useful tool for analyzing what's going on now" (Foucault 1984: 350).

Foucault especially focused his attention on the Hellenistic and Roman ethics of care of the self. The Hellenistic model of conversion and its spiritual exercises provided Foucault with a paradigm for his own conception of philosophy as an "*askesis* or an exercise of oneself in the activity of thought" (Bénatouïl 2016: 370). Foucault suggests that Hellenistic ethics formulates a singular model of the return or conversion to the self that distinguishes it from Platonic and Christian models of conversion: "The Hellenistic model, which I want to analyse was concealed historically and for later culture by two other great models: the Platonic and Christian models. What I would like to do is free it from these two models" (Foucault 2005: 254). As we shall see, in Foucault's Hellenistic-inspired ethics "salvation" or freedom resides not in transcendence to a higher reality through recollection (i.e., Platonic) or through a sacrificial break within the self (i.e., Christian), but in a conversion to the self that takes the form of complete self-sufficiency.

We can say then that Foucault's late genealogy of ethics charts the history of different models of ethics conceived of as practices of self-transformation or self-transfiguration; recovers the Hellenistic model of ethical self-transformation as a "counter-theme" that has been overshadowed by Platonic and Christian models; and importantly, in doing so suggests that this model has significance for contemporary political resistance. Is Foucault right to claim that the Hellenistic model of self-cultivation, or any reconstituted version of it, can facilitate, motivate, or ground political resistance? If critics of Foucault's Nietzschean genealogy of modern power worried that it lent itself to an unconditional, indiscriminate contempt for liberalism and the modern self-reflective subject, the worry regarding Foucault's attempt to reconstitute the Hellenistic ethics of the self lies in what we might conceive as its anti- or nonpolitical conception of freedom. We shall assess this criticism in detail below.

Before turning to Foucault's attempt to connect the ancient Hellenistic and Stoic ethics of the self with the question of politics, we first need to briefly sketch his account of the Hellenistic model. If, as he suggests, we should reconstitute or reinvent a singular, distinct Hellenistic model of the ethics of the self, rather than the other two fundamental forms of experience (the Platonic and Christian models), we need to know what are its essential or necessary elements. Any new, reconstituted version of Hellenistic ethics must share some significant resemblances with its original model. What then does Foucault identify as the essential or constitutive features of the Hellenistic model that must form part of any reconstituted model of the ethics of the self?

Foucault illuminates the singularity of the Hellenistic model by contrasting it with the Platonic and Christian models of self-cultivation. In the Hellenistic philosophies, he suggests, we find a whole array of images of the self turning round to itself: "We must apply ourselves to ourselves, that is to say, we must turn away from everything around us. We must turn away from everything that is not a part of ourselves . . . in order to turn round to the self" (Foucault 2005: 206). In these images of "turning around towards the self by turning away from what is external to us" Foucault identifies what he calls the "central nucleus" of the Hellenistic care of the self, *viz.* the notion of conversion (2005: 206–7). We can therefore clarify Foucault's account of the constitutive features of the Hellenistic model by examining the way he differentiates our fundamental models of conversion: Platonic, Hellenistic, and Christian.

Foucault distinguishes the Platonic and Hellenistic models in schematic fashion. First, whereas the Platonic conversion operates along the axis of transcendence, the Hellenistic conversion operates along the axis of immanence. That is to say, in the Platonic conversion the philosopher ascends beyond this world of appearances to a higher metaphysical reality. By contrast, the Hellenistic conversion does not take the form of an ascent beyond the world, it is a conversion that remains within the immanence of the world, insofar as it takes place through a move from what does not depend on us (external goods or fortune) to what does depend on us (virtue or reason). Second, Foucault suggests that whereas the Platonic conversion requires a radical break of the self with the body, the Hellenistic conversion is the achievement of harmony of the self with itself. Finally, he suggests that in the Platonic conversion the fundamental part of the conversion takes place though knowledge, or recollection of the forms, whereas in the Hellenistic conversion the essential element is much more askesis, exercise, and training rather than knowledge (2005: 210).

Foucault also suggests that in the Hellenistic and Roman culture of the self we discover completely difference processes at work from those in Christian conversion (Foucault 2005: 212). He claims that whereas the Christian conversion requires self-renunciation and rebirth in a new type of being, the Hellenistic conversion does not require a break within the self, but only a break with "what surrounds oneself so that it is no longer enslaved, dependent, and constrained" (2005: 212). In other words, the Hellenistic conversion frees the self from the external world, from the bonds of fortune, for the benefit of the self. "It is a break with everything around the self," as he puts it "for the benefit of the self, but not a break within the self" (2005: 213). The sole objective of the Hellenistic conversion is to return to the self as the only source of invulnerable sovereignty, as a fortress or citadel.

This Hellenistic model of conversion, he claims, develops a mode of knowing nature that makes knowledge an instrument of self-transformation. Foucault suggests that his Hellenistic mode of knowing nature transforms the self in particular ways. First, the Hellenistic mode of knowing of nature enables individuals to become autarkic (self-sufficient); second, it enables them "to take pride in what is their own and not what derives from circumstances . . . establishing a total, absolute, and limitless mastery over that which depends on oneself" (2005: 241). "It is a knowledge of nature, of *phusis* . . . that can transform the subject into a free subject who find within himself the possibility and the means of his permanent and perfect tranquil delight" (2005: 241).

Foucault identifies this modalization of knowledge for the sake of freedom and happiness with the spiritual exercise of the "view from above," "one of the most fundamental forms of spiritual existence found in Western culture" (Foucault 2005: 283; see also Hadot 1995: 238–50). "One of the most distinctive features of [the Hellenistic] care of the self," as Davidson notes, "is its indissociable link with this cosmic consciousness; one philosophical aim of this care of the self is to transform oneself so that one places oneself in the perspective of the cosmic Whole" (Davidson 2005: 129). Foucault takes this spiritual exercise as emblematic of the Hellenistic modalization of knowledge of nature for the sake of the self's conversion, its return to complete self-sovereignty. The view from above enables the Stoic to affirm the whole as the expression of Divine providence: "Understanding the rationality of the world in order to recognize . . . that the reason that presided over the organization of the world, and which is God's reason itself, is of the same kind as the reason we possess that enables us to know it" (Foucault 2005: 281).

Second, the view from above establishes a criterion of value that identifies the good with divine reason and thereby enables the Stoic to

> grasp the pettiness and the false and artificial character of everything that seemed good to us before we were freed. Wealth, pleasure glory: all these transitory events will take on their real proportions again when, through this stepping back, we reach the highest point. . . . Reaching the highest point . . . enables us to dismiss and exclude all false values and all the false dealings in which we are caught up, and to take the measure of this existence . . . and our smallness. (2005: 277)

Taken as a measure of our existence, this Hellenistic/Stoic view from above does two things: on the one hand, it reveals the divine reason of the whole and on the other it "punctualises ourselves in the general system of the universe" (2005: 278).

The upshot of the Stoic view from above is that the sage can affirm the rational necessity of the world; his sovereignty and self-mastery consist in affirming every event:

> What is great down here? It is raising one's soul above the threats and promises of fortune; it is seeing that we can expect nothing from it that is worthy of us. . . . What is great is a steadfast soul, serene in adversity, a soul that accepts every event as if it were desired. In fact, should we not know them if we know everything happens by God's decree? . . . What is great is having one's soul at one's lips, ready to depart; then one is not free by the laws of the city but by the laws of nature. (Foucault 2005: 265)

Hellenistic conversion requires dilating the self beyond itself, bringing about that cosmic consciousness in which one sees the human world "from above" (Davidson 2005: 135). The Hellenistic sage's internal freedom, as Davidson notes, is recognized by all the philosophical schools as the:

> Inexpungible core of the personality, which they located in the faculty of judgment, not in some psychologically thick form of introspection . . . . Internal freedom of judgment leads to *autarkeia*, self-sufficiency, which assures the sage *ataraxia*, tranquility of the soul. The dimension of interiority in ancient thought . . . is in service of a freedom to judge that will guarantee one the independence of wisdom. It is an internal life ultimately concentrated around the sage in oneself, therefore allowing the philosopher to separate himself from passions and desires that do not depend on him. (2006: 138–9)

We can identify the essential feature that Foucault claims distinguishes the Hellenistic model from Platonism and Christianity with what he calls its "self-finalization" thesis (2005: 206). Foucault argues that in the Hellenistic period the self gradually emerged as a "self-sufficient end"; the self, as he put it, became the "definitive and sole aim of the care of the self" (2005: 177). The Hellenistic ethical ideal is to achieve a certain relationship of the self to itself, a relationship of self-possession and self-delight. Its ethical *summum bonum* is just this relationship of self to self.

Foucault elaborates this Hellenistic ideal as a type of "salvation" (2005: 182). In the Hellenistic model, as he conceives it, salvation has a positive meaning: it is training oneself to achieve a continuous "sovereignty over the self" that has as its final aim and end rendering oneself:

> Inaccessible to misfortune, disorders, and all that external accidents may produce in the soul. . . . The two great themes of *ataraxy* (the absence of inner turmoil, the self-control that ensures that nothing disturbs one) and autarky (the self-sufficiency which ensures that one needs nothing but the self) are the two forms in which . . . the activity of salvation carried on throughout one's life, find their reward . . . in a certain relationship of the subject to himself when he has become inaccessible to external disorders and finds satisfaction in himself, needing nothing but himself. (Foucault 2005: 184)

In sum then, Foucault maintains that, in the Hellenistic and Roman philosophy conception of salvation, "the self is the agent, object and instrument, and end of salvation" (2005: 185). The ultimate reward of the Hellenistic care of the self is complete, untroubled self-sufficiency.

It is precisely after elaborating this Hellenistic model of conversion that Foucault maintains we urgently need to reconstitute it because, so he implies, there is "no first or final point of political resistance" (2005: 252), except in the relationship of the self to the self. Yet, as we have already observed, Foucault recognizes that by means of the Hellenistic conversion "one is not free by the laws of the city but by the laws of nature." In other words, he tacitly concedes that the Hellenistic ethics of the self may leave one enslaved by the laws of the city, yet free by the laws of nature. On this view, it seems that the freedom the Hellenistic philosopher aims to realize is not that of participating in political action or citizenship, but rather the philosophical or internal freedom achieved by ascending to a god-like view of nature. Let us briefly turn to this criticism of politics as an ethics of self by looking at Arendt's Hegelian-inspired critique of the Stoic and Hellenistic conception of freedom as nonpolitical.

2. Arendt: Stoicism as Political Retreat

Arendt maintains that Hellenistic ethics identified freedom exclusively with practices of the self that aim at inner sovereignty. Epictetus, she suggests, attempts to show that "man is free if he limits himself to what is in his power, if he does not reach into a realm [the political realm] where he is hindered. The art of living consists in knowing how to distinguish between an alien world over which man has no power and the self over which he may dispose of as he sees fit" (Arendt 1968: 147). According to the Hellenistic ethics of the self, therefore, one can be a slave in the world and yet still be free. "Stoicism" as she avers "rests on the illusion of freedom when one is enslaved" (Arendt 1958: 235). It is this sense, she argues, that Hellenistic ethics formulates a nonpolitical conception of freedom: it conceives freedom simply as a matter of the quality of the will, as the self exercising sovereignty over itself, and holds that this can be achieved in *any* political context or regime; inner freedom or self-sovereignty is independent of the political domain. Foucault himself acknowledges that from the Stoic principle that one must devote oneself to the god within each and every one of us, our divine reason, it follows that we need not concern ourselves with our social or political standing; these are extrinsic, accidents of our existence, not "authentic marks of a mode of being" (Foucault 1986: 93).

Arendt explains away this Stoic ethics as a symptom of the demise of political citizenship:

> It was originally the result of an estrangement from the world in which worldly experiences were transformed into experiences within one's own self . . . into an inwardness to which no other has access . . . inwardness as a place of absolute freedom within one's own self was discovered in late antiquity by those who had no place of their own in the world and hence lacked the worldly conditions which . . . [are] a prerequisite for [political] freedom. (1968: 145)

In the context of Roman Imperium, Arendt claims, Stoics, barred from exercising political freedom, transposed political relations into the relationship of self to itself (see Arendt 1968: 148). The ethics that Foucault draws from the Hellenistic schools seems to entail precisely this transposition of political liberty into the self's relationship to itself. "All the exercises," he explains, "tend to establish a stable and full relationship of the self to itself that can be thought . . . in the *juridico-political form* of full and entire ownership of the self . . . [Freedom] consists in the immanent and concentrated fulfilment of the self" (Foucault 2005: 533; italics added).

Arendt's fundamental complaint about this Hellenistic ethics of the self is that by identifying freedom with an inner quality of the will, a relationship of the self to itself, it necessarily divorces freedom from politics. Political freedom, she argues, is not an attribute or quality of the will, a matter of how the self relates to itself, but a matter of acting in the public domain or the space of appearances. Political action, she argues, therefore also necessarily entails a loss of sovereignty insofar as political agents can never control the meaning or consequences of their actions and are held to account for these uncontrollable outcomes. For Arendt, the Hellenistic ideal of uncompromising self-sufficiency and mastery is strictly nonpolitical because the political actor is necessarily non-sovereign. In the political domain, as she puts it, it is impossible to "safeguard one's sovereignty and integrity as a person" (Arendt 1958: 234).

Arendt argues that not only does Hellenistic ethics turn on a nonpolitical conception of freedom, it also maligns worldly, political action on the grounds that it necessarily jeopardizes this inner, nonpolitical freedom. Because it identifies freedom with the sovereign relationship of the self to itself, Arendt claims that Hellenistic ethics

> accuses [political] freedom of luring man into necessity ... condemns action, the spontaneous beginning of something new, because its results fall into a predetermined net of relationships, invariably dragging the agent with them. ... The only salvation from this kind of freedom seems to lie in non-acting, in abstention from the whole realm of human affairs. (1958: 243)

Arendt then identifies Hellenistic ethics with a nonpolitical conception of freedom that promotes abstention from the realm of human affairs and condemns the political domain as a threat to personal integrity or self-sufficiency. She therefore deplores Stoicism as one of the seminal philosophical and popular sources that legitimates the belief that freedom resides in the self's relationship to itself rather than in the political domain. Politics as an ethics of the self's relation to itself and the correlative notion that freedom resides in exercising power over oneself, she argues, derives from the loss of political freedom, accords absolute superiority to inner freedom, and condemns the political domain, as a "fallen" realm. Does Arendt's critique of Roman Stoicism expose the political limits of Foucault's recourse to this ethics of self-cultivation?

3. Foucault: Stoicism as Political Resistance

In *The Hermeneutics of the Subject*, Foucault addresses a version of this kind of Arendtian objection to Hellenistic ethics: "When salvation is thus defined as the objective of a relationship to self which finds its fulfilment in salvation—the idea of salvation as no more than the realization of the relationship to self—does this point become completely incompatible with the problem of the relationship to the Other?" (2005: 192) Are "the cathartic" (salvation of self) and "the political" (salvation of others), as he puts it, definitively separated?

Foucault, of course, answers this question in the negative. He suggests instead that Hellenistic ethics reverses the Platonic scheme: in the Platonic scheme, one cares about oneself in order to care about others; in the Hellenistic scheme one takes care of oneself "because you are the self, and simply for the self," and care for others comes about "as a supplementary benefit" or as the "correlative effect of the care you must take of yourself, of your will and application to achieve your own salvation" (2005: 192). According to Foucault, the aim of the Hellenistic care of the self is not therefore the removal of oneself from the world, but preparing oneself as a rational subject of action for events of the world.

Here Foucault properly qualifies Arendt's misleading assertion that in Hellenistic ethics salvation lies in nonaction or abstention from the political realm (see also Hadot 1995: 274). More accurately, as he observes, in this art of living, one's relationship to things, events, and the world is refracted through the principle of maintaining the relationship of sovereignty over oneself, of finding salvation in complete possession of oneself. "In the common Stoic attitude," Foucault suggests, "the care of the self, far from being experienced as the great alternative to political activity, was rather a regulating component of it" (2005: 543). Foucault suggests that the sovereign, free individual can act in the world to fulfill his natural duties as long as in doing so he/she maintains this relationship of self-possession or sovereignty.

Foucault elaborates the politics of the care of the self through a brief excursus of Seneca's preface to the fourth book of his *Natural Questions*. By "putting all the sovereignty he exercises . . . within himself, or more precisely, in a relationship of himself to himself," as Foucault explains Seneca's point, the Roman official or functionary "will be able to define and delimit the performance of his office to only those functions it has been assigned. . . . He can exercise his power as good functionary precisely on the basis of this relationship of self to self" (2005: 377–8). By contrast, Seneca claims that individuals who lack self-sufficiency, who seek to secure their value through external goods, are in danger of losing themselves "in the presumptuous delirium of power that exceeds its real functions" (377).

Foucault demonstrates then that the Hellenistic and Stoic "theme of the conversion to the self should not be interpreted as desertion of the domain of activity but rather as the pursuit of what makes it possible to maintain the relationship of self to self as the principle, as the rule of the relationship to things, events and the world" (Foucault 2005: 537–8). Yet, he does not show how any reconstitution of this Hellenistic ethical model might generate political resistance. The Roman official who finds in the principle of self-sufficiency the means of limiting himself to his official functions is hardly an example of political resistance, any more than Weber's ideal bureaucrat is a figure of political freedom. Foucault later slightly modifies his claim about this connection between the ethics of the self and political resistance, seeing the relationship of the self to the self as one among many "possible point[s] of resistance to political power—understood of course, as a state of domination" (1996: 448).

Foucault's qualification helpfully clarifies what he means by political resistance, but at the same deepens these doubts about whether Stoic self-cultivation is a means to achieve this end. Here he suggests that the relationship one has to oneself is a point of resistance not to political power as such, but rather to states of domination. Foucault simply asserts that power is a necessary fact of the world. "I do not think a society can exist without power relations," he remarks, "if by that one means the strategies by which individuals try to direct and control the conduct of others" (1996: 446). Foucault takes as an empirical fact a strategic interpretation of society as a domain of agonistic conflict against a communicative conception of society as oriented toward mutual consensus or recognition.[4] He conceives this agon in terms of a continuum stretching from total domination at one pole to an open-ended network of power at the other. He identifies political power as an open-ended strategic game between individual liberties who compete with one another to control each other's conduct. "Rather than speaking of an essential freedom," as he explains, "it would be better to speak of an 'agonism'—of a relationship that is at the same time reciprocal incitation and struggle, less of a face to face confrontation which paralyzes both sides than a permanent provocation" (Foucault 1982: 790).

A state of domination, by contrast, is a condition that eliminates these "games" of power and with them the possibility of reversals and transformations of who exercises power over whom. As Foucault explains, these are cases in which "power relations are fixed in such a way that they are perpetually asymmetrical and allow an extremely limited margin of freedom" (1996: 441). What distinguishes states of domination from games of power is not that in the former individuals have *no* ability to resist exercises of power, but that their resistance cannot reverse their situation. These individuals might evade some of its deleterious effects, but power relations are fixed such that they cannot overthrow the state of domination. In the context of domination, those subject to control and coercion can never themselves become agents of power capable of controlling or coercing those who exercise power over them. They are permanent victims, never agents.

Foucault then aims to identify practices of the self that allow citizens to play such games of power with as little domination as possible (Foucault 1996: 446). As he conceives them, games of power necessarily entail individuals imposing constraints on or exercising power over others. He wants to identify practices of the self that allow us to play such open-ended games of power. He acknowledges that this requires a revaluation of the "moral" fear of power. Foucault is impatient with this moral convention. He encourages a revaluation of this conventional valuation, partly on the basis of what is, or so he implies, a tacit, universal knowledge at odds with this moral convention. "Power" as he declares emphatically "is not evil. Power is games of strategy. *We all know that power is not evil!* . . . to wield power over the other in a sort of open-ended strategic game where the situation may be reversed is not evil" (1996: 447, emphasis added).

Foucault does not assert that wielding power over others is good. However, he does set out to discover or reconstitute practices of resistance to those forms of domination that significantly limit the scope of individuals' ability to engage in games of power. Foucault values practices of the self to the extent that they make it possible to expand the margin of freedom so that individuals can engage in such games. He does not object to asymmetrical power relations, but only to asymmetries that prevent the emergence of new asymmetries, or to power exercised in such a way as to prevent the play of power. Foucault's political goal then is to find ways to resist states of domination so that individuals can play strategic games "in which some try to control the conduct of others, who in turn try to avoid allowing their conduct to be controlled or try to control the conduct of others" (Foucault 1996: 447). He does not defend political resistance in the name of securing and protecting negative liberty, or freedom from external constraint, or expanding communicative action, but for the sake of sustaining conditions that allow individuals the freedom to play games of power in which they exercise or they have the potential to exercise power over others. The target of Foucauldian resistance is domination, not power.

Are Stoic or neo-Stoic ethical practices capable of cultivating citizens who resist domination for the sake of reclaiming the political domain as a continuous, open-ended agonistic competition for power? Is a reconfigured Stoic care of the self among those practices that are indispensable to such political resistance?

4. Stoicism as Civic Virtue

As we have seen, Foucault defines power as a network of asymmetrical relations that are permanently and necessarily open to reversals of fortune. In this agonistic conception of "the political," victims can always become agents and vice versa. Yet Stoic self-fashioning does not motivate individuals to engage in agonistic power relations in which they are vulnerable to all the turns of fortune's wheel; instead it enables them to perform their natural and public duties by making them indifferent to external goods and reversals of fortune. Its ethical aim is to create rational agents of action who perform these duties no matter what their circumstances. In this particular sense, as we have seen, Stoic self-cultivation does have specifically political effects. Ancient Stoics, as Foucault stresses, conceive their spiritual exercises as essential if individuals are to develop the virtues of good ethical agents. As Foucault puts it "The person who takes care of himself properly ... will at the same time know how to fulfil his duties as part of the human community" (1995: 197).

For the Stoics fulfilling our role as part of the human community requires that we can dispassionately perform our natural social duties. To impartially perform our natural duties, Stoics argue, we must not only know our duties, but we must free ourselves from the cognitive errors, or value errors that constitute the basis of our emotions, and that motivate us to pursue glory, power or wealth. The well-trained Stoic will not suffer from emotions like fear, grief or anger, which jeopardize their impartial performance of natural duties. Foucault shows, for example, that for Epictetus, complete sovereignty as a rational subject may in fact require and make it possible to "observe the order of natural and acquired relationships: those of son, brother, citizen, wife, neighbour, fellow-traveller, and subject and ruler" (*Diss*. 2.14.8; Foucault 1995: 197).

Foucault defends this claim by showing how Epictetus argues that the sovereign, rational self will both know what his natural duties to others are as a communal being and will also be able to exercise these duties because he is untroubled by the passions that lead him/her astray from rational judgments (Foucault 2005: 195–8). Parents who suffer distress at the sight of their sick child's suffering, Epictetus claims, will be incapable of performing their parental duties, whereas the father who exercises Stoic self-cultivation will perform his paternal duties undisturbed by the emotional tumult of fear (*Diss*. 1.II). Likewise, Seneca argues that Stoics who tranquilly affirm death will be able to perform their civic duties, including, for example, sacrificing themselves for their *patria*, while fearful citizens will abandon their natural civic duties (*Ep*. 36). Similarly, he argues that Stoics who judge slights and injuries as matters of indifference will be able to perform their natural civic duties, while angry leaders and citizens will exercise vengeance rather than respect natural law. Foucault notes in passing, the Stoic ethics of anger is located "precisely at the point of connection of self-control and command over others, of government of oneself and government of others" (2005: 374).⁵ Roman Stoics conceived the elimination of anger as a necessary condition of rational political leadership and inter-citizen relationships, and as a necessary political management of angry rulers and angry citizens. As Harris explains, "We can hardly doubt that the early Stoics, already saw that the elimination of *orgē* had political advantages. . . . But it was left to Seneca and Epictetus . . . to bring out the political benefits of this particular Stoic doctrine" (2001: 197). We might say then that the Roman Stoics conceived the care of the self as a necessary condition of civic life, insofar as it can protect the community from the violence of honor-fuelled *orgē*. However, specifying Stoicism as a political therapy of the passions in this way doesn't give any greater traction to Foucault's case that neo-Stoic practices might form the basis of meaningful contemporary political resistance.

We can therefore legitimately acknowledge Stoic practices of the self or "spiritual exercises" as useful for a range of ethical and political purposes, perhaps most noticeably as therapies that aim to cultivate the virtue of constancy or self-command necessary to impartially or "stoically" perform our natural social duties. It is precisely for this reason that early modern thinkers like Justus Lipsius reconfigured versions of the Stoic practices to cultivate virtuous citizens. As Veyne observes of Roman Stoicism, "We must not forget that 'doing politics' did not mean having principles and an opinion about politics or being an activist, as it does to us, but simply 'take part in the public functions of the city, the duty of every free man" (2003: 142). Foucault is right then that Stoic practices aim to cultivate citizens who can fulfill their natural social duties, but they by no means foster individuals willing and able to engage in agonistic competitions for power, glory, or distinction.

One obvious reason Stoicism is necessarily incompatible with this type of political resistance is that it conceives power as belonging among the indifferents when compared to virtue. Stoics aim to extirpate the passions that they claim derive from valuing external goods like power, wealth, and honor. Stoic ethics therefore aims to cultivate virtue, conceived as perfect self-sufficiency, not the desire to exercise power. Stoic practices do not aim to expand the margins of freedom so that individuals can engage in open-ended games of power, but to establish a self-mastery that enables stoics to perform their natural social duties. We can therefore understand Roman Stoicism's care of self as a political therapy that aims to extirpate the passions that it claims (rightly or wrongly) undermine civic virtue. Stoic or neo-Stoic self-mastery does not entail or promote exercising or seeking to exercise power over others.

Indeed, Stoic self-cultivation not only works directly against Foucault's revaluation of political power, and its definition of freedom as the liberty to exercise power over others in an open-ended network of power relations, it also fails to challenge political *domination*. We can see why this is the case by examining some examples of how Roman Stoics refracted their political actions and judgments through the principle of the care of the self. How does Stoic self-cultivation shape the stoic's political response to domination or tyranny?

For the Stoic states of domination do not in any way threaten individual virtue. Stoics judge the tyrant's exercise of power over their "external" goods, including political freedom, material possessions, even their life, as indifferent in contrast with their own sovereign reason. Stoic ethics seeks to transform individuals' judgment such that they can tranquilly accept conditions of domination. It does so by conceiving everything other than reason or virtue as a matter of indifference. Under conditions of domination or tyranny, Stoics remain unperturbed; their "resistance" consists in safeguarding their personal integrity, not in challenging domination.

Seneca, for example, analyzes and illustrates how the Stoic care of the self regulates its response to political domination. Seneca's case suggests that if Stoic virtue is the principle governing citizens' relationship to things, events, and the world, it necessarily mitigates against challenging tyranny. Seneca's articulation of the ethics-politics intersection shows that by making the principle of sovereignty or self-sufficiency the regulating component of political action Hellenistic ethics necessarily (a) gives priority to this inner freedom over political action that challenges political domination and (b) eschews resistance to political tyranny for the sake of maintaining inner purity or sovereignty.

In the *Letters*, for example, Seneca highlights the independence and priority of self-mastery over political freedom. Seneca advises Lucilius that for the sovereign self, losing political freedom, indeed losing any external goods, ought to be a matter of indifference:

> Stilbo after his country was captured and his children and his wife lost, as he emerged from the general desolation alone and yet happy spoke as follows to Demetrius, called the Sacker of Cities . . . in answer to the question whether he had lost anything: "I have all my goods with me!" There is a brave and stout-hearted man for you! Yes, he forced Demetrius to wonder whether he himself had conquered after all. "My goods are all with me!" In other words, he deemed nothing that might be taken from him to be a good. (*Ep.* 9.18-19)

In *On Anger*, Seneca analyzes the right Stoic response for individuals who suffer extreme domination at the hands of a political tyrant, taking the two similar cases of King Cambyses with Praexaspses and the Persian King with Harpagus. Praexaspses and Harpagus both mildly insult their King and in retaliation this tyrant murders their children in front of them. In such extreme cases of tyranny, Seneca indicates that it may be impossible to maintain equanimity or sovereignty, but rather than angrily resisting injustice, which necessarily entails losing oneself in the passion of anger, he advises the victim of injustice to take another course that does not jeopardize his sovereignty:

> To the man whose fortune it is to have a king who aims his arrows at the breasts of friends, and to the man whose ruler stuffs fathers with the guts of their children, I shall say: "Why are you moaning, madman? Why do you wait for some enemy to avenge you by the destruction of your nation, or a powerful king

to fly to your rescue from a distance? Wherever you look, there is an end to your troubles. Do you see that precipice? That way you can descend to liberty. Do you see that sea, that river, that well? Liberty sits there in the depths.... They are escape routes from slavery. Are the exits I show you too difficult, requiring too much courage and strength? Do you ask what is the straight road to liberty? Any vein in your body." (*De Ira.* 3.15)

Stoic freedom consists in preserving the sovereignty of one's reason or judgment, and the Stoic makes suicide the final point of resistance against political tyranny that threatens this sovereignty.[6] Under conditions of political tyranny, suicide is the ultimate road to such freedom.[7] In Isaiah Berlin's words, the "logical culmination of the process of destroying everything through which I can possibly be wounded is suicide" (1969: 164). As Veyne suggests, Seneca's defence of suicide as an act of liberty

> reveals Stoicism's profoundest truth, which is to see life from death's point of view and to make its followers live as though dead. Nothing is of significance but the disembedded self, just barely personal, whose existence can be snuffed out without disadvantage because this self is not waiting for anything ... Jean-Marie Guyau ... put it well: "Death, release from tension, the endless, aimless toil that is life, this is Stoicism's final word" (2003: 114).

In the words of the Delphic oracle, Stoicism requires citizens to "take on the colour of the dead" (Laertius 1925: 7.1).

To conclude, then, if the Roman Stoic care of the self entails any type of political action, it is only insofar as it cultivates a form of self-sufficiency that may make it possible for citizens to dispassionately perform their natural and civic duties. It does not value or facilitate the kind of agonistic political freedom that Foucault champions in opposition to freedom conceived as negative liberty or communicative action. It cultivates virtuous behavior on the part of citizens and officials rather than any broader sense of citizenship as engaged, sometimes critically and transformatively directed public action.

Notes

1 On Arendt and Foucault's different shadings of "biopolitics," see Dolan (2005) and Blencowe (2010).
2 On earlier Greek Stoicism's political theory, see Schofield (1999).
3 Foucault makes this claim about the desirability of reconfiguring ancient practices of the self at the heart of *The Hermeneutics of the Subject* 1981–2 lecture series. In these lectures, he primarily elaborates the late Roman Stoics' practices of the care of the self (see Elden 2016: 154).
4 Despite Foucault's skepticism about the possibility and desirability of realizing "communicative power," Allen argues that it potentially complements rather than contradicts his strategic conception of power (Allen 2002). Foucault himself identifies the

Arendtian communicative conception of power as "utopian" in the pejorative sense of the word, that is, he treats it as symptomatic of "a failure to see that power relations are not something bad in in itself, [something] that we have to break free of" (1996: 446).
5 Yet remarkably in the context of a study aimed at exploring the political significance of the Hellenistic model of conversion, Foucault makes almost no references to Seneca's *On Mercy* (55–56 CE) or *On Anger* (41 CE), one written as advice on leadership to the emperor Nero, the other as advice to his brother the Roman senator Novatus. It is noteworthy that Foucault does not analyze *On Anger* in particular because it elucidates how the Stoic should refract his political judgments and actions through the principle of the care of the self.
6 On the controversy over the Stoic and Senecan defence of suicide, see Rist (1969) Griffin (1986) and Englert (1990).
7 Lodge's frontispiece for his 1620 translation of Seneca's moral works visually represents Stoic constancy in the face of tyranny. Skinner observes of Lodge's engraving "Stoic constancy is shown to triumph over tyranny only through a willingness to embrace death" (2018: 227).

Bibliography

Agamben, G. (1998), *Homo Sacer: Sovereign Power and Bare Life*, trans. Daniel Heller-Roazen, Redwood City: Stanford University Press.

Agamben, G. (2016), *The Use of Bodies: Homo Sacer IV, 2*, trans. A. Kotsko, Stanford: Stanford University Press.

Allen, A. A. (2002), "Subjectivity, and Agency: Between Arendt and Foucault," *International Journal of Philosophical Studies* 10 (2): 131–49.

Arendt, H. (1958), *The Human Condition*, Chicago and London: University of Chicago Press.

Arendt, H. (1968), "What Is Freedom?," in *Between Past and Future: Eight Exercises in Political Thought*, 143–72, New York: Viking Press.

Bénatouïl, T. (2016), "Stoicism and Twentieth Century French Philosophy," in J. Sellars (ed.), *Routledge Handbook of Stoicism*, London and New York: Routledge.

Berlin, I. (1969), *Four Essays on Liberty*, Oxford: Oxford University Press.

Blencowe, C. (2010), "Foucault's and Arendt's 'Insider View' of Biopolitics: A Critique of Agamben," *History of the Human Sciences* 23 (5): 113–30.

Butler, E. M. (1935/2012), *The Tyranny of Greece over Germany*, Cambridge: Cambridge University Press.

Davidson, A. I. (2005), "Ethics as Ascetics: Foucault, the History of Ethics, and Ancient Thought," in G. Gutting (ed.), *The Cambridge Companion to Foucault*, 115–40, Cambridge: Cambridge University Press.

Dews, P. (1987), *Logics of Disintegration: Post-Structuralism and the Claims of Critical Theory*, London: Verso.

Dolan, F. M. (2005), "The Paradoxical Liberty of Bio-Power Hannah Arendt and Michel Foucault on Modern Politics," *Philosophy and Social Criticism* 31 (3): 369–80.

Elden, S. (2016), *Foucault's Last Decade*, Cambridge: Polity.

Englert, W. (December 1990), "Seneca and the Stoic View of Suicide," *The Society for Ancient Greek Philosophy Newsletter*, 184. https://orb.binghamton.edu/cgi/viewcontent.cgi?article=1183&context=sagp.

Epictetus (1995), *The Discourses*, ed. C. Gill, trans. R. Hard, London: J.M. Dent.
Foucault, M. (1971), "Nietzsche, Genealogy, History," in J. Faubion (ed.), *The Essential Works of Michel Foucault Vol. 2, Aesthetics, Method and Epistemology*, 369–92, New York: The New Press.
Foucault, M. (1975), *Discipline and Punish: The Birth of the Prison* [DP], trans. A. Sheridan, New York: Vintage Books.
Foucault, M. (1980), "Prison Talk," in C. Gordon (ed.) and C. Gordon, L. Marshall, J. Mepham and K. Soper (trans.), *Power-Knowledge: Selected Interviews and Other Writings 1972-1977*, 37–55, New York: Pantheon Books.
Foucault, M. (1982), "The Subject and Power," *Critical Inquiry* 8 (4): 777–95.
Foucault, M. (1984), "On the Genealogy of Ethics: An Overview of Work in Progress," in P. Rabinow (ed.), *The Foucault Reader*, 340–72, London: Penguin Books.
Foucault, M. (1986), *The Care of the Self*, trans. R. Hurley, New York: Pantheon Books.
Foucault, M. (1996), "The Ethics of the Concern for the Self," in L. Hochroth and J. Johnston (eds.), *Foucault Live (Interviews 1961–1984)*, trans. S. Lotringer, 432–49, New York: Semiotext(e).
Foucault, M. (2005), *The Hermeneutics of the Subject: Lectures as the Collège de France 1981-1982*, ed. F. Gros and trans. G. Burchell, New York: Palgrave MacMillan.
Griffin, M. (1986), "Philosophy, Cato, and Roman Suicide: I and II," *Greece and Rome* 33: 64–77, 192–202.
Hadot, P. (1995), *Philosophy as a Way of Life: Spiritual Exercises from Socrates to Foucault*, ed. A. I. Davidson, trans. M. Chase, Malden: Blackwell.
Hadot, P. (2011), *The Present Alone Is Our Happiness: Conversations with Jeannie Carlier & Arnold I. Davidson*, trans. M. Djaballah and M. Chase, Stanford: Stanford University Press.
Harris, W. (2001), *Restraining Rage: The Ideology of Anger Control in Classical Antiquity*, Cambridge, MA: Harvard University Press.
Hegel, G. W. F. (1977), *Phenomenology of Spirit*, trans. A. V. Miller, Oxford: Oxford University Press.
Laertius, D. (1925), *Lives of Eminent Philosophers*, Vol. 1, trans. R. D. Hicks, Cambridge, MA: Harvard University Press.
Rist, J. M. (1969), *Stoic Philosophy*, Cambridge: Cambridge University Press.
Schofield, M. (1999), *The Stoic Idea of the City*, Chicago and London: The University of Chicago Press.
Sellars, J. (2019), "Self or Cosmos: Foucault versus Hadot," in M. Faustino and G. Ferraro (eds.), *The Late Foucault*, London: Bloomsbury.
Seneca, L. A. (2001), *Epistles*, trans. R. Gummere, Cambridge, MA: Harvard University Press.
Skinner, Q. (2018), *From Humanism to Hobbes: Studies in Rhetoric and Politics*, Cambridge: Cambridge University Press.
Ucnik, L. (2018), "Ethics, Politics and the Transformative Possibilities of the Self in Hannah Arendt and Michel Foucault," *Philosophy and Social Criticism* 44 (2): 200–25.
Ure, M. (2016), "Stoicism in Nineteenth Century German Philosophy," in J. Sellars (ed.), *Routledge Handbook of Stoicism*, 287–302, London and New York: Routledge.
Veyne, P. (2003), *Seneca: The Life of a Stoic*, trans. D. Sullivan, New York: Routledge.
Wolin, R. (2006), *The Frankfurt School Revisited*, New York: Routledge.

Chapter 10

STOICISM, AMBIGUITY, AND THE DECISION OF SENSE

Barbara Cassin, trans. by Steven Corcoran and Kurt Lampe, with an Introduction by Kurt Lampe

1 Introduction

Barbara Cassin is both a classical philologist and an influential philosopher, several of whose books have reached Anglophone readers in the last five years (2014, 2016, 2018). Still untranslated is *L'Effet sophistique* (1995), from which the following excerpt has been taken. The book's title implies two claims: first, the paradigm of speech we call "sophistic" is an "effect" of the conceptualization of "philosophy," which projects sophistics as one of its negatives. Second, inasmuch as many thinkers actually do speak in this manner, they continue to have an "effect" on philosophy (1995: 7–11, 2014: 28–31). Fundamentally, this effect is to challenge mainstream understandings of how thinking, speaking, and beings should be related to one another. Challenging these normative understandings has political effects, not only because speech is the medium of political action but also because modes of speech are distributed unevenly across genders and sociopolitical categories. The project of *L'Effet sophistique* is to cultivate these effects by analysis of the works of ancient authors usually marginalized in the history of philosophy, such as Gorgias, Antiphon, Aelius Aristides, Galen, Philostratus, and Lucian. Cassin reads these "sophists" alongside canonical ancient philosophers such as Parmenides and Aristotle, as well as an array of modern authors, from Hannah Arendt to Karl-Otto Appel. Most of the arguments developed in *L'Effet* (693pp.) appear in the articles collected as *Sophistical Practice* (370pp.), but without the same systematicity, breadth, and philological detail.

Among the omissions is Cassin's detailed analysis of Galen's *On Linguistic Sophisms*,[1] which adapts Aristotle's *Sophistical Refutations* in order to incorporate and domesticate the Stoic theory of ambiguity (1995: 365–86). Before this, Cassin has emphasized that Aristotle's construction of sophistics[2] revolves around what she calls "the demand for meaning" or "the demand for sense" (*l'exigence de la signification*, *l'exigence du sens*, 1995: 12, 57, 334–5, 386), of which the classic exposition is *Metaphysics* Γ 4-5 (on which see also Cassin and Narcy 1989). Cassin formulates this demand as follows: to speak at all (*legein ti*) necessarily involves signifying or meaning something (*sēmainein ti*), one and the same thing (*to hen*, *to auto*), for yourself and for the other (*hautōi kai allōi*) (1995: 54–8, 334–5). Often a supplement is added: while the "demand for sense" permits meaning without reference, speaking normally aims to signify meanings adequate to beings (1995: 41–54, 104–17, 333–4). *Sophistical Refutations* focuses on regulating the relationship between signifier and meaning in order to reduce equivocation or "homonymy" (*homonumia*, 1995: 342–57). However, Aristotle recognizes that "sophistical" arguments may also play on the relationship between spoken language and signifiers. For instance, the spoken phrase "seeing someone struck with your eyes" signifies differently if expressed "seeing someone struck [pause] with your eyes" or "seeing someone [pause] struck with your eyes" (1995: 363, citing *Soph. Ref.* 177b10–12).[3]

In the excerpt translated below, Cassin argues that precisely this free play between vocalization and signification is highlighted by Stoic philosophy of language, since the Stoics analyze the logic of incorporeal "sayables" and the physics of vocal sounds independently. This makes it possible to acknowledge that what sutures sound, signifier, and meaning is "speech acts" (cf. Cassin 2014: 191–221). It is therefore unsurprising that for Chrysippus, the greatest Stoic authority, "every word is ambiguous [*ambiguum*] by nature" (LS 37N). Cassin suggests that the Stoics have little interest in eliminating homonymy and ambiguity (*amphibolia*), or more generally in excluding sophistics; in fact, they sometimes employ it themselves.[4] Galen's *On Linguistic Sophisms* develops refutations for the types of ambiguity theorized by the Stoics, but only by ignoring their theories of language and excluding the tonal and rhythmic dimensions of speech.

We have included this excerpt from *L'Effet sophistique* because it addresses themes that concern both historians of ancient philosophy and contemporary continental philosophers. Moreover, it does so in a manner that is philologically rigorous and well informed by scholarship. With regard to ancient philosophy, Cassin's emphasis on the sonorous and temporal dimensions of speech could contribute to the elucidation and evaluation of how the Stoics interrelate bodies in the world, rational impressions in the mind, incorporeal sayables, and spoken expressions of those sayables (Atherton 1993: esp. 250–67, 457–70; Gourinat 2000: 168–71). In fact, Cassin's approach to this issue was foreshadowed already in Émile Bréhier's seminal study, *La théorie des incorporels dans l'ancien stoïcisme* (orig. 1908, 3rd ed. 1962). Speaking of the doctrine of sayables, Bréhier asserts,

> This theory suppresses any intrinsic relation between the word and the thing. This is undoubtedly the root of Chrysippus' views on ambiguity. The effect of this theory is that the link between language and thought becomes so loose that a single word can designate a plurality of things. (1962: 15)

Although Cassin does not cite Bréhier, his influence is present in Deleuze's reading of Stoicism,[5] to which she acknowledges her indebtedness.

Deleuze's *Logic of Sense* is a good starting point for thinking about the significance of Cassin's reading for continental philosophy. Deleuze uses the Stoics' examples of speech without meaning, "*blituri*" and "*skindapsos*," to exemplify his theory of the "aleatory instance" that bestows sense on both the language and the world (1990: esp. 36–41, 42–7, 66–73 [Sixth, Seventh, and Eleventh Series]). Let me give a very concise example, starting from the premise that I am composing this paragraph in a cafe. Suppose that a customer looking for a seat were to interrupt me and ask, "What are you *doing* with that laptop?" I might answer, "I'm, uh, you know," my mind racing to coordinate this person's tone of voice (more or less indignant?), my own feelings (more or less apologetic?), the situation in the cafe (more or less busy?), my relationship to the business (more or less valued by the management?), and so on. Here "uh" is a "floating signifier" that holds the place for my chain of signifiers, while "you know" is a "floating signified" that holds a place for the statement that chain will articulate. Both await the "aleatory instance" through which my welter of considerations will snap into a meaningful pattern: "I was just leaving" or "That's none of your business, thank you!" It is in this sense that, as Cassin quotes below, Deleuze says that *blituri* is a floating signifier, "word = x," while *skindapsos* is a "floating signified," "thing = x." Cassin appropriates this Deleuzean reading in order to underline the consequences of what she calls "the word's physical thickness" in Stoic thinking about ambiguity, which remains stable across homonymies, autonymy, and phonematic composition and division. This destabilizes the chain of consistent and stable correlations Aristotle "demands" from speakers (speaking-signifying-communicating-denoting). We must start instead from the dynamic independence of speech's many dimensions, which crystallize as manifestations of personhood, significations of meaning, illocutionary acts, and designations (or rather creations) of a world only through total speech acts.[6]

Cassin's recuperation of Stoic philosophy of language thus bears comparison with several others in this volume. See especially Nicoletta di Vita's synthesis and critical discussion of Giorgio Agamben's various discussions of the Stoic "sayable," and Kurt Lampe's explanation, evaluation, and re-application of Julia Kristeva's critique of the ethics of Stoic judgment. Both of these concern many of the same Stoic doctrines to which Cassin refers, and address similar modern philosophical themes.

B. Excerpt from Barbara Cassin's L'Effet sophistique: Stoicism, Ambiguity, and the Decision of Sense

Galen's scrupulous operation is of a scope that we have not ceased to measure. He not only recuperates the signifying edge of Aristotelian *lexis*, but Aristotelianizes all Stoic lines of deviation.

The Stoics are assuredly, as are we all, Aristotelian, that is to say non-Parmenidean (non-sophistic, non-Antisthenian, in sum, non-pre-Socratic), inasmuch as they distinguish the dimension of meaning that blocks the ontological fusing of being and saying. But their phenomenology, which is to say both the physics of the world they perceive and the logic serving to describe it, is non-Aristotelian. For them, it is the logos that bears sense and not the word, because, or in the same way as, what is primarily at issue are not substance-subjects to which predicates belong, in keeping with some truth/falsity distinction founded for eternity, but actions and events of such nature that there is no truth outside a situation.[7]

Reading the great accounts of their logic, in particular Sextus Empiricus and Diocles's report that Diogenes Laërtius includes in the life of Zeno, one is quickly persuaded that, on the basis of this other understanding of discursivity and in the wake of the Megarian School, the Stoics are far better equipped than Aristotle to reflect on the signifier; that they are interested in it as a dimension with its own laws, a dimension susceptible to being subjugated but not reduced; and that they dispense, by the same token, with all anti-sophistical concern, unless it is to make sophistic *hubris* serve their own ends. This is what Galen cannot tolerate: his treatise is also obviously guilty of doxographic manipulation (cf. Baratin and Desbordes 1981: 27).

To start with, the Stoics were the first, we know, to give a terminological usage to the very word *sēmainon*, "signifier": the signifier is the *phōnē*, the sounds of the voice that one emits and one hears, in their bodily materiality, for example the sound *Dion*. This *phōnē* "shows a signified," *sēmainomenon*, which Sextus Empiricus (8.11f.)[8] describes as "the very thing [*auto to pragma*, well rendered as "content of thought" to avoid confusion with objects of the world[9]] we grasp in place of the sound when it presents itself to our mind along with that sound, but which foreigners do not understand even though they hear the sounds of the voice." It is in this "thing signified" (*to sēmainomenon pragma*), which is not a body but an "incorporeal" (*asōmaton*), for which the name "sayable" (*lekton*) is also coined, that the dimension of the true and the false is situated. Lastly, signifier and signified are tied to a "referent," *tugkhanon*, which is nothing other than the object, the external substrate, obviously corporeal, which corresponds to the word (*to ektos hupokeimenon*): in this instance, "Dion himself."

To clarify what signifier means here, we ought, whatever the risk, to proceed via a comparison with Aristotle, on the one hand, and with Saussure, on the other. For us moderns, the idea that a "sign" is composed of a "signifier" and a "signified" is something we think we owe to Saussure, but that Jakobson, for example, attributes to the Stoics.[10] Let us look at Saussure. To start with, he says, "The linguistic sign unites not a thing and a name, but a concept and a sound-image" (2011: 66); that is, the relationship of designation between language and world, or, more finely, between the sign and the *tugkhanon*, is not to be mistaken for the relationship of meaning, which is internal to the sign—a line thus stretches from Aristotle to the Stoics and to Saussure. Saussure continues: "I propose to [. . .] replace *concept* and *sound-image* respectively by *signified* and *signifier*; the last two terms have the advantage of indicating the oppositions that separates them from each other and from the whole of which they are parts" (2011: 67). This pair of terms is Stoic, but the way they are paired is rather less so. Since the first Stoic observation is that it is possible to have some signifier without signified (for those who do not "understand a language"), where the linguistic entity that Saussure considers exists only as two-in-one (as a "chemical compound" made of signifier and signified, in the image of water made of oxygen and hydrogen

[2011: 103], recto of thought-verso of sound to be cut from the sheet of paper that is language [2011: 113]). This brings us to another difference: the Saussurian signifier and signified are homogeneous, both are "psychological"—Saussure carefully clarifies that with the signifier it is not a matter of "a material sound, a purely physical thing," but of the "psychological imprint of this sound," also present in the inner speech that we undertake, "without moving either our lips or our tongue" (2011: 66). So much so, moreover, that Saussure can characterize the signifier (understood, it is true, as value and as difference, thus opening onto a comparative systematics foreign to simple signification) as an incorporeal: "In its essence, the linguistic signifier is by no means phonic; it is incorporeal—constituted not by its material substance but uniquely by the differences that separates its sound-image from all others" (2011: 118–19, trans. modified). On the contrary, the Stoic signifier and signified are heterogeneous: the first, in contrast with the signifier in Saussure, is a body, whereas the second is a thought-content, which, depending upon the point of view, is more or less incorporeal or embodied (the *semainomenon* properly speaking designates a thought-content embodied in a signifier, but it is an incorporeal *lekton* insofar as it is only virtually stated, and a *pragma* independently of all embodiment [Baratin and Desbordes 1981: 31]). The Stoic connection between signifier and signified is thus thoroughly dynamic, linked not to an abstract conception of language, but to the event of speech acts which incorporate utterables, to such an extent that each of the two series, signifiers and signifieds alike, has its degrees and its autonomy.

What is established in this gap is not only, as we've seen, the plurality of languages (that which barbarians do not understand when they hear Greek) but also the plurality of persons (that which I do not understand, or not as you've said it, when I hear you speak—the incommunicability of the *Treatise of Non-Being*[11]). The gap is even a natural and regular source of homonymy: Chrysippus, reports Aulus Gellius, says that "every word is by nature ambiguous, since one and the same word can be understood in two or more ways."[12] But we ought not to say, along with Diodorus, who Aulus Gellius cites by way of contrast, that what is involved here is "obscurity rather than ambiguity" (*obscure magis [. . .] quam ambigue*), that the signifier is clumsily chosen and lends to confusion that could be avoided with a clearer style. Since ambiguity does not stem from the choice of signifier relative to the signified, it is inherent to the signifier itself, to its physics.

1 The Stoic lexis

This emphasis is necessary in order to understand the classical, and indeed proverbial, example of Stoic ambiguity (*AULĒTRIS PEPTŌKE*), which Galen appropriates, as well as the Stoic classification of signifiers.

The definition of ambiguity comes in, in Diogenes's presentation of dialectic, at the end of the part "on signifiers" (*peri sēmainonta*, 7.62), right before the part on "signifieds" (*pragmata* ou *sēmainomena*, that is to say incomplete *lekta*—"predicates"—or complete *lekta*—"assertions," "arguments," 7.62-3):

> Ambiguity is a *lexis* [a signifier] that signifies, in plain language, in the proper sense, and in the same usage, two or even more *pragmata* [signifieds], so that the several *pragmata* are understood simultaneously in relation to this *lexis*; for example, AULĒTRIS PEPTŌKE: for, by it are indicated both something like this, "a court has fallen three times" (*aulē tris peptōke*) and something like this, "a flute-girl has fallen" (*aulētris peptōke*). (7.62)[13]

We see that an ambiguity is defined first as a *lexis*. Now, the preceding passage very strictly defines the term *lexis* itself, and this definition changes everything in relation to Aristotle's usage of *lexis* as well as that of Galen, and in relation to homonymy. The Stoic *lexis* is effectively the second of the three stages of the signifier, stages which are also three points of view on it. The first stage is *phōnē*: this is at once a generic term, since the study of the signifier is carried out in *Peri phōnēs* treatises, and the base-level signifier, namely the signifier as physical: air impacted through the effect of an animal impulse (*hormē*) or a human reflection (*dianoia*), which goes from emitter to receiver. Thus specified, *phōnē* as such is not articulate (it may be animal, it is an *ēkhos*, an unwritten "noise," DL 7.57[14]) and even less so a bearer of meaning. Then comes *lexis*, which is a *phōnē eggrammatos*, an "inscribable signifer," one might say, and the "letters" (*stoikheia*) that compose it are a guarantee of articulation: for example, *hēmera*, "day." While *lexis* is the properly human level, it is quite remarkably defined as not necessarily bearing meaning. For it is alone the *logos*, final stage of the "vocal sound endowed with sense impelled by a reflection" (*phōnē sēmantikē apo dianoias ekpempomenē*, DL 7.56), that comprises all three at once: voice, articulate, and bearing meaning—for example, *hēmera esti*, the statement of a phrase which thus implies, by means of its conjugation, something like an event, "it is day." Nothing could be clearer than the final summary: "*Phōnē* differs from *lexis* in that *phōnē* may be a noise, whereas *lexis* is always something articulated. *Lexis* differs from *logos*, because *logos* always has sense (*aei sēmantikos*), whereas *lexis* can be void of sense (*kai asēmos*), for example '*blituri*,' but *logos* never"(57).[15] This can be figured as follows:[16]

This sequence demands several remarks. First, in relation to Aristotle, Claude Imbert notes that "the Stoic terms seem to have been purposefully chosen to contradict Aristotelian semantics" (1978: 247 n. 35): it is no longer the word as such, name or verb, that constitutes the signifying unit, as is the case at the beginning of *On Interpretation*, but the statement—this is, manifestly, a wholly other "phenomeno-logy."

The gap also bears on *lexis*. First, Stoic *phōnē* is not Aristotelian *phōnē*. In his treatise *On the Soul*, Aristotle defines *phōnē* as "the kind of sound" (*psophos*) produced by an animate being (2.8 420b5; cf. *History of Animals* 1.1 and 4.9): this "noise" applies to animal as well as to man, and the definition goes from noise to voice via a certain number of physical dichotomies, each determining a class of exclusions (a sound of that which has a soul—not flutes; produced by a movement of the air inside—not fish but dolphins; striking the windpipe—not a cough). This definition seems initially compatible with the Stoic definition until it intersects with another kind of prerequisite, presented as self-evident by means of a simple

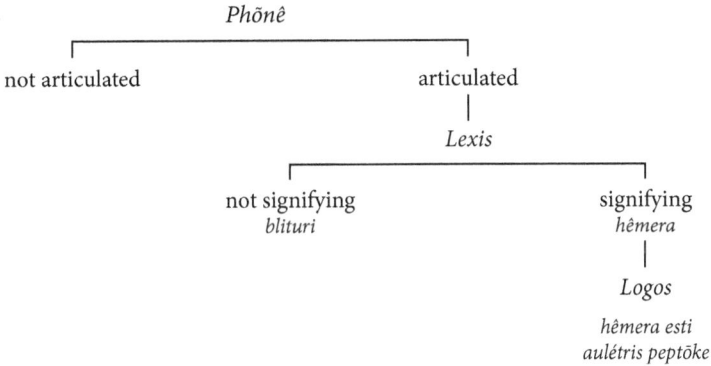

Figure 10.1 *Phōnē*, *Lexis*, and *Logos*.

"and," which I underscore for emphasis: "Not all sound emitted by an animal is a voice, as we have said (since we can make a noise with our tongue or by coughing), but what strikes must be animate and accompanied by a certain representation (*meta phantasias tinos*), since voice is of course a semantic noise (*sēmantikos gar de tis psophos estin hē phōnē*, 420b29-33)." Voice in Aristotle is a species of noise that already involves articulation (it is said to be *dialekton*, bl8, with the same property of articulation as the Stoic *lexis*) and meaning (it is said to be *hermeneia*, b19f., this time with the same property, namely meaning, as their *logos*). So the three levels that the Stoics keep distinct are collapsed here, three levels that in Aristotle gravitate toward, so to speak, this last one, the "end" and the "good," which, beyond animal impulse, constitutes sense for man: "A living being has . . . hearing so that something may be signified to him, and a tongue so that something may be signified to someone else" (435b19-25, and this is the end of the treatise). It might be said that all the Stoics did was to move Aristotle's sequence forward a notch, by naming *phōnē*, vocal sound, what he had chosen to call *psophos*, sound. What this implies, however, is a shift in the very direction of the hierarchies: the important thing is no longer to get as quickly as possible to the point that noise is endowed with sense, but to consider noise itself independently of sense. If the Aristotelian *lexis* is primarily a tool of analysis, as is straightaway implied by the definition of homonymy itself in a relation to the signified,[17] the Stoic *logos* is conceived, by contrast, in terms of the category of the signifier, as a perfected restriction of *lexis*.

2 Blituri *against* tragelaphos

Thus, for the Stoics, "day" and "*blituri*" comprise two examples of *lexis*: one signifies, yet it does so incompletely, while the other has no sense. The one *lexis* is seen to have no sense not because it has an excess of it (in short, homonymy), but because as *lexis* it has the right not to have one—that is the first major novelty: for Aristotle there can be no *blituri*. Truth be told, neither can there be any for Galen. Contrary to the other doxographers, for Galen, it is wrong to consider *blituri* as "absolutely void of sense."[18]

"Why deliberately babble!" he exclaims. In fact, *blituri* designates a sonorous plucking (*De Differentia pulsuum*, 111.4 [= SVF 11.149]).[19] *Blituri* is an onomatopeia that imitates the sound of the harp, the zither or the lyre: depending on the status of the signifier, it is thus either the Stoic paradigm of sound void of sense or the Peripatetic example of the range of sense extending even to music. According to Galen, as well as Sextus and some others, there is another *lexis* void of sense which the Stoics customarily associate with *blituri*, namely *skindapsos*.[20] Now, Galen immediately stipulates that "it is not only the name of a servant, but also that of a musical instrument (*organou tinos*)." It is exotic, insofar as it lacks a known etymology, but it has four strings, is utilized by women, and is akin to a lyre (a "banjo," as it is translated in Timon, as cited by Diogenes Laertius, 7.15). Let us add, however, that this inanimate organon, the *skindapsos*, is also the name of a plant similar to ivy (Clitarchus), of a bird from the Indies (in Hesychius), and that having run through all the species of living beings down to the slave, it ends up meaning "gadget," "thingy," "thing," "what d'ye call it," "so and so" (Artemidorus, 4.2).[21] It fell to Deleuze to interpret the difference between sound and instrument in the light of structure and of what Lévi-Strauss says about *mana*. I cite Deleuze citing Lévi-Strauss:

> Let us return to Lévi-Strauss' paradox: two series being given, signifying and signified, there is a natural excess of the signifying series and a natural lack of the signified series. There is, necessarily, a "floating signifier," which is the servitude of all finite thought, but also the promise of all art, all poetry, all mythic and aesthetic invention." We would like to add that it is the promise of all revolutions. And then there is on the other side a kind of *floated signified*, given by the signifier "without being thereby assigned or realized. Lévi-Strauss propose to interpret in this way the words "gadget" or "whatnot," "something," "*aliquid*," but also the famous "*mana*" (or yet again "*it*" [ça]). This is a value "in itself void of sense and thus susceptible of taking on any sense, whose unique function would be to fill the gap between signifier and signified." (1990: 49–50, 66)

The Stoics thus have a name for the floating signifier, which enables the series to function, *blituri*, and a name for the floated signified, which enables (etc.), *skindapsos*—the whole making it possible for the structure to function, that is to be a structure. "Since Blituri was a Skindapsos, you see. Word = x in a series, but at the same time thing = x in the other series."

Once more, the difference with Aristotle is crystal clear. Instead of *blituri*/*skindapsos*, we have *tragelaphos*, the goat-deer that does not exist but "signifies something":[22] not a signifier on its own, and no more a floating signifier than a floating signified, but rather an always exemplary relation of meaning between signifier and signified under the law of sense, a relation quite simply endowed with some sense without reference. But by no means does this prevent the sense from being—on the simple statement of the word—transparent and eminently figurable: one can draw a goat-deer in a plainer, and even more unigraphic, way than a chimera; whereas a *skindapsos* is not so easily drawn. As for *blituri*, don't even think about it.

3 The Reduction of the Signifier in Stoic Ambuigity

Just as Galen indignantly Aristotelianizes *blituri*, so too does he Aristotelianize Stoic ambiguity. I am probably not—no more than other interpreters who essentially paraphrase or promise—able to understand the internal economy of Stoic classification such as Galen reports it, even on comparing it, like Ebbesen, with the very similar classification that Theon put forward, probably around the first or second century CE.[23] But through and thanks to Galen, it is at least possible to read certain points of anti-Aristotelian violence, all of which pertain, in one way or another, to the weight of the signifier in *lexis*.

The first is tied to combination-division: it will be recalled that one of the Aristotelian examples (which is less anodyne that it appears, since one of the possible senses is to all appearances a nonsense) is *Pentēkont' andrōn hekaton lipe dios Akilleus*. ("Noble Achilles left fifty of a hundred men/a hundred of fifty men," Ar. *Sophistical Refutations* 166a.[24]) This example, which the Stoics also include under their seventh kind of ambiguity, is "one that fails to make plain which signifying part to construe with which other" (*ti meta tinos tetaktai sēmantikon morion*, Galen, *On Sophisms Connected to Expression*. 4 [Edlow: 108][25]). It effectively refers to a problem of construal, as another example given by Theon attests, in which one is uncertain concerning the antecedent of a relative pronoun. But the Stoics, precisely, do not give this example for what they themselves call ambiguity of combination-division. Since, for this first ambiguity of their classification, they propose AULĒTRIS PESOUSA, being the very example, except for the form of the verb, that Diogenes himself puts forward as a paradigm of ambiguity. And it is precisely this example of the flute-girl, worth three times a court,[26] that Galen reprises for the account of his revised taxonomy, under the heading of ambiguity seemingly situated in the statement, whereby we shift focus from the word to the statement (Galen *Soph*. 3.36-41 [Edlow: 100]). I will not comment on the letter of the example, the shift from conjugated verb to participle and withdrawal of the participle:[27] what matters to me is Galen's seizing of the word's physical thickness, and its immediate assimilation in his taxonomy to a movement (*bougé*) of sense, as innocent, and indeed as instructive, as becoming aware of an etymology (one of the examples given alongside AULĒTRIS PESOUSA is that of *Neapolis*, "Naples," in French Villeneuve, the "ville neuve"), or the decomposition of a common expression (*kaloskagathos* says with one word that it is "beautiful and good") [Galen *Soph*. 3.36-41 [Edlow: 100]].

The second ambiguity is Aristotelian homonymy itself: an *andreios* man is a brave man, an *andreios* tunic is a masculine piece of clothing (Galen *Soph*. 4 [Edlow: 106][28]). But the third is typically sophistic-Megarian-Stoic.[29] It concerns a confusion between "existence of the *ousia* and existence of the *ptōsis*" (Galen *Soph*. 4 [Edlow: 106]). "*Ptōsis*" means, in Aristotle as well as in the Stoics, the case, the inflection of a word (fall in the sense of "declension"). But for the Stoics, it designates precisely the inflected word itself, including in the nominative, as attested by Ammonius (*In Ar. De. Int.*, 43, 5-15 = LS 33K) or the scholia in Dionysius Thrax (230, 24-8 = LS 33L). Ammonius compares the straight or direct case, which is to say the nominative (by contrast with the "oblique" cases), with the fall of a stylus: the nominative "falls from thought," as the thought of Socrates falls into a word, whenever we utter "Socrates." *Ptōsis* is thus, according to Ebbesen's proposed translation, a "lexeme." The sense of *ousia*, in itself and probably here as well, is more complex, and in tension between "essence" and "substance." In book Gamma of the *Metaphysics*, *ousia* is for Aristotle the very thing that the word means, the some one thing, *hen ti*, that constitutes its sense (the word "man" signifies the *ousia* of man, in the sense of its *to ti ēn einai*, for example: bipedal animal [cf. Γ4 1006 a31–34]). But the Stoics no doubt adopt the more substantial vection, taking as their starting point the "corporeal," as with Chrysippus, who employs "substrate" (*hupokeimenon*) and *ousia* interchangeably.[30] Let's say that the homonymy arising when one says "man" is prone to being deployed in a complex way. One can set out from the ambiguity between the word's sense (the essence of man) and the word itself (the articulated emission). This ambiguity is tied to the homonymy under the same word—in truth constitutive of the word itself as a sign—of a signifier "man," the sound sequence, and a signified man, the bipedal animal. This confusion leads to another, with which one could also have started: that between the word (signifier and signified) and the referent, the thing that the signified evokes in our mind and that one encounters in the world. And it opens, lastly, onto a third, namely that between the use of the word, which normally serves to signify—to signify something other than itself—and its mention, wherein the word only refers to itself.

Aristotle would clearly never establish this series of confusions in terms of homonymy, since it is not a matter either of two referents or of two distinct senses. Now, this series is at the root of all the major fallacies of the sort "if you say something, it comes out of your mouth. You now say a chariot, so a chariot comes out of your mouth" (DL 7.87 = LS 37R),[31] which Clement summarily refutes. As he puts it:

> But the case is agreed to be an incorporeal. Therefore the renowned sophism is resolved thus: "What you say passes through your mouth." Which is true. "Now, you say a house, so a house passes through your mouth." Which is false. For we do not speak the house, which is a body, but the case, which is incorporeal, beneath which the house falls. (Clem. *Strom.* 8.9.26.5)[32]

The set of distinctions necessary to avoid the sequence of sophisms was deployed with the most subtle of Aristotelian-Stoic detail by Saint Augustine in his *De Dialectica*:

> The word *word* (*quod dixi verbum*) is a word, and signifies the word. The word *sayable* (*quod dixi dicibile*) is a word, and signifies not the word but what is understood and conceptualized in the word. The word *said* (*quod dixi dictionem*) is a word and signifies at once the word itself and that which is produced in the mind by the word. The word *thing* (*quod dixi rem*) is a word, and signifies all that remains, that is to say, all that which is not signified by the three preceding words. But I see that it's necessary to give examples. (*De Dialectica*, 5.8.9-13)[33]

So, it is the difference between "the things signified" and the "signs that signify them" that is required to save Adeodatus, in *De Magistro*, from being taken in by the "man who concluded that a lion came forth from the mouth of his opponent, as is told often in jest," and who was amazed "that, good man that he was, he had discharged from his mouth so savage a beast." But it is the difference between *verbum*, the word as autonym, and *dictio*, that alone enables Adeodatus to reply to Saint Augustine's asking him "if man is a noun," and, since the answer is yes, if when he sees him, he sees a noun; "In this way, since *man* is found to be both a living being and a noun, *man* is sometimes said as a sign, and sometimes as that which it signifies (*illud dicitur ex ea parte qua signum est, hoc qua significatur*)" (*De Magistro* 8.22.4).[34]

For his part, Galen does not come back to this example nor to the category of ambiguity. It is not even certain that he understands the difference between "existence of the essence" and "existence of the *ptōsis*" (*eite tēn ousian eite tēn ptōsin einai*) in a Stoic manner, and not an Aristotelian manner (thus like Edlow, as a difference between the "bipedal animal" and the instance "Socrates," for example). But what is certain here is that there is, in the sequence of the first three Stoic types of ambiguity, which lodge the traditional homonymy (one word for two senses) between two heavy and heterogenous perceptions of the signifier, an extreme kinship with sophistic lines of deviation.

The third point of violence is signaled, once again, by Galen's indignation: "Saying that homonymy occurs when words run together (*kan tois peplegmenois*) is the work of men who do not even listen to words at all (*oud' akouontōn* [. . .] *onomatōn*) (*Soph.* 4 [Edlow: 108])." In my view, his criticism here bears on the sixth type of ambiguity: KAINUKENĒPARELASSEN, in which one does not know "which part without meaning to construe with which other." "Part without meaning" (*asēmon morion*): Long and Sedley understand the expression as referring to the conjunction ἤ, "either . . . or," which forms the interpretation given of the letter H in the verse of the *Iliad* that serves as an example ("Then he would *either* have passed him[35] or rendered victory unclear, 23.382.)[36] But it is clearly no more a matter of *ē*, "either . . . or," taken alone, than of *hēpar*, "liver," with the *ē*—differently accented—as the initial letter, or of *kainē*, "new," with the *ē* last this time—all three possibilities producing sentences all more or less endowed with sense ("He would have driven a liver," "Empty she would have passed him") giving the ambiguity all its spice.[37] For it is a matter of *ē*, understood as *phōnē*, and of the entire sound sequence taken from the point of view of *lexis* and not of *logos*. Besides, this is why this sixth ambiguity resembles the first, our "flute-girl," with the exception that it is not perceived as playing on a silence (*aulē* [. . .] *tris*), but on the manner of pronouncing (with or without aspiration: the rough breathing of "liver," the soft breathing of "either or," and no breathing at all at the end of the word) and of agglutinating a phoneme (*[. . .] ē [. . .]; [. . .] hēpar; kainē [. . .]*). This is also why it is distinct from the seventh ambiguity ("Noble Achilles left [. . .]"), which bears on a *logos* and the construal of sense-laden elements, which is to say, words. In this sixth ambiguity, the sounds jostle and run together (*peplegmenois*), since they are what one perceives, instead of one's watching for sense by tuning into the words (*akouontōn onomatōn*). It is once more the autonomy of the signifier that triggers Galen's reaction. He opts, moreover, to bury the example under a methodological reproach: for him, the distinction between the arrangement of meaning-endowed parts ("Achilles") and the arrangement of parts void of meaning (*kenēpar*) is supposedly a simple distinction of species and not one of type. Note that it would be far more Aristotelian not to see two distinct categories of ambiguity here and instead to focus attention on the meaning alone. And it would have been Galenesque of the Stoics, who have an immediately literal and even alphabetical perception of *lexis* (as articulated, it is a set of letters *phōnē eggrammatos*, reports Diogenes, 7.56[38]), to use it to isolate the amphibological, and therefore also "disambiguating," force of accentuation, and of writing in general.

In a certain manner, the very particular attention that Galen brings to bear on writing, and the distinction, neither Aristotelian nor Stoic, that he makes between the oral form and writing, insofar as it is not simply the mark of human articulation but the imposition of a norm making it possible to remove the ear's hesitations and confusion, have become ours. Our perception of signifiers is very generally confounded with that of *phōnai*. Also, quite simply, sophistics is for us of the domain of the signifier because it sets its course by sound, and because, holding at the same time that there is no elsewhere, no depth that is not surface, it registers sense at the surface, the former being no different to the latter. The linguists' vulgate on the linearity of the signifier is thus in keeping with Aelius Aristides's rhetorical gem regarding speech, "which marches with the same pace as time." "The signifier, being auditory, is unfolded solely in time from which it gets its characteristics," says Saussure (2011: 103). And Martinet puts it that

> every language is thus manifest under the linear form of statements that represent what one often calls the spoken chain. This linear form of human language derives in the last instance from its vocal character: the spoken statements necessarily take place in time and are necessarily perceived by the hearing as a succession. The situation is entirely different when the knowledge is of a pictural type and is perceived by sight. (2011: 21)

Signifiers-voice-tenses are thus linked in the kairotic, homonymic, amphibological, catastrophic combinations-recombinations, which comprise the consistency of the sophistical *logoi*.

When we go from a perception primarily of the spoken to one primarily of the written, and when we, as Galen does, fix the *lexis* in all its letters, what is at stake is something like the loss of the signifier: one fixes the signified in the very place of the signifier. To hear it anew, one must, going against the grain, have a floating attention (a listening without seeing and without idea, someone "who has no eyes at all," as Plato would say of the sophist). Until the stage that logically follows: in which in writing itself the signifier makes a return, just as in the *Étourdit* Lacan wished for,[39] and which is not merely, like the *Treaty of Non-Being*, a cross for translators, but a nightmare for a new sort of philologists—philographers.

Notes

1. Anglophone readers may like to consult Edlow's complete translation of Galen's text (1977), to which I accordingly give parenthetical references.
2. I follow Cassin 2014 in referring to "sophistics" rather than "sophistry."
3. In the first version, the adverbial phrase "with your eyes" modifies the verb "seeing"; in the second version, the same phrase modifies "struck." Aristotle's intended resolution of this sophism is not entirely clear; it is Cassin's plausible suggestion that he has in mind rhythm of speech.
4. But see note 6 below for her cautious and nuanced view on the Stoics' attitude toward the regulation of language.
5. Jean-Baptiste Gourinat discusses and critiques Bréhier's reading of Stoic philosophy of language and its influence on Deleuze in an as-yet unpublished paper (destined for a new edition of Bréhier), which he shared in the conference from which this volume was born.
6. Cassin 2010 emphasizes instead the importance of Lacanian psychodynamics (with the topics discussed here, see esp. 2010: 49–54).
7. My understanding of Stoic dialectic is based on the works, which are not incompatible but not easy to interrelate, of Claude Imbert (some fundamental publications: Imbert 1978, 1986, 1992: I.3 and II.5) and of Gilles Deleuze (1990). The problem for me, if I may put it so crudely, is to know whether the Stoics are rather "sophists" or rather "philosophers"—that is to say, if their perception of language is primarily phenomenological or primarily logological. C. Imbert's reply would be that they are phenomenological, but have an entirely different phenomenology (but in his view these categories are not the right ones), while Deleuze's reply would be logological (this is the spirit of the rapprochement with Lewis Carroll). What may tip the scales in one direction or the other is the Stoic conception of the political, in which case, until proof of the contrary, I hold them to be resolutely "philosophers."
8. [LS 33B. All end-notes added by the editor and co-translator (Kurt Lampe) appear in square brackets.]
9. This is the Baratin-Desbordes translation, 1981: 128. Here is the Greek text, in its incomparable precision, which for all that does not exclude implacable diversions [...] οἱ ἀπὸ τῆς Στοᾶς, τρία φάμενοι συζυγεῖν ἀλλήλοις, τό τε σημαινόμενον κ αὶ τὸ σημαῖνον καὶ τὸ τυγχάνον, ὧν σημαῖνον μὲν εἶναι τὴν φωνήν, οἷον τὴν Δίων, σημαινόμενον δὲ αὐτὸ τὸ πρᾶγμα τὸ ὑπ' αὐτῆς δηλούμενον καὶ οὗ ἡμεῖς μὲν ἀντιλα μβανόμεθα τῇ ἡμετέρᾳ παρυφισταμένου διανοίᾳ, οἱ δὲ βάρβαροι οὐκ ἐπαΐουσι καίπερ τῆς φωνῆς ἀκούοντες, τυγχάνον δὲ τὸ ἐκτὸς ὑποκείμενον, ὥσπερ αὐτὸς ὁ Δίων.
10. Quoted and commented by Imbert 1978: 236 and note 33.
11. [Cassin refers here to Gorgias's *On What Is Not*, which she discusses at length in the first part *L'Effet sophistique* (23–65).]
12. "Chrysippus ait omne verbum ambiguum natura esse, quoniam ex eodem duo vel plura accipi possunt," *Attic Nights* 11.12.1.
13. [LS 37P.]
14. [See all of 7.55-57, part of which is given by LS 33A, 33H.]
15. The progression *phōnē, lexis, logos*, which I forgo from translating, is intelligently rendered in Baratin and Desbordes (1981: 121f.) as "vocal signifier/pronounced signifier/uttered signifier" ("voice/speech/sentence or statement" in Hicks's translation (1925); "voice/word/phrase" in the Genaille "translation" (1965: 70), "voice/word/

language," in *Les Stoïciens* (Bréhier and Schuhl 1962: 35)—all three are misleading but this difficulty can be imputed first to the Aristotelian weight of our categories). However, what bothers me concerning the relation, which changes depending upon the system, between orality and writing, is clearly the designation of *"engrammatic"* by "uttered."

16 Ax, who analyzes all the accounts, proposes a series of variations around this matrix, in accordance with the times and the doctrines (1986: 189, 204-6).

17 [Cassin has explored Aristotle's analysis of ambiguity in terms of homonymy just before the excerpt translated here (333-65; see esp. 353).]

18 Except for Diogenes, the word *blituri* is to be found in Sextus *M.* 8.133, as well as an example of *phōnē* without signification: "Moreover, if the true is in *phōnē*, either it is in a *phōnē* that signifies, or in a *phōnē* that does not signify. If it is in a *phōnē* that does not signify anything, as for example in *blituri* or *skindapsos*, then the truth cannot signify something."

19 τί ληρεῖς ἄνθρωπε ἑκών, καὶ γὰρ τὸ βλίτυρι κροῦμά τι δηλοῖ . . . See Ax's excellent commentary (1986: 190-9). I translate *dēloun* as "designate" to distinguish it in particular from *sēmainein*. The former is the term used in Diogenes Laërtius to say what "proper names" do in contrast with "common names," which, like, "horse" or "man," "signify a quality" (7.58 [LS 33M]). Cf. Graeser 1978. By contrast, let us recall that, in *De Interpretatione* for example, this is the term that serves Aristotle to say what it is that *psophoi agrammatoi* do, the "inarticulate noises" of animals, by way of differentiation from human words, which signify. (2, 16 a28s.)

20 Cf. Ax 1986: 197f., and notes 250, 251.

21 [For the benefit of readers who cannot access Ax 1986, it may be useful to note that this summary concerns a word spelled either *skindapsos* or *kindapsos*, that the reference is to kappa 2730 in Hesychius and that Cassin implicitly alludes here also to Athenaeus 4.183a-b and LSJ s.v. *skindapsos* def. 2.]

22 *Posterior Analytics* 2.7 97 b4-7, *On Interpretation* 1 16a14-17. The rapprochment is already carried out in the ancient commentaries on the *Analytics* and the *Categories* (Ammonios, *in Anal. Pr.* 3.20f. ed. Wallies; Eustratios, *in Anal.* 96.23ff. ed. Hayduck; Olympiodorus, *in Cat.,* 53.16f. ed. Busse), cited by Ax 1986: 196f.

23 Theon *Progymnasmata* 81.3 ed. Spengel, cited and commented by Ebbesen 1981: 36-8, and now also by Atherton 1993, in particular 184-199 (but the criteria that she retains for the principle of the Stoic classification, namely bearer and defect [400f.], never cease to disappoint).

24 [Because the grammar of this verse is ambiguous, so is its meaning. It may mean "Of a hundred men, divine Achilles left fifty" or "A hundred of men and fifty divine Achilles left" or—the translation Cassin claims is nonsense—"Of fifty men, divine Achilles left one hundred."]

25 [Cassin 519-33 offers her own complete French translation of Galen's *On Linguistic Sophisms* on the basis of her own philological judgments about the very difficult manuscripts, though with primary reference to the edition of Ebbesen 1981: vol. 3, 1–26.]

26 ["Flute-girl" is *aulētris*, whereas *aulē* on its own is "court," and *tris* on its own is "three times."]

27 [Cassin refers to the shift from *aulētrispeptōke* in DL 7.63, in which *peptōke* is a conjugated verb, to to *aulētrispesousa*, in which *pesousa* is a participle.] Even less so as Theon provides an intermediate example: AULĒTRISPESOUSADĒMOSIAESTO,

which can be interpreted as *aulētris estō pesousa dēmosia* or *aulē tris estō pesousa dēmosia*.

28 [Galen's enumeration of types of ambiguity is translated at LS 37Q.]
29 Inasmuch as the text is interpreted otherwise than Edlow 1977, see *L'Effet sophistique* 531 n.2.
30 On this point I refer to Goldschmidt 1953: 15–25, in particular p. 17f. [The reference is to the first Stoic "category" or "genus": see LS 28.]
31 "You speak" here is *laleis*, in which one hears the noise made by the lips.
32 I refer the reader to the discussion in LS 33O, via Frede 1978 and Graeser 1978, of whether or not Clement's assertions are Stoic. "Falls" [*se trouve tomber*] renders *tugkhanei* followed by a genitive, in which one should understand also the *tugkhanon*, which we render with the technical term "referent."
33 Ed. Pinborg 1975: 90. This text, whose authenticity no longer seems in doubt, and which was probably written by Saint Augustine around the time of his conversion (he was baptized in 386), puts forward a classification of ambiguity taking into account speech and writing, homonymy and synonymy, and, as part of homonymy technical usage and ordinary usage, but there can be no question here of going into this operation of mastered complexity, which decenters the Stoics by applying Aristotle to them. It's text 45 in Baratin and Desbordes, whose translation I reprise (also see their Introduction, 1981: 52–6).
34 Source for the French text: *Oeuvres de saint Augustin 6: Dialogues philosophiques 3*, intr., trans. and notes by G. Madec, Desclées de Brouwer, 1973: 105–7) citation of 23, then of 24, in the Baratin-Desbordes translation (1981: 235; their text 46).
35 [καί νύ κεν ἢ παρέλασσ'.]
36 "Apparently in this context," they comment, "conjunctions, like ἢ are not considered 'semantic'" (LS vol. 2, p. 232), and they ground this interpretation of Ammonius fragment O by recalling that Diodorus named one of his slaves "However" to prove that every *phōnē* was semantic (*In Ar. De. Int.*, 38, 17–20).
37 [The ambiguity here concerns the string of Greek letters *KAINUKENĒPARELASSEN*. If it is construed *KAI NU KEN Ē PARELASSEN*, in context it would most naturally be translated, "And now he would either have passed him"; if *KAI NU KEN ĒPAR ELASSEN*, "And now he would have driven a liver"; if *KAI NU KENĒ PARELASSEN*, "And now, empty, she passed him." The first four letters could also be grouped "*KAIN*," with a final *H* elided, in order to mean "new."]
38 He specifies "The elements (*stoikheia*) of *lexis* are the twenty-four letters of the alphabet" (Diogenes 7.56).
39 [Lacan's article *L'Étourdit* (1973) is both a key to his late thought about language and famously unintelligible. Cassin devotes a long essay to it, which she opens by claiming it gives us the greatest chances of "escaping Aristotelianism" as a regulatory stance toward the use of language (2010: 12).]

Bibliography

Atherton, C. (1993), *The Stoics on Ambiguity*, Cambridge: Cambridge University Press.
Ax, W. (1986), *Laut, Stimme, und Sprache: Studien zu drei Grundbegriffen der antiken Sprachtheorie*, Göttingen: Vandenhoeck & Ruprecht.

Baratin, M. and F. Desbordes (1981), *L'Analyse linguistique dans l'antiquité classique*, Paris: Klincksieck.
Bréhier, É. (1962), *La théorie des incorporels dans l'ancien stoïcisme*, 3rd ed., Paris: Librairie philosophique J. Vrin.
Bréhier, É., trans., P.-M. Schuhl, ed. (1962), *Les Stoïciens: textes*, Paris: Gallimard.
Cassin, B. (1995), *L'Effet sophistique*, Paris: Gallimard.
Cassin, B. (2010), "L'ab-sens, ou Lacan de A à D," in A. Badiou and B. Cassin, *Il n'y a pas de rapport sexuel. Deux leçons sur "L'Étourdit" de Lacan*, 11–99. Paris: Fayard.
Cassin, B. (2014), *Sophistical Practice: Toward a Consistent Relativism*, New York: Fordham University Press.
Cassin, B. (2016), *Nostalgia: When Are We Ever at Home?* trans. P.-A. Brault, New York: Fordham University Press.
Cassin, B. (2018), *Google Me: One-Click Democracy*, trans. M. Syrotinski, New York: Fordham University Press.
Cassin, B. and M. Narcy (1989), *La décision du sens. Le livre Gamma de la Métaphysique d'Aristotle: Introduction, texte, traduction et commentaire*, Paris: J. Vrin.
Deleuze, G. (1990), *The Logic of Sense*, trans. Mark Lester with Charles Stivale, London: The Athlone Press.
Ebbesen, S. (1981), *Commentators and Commentaries on Aristotle's Sophistici Elenchi*, 3 vols, Leiden: Brill.
Edlow, Robert B. (1977), *Galen on Language and Ambiguity*, Leiden: Brill.
Frede, M. (1978), "Principles of Stoic Grammar," in J. M. Rist (ed.), *The Stoics*, 27–76, Berkeley: University of California Press.
Genaille, R., trans. (1965), *Diogène Laërce: Vies, doctrines, et sentences des philosophes illustres*, 2 vols, Paris: Garnier-Flammarion.
Goldschmidt, V. (1953), *V Le Système stoïcien et l'idée de temps*, Paris: Vrin.
Gourinat, J.-B. (2000), *La Dialectique des stoïciens*, Paris: Vrin.
Graeser, A. (1978), "The Stoic Theory of Meaning," in J. Rist (ed.), *The Stoics*, 77–100, Berkeley: University of California Press.
Hicks, R. D., trans. (1925), *Diogenes Laertius: Lives of the Eminent Philosophers, Volume 2: Books 6–10*, Cambridge, MA: Harvard University Press.
Imbert, C. (1978), "Théorie de la représentation et doctrine logique dans le stoïcisme ancien," in J. Brunschwig (ed.), *Les Stoïciens et leur logique*, 223–49, Paris: Vrin.
Imbert, C. (1986), "Pour une réinterprétation des catégories stoïciennes," in CNRS (ed.), *Philosophie du langage et grammaire dans l'Antiquité*, 263–85, Brussels: Editions Ousia.
Imbert, C. (1992), *Phénoménologies et langues formulaires*, Paris: PUF.
Lacan, J. (1973), "L'Étourdit," *Scilicet* 4: 5–52.
Pinborg, J., ed. (1975), *Augustine: De Dialectica*, trans. B. D. Jackson, Dordrecht: D. Reidel.
Saussure, F. de (2011), *Course in General Linguistics*, trans. Wade Baskin, New York: Columbia University Press.

Chapter 11

ONTOLOGY AND LANGUAGE, BETWEEN CHRYSIPPUS AND AGAMBEN

by Nicoletta di Vita, trans. by Kurt Lampe

1 Philosophy and Language

Of the many connections between philosophy and language in the ancient world, one has received particularly copious attention from researchers. I am speaking of the manner in which philosophy has integrated language into its own tonalities, which today—because of a forgetfulness that is hard to admit—we have difficulty in understanding.

The phrase *logon didonai* (giving a *logos*), which can be found in many places in Plato, is probably the most complete form in which this encounter is expressed.[1] It originates in the domain of music, from which all reflections on language are likewise descended. As Johannes Lohmann has demonstrated, the relations among sonorous tonalities were originally called *logoi* (Lohmann 1970: 8–10).[2] By "giving a tonality," these *logoi* create a harmonic relation between the musical form and the emotional tonality, between the sound given externally and the *Stimmungen* (pitches or moods). It is precisely this "acoustic-musical phenomenon," this need for harmonization, that soon become, according to Lohmann's hypothesis, a "model, among the Greeks, for every kind of knowledge and experience" (1970: 8).

It is widely agreed that all later Greek philosophy ended up making *logon didonai* its proper task (Ildefonse 1997: 38). The result was that all philosophical reflection on *logos* was configured as reflection on *correct* or *orthos logos*, dedicated to an *orthē philosophia*. When Plato, in the *Cratylus* and *Sophist*, makes words and utterances his object of study, he is researching in what form language can be correct. He is testing the medium of his own dialogues, the form assumed by philosophical exercise—in order to evaluate not the power of language but the power of philosophy, of its relation to reality. Similarly, when Chrysippus claims that only the *dialektikos*—in other words, loosely speaking, the logician—possesses virtue,[3] and therefore we must work on language (*dialegesthai*) because it leads to knowledge,[4] it may well be that the goals of his appeal to theoretical work on language are entirely external, strictly speaking, to language itself.

It is possible to read all of this as a decisive step toward heteronomy, as some have already done; in other words, toward the determination of language's status on the basis of its function specifically for thinking: classical philosophy imposed its own norms on language, according to its own needs. Thus Joly has spoken of a "linguistic blockage" (1986: 105–36),[5] of a shadow projected by philosophy *onto* language. The latter has primarily been investigated with regard to either "its instrumental role in the expression of thoughts" or "its mediating function in the representation of extralinguistic reality" (Coseriu 2003: 14), the goal being "to provide a system of expression that apprehends 'things as they are'" (Imbert 1993: 308). In fact, it has often been proposed that the late emergence of linguistic disciplines (grammar, philology, linguistics), that is, of disciplines explicitly dedicated to the investigation of language solely for its own sake, was due to such an original "stranglehold (*mainmise*) on language by philosophy" (Ildefonse 1997: 15).

This situation is in some respects so obvious that it has been possible to speak of a kind of "pillaging" of language's fundamental structures by philosophy. In his well-known article from 1958, Émile Benveniste suggested that when Aristotelian categories were held up to the light, one could see the skeleton of common Greek *verbal* forms of the period: Aristotle "thought he was defining the attributes of objects," he says, but "he only posits linguistic beings: it is language that, thanks to his proper categories, permits him to recognize and specify those attributes." He goes on, "It is what we can *say* that delimits and organizes what we can think. Language furnishes the fundamental configuration of properties that the mind recognizes in things" (Benveniste 1966: 70). Therefore the "stranglehold," so to speak, would be indirect: a tacit but intense reflection on language will have been disguised as an inquiry into the categories of thought and subjugated to those categories.

1.1

At least two points might follow from the foregoing considerations. The first is that language's implication in philosophy has not necessarily caused its own innermost traits to be neglected. To the contrary, it has on each occasion allowed us to glimpse language's ethical, epistemological, political, or religious nature, and therefore to escape language's isolation by apprehending it in the actual constellation of its multiple relationships. It has opened the possibility of approaching language as it participates in all things, by revealing the complexity of its nature.

As Eugenio Coseriu fully appreciated years ago, the disciplines that make language their object "begin" properly "at the point where philosophy of language stops" (2003: 13). They have stopped posing the question surrounding language in order to begin giving, each from its partial perspective, specific answers.

There is thus something more in philosophy's remarkable affection for language. Moreover, this leads us, with our second observation, to the other way of connecting *logos* and philosophy.

2 The Task of Philosophy: An "Unsayable" Passion

In a statement attributed to the Stranger in Plato's dialogue the *Sophist*, we find a rather eloquent expression: "If we were deprived of this [*logos*]—and this would be most serious—we would be deprived of philosophy" (260a). The intuitions of the Italian philosopher Giorgio Agamben and his reading of the ancient world appear to set out from just this point: not only that we understand language via a philosophical perspective, but also, in the ancient world as in today's, that philosophy should be understood precisely in the relation it establishes with language.

In a text originally published in 1984, Agamben had posed the question about the proper task of philosophy very clearly, when he wrote: "The task of philosophical exposition is to come to the aid of speech [*parola*] with speech, so that, in speech, speech itself does not remain presupposed to speech, but comes to speech as speech" (2010: 18). The reference in this curious formulation is to "coming to the aid of" (*boēthein*) in Plato's *Phaedrus* (278c6). In the Platonic passage we read that the only person who merits the title "philosophical" is one who, in their own words, can give a reasonable account of their use of language (278d4). This means, in terms Agamben describes as "modern," giving an account "of the very fact of language," of this presupposition that remains like an *a priori* of every linguistic act. But because this presupposition also and always precedes the person who speaks and the very act of speech, it is a truly "unsayable" and "inexpressible" foundation of that act (2010: 30–4). So the question is the following: How can we philosophically conceptualize and attempt to express this *taking-place* of language, this "originary impossibility?"

This formulation is obviously close to the Wittgensteinian maxim, according to which "was gezeigt werden *kann, kann* nicht gesagt werden" ("What *can* be shown, *can* not be said," *Tractatus* 4.1212): it is not possible to say language itself with language. The mediation of Martin Heidegger is equally manifest: he had assigned to this taking-place, which we cannot express *in* or *with* language, Dasein's opening to itself, "die primäre Entdeckung der Welt" ("the primary discovery of the world," Heidegger 1962: H138). "Not *how* the world is," comments Agamben, "but *that* the world is"—not what one says "propositionally inside of language [*linguaggio*], but *that language is*" (2010: 80).

If this problematic appears peculiarly modern, the merit of Agamben's research consists above all in delineating its archaeology: he discovers the matrix of this demand, which belongs to the twentieth century, in what Plato had already designated as the mark, as Agamben says, "of authentic philosophical exposition," but which only Stoicism, through its original teaching, would have brought to perfect expression.

2.1

It is in fact with a presentiment of impossibility that Agamben first turns to the Stoics. The passage concerns the Stoic theory of the passions, with an innovative take on the Heideggerian theory of Dasein. Dasein faces the opening—which is an opening to language—with *Angst*, anxiety. "This opening has always been traversed by a negativity and a malaise" (Agamben 2010: 82), because Dasein is never master of this opening, of this event that assails and determines it (and which "coincides with the proper place of man's being, with his *Da*," 2010: 83).

Heidegger's thesis that this originary opening is an emotional tonality finds an analogue in the ancient world. It is worth noting that Heidegger himself indicates that Aristotle's theory of the passions was the object of his *Rhetoric* and not of a "psychological" treatise (Heidegger 1962: H38). Even more interesting for us is that, as Agamben emphasizes, the key locus is ultimately to be found in Stoicism (Agamben 2010: 84).

In Chrysippus we discover a fundamental connection between language and passions, *logos* and *pathē*. Only humankind can experience passions, because passions are actually a type of *logos*, a *krisis* or "judgment." They must be defined in relation to *logos*, never in opposition to it (DL 7.111). It is here that Agamben radicalizes the Stoic theory and understands passions as an excess of *logos*, that is, as its "emergence." As both origination and "passion," language remains excessive for individuals; the Stoics give the following definition: "Passions are an excessive impulse or one that exceeds the measure of *logos*" (SVF III.377).[6] Here Agamben obviously displaces to the background the ethical and practical horizon that usually guides analysis of the Stoic theory of the passions. Moreover, he does not directly address the complex way in which the Stoics defined passion: not only as a *krisis* and a *logos* but also as "a movement of the soul that is irrational [*alogon*] and contrary to the nature of the soul" (SVF 3.462)[7]— something that was already deemed "contradictory" in antiquity (SVF III.456-90, LS 65J). That being said, Agamben nevertheless seems to grasp a critical moment of the declension of passions in terms of *logos*: "Ὁρμή ["impulse"]," he specifies, "comes from *ornumi*, which has the same root as Latin *orior* and *origo*, and means . . . an emergence, an origination [*uno scaturire, una origine*] that surpasses the measure of language" (2010: 84). And if passion is not other than *logos* itself, "*the excessive origination must be that of language itself*" (2010: 85).[8] Thus he can conclude that "the theory of the passions, of *Stimmungen*, has always been the place where western man thinks his fundamental relation to language" (2010: 85). And this thought is always the thought of an impossibility: the excessive origination of language, which encompasses the very fact of its existence, appears inapprehensible. It escapes us because of its very excessiveness. Yet for the philosophy that has made language its fundamental theme, it never ceases to exhibit its peculiar demand, which its relation to the passions pinpoints and outlines, but never manages to satisfy.

In antiquity as today, the question can ultimately be formulated as follows: Is it possible to elaborate "a discourse which, neither being reduced to a metalinguistics nor halting in the face of the unsayable, says language and exposes its limits" (Agamben 2010: 34)—which would situate itself at the level of philosophy as "vision of language" (Agamben 2010: 35)? "An ancient tradition of thought," Agamben long ago announced, "sets forth this possibility" (Agamben 2010: 34).

3 Factum Linguae

It is perhaps surprising that Agamben once again refers to ancient Stoicism in order to clarify what is at issue in the "very fact of language." This is indirect at first, when he traces Augustine's and Gaunilo's observations about a situation where someone hears a word unknown to them, and understands it as a word, and not as a simple sound (1982: 45–7). In Augustine's case, the example, taken from *De Trinitate* (X.1.2), concerns a "dead word" (*vocabulum emortuum*), specifically *temetum* (an ancient word for *vinum*, "wine"). Augustine contends that the desire to investigate the meaning of the word testifies to a fundamental condition: that this term is presumed to be a meaningful sign, that the hearer is conscious of being in the presence of something endowed with meaning. Similarly, in his response to Anselm, Gaunilo once again presents the case of someone who, while not knowing the meaning of the voice they hear, still recognizes it as meaningful. Gaunilo's *cogitatio secundum vocem solam* signifies precisely the comprehension of voice *qua* indication of an event of language (*Pro insipiente* 0345b). But a similar observation was already implied by Stoic texts, which Agamben does not cite. According to Sextus Empiricus's testimony (*M* 1.154-8), the Stoics, in order to understand what *logos* is, imagined a circumstance where foreigners (*barbaroi*), having heard the local language, grasped nothing of its meaning. Nevertheless, they will not have doubted that they were in the presence of a language event, and this is because they heard the voice. Diogenes Laertius also attributes to the Stoics a discussion about the fact that a term like *blituri*, although deprived of all meaning, still is easily recognizable as part of a linguistic act (DL 7.57 = LS 33A, SE *M*. 8.133).

But what is this consciousness of a level that, despite being linguistic, remains below the threshold of any question about language in order to recognize it as such? Which is not yet in language, but all the same grasps and expresses it? In other words, what is the place of that which, as Agamben has nicely phrased it in a recent work, "is neither only something linguistic nor simply something factual" (2015: 58)?

4 The "Sayable" alongside Thought, Language, and Things

This question receives a decisive formulation in a recently published chapter "On the Sayable and the Idea," where Agamben discusses the Stoic sayable at length alongside other ancient and medieval theories (2016: 57–122). This happens through, on the one hand, the demarcation and deepening of an interpretation of the Platonic Idea, to which Agamben had already dedicated an essay in 1984, and on the other hand, through an analysis of one of the most important topics in Stoic theory, namely that of the *lekton* or "sayable." The reason is simple: the unsayable, already for Walter Benjamin, is to be "eliminated *in* language" (Benjamin 1995: 325–6, italics my own). It cannot remain outside of language "like an obscure presupposition." "The elimination of the unsayable in language coincides," Agamben observes elsewhere, "with the exposition of the sayable" (2016: 59).

Let us immediately make clear that Agamben's reading of this issue in no way resembles those to which we are accustomed. The theory of the *lekton* is not investigated either on the basis of its inclusion among the incorporeals or in its difficult relation to the theory of propositions. It is instead viewed, one might say, from the point of view of its "demand" (*esigenza*), as a function of its position in the general conception of philosophy. Agamben is obviously fascinated by a certain undecidability in situating the fourth Stoic incorporeal, and the conclusion he reaches is, for that reason, particularly interesting. In his opinion, it is the ancient Stoics who, even if they did not fulfill it, at least recognized philosophy's fundamental task. They managed to find a way of expressing the fact of language, the demand for a philosophical presupposition and thematization.

The interpretation Agamben offers is all the more interesting because it is by no means the product of second-hand analysis or a hasty glance at the sources. To the contrary, his appropriation of Stoic thinking is always conducted with extraordinary philological care.

4.1

The suspicion that the Stoics could provide an important perspective for our inquiry derives from a passage in Ammonius's commentary on Aristotle's *On Interpretation*:

> Here Aristotle teaches us what is primarily and immediately signified (σημαιν όμενα) by them [nouns and verbs], namely thoughts (νοήματα), and by their mediation, things (πράγματα); and he claims that it is unnecessary to conceive of any other intermediate . . . as the Stoics suppose with the name *lekton*. (SVF II.168 = LS 33N)

Alongside language, concepts, and things, Ammonius claims that the Stoics posited a fourth element: the *lekton*. In other words, something else, which cannot be included among things, among thoughts, or even, properly speaking, among words. Its entire place is indeterminate, and so we must, as Agamben himself writes, trace its "cartography" (Agamben 2016: 62).

In order to argue for what was probably a long-standing intuition, he has recourse to a passage from Sextus Empiricus's *Against the Professors* (8.11-12 = LS 33B),[9] which he describes as "the most complete and at the same time the most problematic" for our question (2016: 63). In this passage, which recent historiography has considered a veritable *locus classicus* (Frede 1994: 118), Sextus clearly distinguishes "three aspects" that, he says, "are conjoined" (τρία φάμενοι συζυγεῖν): the *sēmainon*, or signifying sign, that is the *phōnē* or vocal sound, which he stipulates is a body; the *tunkhanon*, that is the object, that which is at issue on each occasion, which is also a body; and finally the *sēmainomenon*, which is not a body, "subsists alongside our thought" (τῇ ἡμετέρᾳ παρυφισταμένου διανοίᾳ), and is not understood by "barbarians," even when they hear the vocal sound. According to Sextus, this is properly the "signified thing" (τὸ σημαινόμενον πρᾶγμα), which is "incorporeal" (ἀσώματον), "revealed by the voice" (ὑπ'αὐτῆς ⟨τῆς φωνῆς⟩ δηλούμενον), true or false, and which, finally, the Stoics call *lekton*.

The passage is well chosen. Without needing to refer to any "fourth" thing, Sextus expresses all the complexity contained in what is *neither word nor thing*, but that, in Ammonius's testimony, has to do with both.

The passage is also interesting because it offers, in a way, a concise abstract of what we might call a "classical" theory of the parts of *logos*.[10] This theory recognizes a tripartition that, in its broad outline, can still be accepted today; more importantly, versions of it can be found in many ancient authors. But in setting this passage before us once more, Agamben takes some important steps. He translates the second τὸ of the expression αὐτὸ τὸ πρᾶγμα τὸ ὑπ'αὐτῆς δηλούμενον as "inasmuch as" (*in quanto*)—"the thing itself inasmuch as it is revealed by" the vocal sound—and emphasizes the description of the σημαινόνενον πρᾶγμα ("the signified thing") as αὐτὸ τὸ πρᾶγμα, "the thing itself."

4.2

It is well known that among modern commentators there is no agreed reading of either this passage or the *lekton* in general. In Sextus's formulation, the *lekton* is entirely reduced to the *sēmainomenon*, the signified, which absorbs many of the features generally assigned by the sources only to the incorporeal.

Isnardi Parente has shown, with regard to the "signification" posited as incorporeal, that "it would be hard to discern what distinguishes it from a simple concept" (2005: 180). That the passage is rather obscure is confirmed by Michael Frede, who remarks, in "The Stoic Notion of a *Lekton*," that "there must be something wrong with Sextus' account" (1994: 119). The difficulty derives not only from the confusion of *lekton* and signified but also, as Brunschwig too elucidates (Brunschwig 1995: 8), from the fact that this is "the only text which attributes to the Stoics the view that there is also a *lekton* corresponding to an expression like 'Dion'" (Frede 1994: 119). Rather than "Dion," Sextus should have written, based on comparison with a text by Seneca (*Letters* 117.113 = LS 33E), something like "Dion is walking" in order to satisfy the propositional character assigned to the *lekton* by the Stoics.[11]

As for the status of the *lekton*, there really is no agreement. For example, some have suggested a reading we might call "Fregean," according to which *lekta* would be "independent contents of thought," that is, entities independent of both thought and language (Frege 1892: 22–50). By contrast, others have insisted on the ontological dependence of *lekta* (Long 1996), which themselves depend on rational impressions (*logikai phantasiai*)—in other words, on that which the Stoics propose as the site and origin of all human knowledge.

An echo of this controversy reaches Agamben as well. Following Schubert's arguments (1994: 15–16), he proceeds to ask himself to what extent the *sēmainomenon* should be understood as the objective content of thought, as in Frege, or as subjective content, more specifically as "the concept present in the mind (*mente*) of a subject (like the Aristotelian *noēma*, according to Ammonius)" (Agamben 2016: 63-4).

If we inflect this question a little and reorient it to our own interests, this amounts to asking whether the *lekton* should be situated among thoughts or among things—whether its place is a *logical* place or exclusively *ontological*.

Although Sextus has identified the *lekton* with the signification of the utterance, and therefore emphasizes its metaphysical status, nevertheless, as Émile Bréhier also says (whom Agamben quotes): "If the 'signified' is a 'sayable,' we by no means see that every sayable is a signified'" (Bréhier 1962: 15)—in other words, that the fact of being sayable is identical with the fact of being signified. Conflating the two is inappropriate, and the issue remains, as Agamben himself says, "aporetic." He suggests that it remained so for Augustine, who, by distinguishing *res* (the bodily thing), *dictio* (*verbum* and *per verbum*, that is, speech in its semantic dimension), and *dicibile* (the sayable), called the latter "speech and not speech," not a *verbum* properly speaking, but *ex verbo*—and did not thereby escape from this confusion (Agamben 2016: 65-6, citing *De Dialectica* 5.8).

Therefore Agamben's suggestion, which may surprise us a little, is that the "*philologically* correct" analysis of the passage in Sextus is the only one to offer a genuine answer to this aporia.

4.3

We can follow Agamben's argument by distinguishing two moments, whose fundamental starting point is Ammonius's indication of the presence of a *fourth element* and whose conclusion is that the *lekton* does not belong to the domain of *thoughts*. A first observation is that Sextus explicitly distinguished the Stoics from those who located "the true and the false" (τὸ ἀληθές τε καὶ ψεῦδος) in "the movement of thought" (περὶ τῇ κινήσει τῆς διανοίας, *M* 8.11 = LS 33B1). Therefore the *lekton*, to which, according to Sextus's statement, the true and the false belong, can in no way coincide with thought. Moreover, Sextus placed the *lekton* "alongside" thought—it "subsists alongside thought" (παρυφισταμένου διανοίᾳ), he says, separating it from things in the mind. The second observation concerns the unusual description of the *lekton* as αὐτὸ τὸ πρᾶγμα, which Sextus mentioned near the passage's beginning, when he says, "the signified is the thing itself inasmuch as it is revealed by it [the vocal sound]." Now, Agamben deliberately translates this as "the thing itself" (*la cosa stessa*). But does this mean that the *lekton* belongs to the world of "things?"

The solution is once again to be found through philological attentiveness. By choosing the word *pragma*, Sextus has not used an equivalent for *tunkhanon*, the real event or object, that which "happens to be" (ἃ τυγχάνει ὄντα). The *pragma* is certainly a "thing" (*cosa*), but its semantic range also encompasses, Agamben asserts, "that about which one speaks," "that which is in question," which is "at stake (*in causa*),"[12] as in the Latin *res*, which signifies "what is at stake in a discussion or a procedure" (2016: 64).[13] Similarly, the verb used here (ὑφεστάναι)—which, we might add, Chrysippus employs for the past and the future in opposition to the present (SVF II.509 = LS 51B)—signals explicitly that we are not dealing with a thing in the proper sense of the term, namely as existent (endowed with *huparxis*).

This is why Agamben's translation of the end of the passage is well founded: the *lekton* is of course a "thing," but only *inasmuch as* it is revealed by the *phōnē* or vocal sound—and this means: *in* its being-revealed by the *phōnē*, considered solely *inasmuch as*, *to the extent that* the *phōnē* displays it. When Sextus stipulates that the *lekton* is "the thing *inasmuch as* it is revealed by" the vocal sound, he precisely indicates, Agamben claims, with an unexpected clarity, "what is in question in speech and in thought: the *res* which, *through* speech and thought, but without coinciding with them, is at stake between a human being and the world" (2016: 65).

The secret of the *lekton* is entirely hidden in such a "being in question" of language in language itself, which is of course even more mysterious. Let us therefore question once more the place of this "inasmuch as." What does it mean that the *lekton*, neither thought nor thing, expresses precisely "that which is in question" in human speech?

5 *The Platonic Idea as Sayability*

A glimmer of illumination comes from Plato. It is not by chance that Agamben has chosen the passage in Sextus; his heavy emphasis on the words αὐτὸ τὸ πρᾶγμα, which appear in an entirely negligeable position in the passage as a whole, is not without purpose. The reason, if we look closely, is rather obvious. In his essay on Plato from 1984, Agamben had already addressed the Idea as "the thing itself" (2010: 15–20). I will not fully retrace his detailed arguments there and in his chapter from 2016; it will suffice to summarize briefly the confrontation he orchestrates between the passage from Sextus and one from Plato's *Seventh Letter* (342a8-d1).

The Platonic passage is relatively well known. There Plato indicates the five elements necessary for achieving *epistēmē*, the science or understanding of "each being," taking as his example the circle. *Epistēmē* itself, as the text explains, is the fourth element. The others are given as *onoma* (name), *eidōlon* (image), *logos*, and a curious "that through which each being is knowable (*gnōston*) and truly is."

We should note that once again Agamben's translation deliberately departs from what is commonly accepted. Plato's text is usually printed and translated as follows: πέμπτον δ'αὐτὸ τιθέναι δεῖ ὃ δὴ γνωστόν τε καὶ ἀληθῶς ἐστιν ὄν, "as fifth, we must posit that very thing *which* is to be known and is truly being" (342a8-b1, italics my own). But in his 1984 essay, Agamben had discussed the need to revise the editions of Burnet and Souilhé in order to restore the manuscript reading (which was the version used by Marsilio Ficino as well). If we retain the passage in its current form, the result will be that the fifth is simply the thing that is the object of knowledge (Agamben 2010: 13). But this would create a pointless circularity by putting in the fifth place that which was presupposed by the entire discourse (in other words, "each being"). It would also confirm Aristotle's interpretation, since he "sees in the Idea a kind of pointless duplication of the thing" (Agamben 2010: 13). By contrast, the manuscripts, according to Agamben (who relies on the work of other scholars),[14] actually read δι'ὅ rather than δεῖ ὅ; in other words, "through which" or "by which" (2010: 14). Therefore Agamben claims that the fifth element is the Idea, whose "technical denomination" in the passage is αὐτὸς ὁ κύκλος ("the circle itself, this circle here")—a formulation very close to Sextus's expression for the *lekton*, αὐτὸ τὸ πρᾶγμα, and, one might say, a rather special way of being a "thing" (Agamben 2016: 68). The interpretive context is soon clarified: in order to analyze the formula chosen by Plato for the Idea, Agamben postulates that *autos*, though it functions adjectivally here, still retains the anaphoric force of its pronominal usage.[15] In "αὐτὸς ὁ κύκλος," he says, the αὐτὸς only designates something, as with all anaphoric pronouns, "inasmuch as this thing has already been signified by means of another term endowed with sense." The anaphoric pronoun, lacking any virtual reference, acquires one through its relation to a term that precedes it.[16] Unlike the case where *autos* appears between the article and the noun (ὁ αὐτὸς κύκλος, "the same circle") and expresses identity (Latin *idem*), in the singular Platonic formulation αὐτὸς ὁ κύκλος, it expresses ipseity (Latin *ipse*). As Agamben puts it, it does not refer to *kuklos* alone (ὁ αὐτὸς *κύκλος*), but to the syntagm *ho kuklos* (αὐτὸς *ὁ κύκλος*) (Agamben 2016: 79–82). Moreover, Agamben observes that the article *ho* is also by origin an anaphoric pronoun. This is to be connected, via a meticulous analysis of the passage, with the expression κύκλος ἐστί τι λεγόμενον, "circle is something said" (Agamben 2016: 79–82).

Agamben can therefore conclude:

> The αὐτὸς, since it refers to a term already anaphorized by the article, resumes the circle in and by its being-said, in and by its being in language.... The circle itself—the Idea—is neither one of the four elements, nor yet simply other than those four. It is that which is in question each time in each of them, and at the same time, it remains irreducible to them: *it is that through which the circle is sayable and knowable*. (Agamben 2016: 82)

5.1

Let us step out of this philological labyrinth for a moment and ask: What does the passage of the *Seventh Letter*, interpreted in this way, tell us about the place of the *lekton*? According to Agamben, there are intriguing affinities between this passage and that of Sextus. The initial listing of elements is similar, and the use of the name "Dion" in Sextus's example recalls the Dion of the *Seventh Letter*—whereas, Agamben notes, Aristotle had substituted the names Choriscus or Callias in his arguments. Moreover, there are also correspondences between the individual elements: to Sextus's *phōnē/sēmainon* corresponds Plato's *onoma*, which indeed he describes as being *en phōnais*; to Sextus's *tunkhanon* corresponds Plato's *eidōlon*, since both are particular occurrences (Agamben 2016: 67–8).

It remains to discover the place of the *sēmainomenon/lekton*. We have already denied that it is thought, so it cannot respond to *epistēmē* in the *Seventh Letter*.

The *lekton* can only correspond to the fifth element in the Platonic passage—to the Idea.

As is often the case in Agamben's texts, the argument comes full circle with impeccable coherence. Did not Sextus describe the *lekton* with the expression αὐτὸ τὸ πρᾶγμα? If we accept Agamben's contention that Plato's Idea is expressed in the anaphoric movement of αὐτὸς ὁ κύκλος, the operation that results is extraordinary: for him, *the Stoics situated the sayable in the same place as the Idea*. This does not mean that they equated the *lekton* with the Platonic Idea, but that they conceptualized the sayable, this strange fourth element, in *the same place between language and reality* that Plato had attributed to the Idea—an uncomfortable place, difficult to express, yet fundamental for Platonism just as for Stoicism.

"The history of post-Platonic philosophy," Agamben says, "can be read, starting with Aristotle, as the history of various attempts to eliminate the Idea or think it differently" (Agamben 2016: 68). In Aristotle's *On Interpretation*, for example, this occurs through an examination of language, whose approach is similar to those we have just analyzed, but adds as its fourth element *gramma* (writing or letter), and deliberately omits the Idea (Arist. *Interpr.* 16a3-7).

Modern commentators—Agamben still refers explicitly to Schubert (1994: 15)—have remarked upon this proximity of the Idea and the sayable, albeit *in the negative*.[17] This nevertheless corroborates Agamben's contention: the Stoics borrowed from Plato the Ideas' mode of existence, modeling the *lekton* on it. Moreover, just as the *lekton*, like every incorporeal, has its "being" as *paruphistasthai*, "subsisting alongside" thought, similarly the Idea is before all else a paradigm—*para-deigma*, what shows itself "alongside (*para*) things."

"The thing itself," Agamben had said in discussing the Platonic Idea, "is not a thing: it is *sayability* itself, the opening that is *in question* in language, which *is* language, and which, in language, we constantly presuppose and forget" (2010: 18). Thus the merit of the Stoics is to have given this fourth element, which they rehabilitated, its proper denomination: the "sayable."

It is easy to see here how not only the Stoic theory of the *lekton* but also the Platonic theory of the Idea receives a new interpretive possibility. Was it not said, in this same passage of the *Seventh Letter*, that the Idea is not "sayable" (*rhēton*) like other objects of learning (341c5-6)?

But Agamben invites us to re-read the passage in the *Parmenides* where Plato, speaking about the Ideas, says that they are "the things you can most grasp with *logos*" (ἐκεῖνα ἃ μάλιστά τις ἂν λόγῳ λάβοι, 135e3). The Idea, in its proximity to the *lekton*, is what is *most* (*malista*) sayable, the place where sayable and unsayable meet—and the Stoics deserve credit for illuminating, with their terminology, the paradoxical place of the fact of speaking, of this *inasmuch as*, this *unsayable sayability*.

Before all else, language is a fact, a fact that escapes us, and yet demands expression. That the *lekton* is a fact, the expression of an event—this is well known; Agamben specifies which fact we are dealing with, namely the fact of speaking.[18]

6 Discussion

At this point we can articulate some critical reflections. Almost all of them derive from the fact that the original question does not really appear to have been resolved by this comparison of *lekton* and Idea. The place that has been identified for the *lekton* remains, despite everything, a problematic position, which clearly exhibits what we understood at the beginning of our discussion as the "excess" of *logos*, the impossibility of apprehending what always precedes us.

6.1 The Logical Value of the Lekton

One might ask—and this is not only the first but perhaps also the most important question—whether the *lekton* should not in every case be understood against the linguistic background of discussions of logic, in which it actually appears, and from which it takes its very name.[19] It is well known that Chrysippus generally spoke of the *lekton* as an *axiōma* ("proposition"), even where it is an incomplete *axiōma*,[20] and thus always highlighted its logical value. Moreover, the most canonical ancient definition, which one might call foundational for our interpretation of the Stoic *lekton*, runs as follows:

> The *lekton* is what subsists in accordance with a logical impression (κατὰ λογικὴν φαντασίαν ὑφιστάμενον), and a logical impression is one in accordance with which the object of the impression (τὸ φαντασθὲν) can be represented discursively (λόγῳ). (LS 33C = SE *M.* 8.70)

This means that the *lekton*, which some modern readers understand and translate as "what is said" (Long 1971: 77), should be understood as something like "the sense of the statement, which the statement exhibits discursively." Some scholars even go so far as to claim that it only exists "in the moment of its utterance" (Ildefonse 1997: 138). But neither the sense of *kata* ("in accordance with") nor the place of *to phantasthen* ("the object of the impression") and its relation to the *lekton* have truly been made clear (Alessandrelli 2013: 65–75). Most importantly, what does it mean to assign the *lekton* to "the domain of logic?"

We should acknowledge that Agamben's reading, by firmly resisting the modern inclination to distinguish what concerns language from what belongs to another area, is exceptionally faithful to the unitary structure of Stoic philosophy. No exteriority is possibly in the Stoic system. The great value of Agamben's analysis, without any doubt, is that he not only recognizes this principle but also brings it to completion. And if this does not yet guarantee that the *lekton* has the ontological value he proposes, at least it clearly makes that plausible.

It is interesting, in any event, that he is entirely aware of this line of questioning. He argues that, although the context in which the sayable appears is almost everywhere linguistic, it is necessary to attend to the traces of its *non*-linguistic status preserved by our sources.

He refers to two passages in this context. The first, once again from Sextus, maintains that the Stoics say the *lekton* λέγεσθαι δεῖ, "must be said" (*M.* 8.80 = SVF II.167). Is it possible to "say" something that is linguistic? A passage from Diogenes Laertius suggests an answer, and Agamben reports it. In the seventh book of his *Lives*, Laertius specifies that προφέρονται μὲν γὰρ αἱ φωναί, λέγεται δὲ τὰ πράγματα, ἃ δὴ καὶ λεκτὰ τυγχάνει: "words are uttered, but things are said, and those things," he continues, "are *lekta*."[21] Agamben's conclusion follows directly from this: "the act of speech," he says, "and what is in question in it are different" (2016: 69).

6.2 The Metaphysical Origin of the Lekton

At this point I would like to concisely call to mind some interpretations of the *lekton* that, at least prima facie, appear similar to those we have just outlined.

That the *lekton* did not originally belong to linguistic theorizing has long been acknowledged by some commentators. Michael Frede, for example, has shown how the term's predominantly linguistic usage was only imposed by Chrysippus, who oriented it toward both the proposition (*axiōma*) and the predicate (*katēgorēma*). Frede speaks of a "*metaphysical* notion, the notion of a *fact*" (1994: 113), at least when it comes to the *lekton*'s first occurrences.

Cleanthes, the first Stoic to have used the term (according to Clement of Alexandria, *Strom.* 7.9), used it "metaphysically": he viewed it above all as the incorporeal effect of a (corporeal) cause,[22] and did not yet view such an effect as an "incomplete (*ellipes*) *lekton*" in the linguistic sense—though the presence of a logical term in the context of physics is, to say the least, "remarkable" (Ildefonse 1997: 189). Note also that Brunschwig views the *lekton* as "defined in terms of *physics*, and not of logic, dialectic, or semantics, at least in the beginning" (1995: 91).

But in truth, we can see that even this is different from Agamben's recuperative reading. The Italian philosopher approaches the *lekton* in relation to linguistic questions, although it is also something more. His attempt to uncover its non-linguistic and "objective" nature (in the sense we have seen) cannot be confounded with what scholars have intended by speaking of the "metaphysics" of the term *lekton*. For Agamben, the *lekton* continues to be the sayable, what can be or must be *said*, "the thing," certainly, but in its sayability and inasmuch as it is grasped in the act of being said. Its value is like that of an *announcement*. Far from being something properly existing or having the function of signifying, it is a sign—the sign that it is possible to speak, that the thing, in entering into language, leaves and expresses the trace of its own sayability. On Agamben's reading, the *lekton* is below the threshold of any action in language, a simple announcement of this possibility itself, an index of the fact of speech, *factum linguae*.

Despite grasping and articulating the common ground of language and ways of being, which is one of the facets of Stoicism that most interests contemporary readers (the verbal nature of the event), Agamben appears to have neglected the full scope of the *lekton*: in other words, from the concept of a predicate to Chrysippus's concept of a "complete sayable." This is because that scope is extraneous to his inquiry into the status of language—as indeed was the case for his commentary on the theory of the passions, whose practical importance he neglected, but whose philosophical force he elucidated in a novel manner. In his work we see for the first time the *lekton*'s role as, before all else, the sign of a demand, which only subsequently branches into its actual, well-known, possibilities, all of them internal to language. Perhaps this reading is better placed to provide an answer to our initial question about the relationship between philosophy and language, below the threshold of any linguistic discipline: it chooses to be a preliminary and almost foundational glance at the *lekton*, the "sayable"—mark and sign of sayability.

Conclusion: Philology and Critique

Does it matter for contemporary thought whether or not Chrysippus acted consciously in expressing the demand of the unsayable? What Agamben wants to show is clear: the Stoics were able to apprehend the "fact of language" before diving into its analysis and comprehension. But that they associated the "announcement of a demand" with the *lekton*, this fourth element that Aristotle would not understand, cannot perhaps be effectively demonstrated except through the arguments we have reconstructed here.

It is obvious that Agamben has identified a hazy area in philosophical thinking and tried to understand it from the outside, so to speak. His approach does not seem to aim at understanding the *lekton*, but rather philosophy through the *lekton*. Perhaps this finds some justification in a claim made by Hülser and many others, namely that the sources for the Stoic *lekton* only furnish us with a very simplified version of the theory. They are "very elementary and not very satisfying: their exposition is essentially incomplete" (Hülser 1987: 832). This inspires us to go beyond the letter of the texts, to grasp the theory's role in the broader preoccupations of ancient philosophy, and, with it, of *philosophy as a whole*, on the basis of a contemporary urgency.

And yet, the most striking feature of Agamben's proposal is its obvious emphasis on philological rigor. All his answers are grounded in the text of his sources, and every connection that might appear illegitimate on the historical plane (perhaps including that between the sayable and the Idea) is, so to speak, justified on the "literal" plane. Every external perspective is complemented and constrained by the most tenacious philological care, which remains entirely delimited and defined by the evidence.

In the short text entitled "Project for a Review" in *Infancy and History*, which was supposed to introduce a program suspended long ago, Agamben locates in "philology" a way of reappropriating the past. "Philology," we read, "awakens the myth from its archetypal rigidity and its isolation, and returns it to history" (2001: 151). It is what recuperates "in a critical manner" "the fracture in speech," which coincides with the division between "content" and its "historical transmission" (2001: 147).

What Agamben adds to the understanding of ancient thought should perhaps be grasped from this angle: a critical philology that aims at the *arkhē* operating in history—not in the sense of a chronological origin, as in Walter Benjamin's famous formulation, but as a presence that still and always proposes itself and makes itself visible in the historical process, though without ever becoming identical with that process.

Thus, archaeological work explores the places where thought—this unique thought that connects and establishes "western history"—finally makes itself intelligible, freed from what makes it inaccessible, ossifies it into fixed categories, and locks away all its hidden potential. This is not simply a matter of dialogue—between us and the ancients, between the contemporary demand of the unsayable and the Stoic expression of the sayable. Stoicism comes closer to us in a concrete sense, alive with the questions it poses and the answers it gives. By suspending thought's allegiance to chronological sequencing, we recognize Stoicism as an interlocutor like others, and better than some others. It becomes not only lively but also influential—"foundational" even, as Pohlenz said, "for western philosophy of language" (1939: 151)—but through a perspective that is original and profuse. The Stoic "revolution in logic," whose motivations lie, as Émile Bréhier writes, "in physics" (1962: 13), becomes with Agamben an extraordinary emergence, the very first, the most foundational, for "ontological" reasons.

Notes

1 Plato *Phaedrus* 95d7, *Cratylus* 426a2, *Theaetetus* 175c8, *Republic* 533c2.
2 For a discussion of the relationship between language and music based on ratios and proportions, see also Koller (1955) and Georgiades (1958).
3 διαλεκτικὸν μόνον εἶναι τὸν σοφόν, DL 7.83.
4 Το τὸ ὁμολογουμένως τῇ φύσει ζῆν (DL 7. 87 = SVF I Zeno 179 = LS 63C), "ethical life in agreement with nature."
5 Grammar is a textbook case. Ildefonse has demonstrated that the Stoics could only "refuse, avert an autonomy" of grammar or other linguistic disciplines, precisely "for philosophical reasons" connected to their project of a "systematic philosophy" (1997: 139).
6 πάθος δὲ πλεονάζουσα ὁρμὴ ἢ ὑπερτείνουσα τὰ κατὰ τὸν λόγον μέτρα.
7 ἄλογόν τε καὶ παρὰ φύσιν κίνησιν ψυχῆς.
8 Agamben clarifies that "in the fragments of the Stoics . . . we nowhere find such an explicit assertion; however, this is the only one that does not contradict the premises of their theory of the passions" (2010: 85).
9 ἦν δὲ καὶ ἄλλη τις παρὰ τούτοις διάστασις, καθ' ἣν οἱ μὲν περὶ τῷ σημαινομένῳ τὸ ἀληθές τε καὶ ψεῦδος ὑπεστήσαντο, οἱ δὲ περὶ τῇ φωνῇ, οἱ δὲ περὶ τῇ κινήσει τῆς διανοίας. καὶ δὴ τῆς μὲν πρώτης δόξης προεστήκασιν οἱ ἀπὸ τῆς Στοᾶς, τρία φάμενοι συζυγεῖν ἀλλήλοις, τό τε σημαινόμενον καὶ τὸ σημαῖνον καὶ τὸ τυγχάνον, ὧν σημαῖνον μὲν εἶναι τὴν φωνήν, οἷον τὴν 'Δίων', σημαινόμενον δὲ αὐτὸ τὸ πρᾶγμα τὸ ὑπ' αὐτῆς δηλούμενον καὶ οὗ ἡμεῖς μὲν ἀντιλαμβανόμεθα τῇ ἡμετέρᾳ παρυφισταμένου διανοίᾳ, οἱ δὲ βάρβαροι οὐκ ἐπαΐουσι καίπερ τῆς φωνῆς ἀκούοντες, τυγχάνον δὲ τὸ ἐκτὸς ὑποκείμενον, ὥσπερ αὐτὸς ὁ Δίων. τούτων δὲ δύο

μὲν εἶναι σώματα, καθάπερ τὴν φωνὴν καὶ τὸ τυγχάνον, ἓν δὲ ἀσώματον, ὥσπερ τὸ σημαινόμενον πρᾶγμα, καὶ λεκτόν, ὅπερ ἀληθές τε γίνεται ἢ ψεῦδος.

10 For instance, Michel Foucault attributes to the Stoics the very invention of this triadic system of signs (1966: 57).
11 Gourinat objects, citing Priscian, that "in antiquity an isolated proper noun, employed as an answer, designates a complete proposition" (2000: 112).
12 [My translation of this phrase follows that of Chiesa in Agamben 2018. (KL).]
13 Note here that, in order to assert the ontological nature of the *lekton*, Agamben does not need the Heideggerian thesis, which he knows very well, about the ontological rather than logical value of the Greek verb *legein*. Cf. Hadot (1980).
14 The principal manuscripts for Burnet and Souilhé are Parisinus graecus 1807 and Vaticanus graecus 1. The reading δι'ὅ was only restored in 1923 by Andreae (Agamben 2010: 23).
15 On the anaphoric use of αὐτὸς, see Chantraine (1968: 143), Ildefonse (2014: 20).
16 On the status of anaphoric pronouns, see Benveniste (1966: 251–7), Jakobson (1971: 130–47).
17 Long notes that a reading of Plato was, for Zeno at least, obligatory; but Zeno's attitude, probably following Antisthenes, was one of suspicion, especially with regard to the separate nature of Ideas and the immateriality of the soul (1996: 18–19).
18 Daniel Heller-Roazen, in the "Editor's Introduction" to Agamben 1999, has already proposed a reading of the Stoic *lekton* in this direction. It is the *lekton*, he writes, which expresses in antiquity "the fact that something appears in language and that language itself, in this appearance, takes place." He also effectively demonstrates the enduring nature of this element in the history of philosophy, notably in the anonymous thirteenth-century *Ars Burana*, where the *enuntiabile* is said to be *extrapredicamentale*, in other words beyond Aristotle's categories and categoriality itself (*predicamentum enuntiabile*); then in the works of Peter Abelard and Gregory of Rimini (fourteenth century), and through the theorization of "objective" contents of thought by Alexius Meinong, which subsist (*bestehen*) without however existing (*existieren*) (Heller-Roazen 1999: 10–12).
19 Hülser says, "von Hause aus ist die Lekton-Theorie kein Thema der Physik, sondern eins der Dialektik" (1987: 833).
20 Think, for example, of the text where Sextus says that what is true (*to alēthes*) is a proposition (*axiōma*), and the proposition is immediately defined as a *lekton* (LS 33P; cf. SE *M*. 7.38 = SVF II.132, Isnardi Parente 2005: 183).
21 Agamben could perhaps have added, in addition to these passages, what Plutarch says. In speaking of the γένος τῶν λεκτῶν, he links it to what is οὐσίαν τῷ λόγῳ παρέχον (Plut. *Adv. col.* 1119f).
22 Chrysippus had clarified (contrary to Zeno, who left it undetermined) that the effect—that "of which the cause is a cause"—is not a body (SVF I.89). He also secured some reality for the predicate, even though it is not an attribute of a body (συμβεβηκ ός), by speaking of entities that "subsist" (SVF II.509; see Sedley 1999: 398).

Bibliography

Agamben, G. (1982), *Il linguaggio e la morte. Un seminario sul luogo della negatività*, Torino: Einaudi.

Agamben, G. (2001), *Infanzia e storia. Distruzione dell'esperienza e origine della storia*, Nuova edizione accresciuta, Torino: Einaudi.
Agamben, G. (2010), *La potenza del pensiero. Saggi e conferenze*, Vicenza: Neri Pozza.
Agamben, G. (2015), *L'avventura*, Roma: Nottetempo.
Agamben, G. (2016), *Che cos'è la filosofia?*, Macerata: Quodlibet.
Agamben, G. (2018) *What Is Philosophy?* trans. Lorenzo Chiesa, Stanford: Palo Alto.
Alessandrelli, M. (2013), *Il problema del lekton nello Stoicismo antico. Origine e statuto di una nozione controversa*, Firenze: Leo S. Olschki Editore.
Andreae, W. (1929), "Die philosophischen Probleme in den platonischen Briefen," *Philologus* 78: 34–87.
Benjamin, W. (1995), *Brief an Martin Buber vom 17. Juli 1916*, in *Briefe*, 6 Bd., Frankfurt am Main: Suhrkamp.
Benveniste, E. (1966), *Problèmes de linguistique générale*, vol. I, Paris: Gallimard.
Bréhier, E. (1962), *La théorie des incorporels dans l'ancien stoïcisme*, 3rd ed., Paris: Picard.
Brunschwig, J. (1995), "Remarques sur la théorie stoïcienne du nom propre," *Histoire Epistémologie Langage* 6 (1): 3–19.
Chantraine, P. (1968), *Dictionnaire étymologique de la langue grecque. Histoire des mots* I, Paris: Klincksieck.
Coseriu, E. (2003), *Geschichte der Sprachphilosophie von der Antike bis zum Gegenwart 1: Von den Anfängen bis Rousseau*, Stuttgart: A. Franke.
Foucault, M. (1966), *Les mots et les choses. Une archéologie des sciences humaines*, Paris: Gallimard.
Frede, M. (1994), "The Stoic Notion of a *lekton*," in S. Everson (ed.), *Companions to Ancient Thought, 3: Philosophy of Language*, 109–28, Cambridge: Cambridge University Press.
Frege, G. (1892), "Über Sinn und Bedeutung," *Zeitschrift für Philosophie und philosophische Kritik* 100: 22–50.
Georgiades, T. (1958), *Musik und Rhythmus bei den Griechen*, Hamburg: Rowohlt.
Gourinat, J.-B. (2000), *La dialectique des stoïciens*, Paris: Vrin.
Hadot, P. (1980), "Sur divers sens du mot 'pragma' dans la tradition philosophique grecque," in P. Aubenque (ed.), *Concepts et catégories dans la pensée antique*, 309–19, Paris: Vrin.
Heidegger, M. (1962), *Being and Time*, trans. John Macquarrie and Edward Robinson, Harper and Row: New York.
Heller-Roazen, D. (1999), "Editors' Introduction," in G. Agamben, *Potentialities*, 1–23, Stanford: Stanford University Press.
Hülser, K. (1987), *Die Fragmente Zur Dialektik der Stoiker. Neue Sammlung der Texte Mit Deutscher Übersetzung Und Kommentaren von Karlheinz Hülser*, 4 vols., Stuttgart: Frommann-Holzboog.
Ildefonse, F. (1997), *La naissance de la grammaire dans l'Antiquité grecque*, Paris: Vrin.
Ildefonse, F. (2014), "Que nous apprend le αὐτός ilidiaque?," in D. Doucet and I. Koch (eds.), *Autos, Idipsum. Aspects de l'identité d'Homère à Augustin*, 19–37, Aix-en-Provence: Presses universitaires de Provence.
Imbert, C. (1993), *Phénoménologie et langues formulaires*, Paris: PUF.
Isnardi Parente, M. (2005), "La notion d'incorporel chez les stoïciens," in G. R. Dherbey and J.-B. Gourinat (eds.), *Les stoïciens*, 175–85, Paris: Vrin.
Jakobson, R. (1971), *Selected Writings* II, The Hague: Mouton.
Joly, E. (1986), *Philosophie du langage et grammaire dans l'Antiquité*, Bruxelles-Grenoble: Ousia-Université de Sciences Sociales de Grenoble.

Koller, H. (1955), "Stoicheion," *Glotta* 34: 161–74.
Lohmann, J. (1970), *Musiké und Logos. Aufsätze zur griechischen Philosophie und Musiktheorie*, hg. v. A. Giannaras, Stuttgart: Musikwissenschaftl. Verlags-Gesellschaft.
Long, A. A. (1971), "Language and thought in Stoicism," in A. A. Long (ed.), *Problems in Stoicism*, 75–113, London: The Athlone Press.
Long, A. A. (1996), "Stoic Psychology and the Elucidation of Language," in G. Manetti (ed.), *Knowledge through Signs: Ancient Semiotic Theories and Practices*, 109–31, Brussels: Brepols.
Pohlenz, M. (1939), "Die Begründung der abendländischen Sprachlehre durch die Stoa," *Nachrichten der Göttinger Gesellschaft* 6: 151–98.
Schubert, A. (1994), *Untersuchungen zur stoischen Bedeutungslehre*, Göttingen: Vandenhoeck & Ruprecht.
Sedley, D. (1999), "Hellenistic Physics and Metaphysics," in K. Algra, J. Barnes, J. Mansfeld, and M. Schofield (eds.), *The Cambridge History of Hellenistic Philosophy*, 355–411, Cambridge: Cambridge University Press.

Chapter 12

MAKING USE OF AGAMBEN'S "STOIC PROVIDENCE-FATE APPARATUS"

A READING OF SENECA'S *CONSOLATION TO POLYBIUS*[1]

Clifford A. Robinson

1 Introduction

Giorgio Agamben's Homo Sacer series uses a wealth of resources from Western poetry, philosophy, and theology to advance a radical critique of present political conditions. My argument proceeds from that critique toward an appreciation of the contribution that ancient Stoicism makes to Agamben's project. I draw upon Agamben's three discussions of Stoicism in the Homo Sacer series, while giving priority to the fifth chapter from *The Kingdom and the Glory* (2011), "The Providential Machine," where Agamben discusses the "Stoic providence-fate apparatus." There, Agamben criticizes Foucault's genealogy of governmentality through a reading of the ancient debate on the Stoic theory of providence, highlighting how the Stoics introduced a decisive split into the being and praxis of God's nature—a separation that ultimately conditions the development of modern governmentality.[2] Agamben's two further discussions of Stoicism in *Opus Dei* (2013) and *The Use of Bodies* (2015) complicate the relationship between his critical, genealogical engagement with Stoic legacies in *The Kingdom and the Glory* and his increasingly affirmative view of Stoic ethical theory. For Agamben, Stoicism stands out among the ancient philosophical schools, insofar as Stoic ethical paradigms render inoperative the problematic operation of sovereign power and economic governmentality.

One difficulty with Agamben's analysis of a "Stoic providence-fate apparatus" arises from his selection of evidence: none of the texts he introduces is simply Stoic. Since Agamben traces the genealogy of governmentality back to the Stoics and their arguments on providence, one would expect that his analysis should deploy Stoic texts as evidence of this philosophical archaeology. The first source he introduces, a close paraphrase of a fragment from Chrysippus's *On Providence* (SVF II.1170) exchanged between Leibniz and Bayle (Leibniz 1951: 258), does at least focus Agamben's analysis of the connection between early modern theodicy and an ancient text fundamental to Stoic arguments on providence (Agamben 2011: 114–15).

The other passages from which he develops his argument all involve distinct philosophical persuasions, from Aristotelianism or Middle Platonism to Neoplatonism or Scholasticism (Agamben 2011: 115–39).[3] Agamben's choice may be justified in part by his concern to demonstrate not only how "the immense debate on providence ... began with the Stoics" but also how that debate "reached almost without interruption the threshold of modernity" (Agamben 2011: 113). Nevertheless, to the extent that Agamben foregoes analysis of ancient Stoic evidence, it remains unsettled whether or not the Stoics can be considered the point of origin for the debate which Agamben's chapter recounts. At the very least, investigation of a surviving Stoic text could support Agamben's genealogy tracing a Stoic origin of the providence-fate apparatus.[4]

For this reason, in the second part of this chapter, I focus on the exemplarity of Agamben's analyses for reading another Stoic text upon which Agamben has never commented. The challenge here is not simply to analyze whether Agamben's theory achieves a historically reliable reading of a Stoic text; rather, the goal is to reveal how unrealized powers of the text's political force, or, as Agamben might put it, its destituent potential (Agamben 2015: 263–79) may be located and developed. Taking direction from Agamben's commentary on Stoicism, I show how Seneca's *Dialogus XI*, the *Consolation to Polybius*, supports Agamben's suggestion of a Stoic origin for the providence-fate apparatus, even as Agamben's thought makes available a contemporary, "common use" of an ancient Stoic source.

I have selected the *Consolation* for this experiment of excavating the destituent potential of a Stoic text because it foregrounds the principal theme of the first volume of the Homo Sacer series (Agamben 1998): the constituting relationship through which sovereign power inaugurates itself by exposing what Agamben calls "bare life," that is, life reduced to its mere biological existence, its "*zoē*," or life void of any "form" or "way" of life, of any "*bios*" (Agamben 1998: 15–67). In the *Consolation*, Seneca treats numerous themes near to Agamben's work—the rule of law and the exception, providential government and negative collateral effects, duty to others and the government of self and others, and finally *oikeiosis* and the use of the self. But, because the *Consolation* situates its author as composing this address sometime between 41 and 43 CE from an exile imposed by the emperor in 41 CE, his very act of writing and the text itself are expressions of bare life exposed to the violence of the sovereign ban (Agamben 1998: 58–67).

By confronting Seneca's text with categories derived from Agamben's Homo Sacer series, it may also be possible to reconceive Seneca's political strategy in the *Consolation*. Others have argued that, beyond the apparent purpose of consoling Polybius, whose brother had suffered an untimely death, Seneca must have had some additional political purpose in writing to him: Polybius was after all a freedman of the emperor Claudius and, as seems likely, the secretary *a libellis*, the official charged with receiving and reviewing petitions to the emperor.[5] But beyond this point, scholarly opinion is divided. Some scholars, following Cassius Dio's criticism of Seneca (61.10.2), have taken Seneca's purpose as obsequious flattery designed to secure his recall from Corsica; others have seen an ironic, satirical message in Seneca's text, so that his purpose was to ridicule the *Princeps* and his supporters (Atkinson 1985: 872–9). I argue that Seneca's performance in this *Consolation*, understood in light of Agamben's philosophy, appears as a subtle deposing of the emperor's power to command and a destabilizing reorientation of its anarchic potential.

2 The Stoic Providence-Fate Apparatus in "The Providential Machine"

In "The Providential Machine," Agamben shows that the Stoics, by initiating a debate that coordinated fate and providence into "a bipolar system" or a subjectifying apparatus, "produc[ed] a . . . zone of indifference between what is primary and what is secondary, the general and the particular, the final cause and the effects" (2011: 122). The "effectual ontology" elaborated through that debate, which only ever worked toward a "functional correlation" of these indifferent oppositions, he claims, "in a way contains the condition of possibility for modern governmentality" (2011: 122). If, as Agamben argues, an apparatus acts as a strategy of governance through which operations of power, lacking any foundation in being, capture living beings as subjects,[6] then the "Stoic providence-fate apparatus" captures all living beings as subjects of a bipolar coordination of divine providence and fate.

In "The Providential Machine," Agamben argues that the ancient debate over providence was concerned to explain how "a divine government of the world" (2011: 114), the paradigmatic form of governmentality, is possible. Agamben's problem here is that "if the Kingdom and the Government are separated by a clear opposition, then no government of the world is actually possible" (2011: 114). There would remain only "an impotent sovereignty and . . . the infinite and chaotic series of particular (and violent) acts of providence," but the divine government of the world only becomes possible when "the Kingdom and the Government are correlated in a bipolar machine: the government is precisely what results from the coordination and articulation of special and general providence" (2011: 114). So here Agamben contrasts two models of cosmological order passed from the Stoics down to Aquinas. On the one hand, there is "the Kingdom" or the *regnum* that Agamben understands with Foucault as the paradigm of sovereign power (Foucault 2009: 227–54; Agamben 2011: 109–13). On the other, there is the "Government" or the *gubernatio mundi*, which Agamben associates with special providence, the series of particular providential actions undertaken by intermediate causes on behalf of the sovereign. This specialized providential action can also be understood as the *dispositio* through which general providence is realized, so that this coordination of special providence with the sovereign's will, understood as general providence, becomes an apparatus, a relation of power through which living beings are captured as subjects.

Through commentary upon three texts, a fragment of Chrysippus's *On Providence* quoted in Aulus Gellius's *Attic Nights*, Alexander of Aphrodisias's *On Providence*, and the essay *On Fate* included among Plutarch's *Moralia*, Agamben establishes that the Stoics first coordinated providence and fate into a subjectifying apparatus. His strategy works analogically across the genealogy through which ancient accounts of providence condition the later possibility of arguments over theodicy. Accordingly, Agamben refers specifically to a paraphrase Bayle had made of this passage of Chrysippus from Aulus Gellius, to show how the Stoics forged "the strategic conjunction of two apparently different problems: that of the origin and justification of evil, and that of the government of the world" (Agamben 2011: 114). In response to the question of whether providence is responsible for such an apparent affliction to humans as disease, Chrysippus seems to have said that "Nature, in preparing and producing many great things excellently ordered and of great usefulness, found that some drawbacks came as a result, and thus these were not in conformity with the original design and purpose" (Aul. Gell. 7.1.7; SVF II.1170; Leibniz 1951: 258; Agamben 2011: 115). These drawbacks, Chrysippus held, "came about as a sequel to the work" and "existed only as consequences which were somehow necessary," but also occurred only "*kata parakolouthēsin* [according to concomitance]" (Aul. Gell. 7.1.7; SVF II.1170; Leibniz 1951: 258; Agamben 2011: 115). This rationalization of afflictions to humanity such as disease or natural disasters opens up a cleavage between one order of providential causality and a second, unintentional order of unavoidable effects.

For Chrysippus, the order of causality and its unintended effects seem to be only two ways of looking at the same providence.[7] The separation between providence and consequences according to concomitance only gradually became a more radical division between general and special providence, as Agamben reveals though his discussion of Alexander of Aphrodisias, an Aristotelian commentator opposed to the Stoics' account of providence. Agamben introduces Alexander because his account reveals how the apparatus which the Stoics constructed would come to involve two distinct but correlated orders of causality: providence as a general cause and fate as a series of specific causes. Alexander objects to the Stoic view that God's providence "looks after both the world in general and particular things" (Agamben 2011: 115), since God must be greater than a master of an estate or a king, neither of whom would trouble himself to manage every trivial matter concerning his property or kingdom. God too must only "prefer to exercise his providence in a universal and general way" (Alexander 1999: 117; in Agamben 2011: 116), not intervening in particular circumstances. Alexander thus argues that, since God "is too high for us to say of him that he looks after men, mice, and ants . . . he rather needs to take into consideration the most important things, while these" particulars "should remain irrelevant for him" (Alexander 1999: 119; Agamben 2011: 116).

A division becomes necessary, Agamben suggests, between providence "in itself" (*kath' hauto*) and providence "by accident" (*kata symbebēkos*) (Alexander 1999: 236; Agamben 2011: 116–18). Providence "by accident" presents a problem, because, although God cannot be so lowly as to fuss over particulars, he also cannot be entirely ignorant of the effect of his general providence on particular things. Alexander resorts to another explanation for God's knowing neglect of particulars; on this model, the divine being may not intentionally make provision for particular cases, but the divine power which we also call "nature" makes subsist the things in which it is found and gives them a form according to a certain ordered connection, but this does not happen in virtue of some decision. Nature does not exercise decision and rational reflection with regard to all the things it does, since nature is an irrational power. (Alexander 1999: 151; in Agamben 2011: 117)

Intermediate between "for itself" and "by accident," Nature acts without volition, yet not accidentally. Through what Alexander calls a "divine technique" (Alexander 1999: 151; in Agamben 2011: 117), nature proceeds independently of general providence to realize an accord with general providence, so that their separation is correlated and coordinated. In this way, unintentional and yet natural consequences may be known by God without "eliminat[ing] their accidental character" (Alexander 1999: 236–40; Agamben 2011: 118). Alexander finally claims, "The being that does not act in view of something, but knows that it benefits and wants it, can be said to provide for it, but neither by itself nor by accident" (Alexander 1999: 236; in Agamben 2011: 117–18).

God's knowing expectation of specific effects caused correlatively by general providence is thus for Alexander the paradigm of governmental action (Agamben 2011: 118–19). Agamben establishes that this theory of providence develops in a contingent way a correlation of the general and particular that amounts to a theorization of the government of the world (*gubernatio mundi*): "Whether providence manifests itself only in the universal principles," as Alexander has it, "or descends to earth to look after the lowest particular things," as the Stoics argue,[8] "it will in any case need to pass through the very nature of things and follow their immanent 'economy'" (2011: 118). For Alexander, though, "the government of the world occurs neither by means of the tyrannical imposition of an external general will, nor by accident, but through the knowing anticipation of the collateral effects that arise from the very nature of things and remain absolutely contingent in their singularity" (Agamben 2011: 118–19). Thus it becomes clear how two correlated causal frameworks form a subjectifying apparatus: general providence anticipates special, collateral effects unfolding according to the contingent series of natural events.

Turning to Plutarch's corpus for a theorization of fate,[9] the last undefined term in the expression "providence-fate apparatus," Agamben explains how providence "by accident" comes to be theorized not simply as natural contingency, but as *heimarmenē* or "fate." Agamben claims that the Platonist author of the essay *On Fate* "follow[s] a Stoic model" that "redouble[s]" ontology into a pragmatics, so that fate must be understood both as *ousia* (substance) and as *energeia* (activity) (Agamben 2011: 120). As *ousia*, fate is "the soul of the world . . . divided spatially into . . . the heaven of the fixed stars, the part containing the 'errant' planets, and the part located beneath the heavens in the terrestrial region" (Agamben 2011: 120). As *energeia*, fate is assimilated by Plutarch to the law of nature (*nomos*), the series of natural causes "determining the course of everything that must come to pass" (*On Fate* 568d; Agamben 2011: 120).

If the paradigm of law governs the connection between fate in general and fate "in particular" (that is, fate *kata meros* or *kath' hekasta, On Fate* 569d), particular facts,

Agamben holds, can only be regarded as the result of efficient causes that follow a general law. He explains, "Plutarch thus identifies what pertains to destiny"—destiny is used as another word for *heimarmenē* or "fate" in the translation—"with what is effectual or conditional (*to ex hypotheseōs*)," or, as he quotes from Plutarch, "with that which is not laid down independently, but in some fashion is really 'subjoined' to something else, wherever there is an expression implying that if one is true, another follows" (*De fato* 570a; in Agamben 2011: 121). According to this account, the claim that "everything happens according to destiny" (*panta kath' heimarmenēn*, 570c) applies only to consequences and effects, never to antecedents, which have the character of hypothetical laws or of "what has been established primarily [*proēgēsamenois*] in the divine appointment of things" (570e). Agamben concludes, "destiny divides what is real into two different levels: that of the general antecedents (*proēgoumena*) and that of the particular effects. The former are somehow *in* destiny" or fate, "but do not occur *according to* destiny, and destiny is that which results effectually from the correlation between the two levels" (2011: 121).

Agamben observes a formal symmetry between the three levels of fate considered as a substance and the three levels of providence. A first providence, providence in the precise sense (573b), is identified as the intellection and will of the primary god (572f). This first providence generates a second providence, "created together with destiny" or fate and "included in the first providence" (574b)—these are the secondary gods who dwell in the heavens. As the third providence, there is the whole array of demonic beings "commissioned to oversee and order the individual actions of men" (Agamben 2011: 121). Plutarch draws an analogy, according to which fate or destiny is ultimately comparable to the law, just as the first providence is comparable to law-giving or "the political legislation appropriate to the souls of men" (573d). The law of fate thus proceeds primarily as *proēgoumena*, primary antecedents, of a hypothetical and general character, which are in fate but do not occur according to fate, and only secondarily as consequences or effects of the *proēgoumena*. Meanwhile, providence presides over that fate as a legislating will and intelligence that gives birth to that law. In other words, Agamben argues that providence in the precise sense stands in relation to fate as a *proēgoumenon* or as a primary antecedent with respect to its consequence or effect, so that fate must be considered a consequence of primary providence.

The ambiguous position of fate, consequent with respect to providence but primary with respect to its particular effects, leads to Agamben's conclusion. He writes of a "functional correlation" through which the general and the particular, the primary and the consequent, and the end and the means are brought into a "zone of indifference," laying the conceptual foundation for what would become modern governmentality. Just as solving the problem of evil was not really in view when Chrysippus characterized god's immanent providence in the world as "government of the world," but the problem of evil nevertheless sprung up once he took his position on providence, so too was the bipolarization of final and efficient causes, means and ends, primary and antecedent, and general and particular not necessarily intended by the participants in this debate, but nevertheless this bipolarization was accomplished.

3 The Stoic Providence-Fate Apparatus in Seneca's Consolation to Polybius

Agamben's "providence-fate apparatus" can be located in Seneca's *Consolation* through the three terms which Agamben considers crucial to any apparatus: first, the living being an apparatus aims to capture; second, the operations of power, cut off from being but nevertheless active among beings; and, third, the subjectivity constructed by the operation of power on the living being.[10] I contend that certain personifications typical of declamatory practice in the first century CE become in Seneca's philosophical rhetoric the operating terms of a providence-fate apparatus: Nature and Fate as providential action, but also Fortune as concomitant effect of providence.[11] Meanwhile, Seneca's persona can be understood through Seneca's notion of bare life, the remainder of life produced by the sovereign ban as an exclusive inclusion from the political order (Agamben 1998: 15–29). His persona is thus particularly worthy of attention here, insofar as he brings the relation between sovereign power and bare life into focus.

The providence-fate apparatus in which Seneca situates himself also involves other subjects, namely, the freedman Polybius, bereaved of his brother and acting as the secretary *a libellis*, and the emperor Claudius, presented as a consoler of Polybius, a champion in the battle against Fortune, and, paradoxically, a coagent of Fortune. Seneca, as bare life separated from all social relations but nevertheless subject to power relations with the emperor, may seem simply to be a mere "secondary effect" of Claudius's will, a mediator performing the *officia* of a consoler within the government of self and others established by Claudius's sovereignty. However, Seneca also makes use of himself, his remaining capacities, and the ambiguities of the providence-fate apparatus to expose—or, even as Agamben might say, to depose—the anarchic potential of the imperial command to which he remains subject even in his exile.

3.1 Seneca's Use of Nature, Fate, and Fortune as a Providence-Fate Apparatus

Chrysippus's providential theology allows for no fracture separating providence and fate; rather, there are only providence's perfect action and the seemingly negative, "concomitant effects" of that action. Much of Seneca's consolatory argumentation is aimed at establishing this position through the dual alliance of Nature and Fate; yet, at the same time, Seneca foregrounds the concomitant effects of providential governance with Fortune's persona and her unpredictably contingent actions. Seneca ultimately provides a perspective in which these personified forces can be reconciled into one paradigm of providential governance.

Seneca's surviving text begins by advancing natural law's universality as a source of consolation and coordinating Nature and Fate as agents of justice, order, causality, and right legal judgment in the cosmos. "The greatest source of consolation," he writes, "is to contemplate that everyone before you has suffered and everyone will suffer what has happened to you; and thus Nature [*rerum natura*] seems to me to have made common what it has made hardest, so that Fate's equality might offer consolation for its cruelty" (1.4).[12] Fate and Nature are conformed to one another, perhaps even treated as interchangeable, so that Nature-Fate is characterized as both a constructive force and as a legal apparatus. Seneca returns to this idea at several other points in the consolation. In the fourth paragraph, advocating that Polybius give up all lamentation, he explains that the "Fates ... stand hard and inexorable; no one can move them with reproaches, no one with tears, no one with their just cause; they never spare anyone from anything, nor do they relent" (4.1). He also joins this mercilessness to Nature, arguing that "the kind of life Nature has promised us" is evident from the fact that "weeping is the first thing humans do after being born" (4.3). Later in the tenth paragraph, Seneca challenges Polybius's claim to possess his deceased brother in terms borrowed from economic exchange and property law: "The Nature of things gave him to you not for legal possession, in the same way she gave to others their own brothers; rather she loaned him. When it seems good to her then, she reclaims him and she does not pursue your satisfaction with him, but rather her own law" (10.4). Again, in paragraph 11, against the claim that an unexpected death is painful, Seneca excuses "Nature," saying that humans must know better or blame themselves, since she "testifies that she will make an exception from her necessity for no one" (11.1). Seneca thus presents Nature and Fate as interchangeable terms for the necessity that governs the world through a consistent legal order.

Fortune is introduced as a third term that challenges the coherence and completeness of Fate and Nature's necessity. In fact, the surviving text begins with two long laments at 2.2-7 and 3.4-5, in which Seneca protests against Fortune's injustice to Polybius and blames her for Polybius's brother's death. Accusations against her persist nearly to the end of the text: at 4.1, reason must bring weeping to an end, because Fortune will not do so; at 5.4, Polybius may show his other brothers an example of courage by enduring this assault from Fortune; at 13.2, Seneca explains that, when the Senate sentenced him to death, it was Fortune who had brought him to this disaster; and at 17.1, she is so bold as to intrude upon Caesar's imperial family by bringing death upon them. Fortune is thus the very personification of recklessly contingent action, appearing in this text as an enemy who brings death and loss without regard for what is orderly, consistent, and good. How can such a force be understood to coexist with Nature and Fate, which supposedly govern the world through universal, legally consistent, and good providential action?

Near the end of the text, Seneca suggests that Fate, Nature, and Fortune could perhaps be reconciled. He writes:

> What pertains to Fortune herself, even if it is not possible now to plead her case before you ... still at some later time I must defend her, as soon as that day comes which will have made you a more balanced judge of her.... For she provides many things to you, with which she may repair this injury. Even now she will give many things, by which she redeems herself. Finally, that itself which she has taken away, she herself had given to you. (18.3)

This passage introduces two problems. First, there is a limitation of perspective which Seneca's discourse takes into consideration: Polybius in his present condition may not be able to appreciate that, though Fortune has deprived him of his brother, she continues to offer him other favors. Second, and more problematically, here Fortune has given Polybius his brother, but in paragraph 10 it was Nature who had given Polybius and his brother their lives (10.4-5). Seneca thus confuses Fortune with Nature so that the incompatibility of their coexistence comes to the fore. Asmis has suggested that Fortune herself may well be only a vanishing reality, a persona who seems to be real from the Stoic progressor's perspective, but, from the point of view of the sage, who knows that there are no misfortunes, her persona must vanish from all causal accounts as nothing more than an imaginary construct (Asmis 2009: 115–27). Asmis's analysis explains how Seneca could credit Fortune and Nature for giving Polybius's brother to him, how Fortune and Nature could cooperate, and, finally, how Fortune could be among the beings who "provides" for Polybius with other compensations. All of these agents—Nature, Fate, and Fortune—are ultimately so many names for providence.

Fortune should not be too quickly assimilated to Nature and Fate, though, so that Polybius's progressor's view of her is simply disregarded. It is here that Agamben's account of the Stoic providence-fate apparatus is especially helpful for reckoning with subjectivities intruding upon the text. Where Alexander associates particular natures with a realm of natural contingency, and where Plutarch establishes a middle zone of primary and secondary causes in which their actions upon particulars are overdetermined, Seneca divides providential action into the actions of Nature, Fate, Fortune, or providence indifferently, even as he identifies the apparently negative concomitant effects of providence with the actions of Fortune. It is only as long as one keeps Fortune's distinction in view that it is possible, with Agamben, to speak of a "Stoic providence-fate apparatus." From the sage's point of view everything collapses into a perfectly coherent causal order in which there is only nature, fate, and providence. The progressor's view of reality is a partial view which records an important fact: the separation between the order of providence and the contingency of fortune. The analysis of perspective has thus brought the argument to a second aspect of the providence-fate apparatus. Beyond the apparatus correlating providence and fate into a bipolarity, the Stoic providence-fate apparatus must also involve living beings captured as subjects through the operations of power.

3.2 Seneca as Bare Life and the Exposure to Sovereign Violence

Up to now I have proceeded as if Seneca has at his command the sage's awareness of the illusory nature of Fortune. In fact, his persona is quite inconsistent. At some times, he transcends every limited perspective and recognizes Fortune and Nature's unity as a sage would; at others, he is so dismayed by the contingency of his bad Fortune that he must be considered unreliable as a consoler. For example, a pitiful *recusatio* highlighting Seneca's diminished capabilities concludes the text: "These things . . . I have composed in a distant region with a worn out and dulled mind. If they seem to answer too little to your intellect or to heal your grief too little, consider that a man cannot be free to attend to the consolation of another, if that man's own troubles keep him occupied" (18.9). Going on to explain how his Latin eloquence has diminished amid the "barbarians' rude grunting" (18.9), Seneca shows himself as clinging to what little humanity he can preserve following his separation from the Roman social order. Taken together with the laments of Fortune's violence which he voices at 2.2-7 and 3.4-5, this complaint at the text's conclusion presents Seneca as a man incapable of reconciling Fate and Fortune, as a subject so downtrodden by the concomitant effects of providence on his fortune that he cannot see beyond her persona.

Though Seneca's posturing reflects a rhetorical strategy rather than a real loss of his expressive powers, it is helpful to understand Seneca's position external to the social order as what Agamben calls bare life (1998: 63–7). Agamben complicates Schmitt's influential definition of sovereignty as both internal and external to the juridical order, insofar as the sovereign decides at the limit of constitutional order on the state of exception, by refocusing his argument on "the relation of exception" between the sovereign and the bare life (Agamben 1998: 15–29). Agamben defines the sovereign exception as an operation performed upon living beings which transforms them by separating their form or way of life from their purely biological existence, their bare life (1998: 25–7, 63–67). Sovereign power thus sustains itself by positing an "exclusive inclusion" of bare life (Agamben 1998: 21–2), a suspended relation or "ban" (Agamben 1998: 28–9) enforced upon the living being by sovereign power.

That Seneca's diminished powers of expression and cognition may involve sovereign violence exacted upon him by the emperor Claudius' decision becomes clear in paragraph 13, as Seneca digresses to mention a trial before the Senate in which he was sentenced to death:

> [Caesar] has not so cast me down, that he would not want me to rise up again—or he has not cast me down at all, but he has supported me, when I have been struck by Fortune and I have fallen, and, as I was rushing headlong, the application [*usus*] of his divine hand has gently put me in my place [*deposuit*] with restraint. He interceded with the Senate on my behalf and not only gave me life but also petitioned it for me. (13.2)

Seneca reveals that, following the Senate's decision to consign him to death, the emperor Claudius interceded so that Seneca was spared (Giardina 2000: 77–9). From external sources it can be established that Seneca's punishment was reduced to relegation, a common form of exile in the imperial period.[13] Situated in this way as beyond the protections of the law and yet not fully outside of its reach, Seneca can be considered bare life in Agamben's precise sense: having been consigned to a social death, Seneca is both restored to the precarity of biological life and deprived of his social identity by the emperor Claudius's decision.

Somewhat surprising, then, is the substitution of Fortune for Claudius as the agent who "cast down" Seneca (13.2). The convict's attitude toward his trial involves this confusion about his position within the providence-fate apparatus: just as Fortune can represent the contingent, concomitant effects of providence, here too she can substitute for the sovereign who reduced Seneca to his bare, biological life through a decision, perhaps indicating a deeper relationship between Claudius's *imperium* and Fortune's contingent action.[14] She represents an anarchic element active within the providence-fate apparatus that upsets the coherence of Nature and Fate, just as Claudius's *imperium* can frustrate the constitutional power of the Senate and its legal and juridical authority. For this reason, Fortune too can exercise sovereign violence upon living beings, when Fortune not only attacks the likes of Seneca and Polybius's brother or leading Republican families (14.2-15.2), but dares "to bring mourning upon" the Caesars by claiming lives from the imperial household (15.2-16.3). Seneca's decline to the non-status of bare life compromises his powers of intellection and expression, so that, like Polybius, he cannot see beyond his grief and mourning to situate Fortune correctly as a concomitant effect of providential action.

3.3 Subject Formation and the Duties of the Consoler

Seneca's diminished condition raises an important question: If Seneca, like Polybius, is a Stoic progressor so compromised by grief for his exile that he cannot see the truth about his situation, why has he appointed himself the task of consoling Polybius, a task to which "a man cannot be free to attend . . . if that man's own troubles keep him occupied" (18.9)? Seneca answers this question at paragraph 13, explaining that he "will apply all [his] effort, so that [Claudius] may not blush to rescue [him]," since the emperor "knows best the time at which he ought to help anyone" (13.3). Though Seneca, as bare life, has been separated from every social relation through the sovereign ban, he nevertheless persists as a subject of power relations with the emperor. His subjection to the emperor's power relations is the only connection to social relations left to him, so, if Seneca wants to make the most of his situation, he must somehow make himself worthy of further clemency from the emperor.

At this point, Seneca is faced with a problem. To act in the service of the emperor, one must have *officia*, or "duties," the fulfillment of which would be well regarded by the emperor, but his relegation to Corsica would have removed him from all conceivable duties. For help here we may turn to Agamben's "The Genealogy of Office" (2013: 65–88), where Agamben argues that Cicero's translation of the Stoic term *kathēkonta* with the Latin *officia* transformed the meaning of *kathēkonta*, which Agamben understands as "what is respectable and appropriate to do according to the circumstances, above all taking account of the agent's social condition" (Agamben 2013: 67). Polybius, for example, has a definable social position as the secretary *a libellis*—the official charged with reviewing petitions to the emperor.[15] In paragraph 6, Seneca explains how Polybius's "great *persona*" disallows certain actions and requires others; that this paragraph concerns *officia* is clear from the use of the word at 6.4. Important here is how the *officia* assigned by Caesar and Fortune indifferently come into focus at the end of this paragraph, where Seneca contrasts the advantages and disadvantages of his and Polybius's respective positions:

Many things are not allowed to you, which are allowed to the lowest and to those lying in some corner of the world; great fortune is great slavery. It is not allowed to you to do anything according to your own judgment: so many thousands of men must be heard, so many applications must be disposed [*disponendi*] ... so that it can be subjected to the *princeps*' most excellent soul according to its order. It is not allowed to you, I say, to weep: so that you can hear the many weeping, so that you may hear the prayers of those petitioning and desiring to receive the pity of the mildest Caesar, you must dry your own tears. (6.4-5)

What Seneca describes here is Polybius's contribution to the functional apparatus coordinated with Claudius's sovereign power. He clarifies how Polybius's self-governance makes possible his governance of others, precisely Agamben's point when he glosses Cicero by saying, "If human beings do not simply live their lives like the animals, but 'conduct' and 'govern' life, *officium* is that by means of which human life is 'instituted' and 'formed'" (Agamben 2013: 74–5). In order to fulfill his duties, Polybius must manage his grief, governing his life in accordance with what his status demands.

Agamben's "The Genealogy of Office" also shows how Cicero's use of *officium* as a translation for *kathēkonta* extended its application to the entire lifespan: "What is decisive," he explains, "is that ... the politician and the jurist's attention is shifted from the carrying out of individual acts to the 'use of life' as a whole; that is, it is identified with the 'institution of life' as such" (Agamben 2013: 74–5). *Officium* may apply to "the condition and the *status* that define the very existence of human beings in society," so that "from this perspective ... Seneca" in his *Ep.* 95 "can speak of an *officium humanum*, of an office that applies to human beings insofar as they are bound with their fellow humans in a relationship of *sociabilitas*" (2013: 75). With this expansion of the Stoic concept through Cicero's translation, it is possible to identify an *officium humanum* that could, even in diminishing degrees, belong to Seneca even as bare life. He need not have a defined social position to have the existential *officium* of *sociabilitas* or "a capacity for socialization." His appointment of consolation as a task for himself now can be understood: though he may not be as well positioned to console Polybius as he could be, as a "member of the great body" of humankind (Sen. *Ep.* 95.51–52; Agamben 2013: 75), he still possesses the potential for social interaction necessary to the execution of this task.

The challenge for Seneca will then be to comport himself in such a way that he might be able to console Polybius. As a human he has the potential for this *officium*, but he has only the necessary condition for the performance of this task, no guarantee that he will be effective. Moreover, he also expresses doubt about himself at 18.9, and even places his confidence in a greater consoler at 12.4 and 14.1-2: the emperor Claudius himself. Seneca's strategy, then, is to vanish behind the voice of Claudius, which he features in an impressive consolatory *prosopopoeia* from 14.2 to 16.3. Once again, Agamben's comments in "The Genealogy of Office" can elucidate this strategy. Quoting a passage in which Varro distinguishes three modalities of human action, "*agere, facere,* and *gerere*" (*De lingua latina* 6.77.245), Agamben observes that the first term corresponds to the Aristotelian notion of *praxis*, action with an aim inherent to its performance, and the second conforms to Aristotelian *poiesis*, action with an aim in the finished product. *Gerere* has no Greek equivalent, and instead it "designates . . . the specifically Roman concept of the activity of one who is invested with a public function of governance" (Agamben 2013: 82–3). *Officium*, Agamben contends, involves action of this kind, not *praxis* or *poiesis*. This way of conceiving the action involved in *officium* illuminates not only the *officia* of Polybius, who acts on behalf of Claudius, but also of Seneca, who conforms "the use of his life" and comports himself as a priestly medium with respect to Claudius, characterized just before the *prosopopoeia* at 14.2 as an oracle: "When [Claudius] speaks, his words, delivered as if from some oracle (*velut ab oraculo missa*), will have an impressive weight; his divine authority will beat the entire force of your grief." To console Polybius effectively, to perform this *officium humanum*, Seneca becomes a means with respect to the end for which he casts Claudius as the primary agent.

Finding a place for himself within the apparatus, Seneca subjectifies himself to Claudius's agency, so that he might have a function in the relations of power and he might comport himself, "the use of his life," and his discourse as an effective medium supportive of Claudius' divine, salvific action. One may thus understand Seneca, Polybius, and Claudius as subordinate, localized causes within the providence-fate apparatus where Nature and Fate are the primary agents, and Fortune is conceived as a secondary providence "by accident." Within this broader, theological apparatus, Seneca's bad fortune—that is, Claudius's decision on his life—may have reduced him to the bare life of an exile, but he still participates in the government of the world as an instrument of primary causes. This potential may seem to subject Seneca so fully to the will of Claudius that the exiled author not only suffers as the bare life excluded through the sovereign ban, but even more he identifies with that subjection as his only potential for right and good action. But, as Agamben observes, "the most ambiguous legacy" of Cicero's *On Duties* arises from his treatment of "the duties . . . as virtues and the virtues as duties": only to the extent that the virtues, understood as an apparatus here, are reduced to the duties does "the life of human beings" become "governable" (Agamben 2013: 76). Agamben does not spell out precisely wherein this ambiguity lies or what it implies, though he does indicate a circularity in which the "effective ontology" deriving from this treatment of the virtues as duty confounds being and praxis (Agamben 2013: 87–8), concealing the possibility of "an ontology of substance" in favor of an "ontology of command" (Agamben 2013: 97–9). On this account, this ambiguity perhaps lies in the unrealized potential for the duties to have been resolved into the virtues, so that the "effective ontology" according to which the subject dutifully becomes "what he has to be" could be rendered inoperative through the tension with the virtues into which the duties were drawn. To comprehend how the virtues may override duties, how this unrealized potential of the tradition might bear upon the *Consolation* and Seneca's choice to perform as an effective medium for the consoling voice of Claudius, it will be necessary to examine the contents of Claudius's speech in light of Agamben's final discussion of Stoicism in the Homo Sacer series.

3.4 *Prosopopoeia and Making Use of the Emperor's Voice*

In "Use-of-Oneself," the fifth chapter of *The Use of Bodies*, Agamben's discussion of Stoic, Epicurean, and Christian sources supports "the hypothesis that . . . the [Stoic] doctrine of *oikeiosis* becomes intelligible only if one understands it as a doctrine of the use-of-oneself" (2015: 49). Agamben's purpose here is to show that the concept of *oikeiosis* depends upon the concept of use, in that it is "only because the animal makes use of its body parts," as he argues, that "something like self-awareness and therefore a familiarity with itself [can] be attributed to it" (2015: 51). Through commentary on Seneca's *Ep.* 112, Agamben explains that the self must be understood "not" as "something substantial or" as "a preestablished end," but rather as "the use that the living being makes of it[self]" (2015: 54). The self is thus the use which the living being makes of itself, of its relations, and of its world. This primordial self-relation, which defines *oikeiosis* primarily as the living being's use of its body, must continue to define the self-relation of the living being in every situation. Even bare life, the condition to which Claudius and Fortune have reduced Seneca, must maintain its own self-relation, its own capacity for *oikeiosis*, and its power to make use of itself. This clarification of Seneca's condition reframes the *prosopopoeia* at 14.2-16.3 as more than an act of interpretation through which Seneca becomes the medium for Claudius's oracular voice; his use of Claudius's *persona* rather involves *oikeiosis*, the appropriation of Claudius's authority, and his power to command.

If this hypothesis can be sustained, there should be some discernible evidence that Seneca's use of Claudius's voice reveals a secondary purpose beyond delivering consolation. At two points the speech seems to reveal the decisive truth about the emperor's reign that it does not rest upon the emperor's virtue and above all his merciful power, celebrated by Seneca at 13.2 and 16.6; rather the source of his power is founding violence and the extra-legal exception. Claudius begins his speech by explaining that Fortune's violence afflicts all alike, so that no house has ever been spared from mourning; the rest of his speech catalogs examples in evidence of this indictment of Fortune. Two examples, Mark Antony and Germanicus, are discussed with irony worthy of further consideration. Introducing Mark Antony as "his own grandfather," Seneca's Claudius portrays the triumvir in a disturbingly tyrannical manner: that is, Antony mourns his brother Lucius Antonius's death—a death inflicted by none other than the first emperor Augustus—by pouring "the blood of twenty legions" (16.2). Along the way, Seneca's Claudius calls out to Fortuna at 16.2, saying, "Insolent Fortuna, what games you make for yourself from human misery!" This exclamation anticipates the lament that just when Antony sat as the "arbiter of life and death over all of his own fellow citizens" (*civium suorum vitae . . . mortisque arbiter*) his own brother was sent to his execution (16.2). Though Claudius does not identify Augustus as the executioner, the irony in which one triumvir decides on the life of the brother of another is precisely what Claudius's exclamation is designed to both highlight and obscure. For, just as Seneca introduces Fortuna to complicate Claudius's role in his exile, so too does Claudius obscure Augustus's agency by crediting Lucius

Antonius's death to Fortuna. The violence of the Principate is thus both raised and concealed, while the sovereign power exercised mercilessly by Claudius's own grandfather is likewise misrepresented as Fortune's play.

As Claudius comes to his last words on this subject, he discusses his deceased siblings as examples of his own bereavement. The emperor is strangely elusive in his presentation of these losses, however, opening with two examples of *praeteritio* as he "pass[es] over all the other examples" and "remain[s] silent . . . about the other funerals" to focus on one example (16.3). These pregnant silences suggest that Claudius's rhetoric may parade as brevity, only to omit uncomfortable details about the Principate's history. He acknowledges that Fortune has deprived his own house of two siblings, but names only the celebrated general Germanicus. Claudius's sister who died in 31 CE, Livilla or Julia Livia,[16] only comes up anonymously, as a second unnamed sibling for whom Claudius once had to mourn. It is possible that Claudius has not named her simply because he is consoling Polybius for the loss of a brother and Livilla was a sister. But his sister's nickname, Livilla, would have also raised unhappy associations with Germanicus's daughter and Claudius's niece, Julia Livilla,[17] named after this sister of the emperor and recently sent into exile and forcibly starved (in truth because of dynastic struggles, but officially for an affair with Seneca, whose own exile also resulted from this alleged affair). Claudius declares that, in mourning for Germanicus, he had "so ruled over his feelings, that he neither left anything undone, which ought to be done by a good brother, nor did he do anything which could be reprimanded in a *princeps*" (16.3). From this perspective, the ironic subtext of Claudius's last claim that he did nothing inappropriate to a *Princeps* can be felt and the violence founding Claudius's power is cautiously but legibly inscribed in his speech.

4 Conclusion

These prominent examples of irony underlining Claudius's sovereign violence show that Seneca is not merely performing as an effective medium for Claudius's divine speech. He also makes use of himself to appropriate the emperor's voice for a new purpose. I conclude by emphasizing two aspects of this act of appropriation: first, how the introduction of a secondary purpose redirects and subverts the providence-fate apparatus in which Seneca situates himself; and second, to what new purpose Seneca consigns Claudius's consolation.

In *The Use of Bodies*, Agamben argues that the most promising way to interact with the apparatuses in which living beings are captured is not to flee them, but rather to advance a new use of these apparatuses which "revokes" and "deactivates" their factical conditions without altering their form (2015: 56–7). The gesture which Agamben advances leaves the apparatus intact, but discovers within it a certain anarchic, "destituent potential" through which the relations posited within an apparatus are deposed and rendered inoperative (2015: 272–4).[18] Agamben reinterprets the factical situation of bare life "beyond every figure of relation" (1998: 55/47), so that its "destituent potential exhibits the nullity of the bond that pretended to hold them together" and "bare life and sovereign power, anomie and *nomos*, constituent power and constituted power are shown to be in contact without any relation" (Agamben 2015: 272–3). Through his commentary on the Stoic providence-fate apparatus, Agamben establishes that the apparatus only ever achieves a "functional correlation" of several bipolarities: final and efficient causes, means and ends, consequences and antecedents, and general and particular. Because the apparatus does not go beyond correlating these terms, they are given to a kind of reversibility or, better, to indifference, so that ends can become means, final causes can become efficient causes, and antecedent terms can become consequent. In the *Consolation*, Fortune names a similar indifference intruding among the coherence and the consistency of Nature, Fate, and, as we have seen, the emperor Claudius's sovereignty. Both in his own speech at 16.1-3 and in Seneca's account of his trial at 13.2, the agency of Fortune substitutes for the agency of various bearers of sovereign power, whether it falls to Mark Antony, the emperor Augustus, or Claudius himself. Claudius's proximity to Nature, Fate, and providence destabilizes the generality of these personified universals; once Claudius is identified with Fortune, the "special providence" that his sovereignty represents can unsettle the unity of Nature and Fate's "general providence." These seemingly cosmic agents can even be considered as contingent consequences of his primary, antecedent role within an apparatus of power/knowledge. In other words, the introduction of an element of contingency—a personified Fortune—into the "Stoic providence-fate apparatus" leaves an opening for Seneca to "make use" of his situation and his intimate power relation with Claudius.

From this perspective, it is possible to understand Seneca's purpose in this consolatory text anew. Far from simply consoling Polybius, Seneca draws attention to his own dubious capacities and his relationship to the emperor perhaps to expose the anarchic potential of that power itself. The emperor's sovereign power to command, to decide on the state of exception, to take or give life, all of these capacities stand revealed for the anarchic, uncontrolled elements which they are. The emperor's "divine authority" may command Polybius's grief into diminution, but it is also beyond even Claudius's control and open to reuse as in Seneca's *prosopopoeia*. Perhaps Seneca's purpose in the consolation is then to reveal this potential for reuse and appropriation even in the worst of circumstances: leaving the apparatus just as it is, he shows its relations to be reversible, indifferent, perhaps even inoperative.

Notes

1. My participation in the Bristol conference would not have been possible without support from the Irish Research Council's Government of Ireland Postdoctoral Fellowship. I also thank Kurt Lampe, Janae Sholtz, John Sellars, Thomas Benatouïl, Carolyn Laferrière, and the anonymous reviewers for their constructive critiques and questions.
2. All of Agamben's discussions of Stoicism in the Homo Sacer series cross-examine Foucault. In *Opus Dei* (2013), he critiques Foucault's analyses of self-government

12. Making Use of Agamben's "Stoic Providence-Fate Apparatus" 211

in *The Government of Self and Others* (2010) and in *The Use of Bodies* (2015) he challenges arguments on the care of the self from *The Hermeneutics of the Subject* (2005).

3 Agamben's entire argument also involves significant passages from Philo, Proclus, Boethius, and Thomas Aquinas (2011: 119–43).

4 I thank an anonymous reviewer for suggesting that Agamben's rigorous approach to ancient sources, as demonstrated by Nicoletta di Vita in Chapter 11 of this volume, may indicate that he knowingly employed an early modern source instead of an ancient one, in order to develop an argument concerning the reception of ancient sources among early modern political theorists. Though Agamben's use of ancient evidence from rival philosophical schools suggests that he is not exclusively concerned with early modern reception (2011: 119–43), he quite clearly means to take Leibniz and Bayle alongside ancient sources such as Alexander or Proclus, in order to investigate an evolving problematic. In any case, Agamben's philological acumen is not really in doubt here; instead I am concerned to develop lines of argument which his essay leaves unexplored.

5 The authors of Polybius's *Oxford Classical Dictionary* entry hesitate to consider Polybius secretary *a libellis*, preferring instead secretary *a studiis* (*OCD* 4 s.v. Polybius (2)). It seems evident from the *Consolation* (6.2-5) that Seneca considered Polybius capable of receiving petitions and interceding with the emperor.

It would be illuminating to know whether Polybius's brother came to his death in 42 or 43 CE due to political intrigue, just as Polybius lost his life by 46 or 47 CE to Messalina's machinations, revealing just how exposed to the vicissitudes of imperial favor powerful freedmen were.

6 Agamben pursues a genealogy of the term apparatus in "What is an Apparatus?" (2009). Proceeding from Foucault and Hyppolite's use of the term *positivité*, Hegel's account of "positive or natural religion," and the Church Fathers' commentary upon a divine *dispositio*, which translates the Greek term *oikonomia* into Latin (Agamben 2009: 3–12), Agamben arrives at Aristotle's *Politics*, where the philosopher uses *oikonomia* exclusively for the management of domestic affairs (Agamben 2009: 8–9). The decisive transformation came, Agamben explains, in the second century CE, when the Church Fathers extended the sense of *oikonomia* to express the Father and the Son's separation as an "economy of redemption and salvation," so that a fracture within the divine being was resolved into a division between God's being and praxis (2009: 9–10). Political and economic action were thus sundered from God's being, and the *oikonomia* or *dispositio*, positive religion, and *dispositifs* could act independently of any "foundation in [the divine] being" (2009: 11). Agamben concludes, "The term apparatus designates that in which, and through which, one realizes a pure activity of governance devoid of any foundation in being. This is the reason why apparatuses . . . must also produce their subject" (2009: 11).

The second half of Agamben's essay redefines apparatuses against the living being. Subjectivity, "that which results from the relation and . . . the relentless fight between living beings and apparatuses" (2009: 14), intervenes as a third term connecting a "massive partitioning of beings" into living beings and "the apparatuses in which living beings are incessantly captured" (2009: 13).

7 Cf. Stobaeus I.79.1-12 (*SVF* 2.913; LS 55M).

8 Plutarch's *On Stoic Self-Contradictions* (1050c-d; *SVF* 2.937; LS 54T) shows that Chrysippus's position actively involves providence in every causal sequence, particular movement, and chance event. Chalcidius's *In Timaeum* 144 contrasts Chrysippus's

view that providence just is fate by another name with Cleanthes's view that "the dictates of providence come about by fate," but also that "things which come about by fate" are not necessarily "the product of providence" (*SVF* 2.933; LS 54U). The position Alexander takes was then already available to the Old Stoa. In Plutarch's *On Stoic self-contradictions* at 1051b-c (*SVF* 2.1178; LS 54S), Chrysippus can even be read as yielding to Cleanthes's position.

9 Since it is accepted that *De fato* (On Fate) was not composed by Plutarch, I refer to the author as Plutarch only for ease of reference.
10 See note 5 above.
11 On the use of these personifications in declamation, see Herington (1982: 529–37).
12 All translations from Reynolds's (1977) edition of Seneca's text are my own. In many places I have checked my interpretation against Basore's (1932) Loeb volume and some of my phrasing may therefore reflect that translation of the text.
13 *OCD* 4 s.v. Annaeus Seneca (2); *OCD* 4 s.v. "relegation."
14 At 6.2, Seneca treats Fortune and Claudius interchangeably, noting how "Fortune positioned [Polybius] in a great light" and how "love of Caesar carried [Polybius] to a higher rank."
15 See note 4 above.
16 *OCD* 4 s.v. Livia Iulia.
17 *OCD* 4 s.v. Iulia (5).
18 Agamben introduced the concept of "destituent potential" to the Homo Sacer series only in the epilogue to its final volume (2015: 263–79). Between the lines one can read a dispute with Antonio Negri concerning his and Agamben's differing views on the prospects for revolutionary political action in the present. Negri (1999) has placed an emphasis on "constituent power" as the ever-decisive source of constituted political order, whereas Agamben claims "destituent potential" is the key to a "coming politics" which will untangle the violent dialectic of constituent and constituted power (2015: 266–7).

Bibliography

Agamben, G. (1998), *Homo Sacer: Sovereign Power and Bare Life*, trans. D. Heller-Roazen, Stanford: Stanford University Press.
Agamben, G. (2009), *What Is an Apparatus? And Other Essays*, trans. D. Kishik and S. Pedatella, Stanford: Stanford University Press.
Agamben, G. (2011), *The Kingdom and the Glory: For a Theological Genealogy of Economy and Government*, trans. L. Chiesa, Stanford: Stanford University Press.
Agamben, G. (2013), *Opus Dei: An Archaeology of Duty*, trans. A. Kotsko, Stanford: Stanford University Press.
Agamben, G. (2015), *The Use of Bodies*, trans. A. Kotsko, Stanford: Stanford University Press.
Alessandro di Afrodisia (1999), *De providentia*, in S. Fazzo and M. Zonta (eds.), *La provvidenza. Questioni sulla provvidenza*, Rizzoli: Milan.
Alexander of Aphrodisias (1998), *La Providenza. Questioni sulla providenza*, ed. S. Fazzio, trans. S. Fazzio and M. Zonta, Milan: Biblioteca Universale Rizzoli.
Arnim, J. von, ed. (1964), *Stoicorum veterum fragmenta, vol. II: Chrysippi fragmenta logica et physica*, Stuttgart: Teubner.

Asmis, E. (2009), "Seneca on Fortune and the Kingdom of God," in S. Bartsch and D. Wray (eds.), *Seneca and the Self*, 115–38, Cambridge: Cambridge University Press.

Atkinson, J. E. (1985), "Seneca's 'Consolatio ad Polybium,'" in W. Haase (ed.), *ANRW II.32.2: Principat: Sprache und Literatur (Literatur der Julisch-Claudischen und der Flavischen Zeit [Forts.])*, 860–84, Berlin and New York: Walter de Gruyter.

Foucault, M. (2005), *The Hermeneutics of the Subject: Lectures at the Collège de France, 1981–1982*, ed. F. Gros, trans. G. Burchell, New York: Picador.

Foucault, M. (2009), *Security, Territory, Population: Lectures at the Collège de France, 1977–1978*, ed. M. Senellart, trans. G. Burchell, New York: Picador.

Foucault, M. (2010), *The Government of Self and Others: Lectures at the Collège de France, 1982–1983*, ed. Frédéric Gros, trans. G. Burchell, New York: Palgrave Macmillan.

Giardina, A. (2000), "Storie Riflesse: Claudio e Seneca," in P. Parroni (ed.), *Seneca e il suo tempo*, 59–90, Rome: Salerno Editrice.

Herington, C. J. (1982), "The Younger Seneca," in E. J. Kenney and W. V. Clausen (eds.), *The Cambridge History of Classical Literature, Vol. II: Latin Literature*, 511–32, Cambridge: Cambridge University Press.

Leibniz, G. W. von (1951), *Theodicy: Essays on the Goodness of God, the Freedom of Man, and the Origin of Evil*, ed. A. Farrer, trans. E. M. Huggard, London: Routledge & Kegan Paul.

Long, A. A. and Sedley, D. N. ([1987] 2010), *The Hellenistic Philosophers, Vol. 1: Translations of the Principal Sources with Philosophical Commentary*, Cambridge: Cambridge University Press.

Negri, A. (1999), *Insurgencies: Constituent Power and the Modern State*, trans. M. Boscagli, Minneapolis: University of Minnesota Press.

Plutarch. (1959), *Moralia, Volume VII: On Love of Wealth. On Compliancy. On Envy and Hate. On Praising Oneself Inoffensively. On the Delays of the Divine Vengeance. On Fate. On the Sign of Socrates. On Exile. Consolation to His Wife*. LCL 405, trans. P. H. De Lacy and B. Einarson, Cambridge, MA: Harvard University Press.

Seneca. (1932), *Moral Essays*, Volume II, LCL 254, trans. J. W. Basore, Cambridge, MA: Harvard University Press.

Seneca. (1977), *L. Annaei Senecae dialogorum libri duodecim*, ed. L. D. Reynolds, Oxford: Clarendon.

Simon, H., Spawforth A. and Eidinow E. (eds.), *The Oxford Classical Dictionary*, 4th ed. Oxford: Oxford University Press.

Varro. (1938), *On the Latin Language, Volume I: Books 5–7*, LCL 333, trans. R. G. Kent, Cambridge, MA: Harvard University Press.

Chapter 13

PIERRE HADOT

STOICISM AS A WAY OF LIFE

Matthew Sharpe

In a series of articles and books beginning in 1972, the philologist and philosopher Pierre Hadot developed a reading of Stoicism as a philosophical way of life that has had widespread influence. Hadot's conception of Stoicism is given its most extended expression in his magisterial 1992 study of Marcus Aurelius, *La Citadelle intérieure: Introduction aux Pensées de Marc Aurèle,* together with a later work, coauthored with Ilsetraut Hadot (2004), on Epictetus's *Handbook* and the Neoplatonist Simplicius's commentary on this text. Since the translation of *La Citadelle intérieure* (1998, henceforth cited parenthetically as IC), alongside Hadot's cognate studies on ancient philosophy more widely in *Philosophy as a Way of Life* (1996c) and *What Is Ancient Philosophy?* (2000), Hadot's conception of Stoicism has been taken up by a range of global, internet-based "Stoic" communities, committed to proselytizing and practising Stoicism as a manner of life.

Section 1 of this chapter examines the bases and sources of Hadot's approach to ancient philosophy as a way of life (*manière de vivre, mode/genre de vie*), situating it in relation to Thomas Bénatouïl's distinction between two traditions in the twentieth-century French receptions of Stoicism. Section 2 addresses Hadot's reading of the Roman Stoic Epictetus, which provides what he terms the "key" to his conception of Stoicism as a lived philosophy: the notion of three exercise-topics or "disciplines" (those of action, assent, and desire) aligned with the three parts of Stoic philosophical discourse (those of ethics, logic, and physics). Section 3 examines Hadot's reading of Marcus Aurelius in this light, attentive particularly to Hadot's remarkable development of the notion of "lived physics" as he finds it in the *Meditations*.

1 Hadot's Way of Reading the Ancients: Sources and Contexts

For Hadot, to become a Stoic in the ancient world was not simply to agree to a set of theoretical claims or to learn to use a distinctive technical vocabulary. It was to undertake to deeply internalize Stoic theoretical discourse, so that it could become one's own inner discourse, reshaping one's beliefs, motivations, and actions (Hadot 2010a: 210–15). To enable this, the student would be enjoined by a teacher to undertake regimens of what Hadot famously called—in the article of 1977 (1996a) bearing this title—"spiritual exercises." Such exercises include practices of listening, reading, and inquiry, like we practice today as students of philosophy (1996a: 81–2). Yet others of these exercises (like forms of fasting or bodily exercise) are not simply or primarily "intellectual," whence Hadot's wider adjective: "spiritual." They instead aim at the therapy of the passions (1996a: 83, 86, 94–5) or transforming students' perceptions of the world, cultivating what Hadot calls an "objective spirit" capable of viewing particular experiences *sub specie aeternitatis* (1996a: 95–101). These exercises call upon the will, imagination, and memory of the agent, as well as their reason—indeed, "the entire psychism" or *esprit* of the philosophical aspirant (1996a: 82).

In his contribution to the *Routledge Handbook of the Stoic Tradition*, Thomas Bénatouil (2015: 541–4) hence positions Hadot within one of two lineages which he identifies in French receptions of Stoicism in the twentieth century. Hadot, Bénatouil contends, belongs within an existentialist-influenced, "experience-" or "will"-based reception of Stoicism. This reception prioritizes Stoic ethics and looks back to Jean-Paul Sartre and before him, Alain (Bénatouil 2015: 541–4). This tradition is opposed to a competing lineage, which positions Stoicism "as a logic of events and a system," as in the works of Émile Bréhier, Victor Goldschmidt, and Jules Vuillemin (546–9). For Bénatouil, indeed, who is here echoing criticisms of Thomas Flynn (2005), Hadot can be read as "appl[ying] to the whole of philosophy as it was pursued in Antiquity the existentialist principle of the priority of choice over knowledge, which Sartre traced back to Stoicism" (2015: 549).

In fact, both the genealogical and the metaphilosophical pictures are importantly more complex than this. Bénatouil rightly points to the formative influence of Henri Bergson on Hadot's thought (Hadot 2009: 9). Hadot also considered writing his doctoral thesis on Heidegger and Rilke, before opting for Marius Victorinus (Hadot 2009: 19). Nevertheless, alongside Hadot's own abiding interest in forms of mysticism—originating in his own youthful experience, "provoked by a sense of the presence of the world, or of the Whole" (2009: 15)—other influences shaped Hadot's approach to Stoicism and ancient philosophy more generally.

The principal question or problem Hadot's readings of ancient philosophy respond to arises from Hadot's training as a philologist, working on the interpretation of ancient texts. To quote Hadot at some length, since the passage so directly qualifies his "existentialist" reception:

> Concerning the genesis of the notion of philosophy as a choice of life or of the notion of spiritual exercises in my work, it should also be said that I began by reflecting on this problem [of] how to understand the apparent inconsistencies of certain philosophers. . . . This is a rather important point, I believe. I did not begin with more or less edifying considerations about philosophy as therapy, and so on. . . . No, it was really a strictly literary problem . . . for what reasons

do ancient philosophical writings seem incoherent? Why is it so difficult to recognize their rational plane? (2009: 59)

In this philological light, it was Hadot's 1959 encounter with Ludwig Wittgenstein, as against Bergson, Heidegger, or Sartre, that would prove decisive in shaping his readings of the ancients. For the later Wittgenstein, Hadot saw, each speech-act gains its significance only within the context of a particular "form of life." It supposes an entire situation or "language game" within which agents with divergent interests and aims are trying to do specific things, according to a series of usually unstated norms and expectations. Outside of this informing context, any utterance will tend to lose or alter its meaning. So, Hadot uses the example of the laconic saying: "God is dead" (1962: 339–40). He compares its significances within ancient religious cults, Christian theology, Nietzsche's *Gay Science*, or a philosopher's mouthing it, having been prompted on camera to "say something philosophical." To understand ancient texts, Hadot hence came to hypothesize, we will need to resituate them within the historical forms of life in which they originated. We should ask questions like: What role did philosophical writings play in teaching, and what relationship did they have to the spoken teachings within the ancient schools? For which readerships were they intended: school insiders or laypeople, advanced or beginning pupils? And what goals did they set out to achieve, not simply at the conceptual level, but in terms of their perlocutionary effects upon these audiences? Could it not be, Hadot came thereby to propose, that the "inconsistencies" we lament in ancient texts hail less from the texts themselves than from our failure to conceive how ancient philosophers were engaged in playing more and different language games than we play in the later modern world (1962: 340)?

Hadot's article "Jeux de langage et philosophie" hence ends with a passage which effectively lays out his research itinerary concerning ancient philosophy for the coming four decades:

> It would be necessary, in this light, to consider as different language games these so profoundly diverse literary genres, whether the dialogue, the protreptic or exhortation, the hymn or prayer . . . the handbook, the exegetical commentary, the dogmatic treatise and the meditation. . . . One will often note that the very fact of being situated in one of these traditions predetermines the very content of the doctrine which is expressed in this language game: the "common places" are not so innocent as one might believe. (Hadot 1962: 342–3)

Arnold Davidson comments (at Hadot 2009: 58) that it is in fact in this 1962 article that Hadot first uses his signature notion of "spiritual exercises."[1] Hadot concurred:

> It was also in relation to language games that I had the idea that philosophy is also a spiritual exercise because, ultimately, spiritual exercises are frequently language games. . . . Moreover, in the same context, Wittgenstein also used the

expression "form of life." This also inspired me to understand philosophy as a form ... or way of life. (2009: 59)

Relative to Bénatouïl's "existentialist" and "systematizing" lineages within twentieth-century French receptions of Stoicism, we begin to see that Hadot might better be positioned as initiating a post-Wittgensteinian *tertium quid* or stream. This stream will look at ancient Stoicism, and philosophy more widely, as a form of life: "a phenomenon in the sense of not only a mental phenomenon, but also a social, sociological phenomenon" (Hadot 2009: 35). It will understand Stoic philosophizing as a situated, embodied, intersubjective activity, with institutional forms, protreptic and pedagogical as well as doctrinal dimensions, and more or less established (if evolving) literary, rhetorical and argumentative conventions. It will begin from an openness to the possibility that ancient philosophers were trying to do different things with words than we do today when we publish monographs, articles, chapters, and reviews. Above all, it will try to read ancient authors' texts in the ways that they understood themselves, within the ancient philosophical forms of life from whence they hailed, in ways we will see vividly in Section 3 below.

To emphasize Hadot's debt to Wittgenstein is not to downplay two other decisive influences on his conception of ancient philosophy and the Stoics. The first of these is Paul Rabbow's 1954 study *Seelenführung: Methodik der Exerzitien in der Antike*, which Hadot tells us that he had read by around 1968 (2009: 35-6). Rabbow contended that the practices stipulated for the Christian aspirant in Ignatius Loyola's work, *Spiritual Exercises*, had antecedents in the ancient pagan philosophical and rhetorical schools. In these ancient schools, Rabbow had argued, we see the prescription of "procedures or determinate acts, intended to influence oneself, carried out with the express goal of achieving a moral effect. . . . It always . . . repeats itself, or at least is linked together with other acts to form a methodical ensemble" (at Hadot 1996b: 127). Hadot's conception of philosophical "spiritual exercises" is avowedly indebted to Rabbow's conception of these "moral exercises," like the premeditation of death or of evils, at the same time as he contests Rabbow's restriction of the adjective "spiritual" to describe only Christian practices (1996b: 126-7).

The second, decisive influence upon Hadot's approach to Stoicism is the work of his wife, Ilsetraut Hadot. When the two met in 1964, Hadot reflects that he had had no idea that Ilsetraut was working on "a doctorate under the direction of Paul Moraux at the *Freie Universitat* of Berlin on the theme of Seneca and the tradition of spiritual direction in antiquity" (2009: 34), which would be published in 1969. His wife's work, Hadot adds, "has exercised a very important influence on the evolution of my thought" (2009: 34). Indeed, to Ilsetraut Hadot's extraordinary study of Seneca, Pierre Hadot discernibly owes several key dimensions of his approach to ancient philosophy: first, his developing understanding of the persona of the ancient philosopher as a "spiritual director":[2] a persona that Ilsetraut Hadot situates within ancient cultures of friendship and patronage, and traces back to Homeric councillor-figures like Phoenix in the *Iliad* (2014: 36-45). Secondly, Hadot will return repeatedly throughout his *oeuvre* to key passages in his wife's book on Seneca and her contemporary article on Epicurean pedagogy, in which she proposes that ancient philosophical teaching was carried out on two planes (Hadot 1969). On the first, in a centrifugal process, the student was progressively exposed to increasingly demanding conceptual material. On the second, in a centripetal movement, the student was frequently returned to the principal teachings of the school, so he would deeply internalize these dogmata as the basis for his way of life. It is precisely as an exercise in this diastolic-systolic spiritual direction that Ilsetraut Hadot proposes we read Seneca's *Letters to Lucilius*, a text to which Pierre frequently recurs, but which he never makes the object of his own dedicated treatment (2014: 116–17).

With these sources of Pierre Hadot's distinct approach to ancient philosophy in place, we turn to his dedicated readings of Epictetus and then Marcus Aurelius.

2 From the Three Parts of Philosophy to the Three Disciplines: Hadot's Epictetus

There can be no question about the centrality of Stoicism within Pierre Hadot's larger conception of ancient philosophy as a way of life. Alongside Plotinus, on whom Hadot continued to work until the end of his life, Marcus Aurelius is the only other ancient to whom Hadot devoted a whole monograph. Stoic philosophy features centrally in Hadot's ground-breaking 1977 "Spiritual Exercises" article, as well as in important pieces on the division of the parts of philosophy in antiquity ([2010b] 1979), the spiritual exercise of the "view from above" (1988, 1993a), the figure of the sage (1991), and the value of the present moment in the ancient philosophies (1993b). Surveying the *comptes rendus* of Hadot's courses at the École Pratique des Hautes Études between 1964 and 1980 (Hadot 2010d), we see Hadot beginning to lecture on Marcus Aurelius from 1971 to 1972, teaching on Stoic logic from 1972 to 1974, then returning to the *Meditations* between 1976 and 1978. Before the appearance of *La Citadelle intérieure: Introduction aux Pensées de Marc Aurèle* in 1992, Hadot had published pieces on physics as a spiritual exercise in Marcus Aurelius (1972), on the interpretive "key" he finds in Epictetus's *Discourses* for the interpretation of the *Meditations* (1978), on Marcus's alleged opium addiction (1984), and on the Stoics' division of the parts of philosophy (1991).

In fact, Hadot takes perhaps the key distinction in his metaphilosophical work on ancient thought, that between philosophy as a way of life and "philosophical discourse," from Diogenes Laertius's account of the doctrines of the Stoics (DL 7.39-41).[3] The Stoics, Diogenes Laertius tells us, divided "philosophical doctrines" (*hoi kata philosophian logoi*) into three parts: ethics, logic, and physics (DL 7.39). Philosophy (*tēn philosophian*), by contrast, was depicted by them as an animal, an egg, a field, a city: "No single part, some Stoics declare, is independent of any other part, but all blend together" (DL 7.40). Moreover, some—like Zeno of Tarsus— "say that these [the distinctions between ethics, logic, and physics] are divisions not of discourse (*tou logou*), but of philosophy itself (*autēs tēs philosophias*)" (DL 7.41). For Hadot, what these passages indicate is the nonidentity for the Stoics between "philosophy itself" and "philosophical discourse," as a more or less systematic doctrine, divisible into different parts (1991: 205–6, 2010a: 220–1). For the Stoics, as Hadot reads them, "philosophy itself, being an exercise of virtue and wisdom, is a single act, renewed at each instant" (2010a: 220). This act, undertaken by an embodied, living person, will be shaped and justified by the philosophical discourse which the student has deeply internalized. But it is irreducible to this discourse: a work of formation, as against information, in one of Hadot's favorite formulations, drawn from Victor Goldschmidt (e.g., Hadot 1962: 341). We have in this distinction between philosophy and philosophical discourse, in effect, the "Stoicizing" template for understanding ancient philosophies as modes of life that Hadot contends can be applied to Epicureanism, Scepticism, and even to the classical Platonic and Peripatetic philosophies (Hadot 2000: 172–233).

So, what then in Hadot's view are the "general characteristics of Stoicism" (IC 74), as such a lived philosophy? In key places, Hadot will refer above all to Émile Bréhier's work to explain his orientation, in a way which again suggests how Hadot triangulates Bénatouïl's "existentialist-systematizing" dichotomy of twentieth-century French receptions of Stoicism. At stake is what Bréhier identifies as the ultimate, unifying ontological grounding of Stoicism. This grounding resides in its doctrine of a single unifying *Logos* which structures physical events and the relations between human beings, with which the human mind—its small fragment—can harmonize itself. Because of this interconnectedness of all things, Bréhier comments, in words Hadot repeatedly cites:

> It is impossible that the good man would not be a physicist and a dialectician, for it is impossible to realise rationality separately in these three domains, and for example to completely grasp the presence of reason in the unfolding of events within the universe without realising, at the same time, the demands of rationality in one's own conduct.[4]

This is not to say, for Bréhier or for Hadot, that we cannot distinguish ethics, logic, and physics, in order to teach and understand. It is nevertheless clear, Hadot stresses, that there was disagreement within the school as to which part of the philosophical *logoi* to teach first, given that each part was so closely interrelated with, indeed in different ways dependent upon the others (DL 7.40-41). This interrelation between the parts of philosophical discourse the Stoics characterized as one of *antakolouthia* ("reciprocal implication"), as Hadot notes, citing Victor Goldschmidt (2010b: 136, 1977: 66). The Stoics hence exemplify what Hadot in his works on ancient divisions of the parts of philosophy describes as a nonhierarchical mode of such division, characterized by "a dynamic continuity and reciprocal interpenetration between the parts of philosophy" (2010b: 135).[5] With Bréhier and Max Pohlenz (a pioneering German scholar of Stoicism) in view, Hadot traces this feature of Stoicism back to its systematic bases:

> This unity of the parts of philosophy is founded on the dynamic unity of reality in Stoic philosophy. It is the same *Logos* which produces the world, which

illuminates human beings in their faculty of reasoning and which is expressed in human discourse, all the while staying fundamentally identical to itself in all the degrees of reality. Physics thus has for its object the *Logos* of universal nature. Ethics ... has as its object the *Logos* in the reasonable nature of human beings. Finally, logic examines this same *Logos* as it is expressed in human discourse. (Hadot 2010b: 135)

There is thus an apparent tension that Hadot faces between the division of the three parts of Stoic philosophical discourse and the single living "act" of Stoic philosophizing he identifies. This tension is resolved by Hadot in 1978 in the pivotal essay, "Une clé des *Pensées* de Marc Aurèle: les trois *topoi* philosophiques selon Épictète." This essay presents for the first time what becomes the organizing claim in Hadot's understanding of Stoicism as a way of life. We mean the claim that the three parts of Stoic philosophical discourse correspond to what Epictetus in the *Discourses* identifies as three exercise-topics or *topoi*. As Hadot acknowledges, the term *topos* is used in Stoic texts to identify the parts of philosophical discourse (IC 90). Yet, Hadot contends that, in Epictetus, the same term is used to also identify "the domains in which the practice of philosophical spiritual exercises should be situated" (1978: 170). Alongside *Discourses* 1.4.11, Hadot's principal proof text for this claim is *Discourses* 3.2.1:

> There are three topics (*topoi*) in philosophy, in which whoever aims to be beautiful (*kalon*) and good (*agathon*) must exercise himself (*peri hous askēthēnai dei*): that of [1] the desires and aversions, that he may not be disappointed of the one, nor incur the other; that of [2] the pursuits and avoidances, and, in general, the duties of life ... ; the third [3] includes integrity of mind and prudence, and, in general, whatever belongs to the judgment.[6]

The third *topos* here, Hadot contends, is readily identified with logic, "which constitutes a method of education of [one's] exterior and inner discourse" (1978: 172). The second *topos*, concerning the duties of life and actions, is readily identified with ethics. The connection between the exercise of desires and aversions and physics "is more difficult to grasp and nevertheless, on reflection, it is also completely evident" (1978: 172). Hadot claims:

> The discipline of desire consists on the one hand of only desiring what depends upon us, and on the other hand, in accepting with joy what does not depend upon us, but comes from universal nature, that is to say, for the Stoics, God himself. This acceptance thus demands a "physical" vision of events, capable of stripping these events of the emotive and anthropomorphic representations that we project onto them, so as to place them in the universal order of nature, in a cosmic vision. (1978: 172)

It is difficult to exaggerate the importance of this claim concerning a "correspondence" between the three parts of philosophical discourse and the three *topoi* "in which whoever aims to be beautiful and good must exercise himself" (Epictetus, *Diss.* 3.2.1) in Hadot's vision of Stoicism.[7] Hadot will call these exercise *topoi*, respectively, those of a lived (*vecue*) logic, a lived ethics, and a lived physics (2010a: 216–20), juxtaposing them to theoretical logic, ethics, and physics as parts of philosophical discourse, as per table 13.1 (IC 90, 44).

Hadot is very open, especially in this 1978 piece, about assigning this key to his reading of Stoicism as a way of life to Adolph Friedrich Bonhoeffer, writing almost ninety years previously, in *Epictet und die Stoa: Untersuchungen zur stoischen Philosophie* (1894).[8] The basis of Epictetus's conception of the three exercise-topics, according to Hadot and Bonhoeffer, lies in a conception of the psyche which seems to have been introduced into Stoicism by Epictetus, perhaps on the model of the Platonic tripartition of the soul (IC 83, 86; I. & P. Hadot 2004: 29).[9] This conception sees it as performing three "fundamental activities" which "cover all the field of reality, as well as the whole of psychological life" (Hadot 1978: 173; IC 84)

The first of these activities is the forming of judgments. Herein, says Hadot, "the soul tells itself what a given object or event is; in particular, it tells itself what the object is for the soul, that is, what it is in the soul's view" (IC 84). Desire and impulse, the activities at play in the other exercise *topoi*, both depend upon this capacity for forming judgments. If we desire something, it is because we have assented to the judgment that it is beneficial to us. If we have the impulse to do something, similarly, it will be because we have assented to the idea that it is a good thing (IC 84). As Hadot comments: "Leaving aside doctrinal refinements, we can say that for the Stoics in general, desire and impulses to action are essentially acts of assent" (IC 125).

The key principle governing Stoic lived logic is that articulated in *Enchiridion* V: that it is not things which trouble people, but their beliefs (*dogmata*) concerning those things. Marcus Aurelius will echo Epictetus's formula, when he comments that "everything is a matter of judgment" for us, or indeed, that "if you are grieving about some exterior thing, then it is not that thing which is troubling you, but your judgment about that thing." (2.15; 8.47; IC, 125-7, 107) The sage will only assent to those representations which are "comprehensive" or, as Hadot translates *kataleptike*, "adequate." As he explains, the usual translation

> gives the impression that the Stoics believed a representation to be true when it "comprehends" or seizes the contents of reality. In Epictetus, however, we can

Table 13.1 Hadot's Epictetan "key" to (later Roman) Stoicism as a way of life.

	Lived logic	**Lived ethics**	**Lived physics**
Psychological function	Judgments, thoughts, and "assents" (*synkatatheseis*)	Impulses (*hormai*) to act and not to act	Desire (*orexis*) and aversion (*enklisis*)
Objects, materials	Concerning truth, rightness, goodness and their opposites	Regarding others, and appropriate actions (*kathēkonta*)	Concerning external objects and events

glimpse a wholly different meaning of the term: for him, a representation is *kataleptikē* when it does not go beyond what is given, but is able to stop at what is perceived, without adding anything extraneous to that which is perceived. (IC 84)

Epictetus accordingly tells his students at *Discourses* 3.8.1-2 that "in the same way that we train ourselves to be able to face up to sophistic interrogations, we ought also to train ourselves to face up to representations (*phantasiai*), for they too ask us questions" (IC 84). What kind of questions? Epictetus illustrates by examples:

> A certain person's son is dead. [What do you think of that?] Answer: the thing is not within the power of the will: it is not an evil. A father has disinherited a certain son. What do you think of it? It is a thing beyond the power of the will, not an evil. Caesar has condemned a person. [What do you think of that?] It is a thing beyond the power of the will, not an evil. The man is grieved at this. Grief is a thing which depends on the will: it is an evil. He has borne the condemnation bravely. That is a thing within the power of the will: it is a good. (*Diss.* 3.3.3 ff.)

This veritable "representation [*sic*] of moral life as a dialectical exercise" (IC 85), as Hadot calls it, hence involves an exercise in restricting what the individual assents to solely to what presents itself in events. We must train ourselves to withhold assent, by contrast, to any and all extraneous "value-judgments" concerning those events: indeed, from any evaluations that do not concern virtue or vice, according to the Stoic teaching that virtue is the only good. A constant self-reflective vigilance is thereby enjoined of the Stoic. As Epictetus adapts Socrates's apology: "The unexamined representation is not worth having" (*Diss.* 3.12.14-15; IC 97, 111, 119).

Turning to the second *topos*: virtue is the only good, for the Stoics. Yet the sage must concern himself with "indifferent" things beyond his control, to the extent that he wishes to act in the world (2010c). The discipline of lived ethics for Hadot concerns itself with the "impulse to act, as well as action itself" (IC 86). Its preeminent material is the *kathēkonta*, "that is, those actions which, in all probability, may be considered as 'appropriate' to human nature" (IC 86), closely related to the Stoics' theorization of the differential value (*axia*) indifferent things have, depending upon whether they accord with, or oppose our nature (IC 203-204). The *kathēkonta*, Hadot notes, are grounded in the natural human impulses to self-preservation and sociability: "Thus, both active impulse and action itself will be exercises above all in the domain of society, of the state, of the family, and of relations between human beings in general" (IC 86). Following Max Pohlenz, Hadot thus distinguishes chapters in Epictetus's *Encheiridion* on duties toward the gods (XXXI-II), and duties toward oneself in the context of one's social relations (XXXIII, XXXV-XLV). At stake in the latter chapters are counsels against engaging in gossip or raucous laughter, making oaths or attending banquets; to moderate one's bodily desires; not to defend oneself against criticisms or take part in spectacles, boast, engage in vulgar obscenities, or be anxious before those in power

(I. & P. Hadot 2004: 37); then again, duties regarding how to relate to women or comport oneself at table, and how to choose a profession (I. & P. Hadot 2004: 38). Here again, Hadot notes the importance that monitoring one's representations plays in the Stoic life, testimony to the *antakolouthia* of the different exercise *topoi*, like the different *topoi* within philosophical discourse (Hadot 1978: 173):

> The last chapters . . . highlight the importance of inner discourse . . . (to say to oneself this or that) which presides over action . . . [F]or example, in the attitudes which we take with regard to the other, it is necessary to tell oneself that the latter has believed himself to be acting well (chapters XLII and XLV) . . . it is necessary equally to know how to find the discourse which will prevent us from becoming angry at another (by telling oneself, for example, not "he has injured me," but "he is my brother"), or which will prevent ourselves from feeling superior to others (chapters XLIII-IV). (I. & P. Hadot 2004: 38)

Lived physics, as we have indicated, has as it goal the reshaping of the desires of the Stoic. In the words of *Enchiridion* VIII, s/he should not "desire that things happen as he wish[es] but wish that they happen as they do happen." We desire things which we consider beneficial and evince aversion toward those things we consider harmful. Yet, Hadot emphasizes, Epictetus is very clear that we can only know what is truly good and bad for us, if we understand our place in the larger Whole of nature: ethics logically presupposes physics. It is necessary thus to "examine what, according to Chrysippus, is the administration of the world, and what place rational animals occupy therein. Then, from this point of view, consider who you are, and what good and evil are for you" (*Diss*. 1.10.10; IC 94). In short, we must try to reflectively shape what we desire "according to nature (*kata phusin*)" as described by Stoic physics. To struggle against what is necessary, because willed by Nature or Zeus, according to the providential order, is an exercise in futility. As the *Encheiridion* counsels:

> If you wish your children, and your wife, and your friends to live forever, you are stupid; for you wish to be in control of things which you cannot, you wish for things that belong to others to be your own . . . (*Ench*. XIV; cf. *Diss*. 3.24.84; IC 119, 111)

Hadot stresses that the goal of lived physics in Epictetus "consists not only in accepting what happens," in a more or less fatalistic spirit, "but in contemplating the works of God with admiration," with a more or less grateful disposition (IC 96). With this in view, he cites Epictetus's exhortation early in the *Discourses*: "For us, nature's final accomplishment is contemplation, becoming aware, and a way of living in harmony with nature. Make sure that you do not die without having contemplated all of these realities . . ." (*Diss*. 1.6.19-25; IC 96). Nevertheless, from 1972 onwards, Hadot develops his thoughts about this discipline of lived physics, in particular, much more in relation to the philosopher-emperor Marcus Aurelius than in relation to Epictetus, the philosopher-slave.

We turn now to Hadot's reading of Marcus Aurelius and his *Meditations*.

3 Hadot's Marcus Aurelius

The history of the reception of Stoicism can be written, in one dimension, according to which of the ancient sources authors have had access to or focused upon: whether the Roman Stoics Seneca, Epictetus, and Marcus Aurelius, or the fragments of the early Stoa. (The works of Musonius Rufus, Cleomedes, Hierocles, and Herculaneaum papyri have not yet made much of an impact beyond highly specialized studies). Hadot's reception of Stoicism focuses primarily upon Marcus Aurelius, with two qualifications. The first is that, following an anecdote Marcus reports in book I of the *Meditations* concerning his teacher Rusticus, Hadot reads Marcus as, above all, a faithful disciple of Epictetus (1.7; IC 9-10, 66-69). The second is that, in contrast to most anglophone commentators, Hadot sees both Epictetus and Marcus Aurelius as in no way epigones, lacking the philosophical rigor of the Hellenistic founders, and prioritizing ethics to the exclusion of physics and logic (IC 64). As Hadot writes, invoking Bréhier and Bonhoeffer,

> Epictetus himself . . . went back to the origins. . . . It can be said that Epictetus subscribes to the most orthodox Stoic tradition: that which, beginning with Chrysippus, apparently continued through Archidemus and Antipater; he makes no allusions to Panaetius or Posidonius. Through Epictetus, Marcus Aurelius was able to go back to the purest Stoic sources. (IC 82)

What arguably most singles out Hadot's reading of the Roman Stoics is his simultaneous stress on the lived dimension of this philosophy *and* his denial that this implies a downgrading of the theoretical dimensions of Stoicism. As we mentioned, Hadot spent three years teaching on Stoic and ancient logic in 1972–4 (cf. 2010d). Émile Bréhier's and Victor Goldschmidt's accounts of the Stoic system remain formative for Hadot's understanding of Stoicism, as we will continue to see. Nevertheless, Hadot sees each part of Stoic philosophical discourse as essential, precisely for the role it can play in shaping the inner discourse, hence the judgments, impulses, and desires of the Stoic. In this sense only might we say that each part of Stoicism is "ethicized," in Hadot, at the same time as it keeps its distinct principles and theoretical integrity.

Hadot's first contribution to the reception of Marcus Aurelius involves his attempt to recover a sense of the literary form of the so-called *Meditations*, so that we can understand its philosophical intentionality. Commentators across the centuries have tried to read the text as the draft of an unwritten treatise, or else as a "*journal intime*" (IC 25-7). In the twentieth century, Dodds claimed to see in the text testimony to Marcus's having suffered an "identity crisis," giving vent to his "morbid" propensities (IC 246); the psychosomaticians, Dailly and Effenterre, discerned in the *Meditations* the symptomatic outpourings of an individual suffering from a gastric ulcer (IC 246-8); while Africa would see the text as issuing from its author's opium addiction (IC 252-5; cf. Hadot 1984). For Hadot, closer here to Ian Rutherford's 1989 work on which he draws on several occasions (IC 13, 257-280; 2014: 243–4, 275), these readings highlight the grave interpretive errors which moderns can make, when they remain unaware of the language games in which an ancient philosophical text was situated.

The literary form of the *Meditations* is, of course, very different from the genres in which scholars write on philosophy today (IC 28-30). The text is divided into some 473 sections and 12 books. Yet the divisions between what we enumerate as books were marked only by two-line breaks in the *Vaticanus* manuscript, and the sections were not numbered (IC 28). Some sections are aphorisms: "receive wealth without arrogance and be ready to let it go" (8.33); or, famously, "the best revenge is to not become like him who has harmed you" (6.6). Others involve reflections spanning over forty lines of modern editions. Yet others are highly rhetorically crafted (IC 257-260). There are staged dialogues (e.g., 4.12) and compelling images, like: "If a man should stand by a limpid pure spring, and curse it, the spring never ceases sending up potable water . . . How then shall you possess a perpetual fountain?" (8.51; cf. 7.59). Perhaps most puzzlingly from our perspective, there is a great deal of repetition, sometimes direct, as for example the phrase: "Nothing is so capable of producing greatness of soul" (3.11.2; X.11.1), but more often with small changes. Hence, compare "how could that which does not make a man worse, make life worse" with "that which does not make a man worse than he is, does not make his life worse either" (2.11.4 with 4.8; cf. IC 49-51).

To approach such a text, Hadot contends (per Section 1), we need to understand for whom it was written and why, placing it in the context of the Stoicism which Marcus Aurelius had embraced in his youth (IC 11-4). It is of the highest importance for Hadot that the text appears never to have been intended for publication, instead being found amid Marcus's mortal remains. Marcus Aurelius himself thus appears to have been the only intended reader of these notes, as the title *Ta Eis Heauton* (Things for Himself) given it—according to Hadot—by Arethas in the ninth or tenth century registered (IC 24). If we look for any Stoic rationale for such an endeavor, we find Epictetus enjoining in the very opening chapter of the *Discourses*, concerning the key Stoic distinctions: "These are the thoughts that those who pursue philosophy should ponder, these are the lessons they should write down every day (*kath'hēmeran graphein*), in these they should exercise themselves" (*Diss.* 1.1.25). Again, in book III, Epictetus enjoins his interlocutors to: "Let these thoughts be at your command (*prokheiron*) by night and day: *write these things* (*tauta graphein*), read them, talk of them" (*Diss.* 3.24.103 [our italics]). To write down the basic principles of Stoic philosophy, these Epictetan sayings indicate, was an essential spiritual exercise in the ongoing efforts of the *prokoptōn* (progressor) to internalize the Stoic principles, so they could be called upon readily, facing challenges of different kinds. Such "memory-aids" (*hupomnēmata*) could then be read over, in order to recall to mind what once had been assented to, in order to "reactivate" these ideas at need (IC 30-4; cf. Foucault 1997). Marcus himself indicates this much, Hadot notes, when he asks himself:

> How can our principles become dead, unless the impressions [thoughts] which correspond to them are extinguished? But it is in your power continuously to

fan these thoughts into a flame. I can have that opinion about anything which I ought to have. If I can, why am I disturbed? (7.2)

In this light, the frequent repetitions and circling around established themes takes on rationality. Many of these fragments (like 2.1, 4.3, 4.26, 7.22.2, 8.21.2, 11.18, 12.7, 12.8, and 12.26), Hadot argues, condense into "chapter-heads (*kephalaia*)"— entire chains of Stoic reasoning concerning ethics, logic, and physics: as such, both reflecting and facilitating Marcus's effort to continually recall these *dogmata* to mind (IC 37-40). Such features of the *Meditations*, and not least the frequency of repetitions, thus do not reflect Marcus's intellectual turpitude, or the work's status as a putative "draft" (IC 25-8). Once we understand the genre of the work as involving *hupomnēmata*, we can see that these features reflect *the sheer difficulty of realizing* the Stoic philosophy in impulse, thought, and deed. As Hadot reflects at the end of *The Inner Citadel*:

> In world literature, we find lots of preachers, lesson-givers, and censors, who moralise to others with complacency, irony, cynicism, or bitterness, but it is extremely rare to find a person training himself to live and to think like a human being ... the personal effort appears ... in the repetitions, the multiple variations developed around the same theme and the stylistic effort as well, which always seeks for a striking, effective formula ... when we read [the *Meditations*] we get the impression of encountering not the Stoic system, although Marcus constantly refers to it, but a man of good will, who does not hesitate to criticise and to examine himself, who constantly takes up again the task of exhorting and persuading himself, and of finding the words which will help him to live, and to live well. (IC 312-3; cf. Hadot 1972: 229)

Are there then no organizing principles, underlying the circumambulations of Marcus's *hupomnēmata*, in Hadot's perspective? As we have indicated, from as early as 1978, Hadot was convinced that Epictetus's division of the three exercise-topics we examined in Section 2 also shapes Marcus Aurelius's *Meditations*. Hadot thus draws our attention to threefold formulations in Marcus's apparently aleatory reflections, which reproduce Epictetus's division of the disciplines of assent (logic), desire (physics), and action (ethics). Thus, consider, with our interpolations:

> What then must you practice? ... [1] thoughts devoted to justice and actions in the service of the community [ethics/action], [2] speech which can never deceive [assent/logic] and [3] a disposition which gladly accepts all that happens, as necessary, as usual, as flowing from a principle and source of the same kind [desire/physics]. (*Med.* 4.33.5; cf. 8.7, 9.7)

> Everywhere and at all times it is in your power to [1] piously acquiesce in your present condition [desire/physics], and [2] to behave justly to those who are about you [ethics/action], and [3] to exert your skill upon your present thoughts, that nothing shall steal into them without being well examined [logic/assent]. (*Med.*7.54)

We cannot examine in detail all the exemplifications and adumbrations of the three Stoic disciplines that Hadot examines in *The Inner Citadel*. What interests us is only what Hadot sees as *different* about the practice of these disciplines in Marcus's text, compared to Epictetus's.

Concerning the discipline of assent, for example, Hadot spends most time in *The Inner Citadel* analyzing *Meditations* 12.3 under the heading of "circumscribing the self" (IC 112-125). *Meditations* 12.3 sees Marcus enjoining himself to "separate yourself" from everything that is not his true self: the *hegemonikon* or "governing part" (IC 119). If you separate yourselves from the four "circles" of what others do and say; the past and future; our involuntary, proto-emotional responses to externals; and "the rushing tide [of external events] which bathes you with its waves," then "you will be able to live the time that is left to you, up until your death, untroubled, benevolently, and serenely." The general principle presiding over this exercise, Hadot notes, is the opening distinction of Epictetus's *Encheiridion* I (IC 114). It is a question of directing attention only to what is within one's control. Yet this exercise is not simply then one of assent: it also implicates ethics, how to respond to others, and physics, concerning "the rushing tide which bathes you" (IC 118). One could be forgiven for supposing here a Platonic influence on the *Meditations* or on Hadot's reading of the text (cf. [Plato], *Alc. I*, 133b-134a; *Phaedo*, 64c-67e).[10]

Concerning ethics or the discipline of action, Hadot again spends a good deal of his time on an exercise that we might associate more closely with the disciplines of assent or desire: namely, the practice of acting with "reservation" concerning our action's *skopoi* (goals, targets), whose achievement is beyond our control (IC 190-3, 204-6). As Hadot notes, this cultivation of a sage caution in action is closely tied to the *praemeditatio malorum*, the effort to anticipate even the worst "outcomes" in advance, so one is not taken by surprise (IC 206-8). Hadot also sees in Marcus a greater interest in justice than we find in Epictetus, so that it "is so important that [concern with justice] is sometimes sufficient to define the discipline of action, as for instance in 7.54: 'To conduct oneself with justice with regard to the people present'" (IC 218). Hadot will even venture that the three exercise disciplines, in Marcus, are aligned with the specific virtues of justice (ethics), temperance (desire), and wisdom (assent), in ways not modeled in Epictetus (IC 323-238; cf. 44).

Nevertheless, it is above all in the discipline of desire or physics that Hadot sees Marcus Aurelius as going farthest beyond his teacher. Marcus's physical reflections were already the subject of Hadot's ground-breaking 1972 essay, "La Physique comme exercise spirituel ou pessimisme et optimisme chez Marc Aurèle," and they occupy the longest chapter in *The Inner Citadel* (IC 128-180). In "La Physique," it is above all Marcus's exercise of "dividing and disenchanting" seductive appearances, skirted above in Epictetus, that Hadot focuses upon. The most famous instance of this exercise involves Marcus enjoining himself to look at Falernian wine as only grape juice; the imperial purple as dyed fabric; and sex as the rubbing together of two bodies, ending in the ejaculation of slimy fluid (6.13; IC 165-6; cf. Hadot 1972: 229–33). Hadot contends that such an exercise, far from expressing Marcus's morbidity, is carried out by the philosopher-emperor "in a quite determinate manner, in accordance with a quite determinate method" (IC

164): notably, when he reminds himself to analytically divide the form, matter, and duration of the thing he might be tempted to valorize (Hadot 1972: 232). Marcus's repeated reminders to recall the transience of phenomena—such as when he asks himself to "acquire a method for contemplating how all things are transformed into each other" (*Med.* 4.48.3; cf. X.11; IC 166, 171)—hence also belong squarely within the Stoic tradition. It is not a matter of pessimism or optimism, so much as an attempt to cultivate a realistic, Stoic view of things that is at issue: in Hadot's words, "to see things in their naked, 'physical' reality" (IC 165), shorn of the anthropocentric values we assign to appearances (IC 164). The flipside of this exercise in disenchantment comes in sections of the *Meditations* which describe how even the most incidental things take on an interest and even a beauty, when they are looked at purely disinterestedly. To cite one of Hadot's favorite sections of the *Meditations*:

> We must also bear in mind things like the following: even the accessory consequences of natural phenomena have something graceful and attractive about them. For instance: when bread is baked, some parts of it develop cracks in their surface. Now, it is precisely these small openings which, although they seem somehow to have escaped the intentions which presided over the making of the bread, somehow please us and stimulate our appetite in a quite particular way.... Ears of corn which bend toward the earth; the lion's wrinkled brow; the foam trailing from the mouth of boars: these things, and many others like them, would be far from beautiful to look at, if we considered them only in themselves. And yet, because these secondary aspects accompany natural processes, they add a new adornment to the beauty of these processes, and they make our hearts glad. Thus, if one possesses experience and a thorough knowledge of the workings of the universe, there will be scarcely a single one of those phenomena which accompany natural processes ... which will not appear to him, under some aspect at least, as pleasing. (*Med.* 3.2; IC 168-69; cf. Hadot 1972: 237-8)[11]

It is only when one achieves what Hadot calls "a cosmic perspective" that things can thus appear as "both beautiful and valueless: beautiful, because they exist, and valueless, because they cannot accede to the realm of freedom and morality" (IC 171). Such a perspective is what is at stake, in Marcus as in other ancient authors, in the exercise Hadot (1998, 1993a) dubs the "view from above." In many sections of the *Meditations*, Hadot notes (9.32, 7.47, 11.1.3, 6.36, 12.32, 7.48; IC 172-173), Marcus enjoins himself to "embrace the totality of the cosmos in your thought" (9.32; cf. 11.1.3), and to look down upon the events that make up human lives. As Hadot writes, this exercise "furnishes powerful instigations for practicing the discipline of the desire" (IC 173). In particular, it enables Marcus to re-perceive just how small and passing are human affairs, in the scale of the Whole, evaluating "indifferents" according to what the Stoics see as their "true proportions" (IC 173). In Marcus as in other authors like Boethius and even Petrarch, this exercise is adduced particularly to quell Marcus's desire for fame. When we recall how "short is the time which each of us lives; [how] puny the little corner of earth on which we live; how puny, finally, is even the lengthiest posthumous glory," our desire for fame—at most a preferred indifferent—is tempered (*Med.* 3.10.2; IC 175-176).

Finally, in *Inner Citadel*, Hadot—whose debts here specifically to Victor Goldschmidt's remarkable study, *Le Système stoïcien et l'idée de temps*, are both clear and acknowledged[12]—lays particular stress upon exercises in what he terms "circumscribing the present." At issue here are those sections in the *Meditations* which lay stress on focusing one's attention upon the present moment. Hadot interprets Stobaeus's claim that for the Stoics "there is no present time, in the proper sense of the term; rather, it is spoken of only in an extended sense (*kata platos*). Chrysippus says that only the present 'actually belongs' (*huparchein*)" (LS 51B) as pointing to a distinction between a mathematical present, infinitesimally small, and the lived present, which "belongs to a subject" and as such has an experiential "thickness" (*platos*) (IC 135-6). Marcus is concerned only with this lived present and the existential importance of its "circumscription." First, such a circumscription serves to diminish our sense of the difficulty of challenges, by dividing them into a sequence of individually bearable, present moments. If we divide a seductive melody into its notes, it will lose its power over us, Marcus notes. Just so, we should "transpose this method ... to life in its entirety" (11.2; IC 133). In doing so, we shall see that it is unprofitable, even meaningfully *unreasonable*, to "trouble yourself by representing to yourself the totality of life in advance ... try[ing] to go over all the painful hardships, in all their varying intensity and number, which might possibly happen" (8.36). Indeed, dividing difficulties into present moments will "make your reflective faculty ashamed" that it could worry about not bearing up to what we might call a sequence of "minutiae" (8.36; IC 132).

Secondly, Marcus's focus on the present moment, as Goldschmidt had identified (1977: 168–86), reflects for Hadot the Stoic perspective which sees it as the only "tense" in which we can act, feel, and suffer, whereas the past is unchangeable, and the future of our worries we cannot presently change. It is, Hadot says, "a matter of increasing the attention we bring to bear upon our actions, as well as the consent we grant to the events which happen to us" (IC 132). In doing so, rather than remaining attached to futural concerns and events we cannot control, we "exalt the consciousness of our existence and our freedom," as Hadot puts it (IC 134). The result is the kind of joy which Hadot asks us to see as overwhelmingly characterizing the Stoicism of Marcus Aurelius (IC 238-242), as when Marcus reflects that

> all the happiness you are seeking by such long, roundabout ways, you can have it all right now ... I mean, if you leave all of the past behind you, if you abandon the future to providence, and if you arrange the present in accordance with piety and justice. (12.1.1-2; IC 134)

4 Concluding Remarks

In this chapter, we have argued that it is imprecise, with Bénatouïl, to align Pierre Hadot's reception of Stoicism with existentialism, because of the stress he lays upon reading Stoicism as a way of life; or indeed, that it is inaccurate to construct just two, more or less mutually exclusive, phenomenological, and systematizing strands of twentieth-century "French Stoicisms."

As we have seen, Hadot instead argues that the exercise disciplines in Epictetus align with the three parts of systematic Stoic philosophical discourse: logic, ethics, and physics. Ethics, the exercise of choice or the will, does not take all. Hadot's reading of the Roman Stoics Epictetus and Marcus Aurelius instead positions them as orthodox inheritors of the Stoic system, as reconstructed by figures like Bréhier and Goldschmidt, to whom Hadot is directly and avowedly indebted. Hadot retains respect for the Stoic systematizing pursuit of knowledge. But, following Wittgenstein, he situates this systematizing activity within a network of philosophical language games. And this approach in his work establishes a bridge between theory-construction and the experiential/existential dimension we see so vividly at work in Marcus Aurelius's *Meditations*. The deepest challenge posed to us by Hadot's re-conception of Stoicism and the other ancient philosophies as ways of life, as well as theoretical achievements, is then that of thinking together both sides of ancient Stoicism.

Notes

1 At Hadot (1962: 58).
2 See, e.g., Hadot (2010a: 211); see I. Hadot (2014: esp. 36–50, 313–19); and Sharpe (2018: 109–18). The author would like to dedicate this chapter to Ilsetraut Hadot, in gratitude and admiration for her work, support, and critique.
3 Similarly, Hadot's emphasis on the importance of the present moment in ancient thought also arguably hails from his engagement with Stoicism, mediated by Victor Goldschmidt's *Le Système stoïcien et l'idée de temps* (1977). See Section 3 below.
4 Bréhier 1961: 303, at IC 74; Hadot (2010a: 221, 1991: 209, 2010b 135–6).
5 Cf. IC 79; Hadot (1991: 208–9).
6 Translations from Epictetus are my own, adapting from the Perseus text by Thomas Wentworth Higginson, and with thanks to Kurt Lampe.
7 Following Max Pohlenz, for instance, Hadot has argued that we can use this "key" to understand the structuring of the fifty-three sections of Epictetus's *Enchiridion* or *Handbook*. The opening chapter, in qualifying the things that are *ephēmin*, already sets out the three domains of exercise: "What depends upon us are value-judgments (*hupolēpseis*) [3], impulses toward action (*hormē*) [2] and desire (*orexis*) or aversion [1]; in short, everything that does not depend upon us" (*Ench*. 1.1). After the opening chapters, chapters III-VI relate explicitly to the discipline of judgment: a fact which Hadot deems pedagogically significant (Cf. 1978: 171.) VII-XI, XIV-XXI and then again XVI-XVIII relate to the discipline of desire, punctuated by sections (XII-XIII; XXII-XXV) concerning what "progressants" in Stoic philosophy should attend to. Chapters XXX-LXV concern the discipline of impulses; while the last part (XLV-LIII) returns to counsels specifically directed at the *"progressants,"* culminating in a final section adducing maxims from Cleanthes, the *Crito* and *Apology* "presenting the fundamental attitude of those who learn to philosophise as a consent to the will of Nature and Destiny" (I. & P. Hadot 2004: 35–40). Long, notably, takes Hadot's reading of Epictetus as authoritative (see 2002: 116–17, 125).

8 Hadot writes of Bonhoeffer: "He has magisterially developed the content of the three *topoi* of Epictetus, clearly recognized this division into three *topoi* was a work original to Epictetus, and even seen that Marcus Aurelius reproduced this division in his ternary schemas" (1978: 189). In private correspondence, William O. Stephens, translator of Bonhoeffer's *The Ethics of the Stoic Epictetus* (1996), has noted that while the connection of the domains and the psychological functions is explicit, their alignment with ethics, logic, and physics is not directly claimed by Epictetus or Bonhoeffer.
9 Epictetus's division of the parts of the psyche, also, is nonhierarchical, like the Stoic division of the parts of discourse (IC 86). Equally, for the Stoics contra Plato, even the passions are not the products of any one, lower part of the soul, but transformations of the entire psyche, including the ruling faculty. See I. & P. Hadot (2004: 29).
10 Compare the criticisms of Hadot, based on his ongoing work on Neoplatonism, in Cooper (2012: 17–22, 402–3 n. 4–5).
11 Hadot talks of a Stoic "realistic aesthetics" (IC 170).
12 Goldschmidt (1977: esp. 168–86); Hadot (1972: 321 n. 1).

Bibliography

Bénatouil, T. (2015), "Stoicism and Twentieth-Century French Philosophy," in J. Sellars (ed.), *Routledge Handbook of the Stoic Tradition*, 541–62, London: Routledge [digital edition].

Bonhoeffer, A. F. (1996), *The Ethics of the Stoic Epictetus*, trans. W. O. Stephens, New York: Peter Lang.

Bréhier, É. (1961), *Histoire de la philosophie*, V1, Paris: Presses universitaires de France.

Cooper, John M. (2012), *Pursuits of Wisdom: Six Ways of Life in Ancient Philosophy from Socrates to Plotinus*, Princeton: Princeton University Press.

Flynn, T. (2005), "Philosophy as a Way of Life: Foucault and Hadot," *Philosophy and Social Criticism* 31 (5–6): 609–22.

Foucault, M. (1997), "Self-Writing," in *Ethics: Subjectivity and Truth*, 207–21, New York: The New Press.

Goldschmidt V. (1977), *Le Système stoïcien et l'idée de temps*, 3rd ed., Paris: Vrin.

Hadot, I. (1969), "Épicure et l'Enseignement Philosophique Hellénistique et Romain," in *Actes de VIIIe Congrès de L'Association Guillaume Budé*, 347–53, Paris: Vrin.

Hadot, I. (2014), *Sénèque: Direction spirituelle et pratique de la philosophie*, Paris: Vrin.

Hadot, I. & P. (2004), *Apprendre à philosopher dans l'Antiquité*, Paris: Livre du Poche.

Hadot, P. (1962), "Jeux de langage et philosophie," *Revue de Métaphysique et de Morale* 67 (3): 330–43.

Hadot, P. (1972), "La Physique comme exercise spirituel ou pessimisme et optimisme chez Marc Aurèle," *Revue de théologie et de philosophie* 22: 225–39.

Hadot, P. (1978 [2002]), "Une clé des *Pensées* de Marc Aurèle: les trois *topoi* philosophiques selon Épictète," in *Exercises Spirituels*, 2nd ed., 165–92, Paris: Albin Michel.

Hadot, P. (1984 [2010]), "Marc-Aurèle: était-il opiomane?," in *Études de philosophie ancienne*, 95–114, Paris: Les Belles Lettres. https://www.lesbelleslettres.com/livre/6 68-etudes-de-philosophie-ancienne.

Hadot, P. (1988), "La terre vue d'en haut et le voyage cosmique: le point de vue du poète, du philosophe et de l'historien," in J. Schneider and M. Léger-Orine (eds.), *Frontiers and Space Conquest*, 31–9, Dordrecht: Springer.

Hadot, P. (1991), "Philosophie, discours philosophique, et divisions de la philosophie chez les stoïciens," *Revue Internationale de Philosophie* 45 (178): 205–19.

Hadot, P. (1992), *La Citadelle intérieure: Introduction aux Pensées de Marc Aurèle*, Paris: Fayard.

Hadot, P. (1993a), "The View from Above, in *Philosophy as a Way of Life*, trans. M. Chase, 238–50, London: Wiley-Blackwell [originally in *Exercises Spirituels* (Paris: Institut d'Étude augustiniennes, 1993)].

Hadot, P. (1993b), "'Only the Present is our Happiness': The Value of the Present Instant in Goethe and in Ancient Philosophy," in *Philosophy as a Way of Life*, trans. M. Chase, 217–37, London: Wiley-Blackwell [originally in *Exercises Spirituels*].

Hadot, P. (1996a), "Spiritual Exercises," in *Philosophy as a Way of Life*, trans. M. Chase, 71–125, London: Wiley-Blackwell.

Hadot, P. (1996b), "Ancient Spiritual Exercises and 'Christian Philosophy'," in *Philosophy as a Way of Life*, trans. M. Chase, 126–44, London: Wiley-Blackwell.

Hadot, P. (1996c), *Philosophy as a Way of Life*, trans. M. Chase, London: Wiley-Blackwell.

Hadot, P. (1998 [IC]), *The Inner Citadel: The Meditations of Marcus Aurelius*, trans. Michael Chase, Harvard, MA: Harvard University Press.

Hadot, P. (2000), *What Is Ancient Philosophy?*, trans. M. Chase, Harvard, MA: Belknap Press.

Hadot, P. (2009), *The Present Alone Is Our Happiness: Conversations with Jeannie Carlier and Arnold I. Davidson*, trans. M. Djaballah, Stanford: Stanford University Press.

Hadot, P. (2010a), "La philosophie antique: une éthique ou une pratique?" in *Études de philosophie ancienne*, 207–32, Paris: Belles Lettres. https://www.lesbelleslettres.com/livre/668-etudes-de-philosophie-ancienne.

Hadot, P. (2010b [1979]), "Les divisions des parties de la philosophie dans antiquité," in *Études de Philosophie Ancienne*, 125–58, Paris: Les Belles Lettres.

Hadot, P. (2010c [1991]), "La Figure du Sage," in *Études de Philosophie*, 233–57, Paris: Les Belles Lettres.

Hadot, P. (2010d), "Comptes rendus des conférences données à L'École Pratique des Hautes Études de 1964 à 1980," in *Études de Patristique et l'histoire des concepts*, 67–167, Paris: Belles Lettres.

Hadot, P. (2014), "Marc-Aurèle et son temps," in *Discourse et mode de vie philosophique*, Paris: Belles Lettres.

Long, A. A. (2002), *Epictetus: A Stoic and Socratic Guide to Life*, Berkeley: University of California Press.

Rutherford, I. (1989), *The Meditations of Marcus Aurelius: A Study*, Oxford: Clarendon Press.

Sharpe, M. (2018), "Ilsetraut Hadot's Seneca: Spiritual Direction and the Transformation of the Other," in M. Dennis and S. Werkhoven (eds.), *Ethics and Self-Cultivation: Ancient and Contemporary Perspectives*, 104–23, London: Routledge.

CONTRIBUTORS

Thomas Bénatouil is Professor of Ancient Philosophy at the University of Lille and member of the CNRS Research team *Savoirs, Textes, Langage*. He has published *Faire usage: la pratique du stoïcisme* (2006); *Musonius, Epictete, Marc Aurele* (2009); and numerous articles on hellenistic philosophy and its French reception.

Barbara Cassin, philologist and philosopher, is Docteur ès Lettres and Emerita Director of Research at the *Centre National de la Recherche Scientifique*. A specialist in Greek philosophy, she works on the power of words. She participated in the seminar at *Le Thor* with Martin Heidegger and René Char in 1969, directed the Léon Robin Center for Research on Ancient Thought, and presided over the *Collège International de Philosophie*. Her research concerns sophistics and the pre-Socratics in particular, and more generally what philosophy presents as other than itself: sophistics, rhetoric, literature (*L'Effet sophistique* [1995]). She was the general editor of the *Vocabulaire européen des philosophies: Dictionnaire des intraduisibles* (2004), which discusses the symptoms she called "untranslatables"; this book, in turn, has been translated, or reinvented, in a dozen languages. C*hevalier de la Légion d'Honneur*, she was elected to the Académie française in 2018, and received the médaille d'or from the CNRS.

Nicoletta di Vita has recently completed her PhD in Philosophy at the University of Padua and at the *École Normale Supérieure* in Paris, with a thesis on the presence of the hymn in ancient Greek thought. The dissertation, against the background of the relationship between poetry and philosophy, aimed to develop a theory of nomination and the voice as the very form and ideal horizon of philosophical language.

Olivier D'Jeranian defended this thesis on "*Responsabilité et engagement dans le stoïcisme*" at the *Université Paris 1 Panthéon Sorbonne* in 2015 and is the author of several translations of Stoic texts into French and articles on Stoicism and Sartre.

Laurent Husson is Professor of Philosophy at the *Université de Lorraine*, Director of the *École supérieure de professorat et de l'éducation* of Lorraine, and coordinator of the transversal seminar "*Le christianisme et ses héritages dans les sociétés et dans* *les textes*." He has published numerous articles on Sartre and the usage of Sartrean concepts.

Suzanne Husson is Professor of Ancient Philosophy at the *Université Paris-Sorbonne* and member of the *Centre Léon Robin* devoted to research on ancient thought. She is the author of *Une cité en quête de la nature. La République de Diogène le cynique* (2011) and of numerous articles on ancient philosophy.

Kurt Lampe, Senior Lecturer in Classics and Ancient History, University of Bristol, is the author of *The Birth of Hedonism: The Cyrenaic Philosophers and Pleasure as a Way of Life* (2015) and of numerous articles on ancient philosophy and its reception, and was Principal Investigator for the UK AHRC international networking grant, *Continental Stoicisms: Beyond Reason and Wellbeing* (2016).

Valéry Laurand is Professor at the University Bordeaux-Montaigne, Director of the unit of research "Sciences, Philosophie, Humanités" (SPH). In 2014, he published *Stoïcisme et lien social : enquête autour de Musonius Rufus*.

Clifford A. Robinson received his PhD in 2014 and is now Assistant Professor of Classics at the University of the Sciences in Philadelphia. He is completing a book on *Self-Consolation: Psychoanalytic Studies of Latin Philosophical Literature*.

John Sellars is Lecturer in Philosophy at Royal Holloway, University of London. He is the author of *The Art of Living* (2003) and *Stoicism* (2006), and *Hellenistic Philosophy* (2018). He is also the editor of *The Routledge Handbook of the Stoic Tradition* (2016).

Matthew Sharpe teaches philosophy at Deakin University. He has published widely on Pierre Hadot and philosophy as a way of life. He is presently co-authoring a study (with M. Ure) on the history of the conception of philosophy as a way of life from Socrates to today (2020) and completing translations of selected essays by Pierre Hadot (with F. Testa).

Janae Sholtz is Associate Professor of Philosophy and Coordinator of Women's and Gender Studies at Alvernia University, the author of *The Invention of a People: Heidegger and Deleuze on Art and the Political* (2015) and co-editor of *Deleuze and the Schizoanalysis of Feminism* (2019). She is a collaborator with the SSHRC Interdisciplinary Research Team, Deleuze and Cosmology, and has published numerous articles on the continental tradition, feminist theory, and aesthetic and ethico-political issues.

Michael Ure, Senior Lecturer in Politics, Monash University, Australia, is the author of *Nietzsche's Therapy* (2008), *Nietzsche's The Gay Science: An Introduction* (2019), and *Reinventing Philosophy as a Way of Life* (forthcoming with Matthew Sharpe). He was the chief investigator for the Australian Research Council grant *Reinventing Philosophy as a Way of Life* (2014–19).

INDEX

accident 8, 19, 21–2, 59, 198–9, 207
Achilles 169, 171–2, 174
actualization/s 7, 57, 60–1, 67–8
  of bodies 60, 68
  of the event 57, 67
Aelius Aristides 161
aesthetic 65, 145, 168
affectations/affections 54, 64, 66–8,
    see also passions
affirmation 28, 39, 47–50, 65, 67, 70, 87,
    113, 116–19, 121
  of chance 87
  Deleuze 65, 67, 70
  versus indifference 113, 116–19, 121
Agamben, Giorgio 5, 10, 143, 146, 163,
    177–212
"Alain" (Émile Chartier) 5–6, 19–23, 216
Alexander of Aphrodisias 70, 109, 198,
    212
All (the) 44–6, 49, 76–8, 84, 85, 88, 89
  One-All 75–7
  Virtual-All 85
ambiguity 5, 44, 161–3, 165, 166,
    169–72, 174–6, 207
Ammonius 169, 175, 182, 184
amor fati 54, 70, 87, 89
anarchic potential 197, 201, 205, 209,
    210
anger 55, 117, 155–7, 159
appropriation, *see* oikeiōsis
Aquinas, Thomas 197, 211
Arendt, Hannah 8, 9, 143, 150–2,
    158–61
Aristo 103
Aristotelian 36–7, 42, 102, 163, 166–9,
    171–2, 174, 178, 184, 198, 206–7
Aristotle 35–6, 42, 47, 88, 161–4, 166–
    70, 174–5, 178, 182, 186–7, 190
  first science 35
  On Interpretation 187

Sophistical Refutations 161–4
  voice and sound 166–70
ascesis, *see* exercises
assent 7, 37, 55, 59, 61, 97, 129, 215,
    222–3, 226–8
assumption (*assumer*) 6, 17, 23, 25–30,
    129, 130, 137
Augustine 170–1, 175–6, 181, 184
authenticity 15–16, 18–19, 22–3, 175
autonomy 3, 58, 60, 64, 145, 165, 172,
    191

Badiou, Alain 2, 4, 75–90
Bataille, Georges 70, 144
being-in-the-world 18–23, 40, 43, 46
Benveniste, Émile 108, 178, 192
Bergson, Henri 3, 76, 79, 81–3, 88,
    216–17
biological 50, 118–19, 121, 196, 204–5
biopolitics 143–4, 158–9
Blanchot, Maurice 79, 88
blituri 162–3, 166–9, 174, 181
bodywithoutorgans 61, 67, 68
Boethius 211, 229
Bonhoeffer, Adolph Friedrich 222, 225,
    232
Bréhier, Émile 3, 5, 11, 26, 32, 39, 41–2,
    46, 51, 57–8, 70, 93, 96, 108, 162,
    173–4, 184, 191, 216, 220, 225, 231

care 6, 10, 124, 133, 143–4, 146–50,
    152–3, 155–9, 182, 190, 211
Cassin, Barbara 5, 161–76
causality 4, 7, 25–7, 35–7, 48, 49, 50,
    54–62, 64–5, 70, 71, 95–6, 124, 189,
    192, 197–9, 201–3, 207, 210
choice
  as original project 16–27
  as *prohairesis* (faculty of choosing)
    22–3

Christianity   99, 110, 119, 123, 144, 146–8, 208, 217, 218
Chrysippus   11, 42, 47, 51, 99, 162, 165, 170, 173, 177, 180, 184, 188–90, 192, 198, 200, 212, 224–5, 230
Cicero   31, 70, 88, 117–19, 121, 206
civic virtue   102, 144, 155–8
Claudius   196, 201, 204–10, 212
Cleanthes   117, 119, 189, 231
Clement of Alexandria   170, 189
commitment   2, 8, 15–22, 25, 30–1, 49, 70, 104, 119–24, 134, 140, 215
  as *engagement*   15–22, 25, 30–1, 49
community   37, 102, 155–6, 227
  civic   102, 156, 227
  ethical   37
  human   155
consciousness   1, 16, 18, 19, 24, 27, 29, 39, 41, 44–7, 49, 62–3, 65–6, 145, 148–9
  cosmic   148–9
  as nihilation/nothingness   41, 49
  pure   28
  self-consciousness   28, 62
control
  and domination or oppression   9, 153–8, 210
  self-control   63, 150
  under our control (ἐo' urur) and not under our control (o a d not und   1–2, 18, 22–2, 27–8, 30, 55, 151, 223–4, 228–30
Cornutus   104–5
corporeal   50, 54, 58–60, 68, 69, 71, 77–8, 84–5, 96, 164, 170, 189
cosmic   45, 53, 56, 60, 63, 66–7, 148, 210, 221
  cosmic city   37
  cosmic cycle   99
  cosmic connectedness   11
  cosmic law   6
  cosmic perspective   56–7, 62, 229
  cosmic reason   54, 56
cosmology   10, 44, 46, 49, 71, 89
cosmos   24, 31, 36–7, 44–6, 48, 50, 53–6, 62–3, 66–7, 70–1, 77, 84, 201, 229
counteractualization   7, 57, 59–61, 66, 68–9, 71
courage   9, 136–7, 139, 158, 202

creativity   5, 99–100, 103, 106
Cynic   127, 129, 133, 138–9

Dasein   179, 180
death   9, 24, 67, 79–80, 82, 88, 98–9, 108, 117, 137, 155, 158–9, 202, 218, *see also* suicide
  death drive   108
  Deleuze and   67, 79–82, 88
  of philosophy   80
  premeditation of   218
  Stoics and   9, 24, 98, 117, 137, 155, 158–9, 202
  time of   99
dehumanizing   20, 29, 30
Deleuze, Gilles   4–7, 11, 26, 53, 54, 56–71, 75–89, 93, 108, 124, 162–3, 168, 173
desire   55, 63–8, 97–101, 108–9, 116, 121, 144, 149, 156, 181, 215, 221, 221–31
destiny, *see heimarmenē*
Diodorus Cronus   165, 175
Diogenes of Babylon   47
Diogenes the Cynic (of Sinope)   129, 137–8
discipline   3, 55, 78, 140, 145, 190, 221, 228–9, 231
  of action   228
  of the All   78
  of assent and judgement   228, 231
  of desire   221, 228–9
  linguistic   190
  self-mastery   3
  spiritual   55
disease   20, 21, 29, 30, 198
distress   8, 9, 117, 155
divination   60, 107
divine   5–7, 22, 24, 35, 37, 48, 50, 56, 71, 78, 84, 98–101, 103, 113, 11–19, 122–3, 148–9, 151, 197–200, 207, 210–11
  authority   207, 210
  law   6, 98–9, 101
  order   71, 113
  providence   48, 56, 84, 113, 118–19, 122–3, 148
  reason/rationality   37, 48, 78, 101, 149, 151

science of 50
substances 35
thought 7, 48
totality 5
will/volition 22, 24, 100, 103
domination 7–8, 145, 153–4, 156–7
dramatization 59, 60, 71
drive(s) 95, 99–104, 108, 140
dualism 17, 22, 24, 27, 35, 39–40, 82, 89
duties 16, 153, 155–6, 158, 205–7, 221–4

embodied 69, 102, 118–21, 165, 218, 220
embodiment 57, 68, 134–6, 139, 165
emotions 1, 7, 17–19, 55, 62, 70, 155,
    see also passions
  and attunement 177, 180
  as *eupatheia* 7
  and impassivity 7, 70, 99
  as involuntary (*prōtopatheiai*) 62, 228
  as transformation of the world 17–19
end, the (Greek *telos*) 24, 53–4, 62, 65,
    118, 128, 149–50, 200
enunciation 95–6, 108, 137, 140
ἐ,' 108,, *see* control
Epictetus 2, 8, 17, 22–4, 27–8, 31, 56, 93,
    96–7, 108, 109, 114, 116–19, 121–4,
    127, 136, 150, 155–6, 215–32
  cosmic perspective 56
  ethical dualism 17, 24
  ethical training/test 114, 116–19,
    121–4
  freedom/sovereignty 150, 155
  Hadot's reading 215–32
  prohairesis 22
  use of impressions 22, 97
Epicureanism 17, 71, 117, 130, 208,
    219–20
epistemology 6, 84, 89
eternity 5, 6, 85, 98– 99, 164
evil 20–1, 23, 116–18, 154, 198, 200,
    223–4
excess 56, 61, 115, 144, 167–8, 180, 188
exercises 53–71, 80, 107, 114–17, 122,
    124, 131, 146, 151, 155–6, 216–19,
    221, 223, 230
  and asceticism 75, 78–81, 85
  and experimentation 54, 56, 66–9
  and improvisation 107
  and life as a test 114–17, 122, 124

existential 6, 18, 22–4, 29, 41, 93, 206,
    230, 231
existentialism 15, 18, 26–7, 216, 218, 230
experimentation 7, 54, 56, 63, 66–70

fate, *see* heimarmenē
fire 37, 104
Foucault, Michel 7–11, 80, 93, 107,
    113–14, 116–19, 121–5, 127,
    130–40, 143–56, 158, 159, 192, 197,
    210–11, 226
freedom 1–3, 5–10, 15–31, 49–50, 55,
    61–2, 100, 107–8, 130, 137–8,
    143–5, 147–54, 156–9, 229–30

Galen 71, 161, 164–9, 171, 172
Gaunilo 181
Germanicus 208, 209
god 4, 6, 7, 23, 35, 37, 46–9, 54, 77, 81,
    93, 96–9, 101, 103–5, 114, 116, 119,
    122–4, 151, 198–200, 217, 221, 224
gods 37, 51, 86, 101, 102, 104–6, 114,
    119, 128, 131, 200, 223
Goldschmidt, Victor 4–7, 79, 93, 96–9,
    108, 175, 216, 220, 230–2
governing faculty (*hēgemonikon*) 128,
    149, 221, 232
governmentality 7, 8, 195, 197, 200
Guattari, Félix 7, 56, 5–60, 64, 68–9, 71,
    80, 85–8

Hadot, Pierre 2, 55, 61–3, 93, 215–33
harmony 49, 103, 113, 115, 148, 224
health 30, 54, 64, 68, 123, 143
Hegel 28, 81, 83, 143, 146
hēgemonikon, *see* governing faculty
Heidegger 6, 35, 42, 45, 51, 87, 179, 180,
    216–17
heimarmenē (English "fate" or
    "destiny") 20, 22–3, 29, 38, 49,
    54, 59, 67, 69–70, 77–8, 82, 84,
    87, 97–8, 113, 119, 121, 124, 131,
    197–205, 207, 210–13, 231
Heracles 31, 122, 123
Hermes 105, 106
heterogeneity 58, 63, 69, 80
Hierocles 101, 102, 109, 225
Homer 80, 105, 106
homonymy 162, 165–7, 169–71, 174–5

hupomnēmata 131, 226–7
Husserl, Edmund 80, 83, 88

idealism 43, 108, 145
imagination 8, 102, 105, 140, 216
  as dimension of language 5, 8,
    95–100, 102, 105, 140, 216
  and repetition 55, 69
immanence 39, 53–6, 61, 65, 67–71,
    147–8
impersonal 7, 63, 69, 71, 79, 88
impossibility 46, 49, 179, 180, 188
impressions, *see* phantasiai
improvisation 103, 107
impulse 1, 55, 70, 100–1, 106, 108, 120,
    138, 166–7, 180, 222–3, 225, 227,
    231
incorporeal(s) 3–5, 26–7, 35–51, 53,
    57–61, 68–71, 76–8, 87, 95–6, 162–5,
    170–1, 179–91, *see also* sayables
  and god 47–8
  as effects or events 57–61, 68, 76–8
  and Sartre's metaphysics 26–7,
    35–51
  as sayables (*lekta*) 3–5, 26, 38–41, 53,
    95–6, 162–5, 170–1, 179–91
  as space or void 36, 37, 41–3, 44–6
  as time 42
indifference 10, 40–1, 55–6, 64, 113–14,
    116–19, 121, 155, 157, 197, 200, 210
  of being in–itself 40–1
  of cause to its effect 48
  as the philosopher's attitude 27, 55–6,
    64, 81, 113–26, 155–7
  as the value of externals 18, 24, 62,
    113, 116, 223, 229–30
  zone of indifference 10, 197, 200,
    205, 210
indifferents 24, 62, 113, 117, 156, 229
inhuman 19, 21–3, 63, 81
jouissance 99, 100, 102, 106

joy 65, 221, 230
joyful 64, 65
judgment(s) 26, 37, 39–41, 55–7, 68,
    130–1, 134, 149, 155–9, 163, 174,
    180, 201, 206, 221–2, 225, 231
Julius Caesar 8, 129, 204–6, 212, 223
Justus Lipsius 156

Kant, Immanuel 42, 80, 108, 140
katalēptikē 11, 222–3
kathēkonta, *see* duties
knowledge 2, 10, 45, 56, 63–6, 81, 85, 98,
    120, 132, 133, 135–6, 139, 140, 148,
    154, 172, 177, 183, 185, 210, 216,
    229, 231
Kristeva, Julia 5, 70, 93–109

Lacan, Jacques 4, 5, 94, 108, 172–3
law(s) 54–5, 62, 101–2, 149, 164, 200
  of the city 101–2, 149–50
  of nature 54–5, 62, 149–50
  of the signifier 164
  and the symbolic order 101–2
Leibniz, Gottfried Wilhelm 77, 79–81,
    88, 195, 198, 211
lekton, *see* sayables
Lévi-Strauss, Claude 168
liberty, *see* freedom
logos 37, 47–8, 131, 136, 163, 166–7,
    171, 173, 177–81, 183, 185, 187–8,
    220–1
Lucretius 38, 80

Marcus Aurelius 10, 21, 30–2, 38, 55–6,
    99, 107, 108, 124, 127–37, 140, 215,
    219, 222, 224–31
masochism 8, 99, 109
materialism 27, 36, 54, 60–1, 84, 86, 90
maternal 94, 99
mathematics 83–5, 87, 89
meditation, *see* exercises
Megarian School 86, 164, 169
Mark Antony 208, 210
metaphysics 3, 4, 35–6, 44–5, 51, 53,
    56–7, 69, 75–7, 80, 88–9, 93, 96,
    108, 118, 161, 170, 189
misfortune 24, 113–18, 121–4, 150, 203
modernity 143–5, 196
mother-child 99, 109
multiplicities 78, 80, 84, 85, 87
music 168, 177, 191
Musonius Rufus 8, 10, 97, 103, 127, 137,
    225

nature 2, 6, 11, 16, 21–2, 31, 36, 42,
    54–7, 59, 62–3, 66–9, 78, 81, 89,
    98, 113–15, 117–18, 120–1, 123–4,

128, 131–2, 134, 136, 140, 148–50, 162–5, 178, 180, 189, 191–2, 195, 198–9, 201–3, 205, 207, 210–21, 223–4, 231, *see also* physics
accordance with   22, 31, 56, 67, 113–17, 224
agreement with   54, 191
and appropriation   120–1, 140
common   55
and diet   103–4
and duties   153–8
and fate   198–205, 207, 210, 231
human   11, 128, 223
and god   81, 224
and mother goddesses   98
and rationality   2, 66, 100–1
and the self   57, 63, 124
of the soul   180
necessity   62–3, 87, 149, 152, 202
negation   17, 26–7, 38, 40–1, 43–4, 46–8, 50–1
neoplatonism   89, 196, 232
Nietzsche, Friedrich   10, 64, 76–7, 80–1, 83, 85, 88, 123–4, 144–5
Nietzschean   66, 67, 144–5, 147
nihilation   41, 43, 45–7, 50
nomadic   7, 79
nonbeing   3, 26, 27, 36–45, 44, 46–9, 172
nonsense   58, 61, 169, 174
norms   10, 133, 139, 145–6, 178, 217
nothingness   4, 15–17, 21, 25–8, 31, 35–6, 38–51

obedience   28, 100
oikeiōsis (English "appropriation")   6, 54, 62, 63, 66, 70, 100–1, 109, 119–20, 131, 196, 208
oikonomia   211
ὅλον, τό, *see* the whole
optimism   18, 19, 22, 229
orexis   222, 231, *see also* desire
organism   54, 66, 100, 104, 109, 118–19, 121
origin   26, 40–1, 43–4, 47–8, 183, 186, 189, 191, 196, 198
ousia   169–70, 199

πᾶν, τό, *see* all (the)
Parmenides   51, 84, 161, 187

parrhēsia   10, 127–33, 136–9
passions   7, 54–5, 60, 63–6, 70–1, 78, 128, 138, 149, 155–6, 179–80, 190–1, 216, 232
phantasiai (English "impressions" or "representations")   6, 7, 11, 18, 22, 23, 31, 55, 97, 105–6, 127–32, 135, 136, 162, 183, 221–4, 226
  cataleptic impressions   7, 11, 55, 222–3
phenomenology   6, 39, 79, 85, 163, 173
Philodemus   137
philology   161–2, 172, 174, 178, 182, 184, 186, 190–1
physics   11, 35–7, 43, 50, 54, 57, 60, 70–1, 79, 80, 84, 97, 118, 162–3, 165, 189, 191, 215, 219–22, 224–8, 231–2
Plato   4, 38, 51, 76, 81, 83–5, 87, 133, 137, 140, 172, 177, 179, 185–7, 191, 192, 228, 232
platonism   76, 80, 83–5, 89, 149, 187, 196
Plutarch   36, 39, 44, 89, 137–8, 192, 199–200, 203, 212
pneuma   37, 41
politics   4, 7–10, 16, 86, 90, 100–3, 106, 108, 136–9, 143–4, 146–7, 150–3, 156, 211–12, *see also* resistance
  democratic   90
  of interpretation   100–3, 106
  and parrhesia   136–9
Polybius   196, 201–3, 205–7, 209–12
Posidonius   38, 225
Priscus, Helvidius   8–9
progress   1, 115, 132–6, 139, 203, 205, 226, 231
prohairesis, *see* choice
Providence-Fate apparatus   10, 11, 195–9, 201–7, 209–12
providential   6, 21, 24, 31, 37, 54, 85, 89, 97, 98, 113, 115, 118, 196–8, 201–3, 205, 224
psychoanalysis   7, 80, 93, 97, 99, 104, 107, 108
psychology   93, 97, 100, 101

quasi-causality   58–61, 69, 71–3

rationalism   102, 107
religion   106, 107, 211

representations, *see* phantasiai
reservation   30, 228
resistance   7–9, 61, 85–6, 133, 143–4, 147, 150, 152–8
responsibilty   5–6, 15–18, 20, 21, 23, 25, 27–32

sage   6, 7, 23, 24, 56–7, 61, 68, 94, 98, 102–3, 131–2, 134, 149, 203, 219, 222–3, 228
Sartre, Jean-Paul   2, 4, 6, 8, 15–32, 35, 38–51, 80, 216, 217
Saussure, Ferdinand   164, 165, 172
sayables   3–5, 26–7, 32, 36–7, 38–41, 47, 50–1, 77–8, 88, 95, 97, 108, 162–5, 170, 181–91, 192–3, 184, 186–91
science   35, 36, 49, 50, 84, 130, 185, 217
self-mastery   3, 49, 149, 156, 157
self-sufficiency   144, 147, 149–53, 156–8
semiology   94–6
semiotic   5, 94–5, 99, 100, 104, 106
Seneca   10–11, 31, 32, 70, 100–1, 108–9, 114–16, 118–25, 127, 131, 133–5, 139, 153, 155–7, 159, 183, 196, 201–12, 218–19, 225
Sextus Empiricus   164, 168, 174, 181–7, 189, 192
sexuality   125, 145
signification   94–7, 99–100, 105, 161–2, 165, 174, 183–4
signifier   5, 38, 95, 162–73
singularities   60, 69, 79, 85
singularity   5, 44, 46, 79–81, 99, 100, 147, 199
situation   6, 16–31, 43, 49, 103, 115, 121–4, 140, 154, 164, 204, 208–10, 217, 218
  and Sartre   6, 16–31, 43, 49
  and Stoic ethics   24, 103, 115, 121–4, 140, 208–10, 218
slavery   28, 29, 98, 108, 137, 138, 151, 168
  and death   98
  Epictetus as   224
  and externals   148, 206
  and parrhēsia   137–8
  and politics   150–1
  and the master–slave dialectic   28–9
  and symbolic meaning   108

Socrates   85, 117, 137, 140, 170, 171
Socratic   85
sophistics   85, 161–76
sovereign power   10, 195–210
  self-sovereignty   148–59
sovereignty   10, 148–59, 195–7, 201, 203–7, 209–10, 212
speech   4, 5, 10, 99, 127, 129, 130, 132, 134–41, 161–3, 165, 172–3, 175, 179, 184, 185, 189, 190, 207–10, 227
Spinoza   64, 65, 67, 71, 76, 79–83, 85, 88, 89
Spinozist   65–6, 83, 85
spiritual exercises, *see* exercises
spirituality, *see* religion; theology
Stiegler, Bernard   10
subjectivity   7, 40, 67, 79, 124, 145–6, 201, 211
suicide   21, 64, 98, 99, 158–60
surpassing (*dépassement*)   6, 28, 30, 44, 63, 65, 180
symbolic   9, 29, 94–5, 99–105

techniques   1, 7, 10, 31, 32, 56, 70, 135, 146
technologies of the self   107, 125
theodicy   48, 195, 198
theology   35–6, 89, 97, 104–5, 195, 201, 217
therapy   10, 156, 216
time, philosophy of   5, 37, 42, 50, 53, 69, 78, 98–100, 108, 229–30
totality   5, 6, 36–8, 43–5, 49, 51, 56, 76–8, 84, 89, 90, 229, 230
truth-telling   10, 127–41
tyranny   8, 156–9

universal   2, 6, 21, 28, 42, 49, 53, 62, 67, 77, 79, 97–8, 101, 154, 198–9, 202, 221
universe   3, 6, 28, 37, 46, 54, 70, 84, 89, 97–8, 149, 220, 229
unsayable   179–81, 187, 190–1
utterance   95, 140, 184, 188, 217

value(s)   9, 16, 21, 27–8, 31, 99–103, 108, 115–16, 118, 121, 129, 133, 145–6, 149, 153–5, 158, 165, 168, 188–9, 192, 219, 223, 229, 231

veridiction, *see* truth-telling
Vespasian   8, 9
violence   16, 23, 30, 137, 139, 143, 156, 169, 171, 196, 203–5, 208–9
virtue   19–22, 24–5, 29, 30, 65, 85–6, 97, 99, 102–3, 109, 113–15, 118, 120–1, 133–4, 144, 148, 155–7, 177, 199, 208, 220, 223
vitalism   79, 85, 88
vocal   5, 162, 166–7, 172–3, 182–5
vocalization   162
volition   5, 24, 37, 97–101, 103, 199, *see also* willing

voluntary   22
vulnerability   64, 68

war   9, 15, 18–25, 27, 29–32, 50
whole (the)   44–6
willing   54–9, 61, 63, 67, 70, *see also* volition
wisdom   1, 3, 6, 29, 50, 82, 134–5, 149, 220, 228

Zeno   42, 54, 100, 104, 164, 191–2, 219
Zeus   24, 31, 37, 98–9, 101, 104, 122–3, 224

www.ingramcontent.com/pod-product-compliance
Lightning Source LLC
Chambersburg PA
CBHW072143290426
44111CB00012B/1957